ROBERT JAY LIFTON is Foundations' Fund for Research Associate Professor of Psychiatry at Yale University. He has for the past ten years been interested in the relationship between individual character and historical change, particularly in China and Japan, and in problems of individual behavior in extreme situations. He has spent more than six years in the Far East, and recently returned from an extensive stay in Japan during which he carried out a study of psychological patterns in Japanese youth, as well as an investigation of the psychological effects of the atomic bomb in Hiroshima.

Dr. Lifton has previously held research and teaching appointments at Harvard University, where he was associated with the Department of Psychiatry and the Center for East Asian Studies; and with the Washington School of Psychiatry.

Thought Reform and the Psychology of Totalism

A STUDY
OF "BRAINWASHING" IN CHINA

Robert Jay Lifton, M.D.

The Norton Library

W · W · NORTON & COMPANY · INC · New York

W. W. Norton & Company, Inc. is also the publisher
of the works of Erik H. Erikson, Otto Fenichel, Karen Horney and
Harry Stack Sullivan, and the principal works of Sigmund Freud.

61-5934

ISBN   0   393   00221   7
PRINTED IN THE UNITED STATES OF AMERICA
6 7 8 9 0

CONTENTS

PREFACE TO
THE NORTON LIBRARY EDITION

The period of a little less than three years which has elapsed since this book first appeared is, by usual standards, a very brief one. Yet when measured against the historical velocity of our present era, it is virtually a lifetime. With the passage of this "brief lifetime," my impression is that the book's subject matter concerns us more than ever. I do not mean that organized programs of "thought reform" or "brainwashing" are more rampant now, in China or elsewhere, than at the time the study was made. The reverse is undoubtedly true. What I do mean is that the larger problem which the book addresses itself to—that of man's psychosocial alternatives in the face of extreme historical situations—increasingly confronts us. For Chinese thought reform, from both the standpoint of the reformers and the reformed, must be seen as taking place against a background of historical dislocation, of the loss of vitality in the relationship of individuals and groups to their own heritage due to the breakdown of the symbolic structure that had been a source of this vitality.

The significance of historical dislocation, in a psychological as well as ideological sense, was made vivid to me during recent work with young Japanese in which I studied the interplay of individual character and historical change. I encountered many of the inner struggles depicted here among Chinese, as well as a variety of additional forms of experimentation and synthesis, originating in a related but different cultural heritage, and operating in a more "open," and therefore more confusing, contemporary environment.

Historical dislocation is not, of course, confined to Chinese and Japanese, or even to non-Western cultures. It is, in greater or lesser degree, a universal affliction, and perhaps a universal opportunity. For Asians and Africans in particular, and for many others in under-developed areas, it is part of a profound revolution, frequently called "anti-colonial" but perhaps more accurately seen as psychological, moral, and ideological. This revolution expresses a sweeping quest on the part of the historically deprived for group-mediated self-esteem and identity. And it is well to keep in mind that one can feel oneself historically deprived in a variety of ways: in an eco-nomic sense (relating to living standard or even the ability to sur-vive); a political-military sense (relating to national power); an educational sense (relating particularly to science and technology); and a racial-exploitative sense (relating to explosive feelings of inferior status and outside domination). This revolution of self-esteem, as we are seeing demonstrated by the Negro movements in our own country at the present time, is one of enormous power, which stems both from the immense numbers of people involved and the moral urgency of their demands.

But revolutions, by their nature, press toward excess, as this book attempts to record. And I believe that by studying thought reform in its historical context we can learn a good deal about some of the puzzlingly belligerent, even solipsistic behavior of Chinese commu-nism on the larger world scene—since the totalist ideology involved relates itself to individual psychology on the one hand, and to group political expression on the other. The book offers no specific remedy, psychological or political, for this extremism. But it takes the strong position, which I would in no way modify now, that we do best to avoid the temptation to meet totalism with totalism, and instead to call upon our intellectual and emotional resources to evolve his-torically relevant alternatives.

Another professional experience I have had within the past year, a study of the psychological effects of the atomic bomb in Hiroshima, has given me an additional sense of the urgency of the problem. Hiroshima represents an even more "extreme" historical situation, one which is an early expression of what might be termed the potentially terminal revolution: the remarkable state of affairs in which man has the capacity to eliminate himself as a species, or at least come perilously close to doing so. Although originally only a by-product of two other revolutions—in the scientific and technological-industrial spheres—this potentially terminal revolution takes on a fundamental reality of its own. It has far-reaching psychological consequences which we have just begun to explore. It is, in fact, a unique problem which dwarfs all others; and yet it bears some relationship to the problem of totalism discussed in this book, particularly to that portion of the final section which deals with "the dispensing of existence" and related tendencies. For such is the nature of our thermonuclear technology that any person or group (of whatever apparent psychological or ideological bent) contemplating or encouraging the use of these weapons enters into a realm of a totalism of consequences. Here we are confronted by the inadequacy of our mental life to our technology—not only in the sense of the former's inability to master the latter, but in the dangerous lag between thought constellations related to the use of nuclear weapons and the potentially terminal consequences of these weapons. Or to put it another way, the totalism of consequences eludes our understanding because it functions, at least as of now, relatively independently of our thoughts and feelings.

This book then is a moral as well as psychological effort toward bridging this kind of gap through gaining a better grasp of one aspect of our historical predicament; Chinese thought reform serves both as a direct object of study and a more indirect path to larger questions. I believe that psychiatry and psychoanalysis have been remiss in addressing themselves to these crucial issues accompanying the unprecedentedly radical social change which now engulfs us. I also believe that psychoanalytic psychiatry, with its capacity for systematic individual exploration in depth, and for disciplined speculation, is potentially equipped to contribute important insights of a very special kind. The problem is that of bringing its classical tool, the clinical interview, into historical perspective —or perhaps that of bringing the psychiatrist into history. For psychiatrists and others in the human sciences to take this step would seem to me nothing less than a moral imperative. It is not that we are capable of supplying transcendent solutions to the world's dilemmas. But if we do not apply ourselves to matters most essential to contemporary existence—or nonexistence—we can hardly consider ourselves students of man.

A NOTE ON THE
GREAT PROLETARIAN CULTURAL
REVOLUTION

Events in China surrounding the Great Proletarian Cultural Revolution, beginning during the summer of 1966 and extending into the present, have extraordinary significance for China, for revolutions in general, and for man's future. They are also an extraordinary challenge to the student of psychology and history, or of "psychohistorical process."

My study of Chinese "thought reform" did not enable me, any more than others following developments on the mainland, to predict such a cataclysm. But I think it fair to say that the psychological environment and general principles described in this book provide a basis for understanding why this kind of upheaval occurred and what happens to people caught up in it. We are in fact witnessing a full flowering of the patterns of totalism which the book delineates. We can now, I believe, see this totalism as part of a quest for what I have elsewhere called "revolutionary immortality"—an effort to create so pure and intense a national environment as to render immortal the revolution itself and the individual's participation in it.

Investigation of the psychological effects of the atomic bomb in Hiroshima led me to a general sense of the significance not only of man's anticipation of death, but his need to survive himself: his urge to "live on" in some enduring principle or "posterity," whether it be biological or biosocial, creative, theological, or natural. The need for a *sense* of immortality is by no means confined to the revolutionary, nor to the dying man. Rather it is a fundamental element of the psychological life in general, essential to psychic vitality. The struggle to retain this sense of human continuity becomes ever more difficult in our age, beset as we are by unprecedented acceleration of the historical process on the one hand, and by threat of nuclear extermination on the other. Under particularly pressing conditions it can, as in China today, take desperate, self-defeating, and dangerous directions.

From this standpoint we may look upon the recent course of the Chinese Revolution as something more than an extreme attempt of an industrially backward nation to catch up with the modern world, or of an ancient culture to rectify a century of humiliation at the hands of the West. China's anguish in many ways epitomizes man's disturbed contemporary efforts to bring significance to his life, to achieve symbolic immortality.

We had better understand that anguish, not only because we must learn to live with the quarter of the world's people involved in it, but because by such understanding we begin to learn something about our own psychological condition.

R.J.L.

Wellfleet, Mass.

PREFACE

This study began as a psychiatric evaluation of Chinese Communist "thought reform," or "brainwashing." It is still primarily this; but it has also, inevitably, become a psychological study of extremism or totalism—and even more broadly, a study of the "closed" versus the "open" approaches to human change.

It is based upon research which I conducted in Hong Kong in 1954–55. It then evolved over four years of additional research and teaching in the United States. My work with Western and Chinese subjects—piecing together emotional details that were both poignant and extreme—and the psychological, moral, and historical challenge of the material have made this study an exceptionally absorbing personal and professional experience.

A book about extremism calls for a special measure of objectivity. This does not mean that its author can claim complete personal or moral detachment. The assumption of such detachment in psychological (or any other) work is at best self-deception, and at worst a source of harmful distortion. And who during this era can pretend to be uninvolved in the issues of psychological coercion, of identity, and of ideology? Certainly not one who has felt impelled to study them at such length.

Instead, I have attempted to be both reasonably dispassionate and responsibly committed: dispassionate in my efforts to stand away from the material far enough to probe the nature of the process, its effects upon people exposed to it, and some of the influences affecting its practitioners; committed to my own analyses.

and judgments within the limitations and the bias of my knowledge.

Much in this book is highly critical of the particular aspect of Chinese Communism which it examines, but I have made no attempt to render a definitive verdict on this far-reaching revolutionary movement. I am critical of thought reform's psychological tactics, not because they are Communist (or Chinese Communist), but because of their specific nature. In the last section of this book, these tactics are compared with practices within our own culture, which also receive critical treatment insofar as they resemble the ideological totalism of thought reform. Instead of contrasting the "good we" and the "bad they," rather, I have attempted to identify and understand a particular psychological phenomenon.

In the pursuit of this understanding, I have recorded all that seemed relevant, including the details of whatever psychological and physical abuse my subjects encountered. I believe that this comprehensive approach offers the best means of contributing to general knowledge, and to the clarification of an emotionally loaded subject; and I hope that this study will thereby ultimately contribute to the resolution, rather than to the intensification, of cold war passions. It is in fact one of the tragedies of the cold war that moral criticism of either side is immediately exploited by the other side in an exaggerated, one-dimensional fashion. One can never prevent this from happening; but one can at least express the spirit in which a work has been written.

Such an approach requires that I inform the reader about my bias in both psychiatric and political matters. Psychiatrically, I have been strongly influenced by both neo-Freudian and Freudian currents: the former through an association with the Washington School of Psychiatry during and immediately after the research study itself, and the latter through a subsequent candidacy in the Boston Psychoanalytic Institute. Both influences were also present in my earlier psychiatric residency training at the State University Medical Center of New York. I have found the theoretical writings of Erik Erikson, especially those relating to questions of personal identity and ideology, particularly relevant for this study. At the same time, I have constantly groped for new ways to bring psychological insights to bear upon historical forces, and do so with a humanistic focus. Thus, I have made extensive use of my subjects' biographical material, and have attempted to include in these presentations a flesh-and-bones description of their life histories in relationship to pertinent social historical currents, as well as a rigorous psychological analysis of their responses to thought reform. This seemed to me the best way to deal with the inseparable relationship between stress and response, and (in William James' phrase) to "convey truth."

My political philosophical bias is toward a liberalism strongly critical of itself; and toward the kind of antitotalitarian (in the psychological terms of this study, antitotalistic), historically-minded questioning of the order of things expressed by Albert Camus in his brilliant philosophical essay, *The Rebel*. No one understood better than Camus the human issues involved in this study.

I should like to mention a few of the many people whose direct personal assistance was indispensable to the completion of this study. David McK. Rioch lent initial support when support was most needed, and always continued to enrich the work through his urbane eclecticism, his provocative criticism, and his personal kindness. Erik Erikson, during many memorable talks at Stockbridge and Cambridge, made stimulating and enlarging suggestions, both about specific case histories and problems of presentation. During the latter stages of the work, David Riesman offered generously of his extraordinary intellectual breadth and his unique personal capacity to evoke what is most creative within one. Carl Binger has been sage and always helpful in his advice. All four made thoughtful criticisms of the manuscript, as did Kenneth Keniston and F. C. Redlich. Others in psychiatry and related fields to whom I am indebted are Leslie Farber, Erich Lindemann, Margaret Mead, and Beata Rank. In the perilous subtleties of Chinese cultural, intellectual, and political history, I was constantly counseled by Benjamin Schwartz and by John Fairbank, both of whom read parts of the manuscript; and earlier in the work by Lu Pao-tung, Ma Meng, Howard Boorman, Conrad Brandt, and A. Doak Barnett.

The literary advice and loving sustenance of my wife, Betty Jean Lifton, can hardly be documented. My father, Harold A. Lifton, also did much to encourage this study.

The Hong Kong research was sponsored for the first seven months by the Asia Foundation, and for the remaining year by the Washington School of Psychiatry. The manuscript was completed under grants from the Ford Foundation and the Foundation's fund for Research in Psychiatry, both administered through Harvard University.

Finally, I must acknowledge my debt to the forty research subjects, Chinese and Western, whose personal thought reform experiences are the basis for this study. The extent of their intelligent collaboration in this work is apparent in the biographical chapters. In these, I have altered certain details in order to protect the subjects' anonymity; but none of these alterations affect the essential psychological patterns.

P A R T O N E

THE PROBLEM

How intoxicating to feel like God the Father and to hand out definitive testimonials of bad character and habits.

Albert Camus

Only simple and quiet words will ripen of themselves. For a whirlwind does not last for the whole morning. Nor does a thundershower last the whole day. Who is their author? The heaven and earth. Yet even they cannot make such violent things last. How much more true this must be of the rash endeavors of man.

Lao Tze

CHAPTER 1

WHAT IS "BRAINWASHING"?

When confronted with the endless discussion on the general subject of "brainwashing," I am sometimes reminded of the Zen Buddhist maxim: "The more we talk about it, the less we understand it." The confusion begins with the word itself, so new and yet already so much a part of our everyday language. It was first used by an American journalist, Edward Hunter, as a translation of the colloquialism *hsi nao* (literally, "wash brain") which he quoted from Chinese informants who described its use following the Communist takeover.[1]

"Brainwashing" soon developed a life of its own. Originally used to describe Chinese indoctrination techniques, it was quickly applied to Russian and Eastern European approaches, and then to just about anything which the Communists did anywhere (as illustrated by the statement of a prominent American lady who, upon returning from a trip to Moscow, claimed that the Russians were "brainwashing" prospective mothers in order to prepare them for natural childbirth). Inevitably, the word made its appearance closer to home, sometimes with the saving grace of humor (*New Yorker* cartoons of children "brainwashing" parents, and wives "brainwashing" husbands), but on other occasions with a more vindictive tone—as when Southern segregationists accused all who favor racial equality (including the United States Supreme Court) of having been influenced by "left-wing brainwashing"; or equally

3

irresponsible usages by anti-fluoridation, anti-mental health legislation, or anti-almost anything groups leveled against their real or fancied opponents.

Then there is the lurid mythology which has grown up about it: the "mysterious oriental device," or the deliberate application of Pavlov's findings on dogs. There is also another kind of myth, the claim that there is no such thing, that it is all just the fantasy of American correspondents.

Finally, there is the more responsible—even tortured—self-examination which leads professional people to ask whether they in their own activities might not be guilty of "brainwashing": educators about their teaching, psychiatrists about their training and their psychotherapy, theologians about their own reform methods. Opponents of these activities, without any such agonizing scrutiny, can more glibly claim that they are "*nothing but* brainwashing." Others have seen "brainwashing" in American advertising, in large corporation training programs, in private preparatory schools, and in congressional investigations. These misgivings are not always without basis, and suggest that there is a continuity between our subject and many less extreme activities; but the matter is not clarified by promiscuous use of the term.

Behind this web of semantic (and more than semantic) confusion lies an image of "brainwashing" as an all-powerful, irresistible, unfathomable, and magical method of achieving total control over the human mind. It is of course none of these things, and this loose usage makes the word a rallying point for fear, resentment, urges toward submission, justification for failure, irresponsible accusation, and for a wide gamut of emotional extremism. One may justly conclude that the term has a far from precise and a questionable usefulness; one may even be tempted to forget about the whole subject and return to more constructive pursuits.

Yet to do so would be to overlook one of the major problems of our era—that of the psychology and the ethics of directed attempts at changing human beings. For despite the vicissitudes of brainwashing, the process which gave rise to the name is very much a reality: the official Chinese Communist program of *szu-hsiang kai-tsao* (variously translated as "ideological remolding," "ideological reform," or as we shall refer to it here, "thought reform") has in fact emerged as one of the most powerful efforts at human manipulation ever undertaken. To be sure, such a program is by no means completely new: imposed dogmas, inquisitions, and mass conversion movements have existed in every country and during every historical epoch. But the Chinese Communists have brought to theirs a more organized, comprehensive, and deliberate—a more *total*—character, as well as a unique blend of energetic and ingenious psychological techniques.

The Western world has heard mostly about "thought reform" as applied in a military setting: the synthetic bacteriological warfare confessions and the collaboration obtained from United Nations personnel during the Korean War. However, these were merely export versions of a thought reform program aimed, not primarily at Westerners, but at the Chinese people themselves, and vigorously applied in universities, schools, special "revolutionary colleges," prisons, business and government offices, labor and peasant organizations. Thought reform combines this impressively widespread distribution with a focused emotional power. Not only does it reach one-fourth of the people of the world, but it seeks to bring about in everyone it touches a significant personal upheaval.

Whatever its setting, thought reform consists of two basic elements: *confession*, the exposure and renunciation of past and present "evil"; and *re-education*, the remaking of a man in the Communist image. These elements are closely related and overlapping, since they both bring into play a series of pressures and appeals—intellectual, emotional, and physical—aimed at social control and individual change.

The American press and public have been greatly concerned about this general subject, and rightly so. But too often the information made available about it has been sensationalist in tone, distorted because of inadequate knowledge, or obscured by the strong emotions which the concept of brainwashing seems to arouse in everyone. Its aura of fear and mystery has been more conducive to polemic than to understanding.

Still the vital questions continue to be asked: Can a man be made to change his beliefs? If a change does occur, how long will it last? How do the Chinese Communists obtain these strange confessions? Do people believe their own confessions, even when false? How successful is thought reform? Do Westerners and Chinese react differently to it? Is there any defense against it? Is it related to psychotherapy? to religious conversion? Have the Chinese discovered new and obscure techniques? What has all this to do with Soviet Russia and international Communism? with Chinese culture? How is it related to other mass movements or inquisitions, religious or political? What are the implications for education? For psychiatric and psychoanalytic training and practice? For religion? How can we recognize parallels to thought reform within our own culture, and what can we do about them?

It was with these questions on my mind that I arrived in Hong Kong in late January, 1954. Just a few months before, I had taken part in the psychiatric evaluation of repatriated American prisoners of war during the exchange operations in Korea known as *Big Switch*; I had then accompanied a group of these men on the troopship back to the United States.[2] From the repatriates' descriptions of what they had experienced, I pieced together a great deal of information about Chinese Communist confession and re-education techniques, and was convinced that this process raised some basic human issues; but the expediencies of the military situation made it difficult to study them with the necessary depth and thoroughness. I thought then that the most important questions might best be approached through work with people who had been "reformed" within China itself.

Yet I had not come to Hong Kong with any clear intention of carrying out this detailed research. I had planned only a brief stopover on my way from Tokyo back to the United States after having lived in the Far East for almost two years, serving as an Air Force psychiatrist in Japan and Korea. But plans can be changed; and such change is sometimes an expression of an inner plan not yet consciously understood by the planner himself. Thus as long as I was in Hong Kong, I decided to make a few inquiries into a subject that seemed so important.

As soon as I did, I discovered that a number of Western scholars and diplomats there had also been asking themselves these questions. They had been shocked by the effects of indoctrination programs applied on the Chinese mainland. They told me of Western missionaries who, after having made lurid "espionage" confessions in prison, arrived in Hong Kong deeply confused about what they believed; of young Chinese students violating the most sacred precepts of their culture by publicly denouncing their parents; of distinguished mainland professors renouncing their "evil" past, even rewriting their academic books from a Marxist standpoint. My Western acquaintances had been both troubled and fascinated by these events, and welcomed my interest in the problem. At my request, they arranged for me to meet a few people like the ones they had described.

The impact of these first encounters was not something one readily forgets: an elderly European Bishop leaning forward in his hospital bed, so deeply impressed with the power of the prison thought reform program he had just experienced that he could only denounce it as "an alliance with the demons"; a young Chinese girl, still shaken from the group hatred that had been turned upon her at a university in Peking, yet wondering if she had been "selfish" in leaving.

I realized that these two people had both been through China's most elemental thought reform programs; and that these programs were much more powerful and comprehensive than the modifications which had been applied to United Nations' troops in Korea. I also realized that Hong Kong offered a unique opportunity for the study of thought reform, although, surprisingly enough, no one was taking advantage of it. I sought a means of remaining there to undertake prolonged and systematic research into the process; and with the help of two research grants, my stay was extended into seventeen months of stimulating psychiatric investigation.

CHAPTER 2

RESEARCH IN HONG KONG

Hong Kong was no ordinary setting for psychiatric research. Many problems arose, some of which I could anticipate, and others which I had to deal with as I went along, but all of which required approaches departing considerably from usual psychiatric protocol. The basic task was to locate people who had been put through intensive reform experiences and communicate with them in meaningful emotional depth. For I felt that this was the best way to study the psychological features and human effects of the reform process. I was not investigating "mental disease" or patterns of neurosis; I was studying individual strengths, as well as vulnerabilities.

I soon found out that those who had undergone this experience fell into two broad groups: Western civilians reformed in prisons, and Chinese intellectuals who had undergone their reform in universities or in "revolutionary colleges." In both groups, it immediately became clear that intensive work with relatively few people was much more valuable than superficial contacts with many. Thought reform was a complex personal experience, destructive of personal trust; it took time for a subject—especially in an environment as full of suspicion as Hong Kong—to trust me sufficiently to reveal inner feelings of which he was not necessarily proud. And with Chinese subjects this was intensified by the East Asian cultural pattern of saying (as both a form of propriety and a means of personal protection) what one thinks the listener wishes to hear. For the first few sessions, Chinese were particularly likely to offer an elaboration of anti-Communist clichés; only weeks or months later would they reveal the true conflicts stimulated by Communist reform.

The twenty-five Westerners and fifteen Chinese subjects whom I interviewed all had experiences which came under the thought reform category. But I could not ignore differences in the two groups, both differences in the type of programs to which they had been exposed, and in their cultural and historical backgrounds. These differences were important factors in my conduct of the research and in the evaluation of the material, and I have also taken them into account in the book's organization: Part II deals only with Western subjects, Part III only with Chinese, and Part IV with a consideration of the basic problems raised by thought reform in general.

Most Chinese subjects were more or less permanent residents of Hong Kong, having left mainland China for reasons often associated with a negative response to thought reform. I was able to interview some very soon after their arrival, but the majority had come to Hong Kong a few years before (between 1948 and 1952) when the first great wave of thought reform was at its height, and it was still not too difficult for educated people to leave China. As refugee intellectuals, many supported themselves through work with press and publishing associations, while others received some form of aid from philanthropic and religious groups. I found it best to approach them, always indirectly and always by means of personal introduction, through members of these various Hong Kong organizations. Work with Chinese subjects was invariably complicated—because of problems of language and culture, and because of their difficult life situation (matters which will be discussed more in Part III)—but at the same time it was extremely rewarding. Their life stories revealed much about the history of contemporary China, and their responses taught me a great deal about Chinese character, all of which was of vital importance for understanding thought reform itself. I was able to maintain relationships with them over long periods of time, some for more than a year; I tried to see them frequently at first (two or three half-day or even full-day sessions per week) and then at weekly, bi-weekly, or monthly intervals. As I do not speak Chinese, it was necessary for me to use an interpreter with eleven of the fifteen subjects; the other four spoke fluent English because they had studied either in the West or with Western teachers in China. I was surprised at the emotional depth that could be achieved in these three-way relationships. Much depended on the intelligence and sensitivity of my two regular interpreters (one of them a Western-trained social scientist) and upon my developing with them an effective style of collaborative interviewing.

The rhythms of work with Western subjects were entirely different. For them, Hong Kong was not a home but an interlude. They would arrive fresh from a grueling prison ordeal, generally remain in the colony from one to four weeks, and then embark for Europe or America. Friends, professional associates, or consular officials would greet them and take care of them; confused as they usually were, they needed assistance. They were also fearful and suspicious, which made it necessary for me to approach them through the people in whom they had greatest confidence, and again on the basis of personal introductions. In order to be able to do this, I made myself and my work known among Western diplomatic, religious, and business groups in Hong Kong. The arrival of a Westerner who had been a prisoner in China was always announced in the Hong Kong newspapers, and I was usually able to set up a first meeting almost immediately.

My arrangements with all subjects were highly flexible, varying with the circumstances of each case. When possible, I had them come to my office-apartment; but it was frequently necessary for me to visit Westerners in homes or mission houses where they were staying, or in hospitals where they were convalescing. I insisted only upon the opportunity to conduct the interview in privacy; although even on this point I had to make one exception when a priest, because of his fears, requested that a colleague remain in the room during our talks.

I tried to spend as much time as possible with each Westerner during his brief stay in Hong Kong; but this time varied greatly, and depended upon the subject's availability, the special features of his case, and my own schedule at the time. Generally, once we had begun, the subject was as eager as I to work intensively together. I averaged a total of about fifteen to twenty hours with each; with some I spent more than forty hours over several months, and in one or two cases, we had just a single interview. A session might last anywhere from one to three hours. Thus, a typical relationship with a Western subject consisted of eight or nine two-hour interviews over a period of eighteen to twenty days.

With most of the Westerners, communication was intense and intimate. Although the majority were Europeans, there was no language problem because English was the *lingua franca* for Westerners in China, and all of them spoke it fluently. Most were under great inner pressure to talk about their experiences; they poured out their stories without hesitation, even if they withheld certain details until later interviews. Some of them, as we shall see, were afraid of people, suspicious of me, or reluctant to reveal what they had done in prison; but in almost all cases, the need to unburden themselves overcame inhibiting factors.

When I had introduced myself and told them a little about my research study (self-identification about profession and affiliations was extremely important in this environment), I would begin to ask them questions about their prison experience—if indeed, they had not already begun to tell me about it. I tried to cover this experience in great detail, at the same time following the general psychoanalytic principle of encouraging the subject to associate freely without interruption. What impressed me most about the material was its immediacy: just a matter of days from their reform ordeal, these men and women still carried with them its entire atmosphere. They had not yet had time to place any distance between themselves and their experiences, or to initiate the distorting reconstructions which eventually occur after any stress situation. (I was to appreciate this immediacy more fully after I encountered such reconstructions during follow-up visits—Chapters 10–12—with many of them in Europe and America three and four years later.) The freshness of the data was tremendously helpful in conveying the actual emotional currents of thought reform.

Why did these subjects originally agree to see me? What was their incentive for taking part in the study? Many, who were in a rather confused state, seemed merely to be following the suggestions of people taking care of them. Some told me that they wanted to make a contribution to the systematic study of the thought reform problem, in order to help future victims, or to combat an evil.

Others said quite frankly that they welcomed the chance to talk over their experiences with a professional person who had some knowledge of this subject, thus acknowledging their need for a greater understanding of their ordeals. Whether stated openly or not, this therapeutic factor became increasingly important with almost every Western subject (and with many Chinese as well) during the course of the interviews. Mostly I listened and wrote, but I did—when they expressed interest—discuss with them such things as mechanisms of guilt and shame, and problems of identity. They needed psychological support and understanding and I required the data which they were able to supply: it was a fair exchange. Most of them told me, before they left Hong Kong, that our interviews had been beneficial to them. Since they were so emotionally involved in the work, we were able to explore their past histories and their general psychological traits, and thus develop a dimension important to the study.

The Western subject group breaks down as follows: total—twenty-five; by profession—thirteen missionaries (twelve Catholic priests, one Protestant minister), four businessmen, two journalists, two physicians, one research scholar, one university professor, one sea captain and one housewife; by nationality—seven Germans, seven Frenchmen, five Americans, one Dutchman, one Belgian, one Canadian, one Italian, one Irishman and one (White) Russian; by sex—twenty-three male and two female; by age—from twenty to seventy, most between thirty-five and fifty.

In my interviews with subjects in both groups, I kept the following questions in mind: What was the nature of the process which he has experienced? What in his emotional responses did he share with the other subjects? How did he as a specific person respond to this process? What relationship did his character and his background have to his particular mode of response? I tried to avoid making premature generalizations and to remain open to the vast array of personal, cultural, and historical data with which I was confronted.

I also made every effort to broaden my background information. In addition to the subjects themselves, I spoke to anyone I could find in Hong Kong (Chinese or Western) who had some knowledge of thought reform, whether as a scholar, diplomat, priest, former Communist, or simply from having observed people who had experienced it. And at the same time, I read everything available about the subject; translations of the Chinese Communist press prepared by the American Consulate were especially valuable, as were additional translations which my interpreters made.

As I proceeded with the work, I realized that one of the main causes for confusion about thought reform lay in the complexity of the process itself. Some people considered it a relentless means of undermining the human personality; others saw it as a profoundly "moral"—even religious—attempt to instill new ethics into the Chinese people. Both of these views were partly correct, and yet each, insofar as it ignored the other, was greatly misleading. For it was the combination of *external force or coercion* with an appeal to *inner enthusiasm through evangelistic exhortation* which gave thought reform its emotional scope and power. Coercion and breakdown are, of course, more prominent in the prison and military programs, while exhortation and ethical appeal are especially stressed with the rest of the Chinese population; and it becomes extremely difficult to determine just where exhortation ends and coercion begins.

I found it very important to consider what was behind thought reform, what impelled the Chinese Communists to carry out such extreme measures on such an extensive scale. The complexities of their motivations will be discussed later on; but it is necessary for us now—before getting into the prison experiences of Westerners —to know something about the Chinese Communist philosophy or rationale for the program.

Their leading political theorists, although reticent about technical details, have written extensively on general principles. Mao Tse-tung himself, in a well-known speech originally delivered to party members in 1942, laid down the basic principles of punishment and cure which are always quoted by later writers. To overcome undesirable and "unorthodox" trends, he specified that

. . . two principles must be observed. The first is, "punish the past to warn the future" and the second, "save men by curing their ills." Past errors must be exposed with no thought of personal feelings or face. We must use a scientific attitude to analyze and criticize what has been undesirable in the past . . . this is the meaning of "punish the past to warn the future." But our object in exposing errors and criticizing shortcomings is like that of a doctor in curing a disease. The entire purpose is to save the person, not to cure him to death. If a man has appendicitis, a doctor performs an operation and the man is saved

. . . we cannot adopt a brash attitude toward diseases in thought and politics, but [must have] an attitude of "saving men by curing their diseases." [1]

The argument continues as follows: the "old society" in China (or any non-Communist society anywhere) was (and is) evil and corrupt; this is true because of the domination of the "exploiting classes"—the landowners and the capitalists or bourgeoisie; everyone has been exposed to this type of society and therefore retains from it "evil remnants" or "ideological poisons"; only thought reform can rid him of these and make him into a "new man" in a "new society." When this argument is applied to Chinese intellectuals, it is also pointed out that they originate from the "exploiting classes" or from the closely related petite bourgeoisie, since only people from these classes had the means to acquire an education. And long philosophical treatises emphasize the need to bring the "ideology of all classes" into harmony with "objective material conditions" [2]—or in other words, to blend personal beliefs with Communist-implemented social realities.

In prisons, Western civilians (and their Chinese cellmates) encounter a special penal version of these principles:

All crimes have definite sociological roots. The evil ideology and evil habits left behind by the old society, calling for the injuring of others for self-profit and seeking enjoyment without labor, still remain in the minds of some people to a marked degree. Thus if we are to wipe all crimes from their root, in addition to inflicting on the criminal the punishment due, we must also carry out various effective measures to transform the various evil ideological conceptions in the minds of the people so that they may be educated and reformed into new people.[3]

Penal institutions are referred to as "re-education centers," "meditation houses," or even "hospitals for ideological reform." Four types of institutions are described in Communist prison codes: [4] the Detention House, the Prison, the Labor Service for Reform Corps, and the Juvenile Delinquents Institute. Westerners spend most of their time in the first, whose function it is "to assume responsibility for understanding the conditions of criminals awaiting sentence." This means that the Westerners' one to five years of imprisonment are essentially devoted to "solving their cases"; and they are not tried or sentenced until just before their release. Some have been sent to the second type, the prison proper, where they engage in various kinds of work. But the large-scale policy of "reform through labor"—the use of prisoners in labor battalions—has been mostly reserved for the Chinese themselves.

In all of this it is most important to realize that *what we see as a set of coercive maneuvers, the Chinese Communists view as a morally uplifting, harmonizing, and scientifically therapeutic experience.*

After the Communist takeover in 1948–1949, there was a brief honeymoon period during which Westerners living in China were treated with great courtesy and encouraged to remain. Then the regime began to use the animosities aroused by the Korean war as well as a national policy of discrediting specific religious and educational groups (and in fact of eliminating all non-Communist Western influence), to make it plain to Western Europeans and Americans that they were not welcome. Most left of their own accord, but others—held by a sense of missionary obligation or by special opportunity for business, scholarship, or adventure—chose to remain. A small number from this group were taken into custody. Most of the arrests occurred in 1951 during the national campaign for the "suppression of counterrevolutionaries," at which time tensions concerning "subversion" were very great. The Westerners were accused, usually on flimsy or even manufactured evidence, of dangerous "espionage" activities. And they were subjected, as few men have been, to a test of the durability of all that had gone into their sense of being.

PART TWO

PRISON THOUGHT REFORM OF WESTERNERS

In dealing with the criminals, there shall be regularly adopted measures of corrective study classes, individual interviews, study of assigned documents, and organized discussions, to educate them in the admission of guilt and obedience to the law, political and current events, labor production, and culture, so as to expose the nature of the crime committed, thoroughly wipe out criminal thoughts, and establish a new moral code.

Chinese Communist Prison Regulations

CHAPTER 3

RE-EDUCATION: DR. VINCENT

I first heard of Dr. Charles Vincent through a newspaper article announcing his arrival in Hong Kong by ship after three and one-half years of imprisonment and twenty previous years of medical practice in China. I was put in touch with him through another subject of mine who had known him in the past. When I telephoned him at the boarding house where he was staying, he readily agreed to talk with me; but when I began to describe to him the location of my office, he showed some hesitation and then made it clear that he wanted me to come and pick him up. I consented to this arrangement and met him in the lobby of his rooming house just five days after he crossed the border. Dr. Vincent was a short, dark-complexioned, muscular Frenchman in his early fifties. He was not emaciated, but he did look pale; and in his eyes was that characteristic combination of fear and distance which has been aptly labeled "the thousand-mile stare."

He said little during the brief automobile ride, but in response to my inquiries about how he was getting on in Hong Kong, he described feeling frightened and nervous. Upon entering my study, he sat down hesitantly, and listened without comment to my few sentences of explanation about my research. When I had finished, he looked at me directly for the first time and asked a quick series of questions: How old was I? How long had I been in Hong Kong doing this work? And then, with particular emphasis, "Are

you standing on the 'people's side,' or on the 'imperialists' side'?"
I told him I was part of the non-Communist world, but that I tried
as much as possible to take no side in order to gain an understanding of the process of thought reform. He went on to explain that
this was important because

From the imperialistic side we are not criminals; from the people's side
we are criminals. If we look at this from the imperialists' side, re-
education is a kind of compulsion. But if we look at it from the people's
side, it is to die and be born again.

Having expressed both his fear and his dilemma—and indeed, the
paradox of thought reform itself—he needed no more prompting to
go into the details of his ordeal. I said little during this first three-
hour interview, and not much more during the remaining fifteen
hours (five additional meetings) which we spent together, for Dr.
Vincent had a great need to talk about what he had been through,
and he did so in an unusually vivid fashion.

As one of the few remaining foreign physicians in Shanghai, he
had been conducting a lucrative practice which included several
Communist officials—until suddenly confronted on the street one
afternoon by five men with revolvers. They produced a warrant for
his arrest and took him to the "detention house" (or "re-education
center") where he was to spend the next three and a half years.

Interrogation and "Struggle"

After a few preliminaries he was placed in a small (8' x 12') bare
cell which already contained eight other prisoners, all of them
Chinese. They were a specially selected group, each of them "advanced" in his personal "reform," each eager to apply himself enthusiastically to the reform of others as a means of gaining "merits"
toward his own release. Their greeting was hardly a friendly one: the
"cell chief" identified himself, and addressing Vincent in Chinese [1]
by his newly-acquired prison number, instructed him to sit in the
center of the cell while the other prisoners formed a circle around
him. Each in turn then shouted invectives at Vincent, denouncing
him as an "imperialist" and a "spy," demanding that he "recognize"
his "crimes" and "confess everything" to the "government." Vincent protested: He was not a spy. He was a doctor. He had worked

as a doctor in China for twenty years. But this only resulted in more vehement accusations: "The government has all the proof. They have arrested you and the government never makes a mistake. You have not been arrested for nothing." Then his cellmates went on to question him further about all the activities in which he engaged as a physician to "cover up" his "spy personality." This procedure in the cell was known as a "struggle," conducted for the purpose of "helping" a prisoner with his "confession," and it was an experience which Vincent had to undergo frequently, particularly during the early phases of his imprisonment.

After several hours of this disturbing treatment, Vincent was called for his first interrogation. He was taken to a small room with three people in it: the interrogator or "judge," [2] an interpreter, and a secretary. The judge opened the session with a vague accusation and an emphatic demand: "You have committed crimes against the people, and you must now confess everything." Vincent's protestations of innocence were countered with the angry declaration: "The government never arrests an innocent man." The judge went on to ask a series of general questions concerning Vincent's activities, professional associations, organizational contacts, friends, and acquaintances during his entire twenty years in China. He answered these as accurately as he could, but was unable to satisfy his interrogator. The judge's demands always contained a tantalizing combination of hint, threat, and promise: "The government knows all about your crimes. That is why we arrested you. It is now up to you to confess everything to us, and in this way your case can be quickly solved and you will soon be released."

After a few hours of this interrogation, questions began to focus more and more upon alleged connections with people from sev- eral groups: his own embassy, American government officials, and Catholic, Japanese, and Nationalist Chinese agencies. By 6 a.m., after ten successive hours of interrogation, he had produced much information; but he still asserted his innocence, denied that he was a spy or had any subversive relationship with these organizations, and again said that he did not understand why he had been arrested. This angered the judge, who ordered handcuffs applied to Vincent's wrists, holding his arms behind his back. He dismissed the prisoner from the room, demanding that he "think over" his "crimes." But when he was returned ten minutes later, Vincent still stated that he could not recognize crimes of any kind. The judge again became incensed, ordered chains placed about Vincent's ankles, and sent him back to his cell. His return there was the occasion for continuous struggle and humiliation.

When you get back with your chains, your cellmates receive you as an enemy. They start "struggling" to "help" you. The "struggle" goes on all day to 8 p.m. that night. You are obliged to stand with chains on your ankles and holding your hands behind your back. They don't assist you because you are too reactionary. . . . You eat as a dog does, with your mouth and teeth. You arrange the cup and bowl with your nose to try to absorb broth twice a day. If you have to make water they open your trousers and you make water in a little tin in the corner. . . . In the W.C. someone opens your trousers and after you are finished they clean you. You are never out of the chains. Nobody pays any attention to your hygiene. Nobody washes you. In the room they say you are in chains only because you are a reactionary. They continuously tell you that, if you confess all, you will be treated better.

Toward the end of the second day, Vincent was concerned only with finding some relief ("You start to think, how to get rid of these chains. *You must get rid of the chains*" [3]). That night, when called for interrogation, he made what he called a "wild confession"—a description of espionage activities which he knew to be nonexistent. As he explained it:

We see in the judge someone who wants to press something on us. And if we show we are a big criminal, maybe we will get better treatment. . . . Everyone of us tries to cheat the government this way. We know they are angry with the Americans . . . so we become a member of an American spy ring . . . I invented a whole organization.

But when he was pressed for details, he could not substantiate his story, and inconsistencies appeared. The confession was rejected, and he was once more summarily dismissed by the judge. The round of interrogation and struggle continued.

On the third night, he changed his tactics. Aware that the officials were greatly interested in his activities and contacts, he began to reconstruct and confess every detail of every conversation with friends and associates which he could remember from the whole of his twenty years in China. He did this because "I thought they were trying to prove I gave intelligence to friends."

Now that he was talking freely, his captors began to press home their advantage. Interrogations, ever more demanding, took up the greater part of each night; these were interrupted every two or three hours for a rapid and painful promenade (in chains) which served to keep the prisoner awake, to increase his physical discomfort, and to give him a sense of movement ("in order to convince you to speed up your confession"). During the day, he was required to dictate to another prisoner everything he had confessed the night before, and anything additional he could think of. When he was not dictating the confessions or making new ones, he was being struggled. Every activity in the cell seemed to be centered around him and his confession. He soon realized that the cell chief was making daily reports to prison officials and receiving regular instructions on how to deal with him. Everything he did or said—every word, movement, or expression—was noted and written down by other prisoners, then conveyed to the prison authorities.

For eight days and nights, Vincent experienced this program of alternating struggle and interrogation, and was permitted no sleep at all.[4] Moreover, he was constantly told by his cellmates that he was completely responsible for his own plight. ("You want the chains! You want to be shot! . . . . Otherwise, you would be more 'sincere' and the chains would not be necessary.") He found himself in a Kafka-like maze of vague and yet damning accusations: he could neither understand exactly what he was guilty of ("recognize his crimes") nor could he in any way establish his innocence. Overwhelmed by fatigue, confusion, and helplessness, he ceased all resistance.

You are annihilated. . . . exhausted. . . . you can't control yourself, or remember what you said two minutes before. You feel that all is lost. . . . From that moment, the judge is the real master of you. You accept anything he says. When he asks how many 'intelligences' you gave to that person, you just put out a number in order to satisfy him. If he says, "Only those?," you say, "No, there are more." If he says, "One hundred," you say, "One hundred". . . . You do whatever they want. You don't pay any more attention to your life or to your handcuffed arms. You can't distinguish right from left. You just wonder when you will be shot—and begin to hope for the end of all this.

A confession began to emerge which was still "wild"—full of exaggerations, distortions, and falsehoods—but at the same time closely related to real events and people in Vincent's life. Every night Vincent would sign a written statement of his newly confessed material with a thumbprint, as his hands were not free for writing. He was so compliant by this time that he made no attempt to check upon the accuracy of what he was signing.

After three weeks, the emphasis again shifted; now he was required to report on others, to make exhaustive lists of all of the people he had known in China, and to write out their addresses, their affiliations, and anything at all which he knew about their activities. Vincent complied, again supplying a mixture of truths, half-truths, and untruths. But after two weeks of this, under the continuing pressures of his captors, these descriptions became exposés and denunciations; friends, associates became drawn into the web. Still the clamor from the judge, officials, and cellmates was the same as it had been since the moment of imprisonment: "Confess! . . . Confess all! . . . You must be frank! . . . You must show your faith in the government! . . . Come clean! . . . Be sincere! . . . Recognize your crimes! . . ."

At this point—about two months from the date of his arrest—Vincent was considered to be ready for a beginning "recognition" of his "crimes." This required that he learn to look at himself from the "people's standpoint"—to accept the prevailing Communist definition of criminal behavior, including the principle that "the people's standpoint makes no distinction between news, information, and intelligence." He described two examples of this process:

For instance, I was the family physician and friend of an American correspondent. We talked about many things, including the political situation. . . . The judge questioned me again and again about my relationship with this man. He asked me for details about everything we had talked about. . . . I admitted that at the time of the "liberation," when I saw the horsedrawn artillery of the Communist army, I told this to my American friend. . . . The judge shouted that this American was a spy who was collecting espionage material for his spy organization, and that I was guilty of supplying him with military intelligence. . . . At first I did not accept this, but soon I had to add it to my confession. . . . This is adopting the people's standpoint. . . .

I knew a man who was friendly with an American military attaché. I told him the price of shoes and that I couldn't buy gasoline for my car. I had already agreed that this was economic intelligence. So I wrote that I gave economic intelligence to this man. But they made it clear that I must say that I received an espionage mission from the American mili-

tary attaché through the other person, to collect economic intelligence.
. . . This was the people's standpoint.

"Leniency" and "Study"

Just as Vincent was beginning to express himself from the
"people's standpoint"—but in a dazed, compliant, and unenthu-
siastic manner—he was suddenly surprised by a remarkable improvement in his status: the handcuffs and chains were removed, he was
permitted to be comfortably seated when talking to the judge, and
he was in turn addressed in friendly tones. He was told that the
government regretted that he had been having such a difficult
time, that it really wanted only to help him, and that in accordance
with its "lenient policy" it would certainly treat him kindly and
soon release him—if only he would make an absolutely complete
confession, and then work hard to "reform" himself. And to help
things along, pressures were diminished, and he was permitted more
rest. This abrupt reversal in attitude had a profound effect upon
Vincent: for the first time he had been treated with human consideration, the chains were gone, he could see a possible solution
ahead, there was hope for the future.

Now he was offered more friendly "guidance" in rewriting (not
once but many times) his entire confession, including descriptions
and denunciations of other people; and his change of fortune gave
him added incentive in applying himself to the task. But he soon
found that this guidance was not to be taken lightly, and on three
occasions when he expressed some measure of resistance, saying,
"This I didn't do," the chains were reapplied for two or three days,
accompanied by a return to the harsh treatment of previous weeks.

Once "leniency" had been initiated, however, Vincent was never
again to experience anything as overwhelming as the assaults of
his early prison period. Given the luxury of eight hours of sleep
a night, of relatively calm and restrained interrogations (he was even
permitted to sit on a chair), of practically no harassment in the
cell, Vincent spent the next two or three weeks doing nothing but
developing in even greater detail his confession material. During
his sessions with the judge, he received further instructions upon
the proper way to apply the "people's standpoint" to all that he was
writing and saying.

Meanwhile, he was initiated into the regular cell routine: carefully regimented arrangements for sleeping and awakening, for eating and for relieving oneself. Freed of the chains, he could join the others on the two daily excursions to the toilet (everyone running head down, to an area with two open toilets, each permitted about forty-five seconds to attend to his needs with sharp criticism directed at anyone who took longer than this), and in the use of the urine bucket in the cell. He was still addressed only by prison number, and continued to receive food adequate for survival but poor in quality. And the sores and infections caused by his chains and handcuffs were given more attention, including local applications and penicillin injections.

Then, three weeks after the beginning of "leniency," he began to take part in the cell's organized "re-education" procedures. This meant active involvement in the group study program—the *hsüeh hsi*—whose sessions took up almost the entire waking existence of the prisoners, ten to sixteen hours a day. Led by the cell chief, its procedure was simple enough: one prisoner read material from a Communist newspaper, book, or pamphlet; and then each in turn was expected to express his own opinion and to criticize the views of others. Everyone was required to participate actively, and anyone who did not was severely criticized. Each had to learn to express himself from the "correct" or "people's standpoint"—applied not only to personal actions, but to political, social, and ethical issues. With each of the prisoners feeling that his freedom or even his life might be at stake, the zeal of the participants was overwhelming.

For a long time after Dr. Vincent joined the group (and probably because of his presence), discussions centered upon past Western insults to China: territorial aggrandizement, infringements upon sovereignty, special privileges demanded for Western nationals. And the message was conveyed to him personally that "under the cloak of medicine" he was nothing but a representative of "exploitation," an agent of the "imperialists," a life-long "spy," whose actions were from the beginning "harmful to the Chinese people."

Discussions starting at an intellectual level would quickly become concerned with personal analysis and criticism. When Dr. Vincent was found wanting in his adoption of the "people's standpoint" or when his views were considered "erroneous," it became necessary for him to "examine himself" and look into the causes of these "reactionary" tendencies. He had to search out the harmful "bourgeois" and "imperialistic" influences from his past for further evaluation and self-criticism. Every "question" or "problem" had to be "solved," according to the "facts," in order to get to the "truth," viewing everything, of course, from the "people's standpoint."

Special "movements" would take place, jolting the prisoners from the ordinary routine into renewed emotional efforts. Sometimes these were part of broad, all-China campaigns, sometimes related to national prison movements, and sometimes locally initiated; but whether directed at "thought attitude," prison discipline, hygiene problems, or personal confessions, they always served to plunge each prisoner into a more thorough and compelling self-examination. Everyone was intent upon demonstrating his own "reform" and "progressive viewpoint." The atmosphere came to resemble that of a great moral crusade.

Dr. Vincent was still receiving more personal attention than anyone else in the cell. At first he simply gave lip-service to what he knew to be the "correct" point of view, but over a period of weeks and months, he began to accept these judgments inwardly, and to apply them to himself.

In the cell, you work in order to recognize your crimes. . . . They make you understand your crimes are very heavy. You did harm to the Chinese people. You are really a spy, and all the punishment you received was your own fault. . . . In the cell, twelve hours a day, you talk and talk—you have to take part—you must discuss yourself, criticize, inspect yourself, denounce your thought. Little by little you start to admit something, and look to yourself only using the "people's judgment."

At times, the prison would take on a highly academic atmosphere. Vincent and his fellow prisoners would focus their attention on applying Marxist theory to Chinese and international problems; prisoners would be referred to as "schoolmates," prison officials would be called "instructors," and all would emphasize that only "discussion" and "persuasion" should be used to teach the ignorant. As Vincent became more and more involved in the process, he began to experience its impact.

They put in evidence, in a compulsory way, the progress of the people. The people have a future. The theories of Marx about history teach us that imperialism is condemned to be destroyed. . . . They put in evidence all the examples of repression by the imperialists in China, the missions, their charity, helping landlords, helping the KMT [Kuomintang, or Nationalist Party]—all against the people. . . . They put in evidence the development of the Soviet Union—its industries, re-education, culture, uplifting of the people, the friendly help of the Soviet to China. They told us of the victory against imperialism in the Korean war, the gradual remolding of Chinese society, the three- and five-year plans in order to arrive at socialist society, the transformation of agriculture, the development of heavy industries, military improvement to defend the people, peace movement. . . . Living conditions of the Soviet state are very high; we see it in the movies, magazines, newspapers. We see the better condition of Chinese people in comparison with pre-liberation times—the hygiene movement in China, the cultural, the economic movement, the rights for minorities, rights between man and woman, free elections, the difference between freedom in the socialist and the imperialist worlds. . . . They solve every problem through discussion—the Korean war, the Indo-Chinese war. . . . They never use force; every question is solved through conference.

But always, the emphasis would shift back to the individual emotional experience—to the "thought problems" which prevented prisoners from making progress. Dr. Vincent learned to express "spontaneously" all of his reactions and attitudes during the discussions and especially to bring out his "wrong thoughts." And as he did so, he became ever more enmeshed in the special problem-solving techniques of this ideological world.

You have to get rid of and denounce all your imperialist thoughts, and you must criticize all of your own thoughts, guided by the official. If not, they will have someone else solve your problem and criticize you more profoundly. . . . You have a problem—you have to denounce it—a schoolmate has to help you—his help has to have "proper standpoint" . . . . I am quiet—they say, "You have a problem"; I say, "I wonder why the Chinese didn't confiscate all of the capitalist properties like the Soviets. I think it might be better to do it like the Russians —this is my problem." They have schoolmates to solve my problem, to demonstrate I am on the wrong side because the Chinese Communists have to proceed in another way. Their way is reform rather than compulsion. He demonstrates that the Soviet revolution was different from the Chinese revolution—that the Chinese capitalist suffered through the imperialists because we imperialists never gave them the opportunity to develop their industries. Now the Chinese capitalists have to be useful to the Chinese government and undergo reform. If they follow the government they will have a bright future. . . . They have to explain the facts until I am convinced. If I am not convinced I must say I don't understand, and they bring new facts. If I am still not satisfied, I have the right to call an inspector—but I wouldn't, I would just accept, otherwise there might be a struggle. . . . You are all day under the compulsion of denouncing your thoughts and solving your problems. . . . You understand the truth of the people—day by day, moment by moment—and you cannot escape, because from your external manifestation they say they can understand your internal situation. If you continually denounce your thoughts, you can be happy denouncing yourself. You are not resisting. But they keep a record, and after one week if you are not saying anything, they tell you you are resisting your re-education. . . . If you think out five or six problems it is a good manifestation; you are progressing because you like to discuss your imperialist thoughts. This is necessary, because if you don't get rid of these thoughts, you can't put in new ones.

When Vincent was too quiet and did not produce enough "wrong thoughts," he was criticized for not being "sincere"—for not taking an active enough part in thought reform. When his views showed the slightest deviation from Communist orthodoxy, he was told that he was "too subjective," "individualistic," or that he retained "imperialist attitudes." When it was felt that he was not wholeheartedly involved in his reform—but was merely going through the motions—he was accused of "spreading a smoke-screen," "window dressing," "finding a loophole," or "failing to combine theory with practice." And after a while he followed the others' lead in seeking out these faults in himself through self-criticism, and analyzing their cause and their significance.

A portion of the study hours each day were devoted to "daily-life criticisms": general conduct, attitudes toward others, willingness to do one's share of work in the cell, eating and sleeping habits. Where Vincent was found wanting in any of these, this was attributed to "imperialist" or "bourgeois" greed and exploitation, in contrast to the "people's attitude" of sharing and co-operation. When considered lax in his work, he was criticized for lacking the "correct labor point of view"; when he dropped a plate, this was wasting the people's money; if he drank too much water, this was "draining the blood of the people"; if he took up too much room while sleeping, this was "imperialistic expansion."

Vincent would still hear talk of men who were shot because

"they resisted"; and on the other hand he heard of the "bright future"—early release or happy existence in China—for those who "accepted their re-education."

Advanced Standing

After more than a year of this continuous "re-education," Vincent was again subjected to a series of interrogations aimed at once more reconstructing his confession—"because after one year the government hopes you understand a little better your crimes." Now from among the great mass of material which he had already produced, the judge focused upon a few selected points, all of which had some relationship to actual events. And thus, "from a wild confession, you go to a more concrete confession." Then, eight "crimes" emerged—including membership in a right-wing French political organization, several forms of "espionage" and "intelligence" in association with American, Catholic, and other "reactionary" groups, other anti-Communist activities, and "slanderous insults to the Chinese people." But now Vincent was more deeply immersed in the "people's standpoint," and the confession had a much greater sense of reality for him than before.

You have the feeling that you look to yourself on the people's side, and that you are a criminal. Not all of the time—but moments—you think they are right. "I did this, I am a criminal." If you doubt, you keep it to yourself. Because if you admit the doubt you will be "struggled" and lose the progress you have made. . . . In this way they built up a spy mentality. . . . They built up a criminal. . . . Then your invention becomes a reality. . . . You feel guilty, because all of the time you have to look at yourself from the people's standpoint, and the more deeply you go into the people's standpoint, the more you recognize your crimes.

And at this point he began, in the "correct" manner, to relate his own sense of guilt to the Communist world view:

They taught us what it means to be a capitalist . . . . to enslave and exploit the people so that a small group of persons can enjoy life at the expense of the masses, their capital coming from the blood of the people, not from labor . . . . that all property comes from the blood of the peasant . . . . that we helped this bad policy, that our mind is the capitalistic mind . . . . and in our profession we exploited everyone. We used our profession to exploit people, as we can see from our crimes.

Then came another fourteen months of full-time re-education. Vincent continued to concentrate upon applying Communist theory to his personal situation, demonstrating an ever-expanding "recognition" of his "crimes."

After two years, in order to show that you are more on the people's side, you increase your crimes. . . . I said I wasn't frank before, there were really more intelligences. . . . This is a good point. It means that you are analyzing your crimes. . . . It means that you realize your crimes are very big, and that you are not afraid to denounce yourself . . . . that you trust the people, trust your re-education, and that you like to be reformed.

By this time his activities were no longer limited to his own case; he had by now become active—and skillful—in criticizing others, "helping" them to make progress in confession and reform. He had become an experienced prisoner, and was beginning to be looked upon as a true progressive. He even came to believe a great deal of what he was expressing—although not in a simple manner:

You begin to believe all this, but it is a special kind of belief. You are not absolutely convinced, but you accept it—in order to avoid trouble —because every time you don't agree, trouble starts again.

During his third year of imprisonment, he was once more called in for a revision of his confession. The document became even more brief, concrete, "logical," and convincing. Now Vincent began to think of his sentence, estimating it from the "people's standpoint" which had become so much a part of him.

You have the feeling that your sentence is coming and that you will be sent somewhere else . . . . and you are waiting. . . . You think, "How long—maybe twenty, twenty-five years" . . . . You will be sent to reform through labor . . . to a factory or to a field. . . . They are very generous about this. . . . The government is very generous. The people are very generous. . . . Now you know that you cannot be shot. . . . But you are thinking that your crimes are very heavy.

Now Vincent was told that his "attitude" had greatly improved. He was transferred to a different wing of the prison—and given treasured privileges, such as an hour of outdoor exercise a day and additional recreation periods in the cell. He found himself living in harmony with his captors, and during the last few months of his imprisonment was even permitted to give French lessons to other prisoners and to conduct medical classes for students brought to the prison for this purpose. All of this was not without its effect:

They used this as a premium in order to show me that they weren't against my work or my profession, but were only against my reactionary mind. To show that my work was well accepted, that they accepted my theories. . . . To show what it means to live among the people, if I become one of the people. . . . To put in my mind that life among the people is good.

Soon he was called in for a formal signing of his confession—both a French version in his own handwriting, and a Chinese translation. Photographers and moving-picture cameramen were on hand, and he also read it for sound recording. With many others like it, it was widely disseminated throughout China and other parts of the world. A short time later he was called before the judge, and after three years of "solving" his case, he was read both the charges and the sentence: for "espionage" and other "crimes" against the people, three years of imprisonment—this considered to be already served. He was expelled immediately from China, and within two days, he was on a British ship heading for Hong Kong.

Freedom

From his story, Dr. Vincent might appear to be a highly successful product of thought reform. But when I saw him in Hong Kong, the issue was much more in doubt. He was a man in limbo, caught between the two worlds.

In his confusion and fear he felt that he was being constantly observed and manipulated. Much of this paranoid content was an internal extension of his prison environment:

I have a certain idea that someone is spying on me—an imperialist spying on me because I came from the Communist world—interested to look and see what I think. . . . When I am doing something I feel someone is looking at me—because from external manifestation he is anxious to look at what is going on inside of me. We were trained this way in our re-education.

And thinking out loud about me, he said:

I have a feeling he is not just a doctor. He is connected with some imperialist organization which will bring me danger. . . . I think maybe someone else is telling you the questions to ask me. . . . But I give you everything, and if tomorrow something happens, I could say, "This is the truth. I have endeavored to tell the truth."

He expressed distrust toward the friend who had arranged for him to see me:

I opened myself with him and told him my ideas. But then I thought, perhaps he will use this against me. We were both re-educated, taught to denounce everybody and not to trust anybody, that it is your duty to denounce.

He later explained the reason for his request that I pick him up at his boarding house:

When you telephoned me . . . I thought maybe he is a Communist. . . . Perhaps an enemy. . . . I refused to come here alone, because I didn't have a witness. . . . This way you come, you are seen, and if I disappear there is a witness.

In this borderline psychotic state, Vincent graphically described his split identity:

When I left China I had this strange feeling: Now I am going to the imperialistic world. No one will take care of me. I'll be unemployed and lost. . . . Everyone will look at me as a criminal. . . . Still, I thought, there is a Communist Party in my country. I am coming out of a Communist world; they must know I have had reform training. Perhaps they will be interested in keeping me. Maybe they can help me, and I will not be really lost. I will go to the Communists, tell them where I came from, and I'll have a future. . . .

But when I came to Hong Kong, the situation changed completely. The Consulate sent a man right away on board with a special motorboat. They took care of me and asked me if I am in need. They told me they wired my government and my family. They brought me to a boarding house, nice room, nice food—and gave me money to spend. The capitalist world is more friendly than I thought it would be.

In his struggle to achieve some sense of reality, his perceptions of his new environment were faulty. He wavered between beliefs, always influenced by his fears:

I had dinner last night at the home of Mr. Su [a wealthy, retired Hong Kong Chinese merchant]. I had the feeling that Mr. Su was a pro-Communist. I had this manifestation. Everytime he spoke, I wanted to say, "Yes." I thought he was a judge—I was sympathizing with Mr. Su because he had a court. He asked me my crimes. I told him all of them in order. He said, "Do you feel guilty about this?" I said, "Yes. I feel guilty about this." I had the impression he was a judge in contact with the Communists and can report everything. . . .

But this morning I wrote a letter to my wife, and I went into detail about my crimes. In this letter I denied completely my crimes. I know my wife—I know her well—she can't do anything to me, so I wrote, "How cruel they were to make a criminal out of someone like me"— and yet last night I admitted guilt. Why? Because there was a judge there. . . .

Today at lunch with the Jesuit Fathers, I know them well—I denied everything because they are my friends. When I feel safe I am on one side. When I have the feeling I am not safe, right away I jump on the other side.

In his constant testing of his new environment, he began to call into question many of the teachings of his thought reform:

When I arrived in Hong Kong, another foreigner coming out of China put me in this difficult position. He told me about the situation in North China—that it was impossible to get meat there, and that there is rationing because everything is going to the Soviet Union. I said—"Impossible! A foreigner likes to exaggerate"—because we never heard about this rationing in jail. I said, "How can it be possible that the Soviet Union needs food from China when they are making such progress?" . . . . In prison we saw their food lists—butter, meat, whatever they like—but now I hear that food is not enough in the Soviet Union. I ask myself, "Where is the truth?"

He found that what he was experiencing more and more came into conflict with his reform, and he felt that this reality-testing was beneficial to him:

They say there is no progress in my country. But I was surprised to see a new steamer from there here in the harbor. I hear that it is an air-conditioned steamer, built since the war. I thought then that my country is not a colony of America—they can have a steamer line come to Hong Kong. I started little by little to come to reality—bit by bit to make comparison of what they told me. The reality is quite good for me. I am thinking that if a school partner [cellmate] could have the possibility of seeing what I have seen in eight days—what could he believe of his re-education? . . . .

And similarly when he read in an American magazine about immense new railroad machinery developed in the United States, he questioned the precepts that "the imperialists are interested in only light industry—to exploit the people" and that "Soviet heavy industry is leading everybody." He commented:

When I saw these, I thought that the Communists were cheating me—cheating everybody.

Midway through the series of interviews, he began to feel restless, neglected, and increasingly hostile to his new surroundings. He reversed the previous trend, and again became suspicious of ulterior motives in his new environment:

Everyday I read the Hong Kong paper I see children are receiving milk and eggs through the help of America. . . . But in prison they are all the time saying that the American imperialists are giving things to people in order to cover up—to show that they take an interest. I see this as a political point—a feeling I have which is strictly connected with re-education.

He became markedly critical of what he saw around him, and more favorable in his references to his prison experience—looking back upon it almost longingly.

Since coming out, arguments and conversation are terribly uninteresting. There are no concrete things. Time is very superficial—people don't solve any problems. They are just going on—spending four hours for nothing—between one drink and another smoke and wait for tomorrow. In re-education we solved every problem . . . . we were given texts to use and had to read them—then new discussions until the moment when there were no more problems. . . . I went to a film last night. I was disturbed by it. Disturbed because it wasn't an educational film—it was just a lot of shooting and violence. I was thinking how much more comforting to have an education film as in the prison—never a film like this there. So brutal—so much fighting and killing. . . .

When we came out of the movie, a Chinese child touched the handbook of a Western lady who was with us. She was very disturbed and kicked the child. I thought, "Why violence, why not just explain to the child that he shouldn't do it?" This has a connection with re-education—because all of the time they told us that relations in society should be on a logical basis, not on a forced basis.

He expressed the loneliness of his new freedom:

There is this kind of freedom here—if you want to do something, you can do it. But there is not the collective way of progress—just an individual way of going on. Nobody pays any attention to you and your surroundings.

Referring back to his prison experience, he said:

It is not that I miss it, but I find that it was more easy.

At this time he also began to feel that I was "exploiting" him for my own professional gain; he "confessed" these feelings to me:

I had a very bad thought about you. I thought that Americans are all the same—when they have need of you they use you, and after that you are a forgotten man.

But during the last two interviews, he became more cheerful and optimistic, more concerned about arrangements for his future. He was now more definite in his conviction that the Communists had wronged him cruelly throughout his imprisonment.

His views on Communist methods became more sharply critical, and more interpretive.

My impression is that they are cruel and that there is no freedom. There is compulsion in everything, using Marxism and Leninism in order to promise to the ignorant a bright future. . . . I was really accepting things in order to make myself more comfortable—because I was in great fear. . . . In this situation your willpower completely disappears. . . . You accept because there is a compulsion all the time—that if you don't go on their road, there is no escape. . . . To avoid argument you become passive. . . .

He described his post-imprisonment change of heart toward his former captors—from toleration to condemnation:

My first few days out I recognized that they were cruel with us—but not in a strong way. There was a religious belief playing on me: if someone does bad to you, don't keep your hate; and another feeling—what I pass through there would be useful for me in the next life. I looked upon it as bad versus good, and I felt I suffered for something. . . . Now my resentment is stronger than it was the first few days. I have the feeling that if I meet a Communist in my country, my first reaction toward him will be violent.

Before leaving for Europe, he began to seek contacts and letters of introduction which he felt could help him in the future. He again wished to do medical work in an underdeveloped Asian setting, but he noted a significant change in the type of position which he sought:

Before I would never accept a nine-to-five job, because it means that you are busy all the time with no time to do what you want. Now—it is very strange—I would like to have such an engagement. I have the feeling that with this kind of job, everything is easy. I don't have to think of what happens at the end of the month. It would give me security, a definite feeling for the future because I have nothing definite in the future.

But Dr. Vincent knew himself well enough to recognize that this quest for regularity and security would not last.

This is not one hundred per cent of my feeling. . . . You see the contradiction—I am just out from the door of the cell—only one step out. But if I take some more steps—and consider what is best for my character—perhaps I will again decide to be by myself. . . . In a Communist country everybody does the same thing—and you accept. Here it is different: you are still the master of yourself.

He felt that the most significant change which he had undergone as a result of his reform was his increased willingness to "open myself to others." And in regard to our talks together, he said:

This is the first time a foreigner knows my character. I believe this comes through re-education—because we were instructed to know our internal selves. . . . I have never talked so frankly. I have a feeling I left part of myself in Hong Kong.

More will be said about Dr. Vincent later on, including his background and character; but first I will return to the prison thought reform process, and to the different inner experience of a man of another calling.

CHAPTER 4

FATHER LUCA:
THE FALSE CONFESSION

I met Father Francis Luca in a Catholic hospital in Hong Kong, where he was convalescing from the physical and emotional blows of three-and-one-half years of imprisonment. He had spent ten years in China, and had just arrived in the colony a few days before; my visit had been arranged by another priest whom we both knew. Father Luca's appearance was rather striking. An Italian in his late thirties, his eyes looked alert and searching, with little of the fear and distance I had seen in Dr. Vincent's eyes. But he had a restless, almost driven, quality which made it difficult for him, despite a partial physical incapacity caused by his imprisonment, to remain seated in his chair. He was interested in and curious about everything—about me, about the hospital, and especially about the significance of his prison experience. One of the first things he told me was that immediately upon boarding the British ship which took him from China to Hong Kong, he had begun writing down all he could remember of his ordeal so that he could record it "before seeing others."

But he too had questions to ask of me: Was I Catholic? And, was I an American? My "no" to the first and "yes" to the second did not seem to trouble him, or to interfere with the ready flow of his words.

Still a little confused during our first talk, he jumped quickly from subject to subject; yet one theme kept recurring. It was not that of the pain or humiliation of his prison experience, but rather his sadness at leaving China. He told me that he had cried bitterly upon boarding the ship, deeply disturbed at the thought that he would never have the chance to return. As he spoke, I noticed that the black robe he was wearing was not clerical garb, but the robe of a Chinese scholar. There were chopsticks on his eating table, and the only complaint among his otherwise grateful remarks about the hospital was the difficulty he had in obtaining good Chinese food, which was the only food he cared to eat. And when another European priest paid a brief visit to the room, Father Luca chatted happily with him—in Chinese. Whatever the success or failure of Father Luca's political reform, he had clearly become a convert to Chinese life.

During the month which he spent in the hospital, I paid him fourteen visits, spending a total of about twenty-five hours with him. Throughout, we were engaged in a common quest for under-standing, and he spoke openly and at great length about the details of his imprisonment and of his life before that.

Father Luca's arrest had not come as a complete surprise, as he had heard that accusations of "subversion" and "anti-Communist activities" had been made against him at public meetings. He had promised himself that, if imprisoned, he would defend the Church and say nothing false. His initial response to interrogation was, therefore, one of forthright defiance. When the judge asked him whether he knew why he had been arrested, he replied, "It must be either due to a misunderstanding or else it is a matter of religion." This angered the judge, who insisted, "There is no matter of re-ligion. We have freedom of religion in China. It is because you op-posed the interests of the people." During subsequent questions about his activities and associations in China, Father Luca noticed that his interrogator began to dwell particularly upon his relation-ship with another priest, Father C, a friend of his whose political and military activities against the Communists Father Luca had himself criticized.

This first interrogation lasted for just one hour, but it served to orient Father Luca for his later confession:

In my mind I had the question, "What will they accuse me of? How will they do it?" Now I began to understand—they would put the question of my relationship with Father C as the important thing. It was good to understand this, but I was not sure how they would go about it. I had heard that the Communists made people confess to all kinds of fantastic charges. But I was then determined not to admit to anything that wasn't true.

He was equally defiant in the cell, penetrating and critical in his observations of his captors. When the cell chief advised him that he would be quickly released if he would "say all you have done," he skeptically replied: "But I have heard that you have been here for six months. Since you must have confessed all of your deeds, how is it that you are still here?" And when he witnessed his first struggle (against another prisoner)—during which the cell chief urged everyone to "help" the man under fire—he thought to himself: "So this is the way of the Communists—using good words to do bad things: *to help* means to maltreat people."

He was awakened from his sleep on the second night and interrogated about Father C's assistants. He was able to tell the Christian name of one, but stated that he did not know the other. The judge heatedly insisted: "It is impossible that you do not know him. You are not being honest or sincere." Father Luca bridled at this impugning of his integrity, angrily insisting that he *was* being sincere, and *was* telling the entire truth. The judge's immediate response was to order chains with twenty-pound weights placed around Father Luca's ankles. He then asked the prisoner the same question, and again received a similar reply. Luca was dismissed and sent back to his cell; there the cell chief, upon seeing the chains, severely castigated him. When called back less than an hour later, his answers still failed to satisfy, and handcuffs were placed about his wrists.

During the third night's interrogation, the judge emphasized the closeness of Father Luca's relationship with Father C, strongly implying that he must have known him before coming to China. When Luca insisted that they had first met in Peking, the judge left the room and Luca was required to sit on the ground with his legs, in chains, stretched out. Unable to maintain this position, he would lean backward; his weight would then fall on his wrists, which were shackled behind his back. Finding the pain of the handcuffs digging into his skin and the general discomfort of his position to be unbearable, thoughts of surrender and compromise came to him for the first time:

It is as I have been told. They will have their false confession. But I don't want to make a false confession. Maybe there is a way to say something that is not totally untrue to satisfy them—but what? . . . . I've said the truth. They don't want the truth. I've only one way to escape: to guess what they really want. With all the circumstances of my life, the most believable thing was that in going back to Europe it was possible to meet him . . . not true, but believable.

He replied that they had met in Europe after the war. The judge was still displeased. And at that point, an assistant passed something to the judge which to Father Luca looked like a photograph.

I thought, "Certainly this can't be a photograph of Father C and myself taken outside of China. It must be the photograph I made with Chinese priests in Rome in 1939 [he had really posed for such a picture]. They must be using this photograph as proof that I had seen Father C there." I don't know how I came to think this. I gave my mind such an explanation because I could not endure the pain. I was coming to the conclusion that they wanted me to say I had seen him in Rome. I thought it might be according to a story which they wanted to put out that Father C was doing espionage work under directions from the Vatican. I knew that this was their line from their propaganda.

So, in answer to the judge's original question about their meeting, Father Luca said: "It was in Rome, in 1939." He was immediately permitted to stand up, experiencing direct relief of the pain, and a few minutes later was taken back to his cell.

The Labyrinth

But the cell chief, acting upon instructions from above, still denounced Luca as not "sincere," and ordered that he remain continuously standing, in order for him to "meditate" on his "crimes." And for the next month—a harrowing maze of nightly interrogations and daily struggles—he was kept constantly awake, his cellmates alternating in their "night duty," pinching, slapping, and poking him to make sure that he did not sleep. Because he was forced to maintain a standing position, his legs became swollen and distended with fluid. He remembers being permitted to sleep on only three occasions: once when he fainted, another time when he became so confused that he could not follow the interrogation, and a third time when interrogations were postponed because of a heavy storm. He estimates that he slept for a total of only sixteen hours during this entire four-week period. He became increasingly confused, and could no longer tell night from day; he found himself constantly straining his faculties in his attempts to understand just what it was he was expected to say:

At the beginning it was only a question of curiosity, but afterwards, when I couldn't endure it and my mind was confused, I thought, "Why don't they say exactly what they want me to say? It is so difficult to get at what they want." After two weeks I would say almost anything they wanted me to say . . . but of course not easily.

In this state, he "confessed" to three major "crimes": use of a concealed radio set to send and receive "espionage" information; organization of a ring of young boys for the purpose of conducting sabotage and writing anti-Communist publications (the public accusation made prior to his imprisonment); and the active participation—as "secretary"—in an "espionage organization" allegedly headed by Father C. All three of these "admissions" were false, built up through half-truths and fabrications.

Father Luca's description of the step-by-step development of these "espionage" themes so graphically reveals the unfolding of his false confession—and his developing belief in some of his own falsehoods—that I have allowed him to speak here at some length. As he told me about the first of these, the concealed radio theme, I was impressed by the complexities of the tortuous process involved:

The first thing about the radio came when the interrogator said: "You have other things which you don't speak about, but you can be sure that the people know them. Don't think that we're not informed." I said that I knew there were some people who said I had a special radio —a short wave set. 1 had heard this accusation before I had been arrested. I told him there was nothing true about it. He said, "You say so, but what is the reality? What have you put in your storeroom immediately after the liberation?"

I said that I had put nothing there. Then I thought, "Maybe there is something—not a radio—but there was a friend of mine who visited me before the Communists came—and entrusted me with some of his things." I tried to think whether I had put some of his things in the storeroom. My mind was not so strong. I said, "Yes—there may be some things that I didn't remember." I also knew that there was a boy who had worked for us who had turned against us and could have reported anything we stored. So, although I did not think there was a radio there, I dared not oppose what the judge said. He said, "Was it a receiver or a sender?" He said it first because I hadn't known the Chinese word for receiver and sender. At first I said that it wasn't either. Then I said, "Maybe a receiver—yes—perhaps a sender." There was a moment when I had the visualization of an actual sender—but I knew best, it was not true. Like sometimes when you are half dreaming and you see something. . . .

Afterwards, when they asked me how it had come into my hands, I also had to tell a story about this. I said that my friend went away and left it for me, and that a servant had helped me to dismantle it. Then the judge said, "You must have been helped by people who understood electricity." . . . Then I brought in two more men, an electrician who worked in the cathedral, and a young boy who liked to tinker with electrical gadgets. . . . The next part also came out logically from what I had said before. I thought if somebody would have a radio the worst place to keep it would be in the cathedral, because it was known that the Communists especially watched churches and frequently made accusations that there were radio senders there. So I said I had put it some other place. At first I said I couldn't remember the street name. When they insisted, I gave them the name: "Ironwall Street." I made it up. When the judge told me the following day that he couldn't find the street on the map, I told him that perhaps I couldn't remember it correctly. . . .

Then I imagined rather clearly a street with a house, a front room, and behind the front room a radio sender. I had a clear imagination of all this without knowing whether it was true. . . . It was like what I have heard about writing a novel—imagining people who act in a certain way—landscapes and circumstances. For writers, it is very vivid —like the real thing—but of course they know that it is not the real thing. With me it was really vivid—yet not having totally lost the idea that it was untrue. . . . I rather tried to have something logical. . . . In the cell, the other prisoners made suggestions and it developed that I didn't only send messages but also received information. . . . So, little by little, it became not only once but many times, with many other people—and also connected with other priests. . . . It became a whole organization. . . . To some extent I visualized the spy organization. I also invented names and many other details.

The second theme, about the subversive ring of small boys, included a personal confrontation:

After one week the judge interrogated me about a certain Chinese boy. I told him the truth, that the name was not familiar to me. Then he confronted me with the boy in person, and I told him again that I did not know him. But the boy said he knew me, and also that I had told him to write anti-Communist pamphlets. I showed some hesitation, as I had contact with a thousand boys as a parish priest.

The judge said I was not sincere—put the handcuffs on me again—and again made me sit in that extremely painful position until I confessed that I knew the boy. From this kind of interrogation, and from the suggestions which were made in the cell, gradually the confession built up. . . . I knew that I had been accused of instigating a boy to write anti-Communist slogans and to throw stones at street lights. . . . Many of the more concrete suggestions came from the cell. The chief would say, "You have already said you have done this, you must have done more. There must have been more boys." Finally a confession somehow developed in which I said there had been twenty-five boys in this organization whose purpose was conducting sabotage and writing anti-Communist publications.

The third, Father C's organization, involved pressures from cell-mates, developing the points which Father Luca had already "admitted" during the interrogations.

They said, "Well, you certainly did something for Father C." I said, "No, that would have been impossible. I had just come to China. I didn't know the situation. I didn't know Chinese." They said, "You didn't know Chinese, but you do know foreign languages." I admitted that I did. And so somehow the suggestion came out that, since I had to be doing something for him, maybe it was writing, some kind of clerical work. This seemed to be the only thing I *could* do for him. So it came to be like a conviction that not only I could do this, but that I had done this. . . . I remembered that Father C had once mentioned an uncle of his and an old lady he knew, both in Switzerland. So I mixed this thing I heard from him with the suggestion I had written letters for him. And so I said I had written letters to that uncle and old lady in Switzerland.

They said, "You say you have not participated in his organization. Now you say you have written letters for him. That is a connection in his organization. Now what was your title? A man who writes letters like this for an organization—what is he called? What is his title?". . . . They didn't say exactly, but the meaning was very clear. I made the reply, "Secretary." After that I knew I must accept the title of Secretary. . . . I did not really believe I had been a secretary but my mind was confused, and I felt it was impossible to refute their [cell-mates] arguments. I did develop the conviction that I had written two or three letters. It came little by little. . . . It is impossible to say exactly how these ideas first developed.

Father Luca's false visualizations (or illusions) varied in duration from a fleeting moment to a period of a few weeks or months, merging into a dream-like state in which

I was mixed up between real and imaginary things and persons. I was no longer able to distinguish what was real and what was imaginary. . . . I had the notion that many things were imaginary, but I was not sure. I could not say, "This is real," or "This is not real."

This inability to distinguish the real from the unreal extended beyond his immediate confession material. Once, just after he had fainted,

I had the idea that I was no longer in prison. I had been put in a small house outside the cathedral. People were going about outside—chiefly Christians. I heard voices and recognized some of them.

But this delusion was by no means completely removed from the confession, because in it he "came out into the garden" and saw two men, remembering the name of one of them but not of the other. And this he related to his interrogators' demands that he name "secret agents" (Chinese assistants to foreign priests), and his inability to remember the name of one of them in particular. The next day he questioned whether all of this had really happened, as it had become to him "half-dream, half-real." He had two additional delusions which also contained fantasies of rescue, but were more elaborate—and more lasting:

I had the idea that in the cell next to mine was a priest whom I knew very well before. He had also been badly mistreated. One day in bright daylight somebody came into his cell and said to him, "You have talked very well. Your affair is very simple and it is now finished. We see that you are not so bad. We'll take you out this afternoon for a trip to the summer palace [in Peking]. After that we will release you."
Then I heard this priest go out with a sigh, and while he was walking past my cell, he spoke in Latin—saying the beginning words of the Mass—"I shall come unto the altar of God." . . . I thought, "Maybe he is saying that because in coming out of jail he is glad that tomorrow he can say Mass. Or maybe he is offering the pain and the suffering experienced to God." . . . I remember that at that moment I coughed to let him know I was there.

So convinced was he that this episode really occurred that one year later, during a special movement for the exposure of all "bad behavior," he "confessed" to having coughed on this occasion to attract the attention of his fellow priest. It was only when he arrived in Hong Kong after his release, and was told that this other priest had never been arrested, that he gave up his belief in this incident. And the same was true of another rather similar episode:

Another time, in bright daylight, I had the impression I heard a European consul speaking—visiting the prison with a group of people. They went to visit another cell—someone else. On their way out, he said, "I have heard that Father Luca was also here." There was no answer from the prison official. He was just before my cell at that moment—so again I coughed—but the officer led him away. I heard him talking in the courtyard and I coughed again to let him know I was there. But nothing happened. . . . Here in Hong Kong I asked the officials of my government whether a consul ever visited the prison. They said no, and that it certainly couldn't be true.

These delusions were also related to his confession material and to a sense of guilt which was building up within him. For all of the characters in them—the other priest, the consul, and himself —had been involved in an incident which he had already confessed in some detail. Father Luca, in attempting to arrange for a young Chinese girl to leave her country and continue her religious studies in Europe, had approached the other priest for assistance, and the consul for the necessary documents. He had been disturbed by this part of his confession because he feared that it might result in the imprisonment of the other priest, and also troubled by the realization that he had chosen to help this girl from among many others because of affection which he felt for her beyond that of religious sympathy. Further, he had come to realize these actions violated Chinese Communist law; and although his captors did not make much of this, he was troubled by having—in approaching the consul—used "political means for religious aims."

This was an especially important issue in Father Luca's case because, despite his confused state, he continued to struggle against any possible betrayal of his loyalty to the Catholic Church. The judge had been exerting great pressure upon him to make some admission of the Church's relationship to imperialistic activities of Western governments. When he refused to do this, he had been required to resume the painful sitting position in which his hand-cuffs dug into his wrists; and the judge further explained, "I don't say that the Catholic Church is imperialistic. . . . I don't ask you to condemn religion . . . but just expect you to recognize that the imperialists used it as a 'cloak' for their invasion." And thus under the pressure of "pain and explanation" Luca made the statement that "the imperialists used the Catholic Church as a cloak to make the invasion of China." For this statement, and for including other missionaries (whom he feared might be consequently harmed) in his confession, he castigated himself severely, and looked upon himself as having been "weak."

Yet through his mental haze, he attempted to understand his ordeal in terms of his religion:

In the first month I decided "Now I am suffering. It is for me a way of having penance for my sins. Now I think also that I have only one outlook and one hope—hope in God."

The "Way"

But toward the end of this first month, Luca's physical and mental condition began to deteriorate. Infections had developed in the areas of his legs swollen by the chains. His increasing confusion made it difficult for him to keep the details of his confession straight. One fabrication required many more to support it, and this "novel," as he called it, became increasingly confused and contradictory. Then, during an interrogation session, he noticed the judge was moving his papers rapidly from one pile to another, until there were almost none left in the first pile. He became convinced that his case was close to being "solved," and this hope was further fed by the judge's sudden order that the heavy chains be removed from his ankles (the handcuffs had been taken off and put back on again several times, and at this point were also off). The judge then told him to sleep for the next two days, but continued to express disapproval concerning the confession, urging that after this long rest he come up with the proper material. Despite his great fatigue, Luca's fears prevented him from sleeping.

This show of leniency did not help him to add anything to his confession. A few nights later, when he had been called for an interrogation, the judge asked, "Now, have you any intention of being sincere?" Father Luca replied, "I want to be sincere and obedient, but I am not certain how to do it. I hope you will show me a way." To which the judge answered, "I will show you a way," and then called in several prison guards and left the room. These newcomers proceeded to gag Father Luca, hold him in a painful position, and then over the course of the night, to inflict upon him a series of painful injuries, mainly to his back. When they had left him about dawn, he lay helpless for about one hour with multiple fractures of his vertebral column. Then a young Chinese whom he had not met before entered the room and began to speak with him softly, in a kind voice, and in Italian—the first time he had heard his own language since his arrest. He was solicitous and did everything possible to make Luca comfortable; then he proceeded to question him in detail about his confession, and mostly about his relations with Father C.

Luca was affected by this human approach ("His way of questioning was objective and impartial. . . . He spoke my own language. . . . It was easier for me to confess"). And he now gave a relatively accurate version of all of these events, quite different from his previous confession. He still felt compelled to exaggerate many aspects of it because "I knew if I told only the truth it wouldn't be sufficient"; but he included nothing that was grossly false. After about two hours, he complained of pain and weakness—both because of his physical condition and his realization that "what remained was difficult." His visitor agreed to end the interview, and shortly afterward, when it was discovered that Father Luca could not walk, he was carried back to his cell on a stretcher. He later learned that he had been interrogated by a "prisoner-official," a prisoner so "advanced" in his reform that he functions essentially as a staff member. So impressed was Luca with the special quality of this session that, when he was in difficulty on several other occasions later on, he asked to see this Italian-speaking prisoner-official again.

He was also at this time examined by a physician who confirmed his fear that his spine had been broken, but spoke to him reassuringly and told him that after some time it would heal.

The months which followed were especially trying. His case was less resolved than ever, and he was now physically completely helpless, dependent upon his cellmates for his every need. After several days of lying on the stone floor, he was given a hard wooden bed with a rough blanket. He was visited on just one more occasion by the doctor, who arranged for his cellmates to request additional clothes and blankets from Father Luca's mission organization, which still existed on the outside. Luca derived some comfort from this because "I felt better about their beginning to take care of me." But the only medical treatment he received at this time was the prescription of some leg exercises. His requests for assistance with urination or defecation were frequently refused; this, combined with his partial loss of control over both his urinary and anal sphincters (on a neurological basis due to his injury) resulted in frequent soiling of his bedclothes and the cell. The odors caused further resentment and severe criticism from his cellmates, living as they were in an intimacy which made every occurrence the experience of all.

In addition, Luca's immobility led to the development of severely infected bedsores on his back, thighs, and toes. At first these were treated very inadequately with iodine and other topical applications; but after objections had been raised by his cellmates to the odor that emanated from them, he received more effective treatment in the form of careful bandaging and penicillin injections.

Luca constantly maintained attempts to recover his physical capacities. After a short period of time he began to exercise his toes; after three months he could begin to sit up; after one year, he could stand, leaning against the wall. Not until fifteen months after his injury was he able to walk to the toilet. His cellmates at first assisted him in his exercises, but their "help" was frequently so rough that it caused him great pain—and on one such occasion he cried out so loudly that a prison official heard him, and came running into the cell to find out what the trouble was. After this, his cellmates offered little assistance.

Despite his physical incapacity, Luca was required to take part in cell activities—confession and reform. Immediately after his injury, this consisted of answering "little papers" sent down from the officials, asking specific questions about such matters as his relationship with Father C, and his activities on behalf of Catholic organizations in China. Not long afterward more exhausting activity was required of him: he had to participate in the interminable cell "study" activities. When he would doze off—as he did frequently—the cell chief would strike him smartly on top of his head with a straw brush.

Luca's inner experiences during this period were those of extreme humiliation, helplessness, and depression:

I could do nothing for myself. . . . During the night if I had to urinate, I had to wake the man near me. . . . I was sorrowful. . . . I thought, "I can never be well again. My legs will never be cured. I will be helpless in everything. . . ." I thought much about my parents, how they must be suffering about me. . . . I wept several times, chiefly during the night.

He found comfort, reassurance, and an outlet for his feelings only through his fantasies, which usually concerned rich emotional experiences he had known in the past: places and people he had loved, songs with special meaning, his home, and his mother.

I was thinking mostly at night of places I had been—walking with my parents, my brother and sister . . . chiefly of home . . . and of holiday journeys. . . . Once I had the strange feeling I had come back to Europe to my parents. . . . I had another thing—not exactly a dream —but like an obsession, maybe a pastime. I would try to remember geographical names—names of towns I knew all over the world— sometimes of rivers and seas also—a kind of geographical hobby. . . . I have always been rather interested in geography. . . . When I was in very bad condition, I would sing, externally or internally—chiefly rather sorrowful songs: Negro spirituals—*Swannee River, Josiah, Old Kentucky Home, Home on the Range*—these songs in English . . . also, European songs and songs I sang with the Legion of Mary and other religious groups . . . religious songs from Holy Week, also rather sad. They gave me a remembrance of my life in the Church with the youth in China. . . . When I was particularly in bad shape, I sang Negro spirituals . . . and also one song my mother sang to me when I was a little boy—a Negro baby song. . . . It was sorrowful, but an opportunity to express oneself, a kind of relief.

Later in his imprisonment, he was able to share some of these emotions:

There was in my cell for a while a young fellow, a Chinese Catholic. I knew he was a Catholic, but it wasn't possible for us to say anything or to speak about religion. But at recreation time, we sometimes sang songs. He was fond of music and knew many songs—Schubert, Beethoven, Christmas carols. He would sing the tune, then I would sing—sometimes together. It was a way to express a community of feelings—the others didn't understand. . . . He was on the outside a good prisoner—he said nothing against the Communist doctrine—and if not for the singing I might have doubted that he still had the Catholic faith. . . . He was also a comfort for me.

Beginning All Over

Three months after the injury (and four months after his arrest), Luca had an unexpected visitor in the cell: the judge appeared to announce a dramatic reversal in the official attitude toward the confession material. He told Luca that it was confused, inaccurate, and incomplete; and he gave an example of what he meant ("Why, as for L. [a Chinese allegedly the 'chief' of an 'espionage' organization], you probably don't even know him.") He urged the prisoner to "begin all over again" and this time "tell only the truth." He informed him that he was to be transferred to a new cell "where you will be better able to write things."

Luca was struck by the irony of the judge's statement—not too long before his reluctance to confess to an incriminating relationship with this same L. had resulted in his being placed in chains. But he was immensely pleased at what seemed to be an opportunity to clarify things and rid himself of the painful burden of maintaining his falsehoods. His hopefulness increased when he noted an improved atmosphere in the new cell and more considerate cellmates.

But his sense of relief was transient. When he began to dictate a denial of his three major "crimes" and a more accurate statement of his activities and associations (his limited knowledge of written Chinese, and poor physical condition prevented him from writing it out himself) the cell chief refused to accept the retraction; he told Luca that he was not yet "psychologically fit" to prepare his materials, and that if what he said were true, and he had really done nothing wrong, he would certainly not have been arrested.

Luca's dilemma was now greater than ever:

The judge said—"You must not tell untrue things." On the other hand, when I told only real things, this was considered insufficient and I was not allowed to write them. I was in great psychological pain. I felt it was impossible to satisfy these people.

There followed a return of the vindictive treatment—struggles, angry denunciations, and physical abuse: thumbs, pencils, or chopsticks pressed under his chin or between his fingers, and painful ear-pulling. Attempts to tell the truth brought no relief.

Finally Luca came upon what seemed to him to be the only solution:

I thought, "I must find a way. There must be a way of giving real facts—and then presenting them as being bigger [more incriminating] than they were." . . . Maybe this would satisfy them. . . . From this time on I had this idea.

Soon afterward, during a prisonwide confession and self-accusation movement, he found himself implementing this new approach. As confession pressures mounted and competitive feelings developed among the prisoners ("I can tell one guilty fact. . . . I can tell three guilty facts . . ."), Luca was himself heavily struggled and at the same time drawn into the group emotions.

Now—and for the remainder of his imprisonment—he began to make "real things bigger." He imbued with an aura of espionage and intelligence such events as conversations with young girls in his religious groups and routine comments made to colleagues about the Chinese political and military situation during the Civil War. In this way he built up an impressive series of admissions: "Passing military information" to Father C, conveying "political and economic intelligence" to "imperialists" in Hong Kong, engaging in "reactionary activities" in the Legion of Mary (a militant, partly clandestine Catholic organization greatly resented by the Communists), and many additional "crimes"—all distorted exaggerations of his real activities, rather than the more "creative fantasy" of his earlier false confessions.

And in response to continuing pressures, he began to dictate to a fellow prisoner (and later write out himself) a lengthy account of his entire stay in China, covering "generally speaking all of my behavior, although emphasizing what could be considered misbehavior." His efforts were well received ("The cell chief now looked upon me as a man with whom it is possible to do something"), and he felt the urge to produce more and more material.

This urge was intensified when, after one year, a general prison reorganization took place in which a new and more moderate

policy was instituted.[1] Through manipulations from above, the
cell chief was struggled and severely criticized for his encouragement of physical abuse, and then he (along with everyone else in
the cell except Luca) was transferred and replaced.

After this Luca received no more beatings or physical pressures
of any kind; but the new chief instituted a regime of increased
psychological demands ("Although caring for my body, he was
rather unpleasant to my spirit"). These demands took the form
of twice-daily sessions during which all prisoners were required to
write down and discuss their "bad thoughts," as well as increasing demands upon Luca to condemn Church activities and to record
"bad behavior" of any variety. Now Luca began to pour out in great
detail information about all of his clerical activities in China as
well as activities of his associates, especially emphasizing whatever
could be constructed as "reactionary."

I thought—it is so difficult to find out what they think is bad—so
the best way I had was to write everything. . . . The idea came to
me that if I don't confess something that is true, I won't be able to get
rid of the things that are false.

He even began, like others in his cell, to invent "bad thoughts":

Formerly it was a pressure to invent facts about before I was arrested.
Now it became a pressure to invent ideas. . . . I had to say, for instance, that I had all kinds of good feelings about President Truman,
which was a bad thing—although I really had no special feeling either
for or against him.

For a period of two weeks he did nothing but write out material
about himself and others. Under this impulse to tell all, he confessed for the first time that he and some other priests had arranged a code together, used mostly in mail to inform friends and
relatives in Europe of their personal safety and of the state of the
Church in China. He gave this information now, even though he
had carefully held it back during his confused state in the first
month, and also in the more "relaxed" interview which just followed his injury. Much to his surprise, the judge made little of
it, and it was never included as part of his formal confession; nonetheless, he regretted it later on when he discovered, after his release, that one of the priests involved had been arrested.

He began to feel his efforts were being encouraged. The judge
paid another visit to his cell, and this time was even more friendly
in his assertion that Luca had a perfect right to deny any accusation which was not completely justified. Yet despite this, Luca continued over the months to experience increasing emotional tension,
especially when he was criticized in connection with his religion.
The problem came to a head during a special confession movement,
when he strongly objected to the cell chief's assertion that he "used
religion only as a cloak" for his alleged espionage activities:

I replied violently, "This is not a cloak. A cloak is easy to remove. But
for me if you want to take off my religion, it is necessary to take out my
heart and to kill me."

The cell chief then told him that although he had improved in
many ways, his anger was a form of bad behavior which he should
take up in his self-criticisms, and that there must be still in his
soul something which prevented him from having full confidence
in the government.

Luca admitted that there were things still disturbing him, but
said that he was unable to discuss them in the cell, and requested
that he be allowed to see the prisoner-official who had spoken to
him kindly and in his own language just after his injury. This was
arranged, and Luca took part in two remarkable therapeutic sessions with this man, which ushered in a period of greater intimacy
between himself and his captors. During the first, speaking "frankly
but with caution," he said that he was still "grieving" about his
deformed bodily state (avoiding any direct accusations, and speaking of it as "illness"); that he was still concerned about young girls
in the Legion of Mary who had been beaten in their schools; and
that he still had great doubts about whether there really was freedom of religion in China. In saying these things Luca felt the mixed
motivations characteristic for the thought reform experience:

I felt that these would be bad things to say in the cell because there
they would cause me trouble. But I knew that to say something would
give me relief. I also knew it would have a favorable result—that the
officials would consider me frank and would have understanding for
me.

One month later a second meeting was arranged during which
the prisoner-official gave a startlingly "reasonable" answer to the

points which Luca had previously raised—including the first semi-official recognition of fallibility on the part of the government:

It is true that there have been wrong things in your case, but you must remember that your behavior was at first very antagonistic to the government. . . . When you spoke in a such a confused manner, the judge lost his temper. This, of course, was not right, but in any case you should try to understand the circumstances . . . perhaps some people have been mishandled in prisons—but you must remember that in seventeenth-century England and during the French Revolution, this also happened. And if you will take a look at the greater picture, you will see that there is better control of the population in China now to prevent these excesses than there was in either England or in France during these other periods.

This explanation deeply impressed Luca although it did not completely dispel his belief that the Communists should have gone a step further and made public admission of and reparations for their excesses.

Near the end of his second year of imprisonment, he began to work on what eventually became his final confession document. Told first to write it out in his own language, he summarized the main points of his prison-prepared "autobiography," and then translated these himself into Chinese. Next he was brought before a new and apparently high-ranking judge for a one-week period of severe, "rather correct," but sometimes threatening interrogation: "I see you do not yet have a good knowledge of your sins. You really ought to be punished very severely, perhaps ten years in prison." With the aid of the old judge, the new judge, and the prisoner-official, Luca evolved a four-point confession full of "intelligence" implications, but so close to actual events that Luca himself felt it to be "almost real."

Church Under Attack

During Luca's remaining eighteen months of imprisonment, the cell study program put great emphasis on a critical analysis of the Church's activities in China. Luca admitted that certain priests were out of line in their political and even military activities in China (he had criticized colleagues for such behavior even before his arrest); but at the same time he emphasized that the great majority were concerned only with their religious activities. This attitude, he was told, was not progressive because it did not take into account the principles of "collective responsibility":

If one in a family makes a mistake, it is the fault of the entire family; if one priest does something wrong, and is not stopped by the higher authorities, the Church authorities are at fault.

When Luca would try to point out the good that the Church had done, its service to the sick and to the poor, he met this argument:

This is still a form of aid to imperialism, because the sick and the poor and other Chinese people are led to believe that good is emanating from foreigners, conveying a favorable impression of foreigners in general, and therefore making propaganda for and serving the purposes of the imperialists.

Similarly, when Luca responded to arguments against the "old China hand" attitude of many priests—their lavish living habits and distance from the common people—by pointing out his own integration into Chinese life—Chinese friends, services conducted in Chinese, living in the Chinese manner—he was told that his behavior was even worse, because it "deceived the people."

Luca found this kind of argument extremely disturbing:

It was the most difficult of their reasoning to counteract. . . . What you do that is good—is bad—precisely because it is good!

He continued to experience his greatest inner pain whenever religion was discussed; and because of his imperfect attitude, he was frequently criticized as "stubborn," "subjective," and "having backward ideas." But increasingly he stifled whatever inner protest he felt, and began to express himself cautiously, in a manner consistent with the Communist point of view wherever possible; at the same time he immersed himself in "facts and logic"—in the elaboration of small detail.

He was considered to have made some "progress." Toward the middle of his third year of imprisonment, he was sent to a different compound with a more liberal routine: exercise periods in the courtyard, more leeway in going to the toilet, and less suffocating discipline. Here *hsüeh hsi* was the main task, and Luca was criticized repeatedly for not telling his real thoughts. This accusation was upsetting because it was partially true.

Sometimes I dared not say some things. . . . Sometimes I really was telling what I thought. . . . And sometimes when I was, they still said I wasn't telling enough.

Even during this "improved" period, Luca was not free of outward signs of psychological disturbance, and suffered from insomnia and "general nervousness." When in response to cellmates' questions he admitted that he was praying at night, he would be told that he shouldn't do this, since it must be what was keeping him awake.

About nine months before his release, he was confronted with what turned out to be the last major demand for "betrayal." The judge insisted that he write a letter to one of the young girls who had been most actively associated with him in the Legion of Mary, telling her that the Legion was a "reactionary organization led by spies" with "nothing religious about it," and that she should confess to the government all of her "reactionary activities." Luca was warned, "Remember, your future depends upon how you write this." After much pressure and conflict ("because of fear, and because I could not resist the moral pressure"), Luca finally wrote the letter. His first draft—which made some mention of things done for religion—was rejected; and in his final draft, he stated that he had deceived them in leading them to join the Legion of Mary, that he was wrong in telling them to "resist the government," and that he had done so because of his "imperialistic relations."

His letter did not go quite as far as the original request: he did not, for instance, include the phrase, "nothing religious about it." This served to give him some sense of a small victory; but the entire incident was a source of such great pain that it was one of the matters he found most difficult to discuss with me.

After that—this was my chief grievance—I felt I was a coward. I said something that was to be used to trouble people, and while not contrary to the essentials of the Church, could make a lot of trouble for religious work. . . . And I felt that these girls and other people had probably been more firm than I. . . . I should have been their leader —but I was not as strong as they.

A short time later, he was told by his cellmates, "You are nervous, full of fear. . . . You must have more things to say." He was then called before an official to discuss this matter. Luca approached this man openly, and asked him two questions which had long been troubling him: Would it be possible for him to remain in China after his release from prison? What was the real point of view of the government about religion? He was told that the government was not opposed to foreigners living and working in China, and that he would be able to stay; that the government did not oppose religion; and all those who did not oppose the religious reform movement could continue their religious activities. The reform movement referred to was the Communist-sponsored, nationwide, "triple autonomy" campaign for all of Chinese Christianity, advocating Chinese rather than foreign direction of worship, funds, and organization. To the Communists, this movement was merely a way to cast off outside "imperialist" influence and form a "national church"; but most of the Catholic missionaries saw it as a way to get the Church under direct Communist control. The Legion of Mary was strongly opposed to the reform movement, but Luca himself had favored a much more moderate position than some of his superiors. In this discussion, the official conceded that Luca "was not like other foreigners," as he had always been against the presence of foreign troops and Western concessions in China; but at the same time the official strongly condemned Luca for his repeated defense of the Church in the cell, and insisted that he was attempting to influence the cell chief, a Chinese Catholic who was bitterly critical of Church activities. In this and other talks with officials, there was a sense of better mutual understanding than in previous talks, although Luca nonetheless encountered periodic outbursts of personal "struggles" and vindictive criticism, largely relating to the issue of the Church.

There were also indications that Luca's imprisonment might soon come to an end: the appearance of other foreigners, including another priest, in his cell; more rewriting, translating, and summarizing of his confession with the help of his compatible prisoner-official; orders for the foreigners to send for their luggage. His confession, simplified and clearly damning, was finally pruned down to just two points: his relationship with Father C, and his Legion of Mary activities. In the first, "espionage" was still mentioned;

and in the second, a new emphasis was placed upon details of organizational structure and membership. The confession was accurate to the extent that it included only real events; it was distorted only in the interpretation of these events. When the confession was in final form, Luca was called into a special room, where he was photographed and recorded reading it aloud.

During his last weeks of imprisonment, Luca experienced what was perhaps his highest point of co-operation with his captors. During a last "confession movement," he brought out yet more details about his resistance to the government in his Legion of Mary work. After this, he became actively involved in helping two newcomers to confess. With one of them, he felt justified:

I believed that his attitude wasn't good—he had done bad things— beatings and possibly killing people. There was no use for him not to confess.

But the other man was a Chinese Catholic priest, which put Luca in a difficult situation:

It was for me a very great strain. I dared not stay out of helping him, but I would not enforce upon him things I felt were wrong. I tried to make a compromise—to find real facts which were not against religion, to let him use words that didn't imply something. But either he did not understand my tactics, or else he just would not use them.

These incidents of co-operation—and especially the second—were also difficult for Luca to discuss.

His final sessions with judges and officials were held in an atmosphere of friendly exchange between reasonable people. There was, however, some talk about a ten-year sentence. Luca admitted some of his "errors," and certain specific "bad behavior" concerning his relationship with Father C and with the Legion of Mary; but he emphasized that at the time, he had been unaware he was committing a "crime." The judge said:

We know we made mistakes with you—that is, with your body—but when you go away you must also admit that you had some faults, and you must not exaggerate what happened here. . . . You must realize that at the beginning it was difficult for us to fully master the prison situation—we had many bad people among the other prisoners—and now all of the beatings have stopped, which shows that our real policy is not so bad as might seem if one were to consider only what happened to you during the first year.

Luca responded by agreeing that he had observed these improvements in prison procedure.

During one of these interviews he was told for the first time that he was to be expelled from China; official confirmation came a few minutes later when he was taken before another judge and another official, who read the formal sentence. The "crimes" named had been reduced to three: the "military information" to Father C, his Legion of Mary activities (both included in his last confession), and "information to imperialists" transmitted in letters written from China.

Luca had mixed feelings about the resolution of his case:

Of course I felt some relief—the feeling that now it is all finished—no more strain. But at the same time I had the feeling that the conclusion is not totally satisfying—I didn't want to be out of my missionary work—and not see the many friends—the Christians left there—and no longer have any connection with them. . . . I also had the feeling that the things I said in the beginning were retracted—but that all of the case was not totally clear.

Release and Search

He still had these mixed feelings when he boarded the ship which took him from China to Hong Kong. On the way, he experienced transient beliefs that there must be Communists among the sailors who would report on his shipboard behavior. He also observed and described to me the sequence of his feelings about his experience: the first day, sadness at leaving China; second day, chagrin at his "needless suffering" in an experience so "stupid and meaningless"; third and fourth days, the feeling that the Church had made mistakes in China which should be corrected; fifth and sixth days, a vague melancholy. When he landed in Hong Kong on the seventh day, he was quoted by reporters as saying that his arrest had been due to a "misunderstanding"—avoiding then any strong statement or condemnation.

When I saw him a few days later, his paranoid thinking had disappeared, his depression had diminished, and his attitude was no longer neutral. He was once more the dedicated Catholic priest, preoccupied with the problems of his Church, cared for, attended to, and continuously visited by his religious colleagues. His principal regret was his inability to maintain allegiance to both the Church and to China:

To leave the prison was to be expelled—if I could have left the prison without having been expelled, I would have liked that most.

By the second interview (just two days after the first) little confusion remained: he spoke clearly of the "false accusations" made against him, of his conviction that he had been "unjustly" treated. But he did not stop with these condemnations; rather, he embarked upon a determined search for understanding of his ordeal. He sought—through meditations, talks with me, and his writings—to discover why the Communists had behaved as they did, what mistakes the Church had made in China which might have contributed to this behavior, and how he, as a priest who had undergone an ordeal, could help his Church to improve itself in the future. He told me of the detailed reconstruction of his entire imprisonment which he had begun while on the ship, essentially for his own use; of the special reports he was preparing for Church authorities; of the articles he was writing for Catholic periodicals. One of these articles dealt with apologetics, and refuted the Communist point of view on religion. Another article was a detailed report on the activities of the Legion of Mary in China.

When I was in jail they had me write very much about this. Now I would like to write freely about it and have a good look at the thing. . . . My aim is to have a document that a few people can study to see whether we made mistakes, and how these can be corrected. . . . And to show what were the false accusations that the Communists made against us.

Others were more simple vignettes of Catholic faith: he told of praying to the Virgin Mary during a painful ordeal of struggle and beating, which resulted in the immediate arrival of prison officials who stopped the abuse; and of the progress of a little Chinese girl, at first "naughty" and "fierce," whom Luca had succeeded in converting to active Catholicism despite the initial opposition of her parents. So preoccupied was he with these activities that it was not until the third session with me that he went into any detail about his prison experience.

When he did, it was usually in a self-deprecating manner. He spoke of his "weakness," his "cowardly behavior," of his failure to set a proper example as a leader of Chinese Christian youth. Nor could he always find comfort from talking with his fellow priests in Hong Kong: some would express amazement at his having made such a false confession, and he would interpret this as a feeling on their part of his having let the Church down; others received him as something of a hero, and this made him feel no better.

People now say, "You are wonderful. You have suffered so much—like a martyr." I become uncomfortable and confused when they say this. There are so many things I should have done better.

Martyrdom was for him an ideal which he felt he had failed to live up to, and he viewed his imprisonment as a missed opportunity.

I felt not too useful because I had an insufficiently good attitude—and because I had confessed to false things. I had the idea of a somewhat wasted occasion.

He summed up his feelings in the language of the Church:

I am guilty of many sins, but not the ones that the Communists accuse me of; and I hope to make amends for my sins.

Yet it did mean a great deal to him to be once more living in a world of priests, nuns, and fellow Christians. He was especially pleased when he received visits from young colleagues, former students, or from Chinese Christian youths who told him of the inspiration they had derived from his leadership in the past.

As he continued his explorations, he remained thoughtful and moderate in his views about the Communists as well as about his own Church, and always qualified his judgments. Concerning his own treatment, he said:

I think it is wrong to seek by evil means such guilty interpretation of my behavior. . . . I feel that they treated me wrongly. . . . Of course it is better that they admitted their mistakes—and let me retract. But even when they admit their mistakes, they don't go to the bottom of the question of why they make mistakes.

The reasons for these Communist "mistakes" were, he felt:

They are prejudiced against the Catholic Church. . . . They are too confident about their own judgment. . . . They are not sufficiently correct about criticizing or punishing their own misbehavior, or that of their semi-official associations.

He had some praise for the Chinese Communist regime as well; he recognized its accomplishments in building and industry, he was impressed with their planned production, and he felt that many of their concepts about economics were "logical." And although he himself had long been critical of the Nationalist Regime which preceded the Communists, its shortcomings, and especially its corruption, had become more vivid to him: "I have somewhat more understanding of the reason why so many people in China were discontented with the old order."

Nonetheless, he believed that the Chinese people were paying a heavy price for their accomplishments—especially in the "great strain" being imposed upon them, and in the limitations upon their thought. He thought the Communists were particularly deficient in "the question about how to let people have their own ideas, and especially about a way of making justice in the courts." There had been some improvement, he felt, but not enough:

At the beginning they were totally wrong; since three years ago, they have been in some ways better, but not sufficiently so that one could say that their ways were good.

Father Luca also had pointed and specific criticism for his own Church. He especially disapproved of those among the Catholic priests who became involved in military activities against the Chinese Communists, both on ethical and practical grounds: "I think it is not according to the Christian way of proceeding—and it is of no use." He claimed that he had always disapproved of these activities, but he had been made to feel during his imprisonment that he had "indulged" those among his friends who pursued such policies, and now his opposition was more firm. He was also critical of foreign priests who lived too lavishly in China ("They forgot the spirit of poverty"), and more basically of the Church's failure to build up a highranking Chinese hierarchy, and its tendency to keep foreign priests in the senior positions in China. He felt that both the Communists and the Church should mend their ways: that the former should admit and correct their mistakes and develop a "more fair attitude" towards religion; and that the latter should "see more what was wrong in our attitudes" and then seek to change them.

In all of this, Father Luca maintained a distinction between the fallible actions of individual priests, and his more basic religious convictions:

When there was criticism of priests, I knew that much was true, and I admitted it. But about the existence of God—I was convinced of the emptiness of their arguments when they said there was no God.

His religious feelings aside, Luca felt he had undergone an important personal change. He found himself more willing to listen to others' opinions, more patient, and less quick to "get in anger." He also thought that he had become more articulate, and had largely overcome a previous tendency to "feel nervous because I couldn't express the things I wanted to say."

During the month in which we were working together, Luca showed periodic signs of restlessness, "nervous diarrhea," and anxiety concerning his future. But these gradually diminished as he became increasingly focused and relaxed within the Hong Kong Catholic setting. His physical condition also improved, although he was told that he would never be well enough for the active life of a parish priest. He showed throughout an obvious reluctance to leave Hong Kong; although it was not China proper, it had at least a partial Chinese atmosphere, and permitted him to use the Chinese language. At first he expressed this directly: "I regret the possibility that I may have to go back to Europe." But gradually, he began to accept the inevitable, and when he finally left, he was looking ahead to future work. Yet he also looked back to his life in China—and his mood was one of sadness.

CHAPTER 5

PSYCHOLOGICAL STEPS

There is a basic similarity in what both Dr. Vincent and Father Luca experienced during Communist imprisonment. Although they were held in separate prisons far removed from each other, and although they differed very much in their responses to reform, they were both subjected to the same general sequence of psychological pressures. This sequence was essentially the same despite the fact that these men were very different from each other, with different personal and professional life styles. Nor was this thought reform pattern common to just these two: it was experienced by all twenty-five of the Westerners whom I interviewed.

The common pattern becomes especially important in evaluating the stories these Westerners told me. Each was attempting to describe, in most instances as accurately as possible, the details of an ordeal from which he had just emerged. But what each reported was also inevitably influenced by his immediate life situation—his psychological transition between the two worlds, his personal struggles for both integrity and integration, his feelings about succoring and threatening colleagues and strangers in Hong Kong, his view of me as an American, a physician, a psychiatrist, and a person. All of these circumstances could affect his account, and especially its emotional tone. Therefore, both during the interviews and in the later study of my notes, I had to sift out what was most characteristic and most consistent, to evaluate this information in terms of my understanding of the people supplying it, and then to piece together a composite analysis of the process itself.

Death and Rebirth

Both Dr. Vincent and Father Luca took part in an agonizing drama of death and rebirth. In each case, it was made clear that the "reactionary spy" who entered the prison must perish, and that in his place must arise a "new man," resurrected in the Communist mold. Indeed, Dr. Vincent still used the phrase, "To die and be reborn"—words which he had heard more than once during his imprisonment.

Neither of these men had himself initiated the drama; indeed, at first both had resisted it, and tried to remain quite outside of it. But their environment did not permit any sidestepping: they were forced to participate, drawn into the forces around them until they themselves began to feel the need to confess and to reform. *This penetration by the psychological forces of the environment into the inner emotions of the individual person is perhaps the outstanding psychiatric fact of thought reform.* The milieu brings to bear upon the prisoner a series of overwhelming pressures, at the same time allowing only a very limited set of alternatives for adapting to them. In the interplay between person and environment, a sequence of steps or operations [1]—of combinations of manipulation and response—takes place. All of these steps revolve about two policies and two demands: the fluctuation between assault and leniency, and the requirements of confession and re-education. The physical and emotional assaults bring about the symbolic death; leniency and the developing confession are the bridge between death and rebirth; the re-education process, along with the final confession, create the rebirth experience.

Death and rebirth, even when symbolic, affect one's entire being, but especially that part related to loyalties and beliefs, to the sense of being a specific person and at the same time being related to and part of groups of other people—or in other words, to one's sense of inner identity.[2] In the broadest terms, everything that happened to these prisoners is related to this matter. Since everyone differs from everyone else in his identity, each prisoner experienced thought reform differently, nor did anyone respond completely to all these steps; at the same time, the experiences had such magnitude that they affected every prisoner in some measure, no matter what his background and character.

1. THE ASSAULT UPON IDENTITY

From the beginning, Dr. Vincent was told he was not really a doctor, that all of what he considered himself to be was merely a cloak under which he hid what he really was. And Father Luca was told the same thing, especially about the area which he held most precious—his religion. Backing up this assertion were all of the physical and emotional assaults of early imprisonment: the confusing but incriminating interrogations, the humiliating "struggles," the painful and constricting chains, and the more direct physical brutality. Dr. Vincent and Father Luca each began to lose his bearings on who and what he was, and where he stood in relationship to his fellows. Each felt his sense of self become amorphous and impotent and fall more and more under the control of its would-be remolders. Each was at one point willing to say (and to *be*) whatever his captors demanded.

Each was reduced to something not fully human and yet not quite animal, no longer the adult and yet not quite the child; instead, an adult human was placed in the position of an infant or a sub-human animal, helplessly being manipulated by larger and stronger "adults" or "trainers." Placed in this regressive stance, each felt himself deprived of the power, mastery, and selfhood of adult existence.

In both, an intense struggle began between the adult man and the child-animal which had been created, a struggle against regression and dehumanization. But each attempt on the part of the prisoner to reassert his adult human identity and to express his own will ("I am not a spy. I am a doctor"; or "This must be a mistake. I am a priest, I am telling the truth") was considered a show of resistance and of "insincerity," and called forth new assaults.

Not every prisoner was treated as severely as were Dr. Vincent and Father Luca, but each experienced similar external assaults leading to some form of inner surrender—a surrender of personal autonomy. This assault upon autonomy and identity even extended to the level of consciousness, so that men began to exist on a level which was neither sleep nor wakefulness, but rather an in-between hypnogogic state. In this state they were not only more readily influenced, but they were also susceptible to destructive and aggressive impulses arising from within themselves.[3]

This undermining of identity is the stroke through which the prisoner "dies to the world," the prerequisite for all that follows.

2. THE ESTABLISHMENT OF GUILT

Dr. Vincent and Father Luca found themselves unanimously condemned by an "infallible" environment. The message of guilt which they received was both existential (you *are* guilty!) and psychologically demanding (you must learn to *feel* guilty!). As this individual guilt potential was tapped, both men had no choice but to experience—first unconsciously and then consciously—a sense of evil. Both became so permeated by the atmosphere of guilt that external criminal accusations became merged with subjective feelings of sinfulness—of having done wrong. Feelings of resentment, which in such a situation could have been a source of strength, were shortlived; they gave way to the gradual feeling that the punishment was deserved, that more was to be expected.

In making their early false confessions, Dr. Vincent and Father Luca were beginning to accept the guilty role of the criminal. Gradually, a voice within them was made to say, ever more loudly: "It is my sinfulness, and not their injustice, which causes me to suffer—although I do not yet know the full measure of my guilt."

At this point their guilt was still diffuse, a vague and yet pervasive set of feelings which we may call a free-floating sense of guilt.[4] Another prisoner expressed this clearly:

What they tried to impress on you is a complex of guilt. The complex I had was that I was guilty. . . . I was a criminal—that was my feeling, day and night.

3. THE SELF-BETRAYAL

The series of denunciations of friends and colleagues which both Dr. Vincent and Father Luca were required to make had special significance. Not only did making these accusations increase their feelings of guilt and shame, it put them in the position of subverting the structures of their own lives. They were, in effect, being made to renounce the people, the organizations, and the standards of behavior which had formed the matrix of their previous existence. They were being forced to betray—not so much their friends and colleagues, as a vital core of themselves.

This self-betrayal was extended through the pressures to "accept help" and in turn "help" others. Within the bizarre morality of the prison environment, the prisoner finds himself—almost without realizing it—violating many of his most sacred personal ethics and behavioral standards. The degree of violation is expanded, very early in the game, through the mechanism of shared betrayal, as another priest described:

The cell chief kept asking information about Church activities. He wanted me to denounce others, and I didn't want to do this. . . . A Chinese Father was transferred into the cell, and he said to me, "You cannot help it. You must make some denunciations. The things which the Communists know about any of your Church activities you must come out with." . . . Much later I was put in another cell to bring a French priest to confession. He had been stubborn, and had been in solitary for a few months. He was very fearful and looked like a wild animal. . . . I took care of him, washed his clothes for him, helped him to rest. I advised him that what they might know he might as well confess.

Although there is a continuing tension between holding on and letting go, some degree of self-betrayal is quickly seen as a way to survival. But the more of one's self one is led to betray, the greater is one's involvement with his captors; for by these means they make contact with whatever similar tendencies already exist within the prisoner himself—with the doubts, antagonisms, and ambivalences which each of us carries beneath the surface of his loyalties. This bond of betrayal between prisoner and environment may develop to the point where it seems to him to be all he has to grasp; turning back becomes ever more difficult.

4. THE BREAKING POINT: TOTAL CONFLICT AND THE BASIC FEAR

Before long, Father Luca and Dr. Vincent found themselves at an absolute impasse with their environment. Each was looked upon not only as an enemy, but also as a man completely out of step. They were aware of being in painful disagreement with alleged truths about their past, and yet at this point they were unclear about what these "truths" were.

At the same time, they had been impressed with the inflexibility of their milieu. The government, being infallible, would not give way; it was the "stubborn criminal" who had to "change." Their situation was like that of a man taken suddenly from his ordinary routine and placed in a hospital for the criminally insane, where he is accused of a horrendous but vague crime which he is expected to recognize and confess; where his assertion of innocence is viewed as a symptom of his disease, as a paranoid delusion; and where every other inmate-patient is wholly dedicated to the task of pressuring him into a confession and a "cure." [5] The sense of total reversal is like that of Alice after falling down the rabbit hole; but the weirdness of the experience is more that of a Kafka hero.

The prisoner's dilemma leads him to a state of antagonistic estrangement. He is not totally estranged from the environment, because even antagonism is a form of contact; but he is totally cut off from the essential succor of affectionate communication and relatedness, without which he cannot survive. And at the same time, his increasing self-betrayal, sense of guilt, and his loss of identity all join to estrange him from himself—or at least from the self which he has known. He can contemplate the future with only hopelessness and dread. Literally and emotionally, there seems to be no escape from this hermetically-sealed antagonism.

As the assaults continue, and as they are turned inward, he begins to experience one of the most primitive and painful emotions known to man, the fear of total annihilation. This basic fear [6]—considered by some the inherited forerunner of all human anxiety—becomes the final focus for all of the prison pressures. It is fed by every threat and accusation from without, as well as by all of the destructive emotions stimulated within. The fear is compounded by the horrifying realization that the environment seems to be making it come true. Dr. Vincent did not only fear annihilation; he actually felt himself to *be* annihilated. It was this confirmation of a primitive fear which led him to hope for relief through quick death.

This is the point at which physical and mental integration break down. Some prisoners may be brought by their severe anxiety and depression to the point of suicidal preoccupations and attempts:

They scolded me in a nasty way. I had the feeling that everyone was cross with me and despised me. I thought, why do they despise me?

What have I done? . . . I was eating very little. . . . I refused to eat or drink. . . . I felt very much down. I felt there was no chance for me. . . . It was so utterly hopeless. For six weeks I did nothing but think how I might kill myself.

Others experience the delusions and hallucinations usually associated with psychosis:

I heard investigations taking place below, and one day I heard my name called. I listened while Chinese were indoctrinated to testify how I had been gathering information on troop movements. . . . The next day I recognized the voice of my Chinese accountant who was told that I had confessed everything and therefore his confession better agree with mine. . . . Once I heard the guards saying in a social conversation with a German that they would soften me up by locking me in a cage which used to be used by the KMT. . . . I was near going nuts.

Such symptoms are clear evidence of the loss of the capacity to cope with one's environment. At the same time, they represent —as do any psychiatric symptoms—protective efforts, attempts on the part of the human organism to ward off something perceived as an even greater danger: in these cases, the anticipation of total annihilation.

Many of Father Luca's transient delusions represented just such a combination of breakdown and restitution. His imagining (and believing) that his consul was visiting the prison, or that he was once more among his fellow Christians, were evidence he had lost the ability to discriminate between the real and the unreal. But in experiencing these same delusions, the content of which reinforced his fantasies of rescue, Father Luca was clinging tenaciously to his own life force, and at the same time warding off his basic fear.[7]

No prisoner, whatever his defenses, ever completely overcame this fear of annihilation. It remained with each in greater or lesser degree throughout imprisonment, and in some cases for a long time afterward. It was a constant inner reminder of the terrible predicament he might again be forced to face should he further displease his captors.

At this point, the prisoner's immediate prospects appear to be physical illness, psychosis, or death. If his death is to remain symbolic—and psychic damage kept from progressing beyond the reversible stage—some form of desperately needed relief must be supplied.

5. LENIENCY AND OPPORTUNITY

A sudden change in official attitude—the institution of leniency —supplies this relief. The unexpected show of kindness, usually occurring just when the prisoner is reaching his breaking point, breaks the impasse between him and the environment. He is permitted—even shown how—to achieve some degree of harmony with his outer world.

"Leniency" does not mean that the milieu budges from any of its demands, or even from its standards of reality. It simply lets up on its pressures sufficiently for the prisoner to absorb its principles and adapt himself to them. When Dr. Vincent, after two months of imprisonment, suddenly encountered friendliness and consideration in place of chains and struggles, there was no cessation of the pressure for confession. In fact, the effect of leniency was to spur him on to greater confession efforts. He was able to make these efforts because his leniency was accompanied by guidance; he had a chance to learn and act upon what was expected of him. Father Luca had no such good fortune. He, too, after one month, was given a respite: the removal of chains and handcuffs and the opportunity to sleep; but his was the unusual experience of leniency without guidance. He was willing to comply (his false confession was, among other things, a profound expression of compliance); but he was unable to find the desired approach. In his case, therefore, a new impasse was created, which resulted in a brutal interruption of his leniency.

The timing and the setting of leniency can be extremely dramatic, as it was for another priest.

It was Christmas Day. I was brought to see the judge. For the first time I found the room full of sunlight. There was no guard and there were no secretaries. There were only the kind faces of the judges offering me cigarettes and tea. It was a conversation more than a questioning. My mother could not have been much more good and kind than the judge was. He said to me, "The treatment you have received here is really too bad. Maybe you are unable to stand it. As a foreigner and a priest, you must be used to good food and better hygienic standards. So just make a confession. But make it really good, so we can be satisfied. Then we will close your trial and finish your case."

In other cases, leniency was utilized to confront the prisoner with a threatening life-or-death alternative. It might include a new "good" interrogator who replaces or alternates with the "bad" one:

An inspector had talked to me nastily and I collapsed. Soon after, a nicer inspector came to visit me. He was worried—very friendly to me—and asked me if I had heart disease. . . . He said, "Your health is not good; you must have a better room." He called on me again and said, "We must get your case settled now. The government is interested in you. All you must do is change your mind. There are only two ways for you to go: one way leads to life, and the other to death. If you want the road that leads to life, you must take our way. You must reform yourself and re-educate yourself." I said, "That sounds very good." I felt light of heart and told the other cellmates about it. They said, "That's good. Write your confession about how wrong your old political ideas were, and how willing you are to change your mind—and then you will be released."

This threat also was clear in the experience of another prisoner who had been transferred to a hospital after an attempt at suicide:

At first they told me that I had tried to kill myself because I had a bad conscience. . . . But the doctor seemed very kind. . . . Then an official came to see me and he spoke to me in a very friendly voice: "The government doesn't want to kill you. It wants to reform you. We don't want to punish you at all, we just want to re-educate you." . . . It was my first glimmer of hope. I felt finally there might be a way out. I wasn't feeling so hopelessly alone any more. The official had actually shown some human quality.[8]

Apparent in all these examples is the immense stimulus which leniency provides for the prisoner's reform effort. Total annihilation is no longer all he can visualize. He has been offered rest, kindness, and a glimpse of the Promised Land of renewed identity and acceptance—even freedom; annihilation is now something he can avoid, and in fact *must* avoid at all costs.

The psychological decompression of his environment serves to win him over to the reform camp, especially to that part of the reform camp which is working on him. In other words, he becomes motivated to help the officials achieve what they are trying to do to him. He becomes, as did Dr. Vincent, their grateful partner in his own reform.

6. THE COMPULSION TO CONFESS [9]

Long before any suggestion of leniency, Father Luca and Dr. Vincent had perceived the dominant message of their milieu: only those who confess can survive. Indeed, everything in the way of assaults and leniency—all pressures of breakdown and promised restitution—served to reinforce this message. In such a climate, the two men had no choice but to join in the universal compulsion to confess. Their first expression of this compulsion was the early elaboration of false "crimes." Even when a prisoner was aware that his confession was "wild"—as was Dr. Vincent—he had begun to submit to the confession requirement, and to behave *as if* he were a criminal. This was even more true, and the guilt even more profound, for those who, like Father Luca, came to believe in their own falsehoods.

These first confessions are preliminary (although prison officials do not necessarily mean them to be such) to the main manifestation of the compulsion to confess—the *total* soul purge. Both Dr. Vincent and Father Luca, when their false confessions were rejected, hit upon the expedient of simply confessing everything, with special emphasis on what might be considered most sinful. In doing so, they moved beyond mere playing of the criminal role. They were beginning to accept as valid parts of themselves the two basic identities of thought reform.

The first of these is the identity of the repentant sinner. The prisoner in effect says: "I must locate this evil part of me, this mental abscess, and excise it from my very being, lest it remain to cause me more harm." This leads directly to the second identity —that of the receptive criminal, the man who is, at whatever level of consciousness, not only beginning to concur in the environment's legal and moral judgment of him, but also to commit himself to acquiring the beliefs, values, and identities officially considered desirable. The acceptance of these two identities led both Dr. Vincent and Father Luca to express the idea that one had to get rid of old thoughts and emotions in order to make room for the new ones. Precisely this compulsion to reveal everything provides the continuity between breakdown and restitution, between confession and reform.

The compulsion to confess is not static; it continually gathers momentum, and provokes an increasing sense of submission—as described by another priest:

> After a while one wants to talk . . . they press you, so you feel you must say something. Once you start you are deceived: you are at the top of the tree and you go down. . . . If you say the first word, there is always something more: *"Lao shih"*—No, no, be a good boy! Say the truth!—, *"t'an pai"*—Confess!—are constantly repeated every two minutes. I felt myself wanting to say more to make him shut his mouth, he was so insisting. . . . It made me weak; it made me want to give in.

Equally important, as both Dr. Vincent and Father Luca discovered, is the "creative" participation which each prisoner develops in his confession process. His inner fantasies must always make contact with the demands from without. To be sure, these fantasies are painstakingly and selectively molded by officials and cellmates. But they are never entirely divorced from the man who produces them. This means that a good deal of the energy involved in the confession comes from within the prisoner himself. His compulsion to confess dedicates him to the task of continuously carving out and refilling his own inner void—under the active supervision and broad moral guidance of his captors.

7. THE CHANNELLING OF GUILT

Once the compulsion to confess is operating, the prisoner is ready to learn a more precise formula—thought reform's conceptual framework for his expression of guilt and repentance. By adopting the "people's standpoint," he channels nonspecific feelings of guilt into a paranoid, pseudo-logical system. His sense of evil, formerly vague and free-floating, is now made to do specific work for reform. He takes this step, as Vincent so clearly described, by learning to see evidence of personal evil and destructiveness in specific past actions. What was most prosaic, or even generous, must now be viewed as "criminal."

This reinterpretation of events, as absurd as it may sound, has a strong impact because it stimulates forces within the prisoner himself which support the contentions of his environment. He has, like everyone else, struggled with feelings of curiosity, hostility, and vindictiveness not acceptable for public display, but retained as part of his own secret world. Now the awareness of these feelings within himself, and especially of the secretiveness which accompanies them, makes him feel like the "spy" he is accused of being. It is a relatively easy step for him to associate this image of himself as a conspirator with the past events under consideration. Indeed, in making a casual comment about approaching Communist armies, one part of him might really have hoped that this information would reach and benefit the other side; and even if this were not true, it becomes fairly easy for him to imagine that it had been.

Since the people's standpoint is an ultimate statement of bias, its acceptance also involves a basic negative commitment. The prisoner joins in condemning himself less for what he has *done* than for what he has *been:* as a Westerner—and therefore an "imperialist"—he is guilty. For him, this is the real significance of the people's standpoint, and its use of news, information, and intelligence is merely a method of implementing its prejudgment.

The more the prisoner submits to these black-and-white judgments, the more he surrenders all that is subtle or qualified—as another missionary described:

At first I was always making this distinction: as far as my conscience is concerned, it is no sin, but from their point of view it is a crime. I knew that the judgment would be standing on their point of view. . . . The same action was seen by me and them from a completely different morality—seen through a different window. They are looking through from the outside in, me from the inside out. . . . They said the government is infallible, so what it discovered cannot be untrue. That puts me in a bad position. I said, "I admit the government is infallible." They took my words like rubber. . . . Later I asked the government for a lenient sentence. I could not say that they were unjust, as I was standing on their point of view.

As the prisoner accepts this "higher" group morality, its most harsh judgments make common cause with the most tyrannical parts of his own conscience; through this joining of forces, he is changed from a man who merely feels guilty into one who feels guilty about exactly those actions which the environment considers criminal.

8. RE-EDUCATION: LOGICAL DISHONORING

While Father Luca and Dr. Vincent, in a general sense, began their re-education the moment they were imprisoned, its formal inception occurred with the stress upon group study (*hsüeh hsi*) just after the institution of leniency. Both men found that it was not Communist doctrine per se which mattered, but rather the use of Communist doctrine and its reasoning techniques to broaden their own self-exposure.

It was no longer enough to admit guilt, to feel guilty, or even to recognize specific guilty actions. The prisoner had to extend his self-condemnation to every aspect of his being, and learn to see his life as a series of shameful and evil acts—shameful and evil not only in their possible opposition to Communism, but also because they violated his own cherished ideals.

With Father Luca, this desecration of identity took the form of convincing him that he and his missionary colleagues had been "un-Christian" in their conduct in China. Personal dishonoring of this kind was applied to both priests and laymen. It is illustrated in the following exchange between another priest and his prison instructor:

Instructor: "Do you believe man should serve others?"
Priest: "Yes, of course I do."
Instructor: "Are you familiar with the Biblical saying, 'I come on earth to serve, not to be served?'"
Priest: "Yes, as a priest it is my creed."
Instructor: "Did you have a servant in your mission?"
Priest: "Yes, I did."
Instructor: "Who made your bed in the morning and swept the floor?"
Priest: "My servant did this."
Instructor: "You did not live up to your doctrine very well, did you, Father?"

This same priest explained the process of logical dishonoring in Marxist terminology and with a good deal of psychological insight:

They believe that in each person there is a thesis—his positive element, work, or creed; and an antithesis—his weakness which works against this. The thesis in my case was the Catholic and my missionary work. My antithesis was anything which worked against this due to my personal shortcomings. The Communists attempted to wear down my thesis and encouraged the development of my antithesis. By making the antithesis stronger and the thesis weaker, they seek to have the antithesis replace the thesis as the dominant force in the individual.

The antithesis of which the priest speaks is his negative identity [10]—that part of him which he has been constantly warned never to become. A priest's negative identity is likely to include such elements as the selfish man, the sinner, the proud man, the insincere man, and the unvigilant man. As the reformers encourage a prisoner's negative identity to enlarge and luxuriate, the prisoner becomes ready to doubt the more affirmative self-image (diligent priest, considerate healer, tolerant teacher) which he had previously looked upon as his true identity. He finds an ever-expanding part of himself falling into dishonor in his own eyes.

At this point the prisoner faces the most dangerous part of thought reform. He experiences guilt and shame much more profound and much more threatening to his inner integrity than any experienced in relation to previous psychological steps. He is confronted with his human limitations, with the contrast between what he is and what he would be. His emotion may be called true or genuine guilt, or true shame—or existential guilt [11]—to distinguish it from the less profound and more synthetic forms of inner experience. He undergoes a self-exposure which is on the border of guilt and shame. Under attack is the deepest meaning of his entire life, the morality of his relationship to mankind. The one-sided exploitation of existential guilt is thought reform's trump card, and perhaps its most important source of emotional influence over its participants. Revolving around it are issues most decisive to thought reform's outcome.

Why call this process *logical* dishonoring? Surely it is not logical to have one's identity so disparaged—unless one sees this disparagement as a small but necessary part of a greater system of events. And this is precisely the kind of systematic rationale which the Communists—through their ideology—supply. A prisoner's inconsistencies and evildoings are related to historical forces, political happenings, and economic trends. Thus, his acceptance of his negative identity and the learning of Communist doctrine become inseparable, one completely dependent upon the other. The realignment of affirmation and negation within one's identity requires an endless repetition, a continuous application of self to the doctrine— and indeed, this is the essence of re-education. The prisoner must, like a man under special psychological treatment, analyze the causes of his deficiencies, work through his resistances (or "thought problems") until he thinks and feels in terms of the doctrinal truths to which all of life is reduced. In the process, he may be guided by a particular "instructor" (sometimes referred to as "analyst" or "case analyst") who has special charge of his case, keeps all personal records, and conducts many individual interviews with him. The prisoner's psychological strengths and weaknesses become well known to his personal instructor, then to other officials as well, and are effectively utilized in the undermining process.

What we have said so far of "re-education" hardly lives up to the name: we have talked more of breakdown than of remaking. In actuality, the remaking is also well under way. Even during the earlier stages of identity assault and compulsion to confess, the prisoner experiences stirrings of restitution. The buildup of his negative identity, along with his developing acceptance of Communist doctrine, provide the first contours of something new. He continues, during the years of imprisonment, to loudly proclaim his own demise; but as his re-education proceeds, he finds himself first announcing, and then experiencing, the refashioned identity which is emerging. His sense of nakedness and vulnerability nourishes the growth of the "new man."

9. PROGRESS AND HARMONY

The prisoner's new self requires emotional nutriment if it is to continue to develop. This nutriment is supplied by the prisoner's achieving a sense of harmony with his no-longer-strange surroundings. Harmony is partly a matter of gradual adaptation, as both Dr. Vincent and Father Luca made clear. Adaptation in turn is contingent upon progress in reform; and only when this progress has been demonstrated does the prisoner begin to receive the recognition and acceptance which is so precious in such an environment.

Then, as Dr. Vincent described, the prisoner can experience the deep satisfactions of solving all problems; of group intimacy in living, working, and suffering; of surrendering himself to an all-powerful force, and sharing its strength; of laying himself bare in the catharsis of personal confession; of sharing the moral righteousness of a great crusade of mass redemption.

Toward the end of their imprisonment, both Dr. Vincent and Father Luca were living under quite comfortable circumstances. The improvement in their physical surroundings was important enough; the atmosphere of frankness and of being met halfway was exhilarating. Both had regained the status of being human. Talks with judges were man-to-man encounters between people who understood each other and considered one another's feelings. Indeed, Father Luca felt free enough to voice doubts and criticisms; and although he did this partially as a tactic, he was at the same time accepting therapeutic assistance from his captors.

To appreciate the emotional appeal of harmony, one must—as the prisoner invariably does—contrast it with the basic fear and estrangement of the earlier phases of imprisonment. Instead of antagonism and total conflict, he feels in step with a milieu which appreciates him. Identified as a "progressive," he is permitted (and grasps at) a more direct form of self-expression. To be sure, he is still partly the actor; but performance and life have moved closer together, and he is not acting as much as he thinks he is. As he achieves a more intimate communication with his reformers, his entire experience takes on a much greater feeling of reality. Officials in turn show a beginning willingness to accept the prisoner as he is —by no means perfect in his reform, but at least more genuine in his partial reform.

10. FINAL CONFESSION: THE SUMMING UP

In this atmosphere of harmony and reality, the prisoner is ready to make a conclusive statement of what he is and what he has been. The confession has long been developing, of course, but it is likely to take its final shape only after he has achieved sufficient "progress" to produce and believe in a "correct" version.

In Father Luca's case—which is especially illustrative for the entire confession process—the two short paragraphs of his final confession seem almost anticlimactic after the millions of self-accusatory words he had already poured out. Yet this briefest of confessions was both a symbol and a summation of all that had gone before. For the officials, it was *the* confession, the statement for the record. For Father Luca, it was the last of an arduous series of confession identities. To understand this, we must review the sequence of his confession responses and his existential involvements, since any confession, whether true or false, contains an interpretation of one's present and past relationship to the world.

Luca's first confession statement (so unacceptable as a confession that it might better be called his pre-confession statement) was his defiance. In claiming that his arrest was either a mistake or a consequence of his faith, he was clinging to the identity of the priest with integrity. But as he began to surrender more and more of this part of himself, and became lost in the labyrinth of his own false confessions, he took on two additional identities: the secret conspirator and the "novelist," or creative confabulator. His belief in his own falsehoods indicated both the degree to which his identity had broken down and the strength of the image created within him of this conspiratorial self. When he consented to speak about his clerical colleagues, and give details about Catholic groups, he was assuming the imposed identity of the betrayer, and especially the self-betrayer. Then, when the "novel" was abandoned, and he began for the first time to confess *everything*—to lay before his reformers all that came to his mind—he became the ignorant supplicant, groping for acceptance. Next, in organizing specific points in an acceptably self-damning fashion, he was simultaneously the repentant sinner (he could be repentant because he knew better what his sins were) and the relatively advanced confessor (one who had learned the techniques of his environment). In the two paragraphs of his final confession—in which he referred to his "espionage" relationship with another priest, and to his "illegal" church activities—he took on (although hardly completely) the final identity of the "confirmed" criminal.

The reformers thus ended precisely where they had begun. From the beginning they had labelled Luca a criminal; and these two "crimes" were clearly the ones they had originally selected for him to "recognize." Why, then, did they put everyone to so much trouble?

They did so because confession is as much a part of re-education as re-education is of confession. The officials demanded that their accusations become the prisoner's *self*-accusations, and that the confession be made with inner conviction. They required that he present himself in the evil image they had constructed for him—and their reasons for requiring this, as we shall later discuss, are by no means completely rational.

Father Luca's sequence of confession was neither unique nor accidental; the sequence was essentially the same for Dr. Vincent also, and for almost all other prisoners. There is first the attempt at accuracy, then the wild confession, then the return to real events in distorted focus, and finally, the brief "criminal" confession. Since the development of the wild confession usually occurs during the first few days or weeks (Father Luca's lasted for an exceptionally long time), the main trend is a shift from the imaginary to the concrete. Although fantasy and falsehood are by no means eliminated, this shift does give the prisoner the sense that he is moving in the direction of truth. His confession changes from an uncontrolled dream-like (or nightmarish) vision to a more responsible reinterpretation of his own life. Thus he becomes more "engaged" in the confession process, more closely bound to his own words. At the same time, the effect of his wild confession has not been entirely lost upon him; he is apt to retain feelings of guilt over it, as if he had really done the things he described.

While each step in the confession is the result of changes in the strength and tone of the environmental pressures, the prisoner experiences many of his responses as personal discoveries. Both Luca and Vincent, in shifting from falsehood to exaggeration, thought they had hit upon a useful and ingenious technique; only later did each realize that the officials' manipulations had made this reaction inevitable. Each step in the confession, then, is a means of adaptation; and it is also, for both prisoner and reformer, a compromise: he wishes to say less, and they demand more.

In this confession sequence, there is a good deal of structuring and planning on the part of prison officials. But they too can be victimized by their impulses, and by the contagious paranoid tones of the environment; their confusion over what is true and what is false—so evident in their treatment of Father Luca—can add to this general emotional turmoil.

The confession thus embodies demand and response, molded creativity, adaptation, compromise, working through, and a good deal of confusion on all sides. Its final version is the prisoner's subjective perception of the environment's message, guided by his reformers, but also including his own guilty re-evaluation of his past actions. Its beginnings in real events, the "logic" of its distortions, and its documented flavor may make it quite believable—both to the outside world and to its creator as well.

11. REBIRTH

Just before his release Dr. Vincent became once more the physician and teacher, and at the same time he became the advanced and sympathetic student of Chinese Communism. At the end, reformers made it clear he should combine these two aspects of himself. He was expected to bring the scientific and technical emphasis of his profession to his study of Communism, and to carry over a "progressive" approach (pedagogical shortcuts geared to the needs of "the people") to his medical teaching.

The same principle was applied to Father Luca. Toward the end of his imprisonment he was more and more recognized as a priest with the right to hold his religious views, even if the officials would not go so far as to allow him to practice his religion—an enemy ideology—in the prison. Simultaneously he reached a stage of maximum participation in the Communist movement. This combination is best symbolized in his assuming the role of the reformer, working on a Chinese Catholic priest to bring him to confession. The foreign European missionary who had helped to train Chinese colleagues was once more taking the role of the spiritual mentor, but this time under the imposed sponsorship of the Chinese Communist movement which now encompassed them both.

They did not cease to be priest or physician; rather each became a priest or physician sympathetic to, or at least in a working relationship with, Chinese Communism. Although much of their former identities had been dishonored during imprisonment, they had suffered only a temporary, controlled, and partial "death." If anything like a whole man is to walk out of prison, a good deal of the prisoner's old self will have to be resurrected. This resurrection, however, can be permitted only when the imposed thought reform elements are strong enough to dominate the new combination. For it is just this confluence of identities—the bringing together of evil criminal, repentant sinner, student of Communist doctrine, and the man originally imprisoned—which constitutes the rebirth. Heralded by all of the identity shifts of previous steps, this confluence is likely to occur only after prolonged re-education. And since even the prison identities must be carved out of the prisoner's own emotions (albeit with a powerful knife), rebirth means a basic modification, but not a total replacement, of the former self.

It is a modification strong enough, as in the case of Dr. Vincent, to create a profound change in the prisoner's view of the world, and in his personal relationship to the world. He reinterprets his thought and behavior, shifts his values, recodes his sense of reality.[12] The Communist world, formerly considered aggressive and totalitarian, is now seen as peace-loving and democratic. He identifies with his captors, and is happy in his faith.

12. RELEASE: TRANSITION AND LIMBO

At this point, the prisoner is ready for release, although the actual timing of a Westerner's release has been determined more by international political considerations than by his progress in reform. In recent cases, a public trial, replete with prosecuting and defense attorneys, has formalized both the conviction and the rebirth. Before an outside audience, the prisoner once more admits his crimes and expresses his new point of view, while the defense attorney makes a plea for additional "leniency." More frequently, the prisoner is simply read his charge and sentence while still within the prison, as happened to both Vincent and Luca. On rare occasions, a Westerner is sentenced to serve additional time in a new setting (considered a true prison) where he undergoes "reform by labor," a procedure of much less emotional involvement. Whether publicly or privately sentenced, the great majority of Western prisoners have been immediately expelled from China.

But release and expulsion, as Vincent in particular discovered, do not put an end to one's troubles. Instead they thrust the Westerner into an environment which immediately questions all that has been so painstakingly built up during the years of imprisonment; and they precipitate a new identity crisis just as severe as the one experienced during incarceration. Although this crisis occurs outside the thought reform milieu, it must be regarded as the final "step" in reform; it cannot be separated from what has gone before. The presence of this post-release identity crisis in virtually all of my Western subjects during the time of our interviews was what enabled them to describe so vividly the identity conflicts of their thought reform experiences.

Upon arriving in Hong Kong, Dr. Vincent discovered that what he had become in prison was of absolutely no use to him in his new milieu. Alone with his emotions, he found himself in a devastating predicament: he had internalized enough of his prison environment to feel a severe distrust of the non-Communist world, but was sufficiently receptive to the evidence around him to be highly suspicious of the Communist point of view as well. The security he had known during the latter part of imprisonment suddenly vanished, and his identity was shaken to its foundations. Should he still be the "Communist physician" of his rebirth and seek employment through a European Communist party? or should he return to his freelance medical work in underdeveloped countries? In his personal limbo he was unable to feel "safe" (or whole) in either world; instead he felt deceived by both.

He longed nostalgically for the relatively simple, ordered, and meaningful prison experience, now glorified in his memory. He could relinquish this longing only as he began to be able to trust his new environment; this trust in turn depended upon the capacity to trust himself. Once more he underwent a painful identity shift, encompassing what he had been before, what he had become in prison, and what he was in the process of becoming after release.

Father Luca experienced a similar crisis, in some ways attenuated by his immediate welcome into the motherly embrace of the Church. He knew clearly that he was still the dedicated Catholic priest (although it was not easy for him to give up being a "Chinese" Catholic priest). But he retained profound doubts about his own integrity, and especially about the morality of his missionary work. The dishonoring had struck deep chords in him, and had stirred strong anxieties. His problem was not so much whether or not to continue being a Catholic priest—he could conceive of no alternative to this—but rather one of regaining respect for the clerical missionary life to which he was committed.

Nor were Dr. Vincent and Father Luca alone in these conflicts; immediately following release, all prisoners experienced profound struggles about their integrity, their ability to trust, and their search for wholeness. None escaped the personal crisis of this transitional period any more than he could avoid involvement in the other steps; but each man's crisis was his own.

CHAPTER 6

VARIETIES OF RESPONSE:
THE OBVIOUSLY CONFUSED

In discussing in Chapter 5 the twelve psychological steps of prison thought reform, I emphasized the similarities in the emotional responses of the people who were put through it. These similarities were due both to consistent pressures and to universal human characteristics. In this chapter, I shall turn to the equally important individual variations which I was able to observe. Each subject, during and immediately after his reform, demonstrated his own special combination of emotion and belief, his particular pattern of strengths and susceptibilities. The quality of this personal response depended largely upon the character traits of the man who was imprisoned, upon the configurations of emotions and identities developed within him during the course of his entire previous life.

Since no two men are the same, we could delineate as many types of response as there were subjects interviewed. It is convenient, however, to distinguish three general categories, based upon the beliefs these men expressed and the emotions which underlay those beliefs at the time of our interviews. These categories—*the obviously confused, the apparent converts,* and *the apparent resisters* —each describe a broad style of response characteristic for the time of imprisonment as well as for the post-release period. Despite the complexities involved, and the inevitable overlapping, these three categories allow us a deeper appreciation of both the inner effects of thought reform, and the relationship of these effects to already existing patterns of behavior.

Dr. Vincent and Father Luca, as different as their reactions were, both exhibited the first and most frequent variety of response. Both felt confused and said so. Each could recognize that he had been affected by some of the Communist message, and each felt a need to reconsider the problems of who he was and what he believed. This combination of admitted confusion and conscious search was characteristic for fifteen of the twenty-five Westerners.

Although I have said much about Dr. Vincent and Father Luca, I have included very little about the man behind the response or the child and youth behind the man. The following examination of their preprison life patterns makes obvious what psychiatrists and psychologists have learned to expect—that all men have a hidden history of struggle and conflict, whether they are patients or "normal" research subjects.

Dr. Charles Vincent: The Mystical Healer

Born and brought up in southern France in a pious, middle-class family (his father was a painter who limited his creations to Catholic religious art), Charles Vincent began to express during his earliest years an antagonistic urge to cut himself off from people around him:

My father looked at me as a wild child. . . . He was telling me all the time I didn't have any relationship with him. . . . We were in the same house but not in fusion. . . . He didn't succeed to have my inside. . . . I thought, no matter what—you are wrong and I am right.

Charles sought always to escape the confinement of his house: "I didn't like to sleep in a bed. I wanted to sleep in a tree." He remembers his father, on one occasion, chaining him to the house, but to no avail: "I succeeded in escaping and I was happy."

His father felt that the best cure would be a strict boarding school. Charles attended four of these schools, most of which were run by Catholic authorities, between the ages of ten and seventeen. In each case he did well enough in his studies, but he recognized no rules, and kept himself emotionally aloof.

It was difficult for me. . . . my temperament was to go against every-body, to keep me tight with no external manifestations. . . . I was not interested in people around me, you understand—just looking only my way—just wanting to be out because I thought that way I could be more independent—to put a distance between persons who might still influence my goings on.

Vincent (with a certain pride) remembers school authorities complaining to his father: "Your son has been here for four years and we don't even know him." After a period of time, he was usually expelled.

But through all this combat, he felt deep within him that he was bad and guilty and that they—his father and other strict authorities —were justified in punishing and seeking to reform him.

I never fought with my father. He was a good man. He gave me a profession. If he used a strong way with me, I think he was right. . . . I felt, "My father is my father, and I cannot go against him." The fault was with my character, but I couldn't by myself correct myself.

This pattern continued through his teens, with his father still his main antagonist. His mother was apparently also on the side of authority, but Vincent's evasiveness about her suggests that what-ever else they shared was either too intimate or too painful to be easily recalled or revealed.

At the age of nineteen, his distorted emotional patterns reached a bizarre climax in his first encounter with love. Feeling enamored of a fourteen-year-old girl, he decided that "she *must* fall in love with me," but he neither made physical advances nor even spoke of his feelings. Instead, he studied an anatomy book to find out where on his body he could shoot himself without causing perma-nent damage, took his father's pistol, and put a bullet through his shoulder. In telling me about this, he showed me his scar. Just be-fore shooting himself, he sent the girl a one-sentence note, telling her what he was about to do, and ending with the phrase, "only you cut my youth." He told me that he had done all of this "be-cause I wanted this girl to know I was in love with her—to be moved." Vincent spent two months in a hospital recovering; and the incident appeared to have more effect upon his parents than upon the girl: "My father said it was a surprise for him, a surprise to my mother also, to everybody." He looked upon his actions as a necessity, the only possible course for a man of his character:

I realized I was foolish, but I had to go through my experience. If someone had said "You are foolish," I never would have agreed. I was sure that in this way she would have to have love for me. . . . From this example you can see how straight I was going through to my aim through my personal experience. I never had a thought to touch the girl—to let her know I was interested in her. But only through myself, you see, I did it. I am the master of myself, and do what I want to myself.

With this deed, Vincent was acting out his conflicts on many levels: he was getting even with his father and mother, and with all other authorities whom he "surprised"; he was substituting destructiveness (actually self-destructiveness) for love or affection; and through this act of self-punishment, he was atoning for his guilt. But what is most remarkable is his need to experience—and to manipulate—all thought, feelings, and actions through the medium of his own body. Such extreme narcissism, and such bizarrely symbolic behavior are usually found only in people so cut off from other human beings as to be considered psychotic. Indeed, one might well have expected such a youth to become a psychiatric casualty, if not a ne'er-do-well or a criminal. Certainly his extreme self-absorption, his disregard of all social rules, and his destructive behavior toward others and toward himself did not seem to offer much promise for his assuming a place or a function in any society.

Vincent had, during this stage of late adolescence, experienced a crisis precipitated by the conflict between his asocial style of remaining the "master" of his own "insides," and a sudden urge toward intimacy with another human being. At this age, some form of identity crisis—of a struggle to achieve direction while suspended between the child of the past and the adult of the future—occurs in everyone;[1] but in Charles Vincent, it assumed dangerously pathological proportions.

Yet a solution appeared, a means of directing his energies into constructive channels and finding a socially possible way of life. Charles embarked on the study of medicine, with a passion for his subject which almost totally consumed his intellect and his emotions. He worked night and day, first on the theoretical and then on the practical aspects of medical study; he devoted all his spare time to extra work in clinics, and he graduated at the top of his class at the age of twenty-six. This vocational (and nonideological) solution to his identity crisis supplied the anchor for a life threatened by dangerously disruptive emotions. He had undergone a personal "death and rebirth"; but in his mystical view, he saw it as a continuation rather than an interruption of his previous life:

I always wanted to be a doctor. I thought, it is the best profession. To talk to me about engineering, law, means nothing—but to be a doctor —I liked it by instinct.

Charles remained in Europe only long enough to take his licensure examinations and acquire a wife; on their wedding day they embarked for China. Again acting both intuitively and decisively, he had responded to the lure which China held for Europeans and Americans during the first decades of the twentieth century. He had spoken to many returning missionaries, and had read many articles; he was excited by the challenge of the difficulties, and by the absence of hospitals, physicians, and even rudimentary sanitary conditions. This opportunity for lonely accomplishment and exaggerated autonomy was probably the strongest attraction for him:

In my training I always liked to do things for myself, to do what is necessary. For a doctor to be master of himself is what the patient needs. . . . I took to China my microscope, all of my books and equipment, and a small microtome so I could do everything for myself and be completely independent.

China more than lived up to his expectations. As a much-needed physician in an alien setting, he was able to do useful work and at the same time live in his own idiosyncratic fashion. He worked with other doctors only at the beginning in order to learn something about local conditions and about Chinese medical vocabulary. Then he developed a self-sufficient pattern of private practice and part-time employment with European governmental representatives; he had daily clinic hours and also made broad bacteriological surveys. For a while he did research at a large medical center, but he discontinued this when a paper of his was criticized and at the same time a distinguished scientist arrived from Europe: "The competition started, so I left." Once he considered accepting a tempting offer to head a large missionary hospital, but abruptly backed out of the arrangement as soon as he discovered a clause in the contract saying that he would not be permitted to leave the hospital area without the permission of the Mother Superior.

He maintained throughout his years in China an intensive absorption in his medical work, treating Chinese and foreigners of all walks of life. But he scrupulously avoided intimate personal relationships with anyone, as he considered these a threat to his freedom. "If I have a friend I have to invite him, and I don't like to be a slave to convenience." He much preferred such individual pursuits as writing, painting, and hunting. "Instead of going to a dinner party, I can go to the country. I was a man who knew a better place." As might be expected, other Westerners in Shanghai disliked Dr. Vincent, viewing him as strange and somehow evil.

After the war he decided, because of past political affiliations (although never interested in politics, he had joined a French rightist party in his country for the practical advantages this then afforded him) to move his practice almost entirely into the country. He began to care for patients over a wide area—traveling by motorcycle, horsecart, mule, small boat, or on foot. He kept three separate clinics in the country, always choosing the sites so that they would be near hunting areas. He ignored real danger from troops of both sides during the Chinese Civil War, and pursued with impersonal mystical enthusiasm both his healing art and his communion with nature:

I lost myself completely living this kind of life. In the early morning and in the evening I would fish and hunt. I would work all day, sometimes traveling three hours to get to a patient, sometimes sleeping at his home. . . . I enjoyed living with the patient because to me he was not just a case. . . . There was no other doctor, and I was giving life to plenty of patients. . . . It was a necessity to see life in contact with poor people and with nature in order to have emotions—emotions which I can translate into writing and painting. . . . There was no man as happy as I.

Dr. Vincent maintained a similar personal distance in his relationships with his wife and children. He spent little time with them, referring to his wife as "a very nice woman" because "she never gave me any trouble and always respected my freedom." He arranged for his family to leave for Europe just before the Communist take-over in 1948. He had virtually lost contact with his mother and father.

In 1949, with the new regime installed, he found his services more in demand in the city, where he again began to conduct most of his practice. He established what he considered to be good relations with a few Communist officials, treating them at his private clinic, and he thought that with so few foreign doctors remaining, his future was "bright." He disregarded numerous warnings from his embassy advising him to leave because the situation was becoming dangerous. On one occasion, he did make reservations to go; but he decided to cancel them, because "I felt that to stay was more in keeping with my character."

An important feature of Dr. Vincent's pre-thought reform character was his manner of combining extreme and potentially disruptive emotional patterns from early childhood with techniques learned during young adult training to shape a highly personal and unusual style of life. It is true that a psychiatrist might well have noted prominent schizoid and paranoid character trends; to put it more simply, he was a man unable to love. Yet he had developed a stable and workable identity as a mystical healer—a lonely adventurer, ever courting new dangers; an isolated seeker of high aesthetic values, ever replenishing his store of sensations; a magical manipulator who could master his environment only through maintaining his distance from other people.

Incorporated in this self-image were three convictions which he had been seeking to prove to himself almost from the day of his birth: *I need no one. No one can have my insides. I transcend other mortals.* To maintain these personal myths required ever-strenuous but ever-exhilarating efforts. He was always on guard against his own inner urges in the opposite direction: his tendencies to seek intimacy, work co-operatively, and rely upon other people. These social and co-operative urges were, ironically enough, his negative identity. He had to keep warding them off as dangers to his personal myths, and to his exaggerated sense of individual mastery which held together the entire configuration.

Like anyone who rebels strongly, he carried with him, through identification, much of those people from whom he sought to free himself. He had become, like his father, an artist and something of a tyrant. (What he took from his mother is less clear.) The powerful emotions he had expressed in his early defiance of authority also left him with strong feelings of guilt. His guilt feelings were not obvious, and he may even have appeared to some as a man without a conscience. Instead, he suffered from a more repressed and potentially malignant sense of evil and need for punishment, which revealed itself only in disguised form: in his self-injury at nineteen, his courting of danger, and his remaining in China long after he had been warned to leave. But the life pattern of the mystical healer could, under most circumstances, keep these emotions under control.

When Dr. Vincent was imprisoned, however, everything was suddenly overturned: the manipulator was now being manipulated, the healer was considered "ill" and in need of "treatment," the aesthetic wanderer was thrown into a crowded dingy cell, the isolate was forced to lay himself bare before strangers. Nothing in his former identity seemed to fit the new circumstances.

In making his wild confession, he did attempt to maintain his emotional distance and call his manipulative powers into play. A man without binding group loyalties or devotion to any shared set of truths, he cared little for the pros and cons of Communist ideology; his concern was to survive. But thought reform assaults very quickly undermined his efforts to maintain control and stay uninvolved; he was drawn—as all had to be—into an intimate world of personal relationships and of ceaseless self-probing.

Under these circumstances, his personal myth of absolute independence and superhuman self-mastery was exploded. He had no choice but to become emotionally engaged in a human society, perhaps for the first time in his life. This reversal of such a basic identity pattern was a mark of thought reform's power; but it was achieved only through the reformers' success in bringing out Vincent's long-buried strivings toward human involvement, strivings which he had until then successfully denied. They had also made contact with his concealed guilt susceptibilities: as he was made to feel more and more guilty, he could surrender his precious isolation (indeed, he had to, as his flight from people had been one of the original sources of his guilt), and become more and more what the environment wished him to be.

When this began to happen, he could call upon no broad beliefs and no social self to protect him. Dazzled by the sudden filling of a long-standing emotional void, he took on much of the coloring of his new milieu. He accepted, and by no means superficially, much of the ideology and many of the visions of Chinese Communism. For he was a man no less vulnerable to human influence than others; behind his lifelong avoidance of people was both a fear of and a desire for such influence.

In his process of rebirth, much of his old identity could be drawn upon. He was able to find a new focus for his mysticism in the Communist version of "the people"; he could resume his manipulative healing in "helping" his cellmates ("the Communists, too, bind body and spirit," he told me); and he could make use of a "scientific methodology" which appealed to the more concrete and logical side of his character. His rebirth culminated in his re-emergence at the end of his reform as the teaching physician. He gave the impression that during the last part of imprisonment he had brought his new identity configuration into good working order; at the moment of release, he was in a fairly integrated state.

When he was thrust into the Hong Kong environment, however, his new identity was in turn shattered. I have already described the identity crisis precipitated within him through his inability to trust himself in relationship to either the Communist or non-Communist world; this information about his background reveals why his crisis of trust was so extreme. What was most devastating to Vincent was his loss of the exaggerated sense of mastery, which he had always been able to call forth in a non-Communist environment. Having functioned for so long on the assumption that he could trust nothing and no one outside of himself, the absence of this self-trust was crucial, and the paranoid psychosis which this personal faith had always warded off threatened to engulf him.

He was, in fact, closer to psychosis after release than he had been during the worst assaults of imprisonment. True, it was during thought reform itself that he had been deprived of his self-mastery; but then he had been offered a workable identity configuration in return, along with a strong sense of order and a series of pressures so involving that his emotions were absorbed by the constant struggle to keep in step. In Hong Kong he faced a milieu which offered neither controls nor support; instead it presented a peculiar combination of freedom, colonial flavor, inequalities, artificiality, and a certain tentativeness. To be deprived in such a place of his only dependable identity mechanism meant facing for the first time the full consequences of his loss—facing both outer chaos and inner confusion.

Consequently, Dr. Vincent showed a tendency to relapse into the identity of the repentant criminal, as, for instance, when he reacted to the Chinese businessman as an accusing judge. He also had the—to him—novel experience of suffering from, rather than thriving upon, loneliness. In his encounters with friends, casual acquaintances, and with me as well, he sought help in the struggle to regain his lost sense of integration and mastery. But he was ill-equipped for close relationships, both because of his oldest life patterns and because of his newly-magnified suspiciousness. He quickly sensed that hope lay, not in the imposed emotional patterns of thought reform, but rather in a reversion to what he was best equipped to be—the mystical healer.

Once he was permanently removed from external thought reform pressures, this reversion was inevitable. The clearest evidence of his return to his old pattern of experiencing all of life through his own mind and body is expressed in the following extraordinary statement made during our final interview:

What happens is strange—this experience is useful to me—because I proved everything in China . . . to be in jail and to be accused is part of myself. . . . It is difficult to explain. . . . Now I have had the experience of the reality of that world. I know what they do. . . . My mind is more enlarged.

I know everything about them—how cruel they are—their different mind—their materialistic way to see things—their logic. . . . You cannot know—you cannot understand what the chains and the *tou-cheng* [struggle] mean—about the compulsion they use. . . . I know everything about the step-by-step method . . . it is the difference between a man who studies anatomy in a book and a man who studies anatomy on the body.

I can see the situation through my experience, a personal experience—physical and spiritual. Now if somebody said to go back to China, I would say no; without my experience, I would say I have to go back.

Here are echoes of the youth who put a bullet through his own shoulder to express his love for a young girl: the experience must be his, or it is no experience at all. This basic core of character had survived parental criticism, strict Catholic schools, medical study, twenty years of life in China, and even thought reform itself.

Dr. Vincent's confusion and search was, on the whole, non-ideological. Communist and non-Communist beliefs were, as always, important to him only as they affected his immediate life experience. Even his confusion about ideas, manifested in the jump from one side to the other, was mainly an involuntary emotional experiment, a form of identity testing. His search led inevitably back to that part of him he knew best. But the effect of the Communist view of the world and the thought reform identities which he had absorbed during his imprisonment cannot be completely dismissed. These remained within him as an alternative self, ready again to emerge—as they did during our interviews together—should he feel wronged or neglected during his future life in the non-Communist world.

What about his statement that he had never "talked so frankly" as he had to me, and that this was an effect of his re-education? I think he answered this question in his last sentence: "I have a feeling I left part of myself in Hong Kong." This remark can be interpreted in more than one way. It contains the suggestion that through thought reform, he had learned to surrender his "insides," and had therefore been able to reveal more of himself to me than he had to anyone before. But it implies also, and perhaps more importantly, that in leaving part of himself in Hong Kong, he was shedding one of his skins in order to free himself for what lay ahead. He was leaving behind the newest, least comfortable, and most expendable part of himself, the reformed man. He was aware that thought reform had taught him to "open" himself to others; but having done so, first in prison, and then with me in Hong Kong, he was bent upon unlearning his lesson.

Anthony Luca: Liberal Father Confessor

Father Luca's confusion and search took a very different form, influenced by his own special background and character. Born in East Africa, son of a prominent Italian colonial official, Anthony grew up with a dual allegiance. He was very much a European boy —living among "natives" he was made especially aware of this; but he was also a child of Africa. He spent nine of his first eleven years there; and when he was sent to live in Europe from the ages of seven to nine, he had longed for the freedom of "the land . . . the river . . . a whole little world of our own" in Africa. An excellent student during his early years, his work suffered in Europe. But more disturbing to him were his social difficulties there among the "rough and rather unpleasant" boys in his class, who spoke a kind of slang he could not understand. And when Anthony, without thinking, used the common language of Europeans in Africa—African words mixed with his own language—he was laughed at and teased. His companions, with the merciless psychological accuracy of schoolboys, summed up his conflict when they tauntingly dubbed him "the white Negro."

His family relationships perpetuated this conflict, and also presented him with an additional emotional duality. The family had in many ways a classical European constellation: a stern, strongly opinionated, "authoritarian" father; a less talked about, but more intimate mother; a "very reliable" older brother and a more erratic and attention-getting younger brother among Anthony's five siblings.

His feelings toward his father alternated between fear and love, meeting in a common denominator of respect. He happily recalled the long walks which they took together in the open African countryside, during which his father would tell him informative and interesting stories and teach him the alphabet to prepare him for school. But his father also had a more frightening side, so that Anthony had a "double idea about him"; he was demanding and critical, and would frequently beat the boy for misbehaving. Anthony resented his father's tendency to "say what was wrong but not use many words of explanation or justification." Despite this conflict, he was deeply impressed with his father's "great sympathy for the black man," and his energetic defense of Africans in their conflict with Europeans.

He received affection and solace from his mother, but he was troubled by her "nervousness"—and he sometimes felt that both of his parents neglected him in favor of their own cultural and intellectual interests. Despite these problems he deeply missed his parents when, on medical advice, he was sent to live with relatives in Europe because of the discovery of what was then diagnosed as a kidney ailment. Put on a closely-supervised medical and dietary regime, and beset by emotional conflicts, he at first felt weak and worthless: "I was little, had no strength, and the other boys despised me." But these feelings were soon overshadowed by a new pattern which quickly became a major concern—his "badness."

As a child in Africa, Anthony had an occasional show of temper and was considered to be a bit reckless, sometimes self-destructively so: he would experiment with his environment by putting dirt in his mouth "to see what it tasted like," or by running across the street just in front of an automobile "to see if I could run quickly enough." But later in Europe, feeling lonely and persecuted, he became more generally ill-tempered and disobedient; and a continuing struggle with his aunt and uncle developed (or with his father during visits). The conflicts began with Anthony's misbehavior, and ended either with his being sent to bed without dinner, or, more frequently, with his being placed in the "black cellar," despite all his infuriated cries and kicks.

This pattern diminished somewhat when he returned to Africa; but when he was in Europe during his teens—he had entered boarding school there at the age of eleven—his "badness" took another form, a disturbing new sexual awareness. He experienced anguished feelings of guilt and shame about his masturbation and his sexual interest in girls, and also in connection with a physical approach made to him by another young boy.

After a while, he did begin to earn some respect in school because of his fine grades, his rapid body growth, and his developing ability in sports; he made more friends and felt more accepted by others. But he was aware of a "contradiction" in his character, one which always remained with him: in his relations with other people he alternated between shyness and fear on the one hand, and overly assertive and dogmatic attitudes on the other.

This "bad" (and sexually aware), "weak" (but athletically competent), able and intelligent, shy-domineering, "white Negro" adolescent sought some way to integrate these painfully unmeshed aspects of himself and become a person whom he and others could respect. He found it through religion, and specifically through the clerical ideology of the Catholic Church.

He was embracing a doctrine which had always been available to him. As a son of "good" (although not fervent) Catholics, he had begun to attend Mass in Africa when still an infant and had been instructed there by missionary fathers. He had not, however, demonstrated a particularly strong interest in religion until the time of his troubled adolescence, when he began to seek comfort through long periods of prayer in the chapel of the dormitory (run by

Catholic fathers) where he was living. During the course of this inner search, he developed the conviction that his mother and father had not been sufficiently pious or serious in their lives. His resolve to follow a more purposeful existence carried him closer to an ideological solution of his identity crisis.

It was something of thinking that there must be some great interest in life to help others—to have a lasting aim—a broader point of view that embraced the whole of things which could help people who underwent unpleasantness.

At the age of fourteen he participated in a Catholic retreat supervised by one of the fathers—three-and-one-half days devoted to prayer and meditation, while completely withdrawn from worldly activities—which he considered a crucial interlude in his life. During the retreat, he thought a great deal about what he considered to be his two main faults—his sexual ideas (especially the guilt accompanying masturbation) and his bad temper; he sought ways to overcome these and to "correct myself." His plans became more specific and affirmative: "I emerged with the resolve to be good, to be active in the world, to have an aim for religion." He dates his urge to enter the priesthood from this retreat; but at the time he told himself it would not be possible because he was too unworthy. At the age of sixteen he made his definite decision, strongly influenced by a young priest whom he greatly admired and who planned to do missionary work in China.

Anthony was then certain that he too wished to become a missionary, either in Africa or China. A schoolmate's interest in China and his friendship with Chinese Christian students played a part here. Like many European Christians of this period, he viewed China as the great missionary challenge: "I thought that what I could do best was to be a missionary in China . . . the biggest country . . . the most people . . . to be a parish priest was not so necessary."

His family was not pleased with his decision. His father, whose aspirations for the boy included a brilliant and conventional career, particularly objected to his choosing a small, unknown missionary order rather than a famous society like the Jesuits. But Anthony succeeded in winning over his mother, who in turn combined forces with the seminary Superior to obtain reluctant agreement from her husband.

During his six years of seminary training and theological study, the emphasis was upon "self-examination" and "internal discipline." Anthony found it quite demanding, particularly since "I always had difficulty in exactly stating my feeling," but he felt that he profited from the training and had "good memories" of these years. He went on to take advanced theological studies, completing a doctoral dissertation relating to the psychological aspects of faith; and he also did work in medicine and Buddhist philosophy to prepare him for his Asian missionary assignment.

His departure was delayed by the war, and he remained in Europe for three additional years. He became involved with anti-Fascist underground activities, and worked closely with guerrilla forces. During this time he demonstrated unusual bravery, volunteering for dangerous missions, and on one occasion approaching unarmed a group of enemy deserters to convince them to give up their weapons. He attributed his lack of fear to his firm conviction that what he was doing was right; and he was widely praised for his courage.

When he was finally sent to China, Father Luca was quickly enthusiastic and successful in his missionary work. He responded strongly to the country, the language, and the people. He developed particular affection for the young Chinese he guided and taught, and they in turn regarded him with great respect and affection. But he was still troubled by the emotional problems which had plagued him since early adolescence. His sexual conflicts emerged in his experiencing "great affection" and "intimate feelings," on two occasions, for young secondary school girls with whom he was working; and his difficulties with authority came out in his frequent resistance to those above him, and his fluctuation between overbearing and self-effacing attitudes. He continued, as in the past, to overcome these problems through meditation, prayer, and especially religious confession.

But after the Communists took power, Father Luca found himself in conflict with both the representatives of the new government and with many of his own colleagues. Much of his activity was devoted to organizing Chinese youth into the faith-propagating Legion of Mary. The Legion, as well as all other religious organizations, was soon required to register with the new regime, and it was bitterly criticized and constantly harassed because of its opposition to the regime's triple autonomy movement. At Communist mass meetings, the Legion of Mary was denounced as a "reactionary" organization devoted to "espionage," and Father Luca heard that on one such occasion he was publicly accused of inciting young boys in his youth groups to "sabotage" and to various forms of vandalism.

Father Luca favored moderate behavior on the part of the Church in meeting this crisis. He especially opposed arbitrary attitudes of individual Catholic officials and was critical of those who indulged in political—and in some cases military—action against the Communists. He argued against the thesis that all Communists were evil *per se*, expressing the Christian point of view that they were human beings after all, sometimes guilty of wrongs, but capable of redemption. Father Luca felt strongly about the Church's need to find a means of surviving in China, and about his own personal desire to remain there and continue his missionary work. He repeatedly ignored his colleagues' advice to leave despite what they considered to be his precarious personal position.

The man who was imprisoned, then, was an effective and integrated human being, one able to work and to love. Crucial to his identity was his sense of being a man of God, a representative of the Faith and of the Truth, a responsible official of the Catholic Church, a friend of the oppressed, a searching and open-minded scholar, a brother and father of Chinese youth, a lover of China and of the Chinese, and a foreign member of Chinese culture. But ever lurking in the background was another much more derogatory self-image, a view of himself as impure (sexually) and unhumble (in his dealings with superiors). Also part of this negative identity, we suspect, were old feelings of weakness, as well as the fear of alienation from friends and colleagues. These negative and positive elements were both included in his over-all identity of the liberal "Chinese" father confessor.

His liberalism was related to his past identity struggle: torn apart as a child by the conflict between his African and European selves, deeply attached and yet a bit unsteady in his family identifications, experimental and inquisitive since earliest childhood (even to the point of swallowing dirt), he had early learned to be receptive to the other person's convictions and way of life. With him, as with anyone truly receptive, this meant not just standing by with tolerance, but actually becoming each of the things which challenged his sense of identity—whether African child, European schoolboy, or Catholic priest and missionary. Thus he became more "Chinese" than his colleagues, closer to and better loved by those whom he guided and instructed. At the same time, his capacity to understand and sympathetically enter into the other person's point of view made him more prone to moral conflict and indecisiveness. Such is likely to be the identity constellation and the dilemma of any "liberal," no matter what his cause.

Priests have been called "father-confessor" since the Church's early days. For each priest this title has a shared as well as a special meaning; in Father Luca's case, it symbolizes much of his character. He was even more the "father" than the average priest, since almost all of his professional career had been devoted to work with youngsters, and he liked to do this work best. He was a "confessor"— as a priest, novice, naughty child (and later as a prisoner)—in all three meanings of the term: he made confessions, he heard confessions, and he also "avowed and adhered to his faith under persecution and torture without suffering martyrdom."

Confession, then, had long been for him a personal style, even a way of life. It was not without its difficulties: the small boy was not always clear about what wrong he was expected to "confess"; the novice could not easily express his exact feelings. Whatever inarticulate and repressive forces worked against it, however, confession had served him well. Through it he had been able to face, and share with sympathetic colleagues, the disturbing feelings which had fed his negative identity. It had been especially important in subduing (although never fully conquering) his sexual urges and aggressive tendencies.

Nonetheless, the sense of evil which accompanied these sexual and aggressive urges could not easily be stilled. Confession helped to keep these feelings conscious and manageable (rather than inaccessible and more dangerous, as with Dr. Vincent); but it also required him to search out his own evil, to look constantly upon himself as one who is guilty. His susceptibility to guilt, present from early life, was thus ever stimulated anew. Managed reasonably effectively by his tie to the Catholic Church, his guilt was a point of vulnerability for any new authority which might seek to manipulate his loyalties; it was, in fact, the royal road to his negative identity.

Father Luca's complex adult configuration was largely the product of emotional compromise. In dealing with his father and all later authorities, he had alternated between submission and rebellion. He had, in a sense, defied his father in becoming a priest, and especially in a small missionary order; but he was remaining within a Catholic ideology which his family held sacred. Moreover, he became, like his father, at the same time both a champion of the rights of "natives" and a loyal servant of a European institution. He also possessed a tenderness which—as his prison memories suggest—must have been derived from a relationship of love and intimacy with his mother; a relationship which may have been responsible for much of his submissiveness, receptivity, and penchant for suffering.

In his ideological solution to his identity crisis, Father Luca (unlike Dr. Vincent) acquired a comprehensive if constricting view of the world, and a strict code of conduct for relations with other people; he took on a sense of loyalty and near-total submission to an institution greater than himself. His concern was no longer simply, "Where do I stand?" and, "What can I do about my badness?" Badness and commitment still had to be dealt with, but not on an individual basis. Instead, he asked himself, "How can I purify and humble myself in order to better serve the Church? How can I be more consistent in my life, and mean what I say and do? How can I, as a Catholic priest, be fully *sincere?*"

It is therefore not surprising that Father Luca objected strenuously to the judge's impugning his sincerity. He stated his position at the beginning—"a mistake or a matter of religion"—which made him, as he stood before the judge, both a man defending truth and a representative of a sacred institution. The fact that he had doubts about his own sincerity, at whatever level of consciousness, made him fight all the harder: one does not reveal inner weakness before the enemy. Moreover, by this same initial statement, he had declared his imprisonment a test of his sincerity; he assumed the posture of the confessor who is the defender of his faith against those who would persecute it.

The irony of his situation was that his reformers meant something a little different by "sincerity": for Chinese Communist officials, both in prison and out, to be sincere is to yield to them as representatives of the Way and the Truth. "Insincerity" or resistance is the one attitude which they will not tolerate, and they regarded Luca's behavior as provocative. This, plus their prior identification of him as an enemy—he was not only a Catholic priest, but a leader of a militant Catholic organization—led to their use of force and brutality to a degree unusual even for a Chinese Communist prison. As on earlier occasions in his life, Luca could not grasp or articulate what he was expected to confess; and although the reformer's contradictory demands may have been mainly responsible for this, it is very likely that Luca's lifelong resistances to confession also played a part, as he seemed to have much more difficulty than most other prisoners in reaching an understanding of the situation. In any case, he experienced a more profound physical and psychological breakdown than did Dr. Vincent.

Father Luca's false confession reflected both a disintegration of his sense of reality and identity, and an outpouring of his sense of evil. His experience was like that of a man, who, troubled by feelings of guilt, dreams that he is a criminal being punished. Luca was a "criminal" being punished in jail, "dreaming" of having committed the kind of crime of which he was accused—his dream work much assisted by his surroundings, and closely supervised by judge and cellmates. In a twilight state of fatigue, pain, and altered consciousness, he was both responding to the prison message and at the same time reverting to his own familiar confession idiom.

No other prisoner I encountered confessed more extensively than did Father Luca; nor did anyone else sustain for as long a period such a grossly false story. He could do this and even believe in his confession, not only because the environment encouraged this belief, but also because his confession had for him the ring of psychological truth. That is, it expressed "subversive" things about himself, albeit in the language of the Communist police system rather than that of the Catholic Church. It was an extreme version—a caricature—of his own negative identity. As an experienced confessor (and a man who had done some writing) Father Luca could be creative, prolific, and convincing in using this caricature to develop his confession-novel.

The direct physical assault, coming at the height of the false confession, showed a loss of control on the part of the Communist officials. They had begun to check Father Luca's false confession, apparently after having believed a good deal of it, and had found it to be "insincere" beyond words—in both the conventional and their own special meaning of the term.

Luca himself, once injured (and physically punished), rose to impressive heights of courage and strength. He had given indications of his will to survive even before the injury. His delusions had included fantasies of self-affirmation—of recovery, rescue, and return to priestly activities—along with elements of guilt. At that time, too, he could summon faith in the religious purpose of his suffering ("penance for my sins"). Crippled and helpless, he was able to reach more profoundly into his emotional being and remind himself of the most basic forms of trust he had known in the past: religious comradeship, earthly places, both beautiful and permanent, and most of all, sad songs which took him back to maternal love and tenderness. His identity collapse had been temporary; now he sought always to reaffirm that in himself which he most valued and could depend upon. And at the same time, he kept his inner experience within his own religious idiom. His imprisonment was a continuation of his lifelong self-purification. His faith was a powerful ally, one he would under no condition surrender: hence his dramatic assertion that "to take off my religion it is necessary to take out my heart and to kill me"—both a statement of creed and a quashing of self-doubt.

This very creed and his devotion to the Church behind it led to his greatest pain during reform. As a "liberal" he had already been in conflict with "illiberal" (and militaristic) colleagues, with whom he was now accused of conspiring. As a "liberal," he could also "feel" the validity of some Communist objections to official and nonofficial Church activity. He was especially vulnerable to accusations that the Church did such apparently "good" things as helping the sick and poor for its own selfish reasons: this would be "insincerity" at its worst. But he was susceptible not only because he was liberal; it was precisely in this issue that he found his guilt, both personal and existential, most exploited. A negative image here—of self and Church—was both intolerable and unavoidable.

Luca's quest for "sincerity," as well as his "Chineseness," served, toward the end of his imprisonment, to bring him into a position of harmony with the officials: all became increasingly "frank" and "sincere." But it was sincerity at a price, and led him to the incongruous position of "helping" a fellow-priest make a criminal "confession"—his furthest venture into "betrayal." He was, to be sure, still "hearing confessions'"; but now "sincerely" in harmony with the opposition.

Yet this too was only partial and transient. Immediately upon release, he was identified by his religious colleagues once more as the dedicated Catholic priest, which he had never really ceased to be. He also faced the delicate problem of restoring his identity as a liberal confessor, deeply committed to an authoritarian Church. His identity flexibility required that he scrutinize the Communists, the Church, and himself. In his profound sense of shame and guilt over having betrayed the Church (and himself), he felt the need to both relive and reformulate his relationship to it. Thus the story of the "naughty little girl" converted to active Catholicism despite parental opposition retells his own experience in entering the priesthood. His "liberalism" had obliged him to give a hearing to some of the Communist message; but this involved him much less than his personal, credal, Catholic search. Now, as before, he could deal with his conflicts within his religious framework.

He conveyed the feeling that his imprisonment had made him more open to others' influence, more submissive; these could be important changes, but as heightening of traits already present, rather than as new characteristics. Perhaps an even more profound upheaval for Father Luca was the need to surrender much of his "Chinese" self, leaving him in a state of mourning which began not with imprisonment, but after release. He gave me the feeling, however, that from his careful, painful, and conscience-ridden weighing of ideas and emotions, a somewhat remodeled, but still liberal (and not entirely un-Chinese) father-confessor was re-emerging.

Professor Hermann Castorp: The Submissive Scientist

Let us now examine the experience of another man who falls into this general category of the obviously confused, yet responded quite differently from either Dr. Vincent or Father Luca. A biologist from Central Europe in his mid-fifties, Professor Castorp was introduced to me by a member of his consulate in Hong Kong. Two or three of my other subjects who had met him in prison told me he had been "very progressive"; but when he came to see me just a few days after his release, he could best be described as "lost." In addition to the typical post-imprisonment fear and suspiciousness, he was overcome by loneliness, and sought group protection whenever he could: "Even when crossing the street, I waited for a few people and crossed with the group." He welcomed the opportunity to talk things over with me, and so clearly enjoyed our three half-day sessions together that each time he was reluctant to leave. Yet despite his voluble answers to my questions, and his eagerness to prolong our talks, his manner was vague and distant, much like that of the stereotype of the "absent-minded professor."

Both in his native Austria, and during his twenty-five years in China, Professor Castorp had lived the quiet and detached life of the scholar. A hard worker and a capable, well-liked teacher, he put a premium upon meeting—or even exceeding—the demands of others:

I have always had the tendency to satisfy people. . . . I have never wanted to displease anyone. If I am given work, I try to do better than what is expected. . . . If you give me a salary that is satisfactory, my entire energy is yours.

He attributed these traits to his "strongly Catholic" and "very conservative" Teutonic upbringing; to his stern and "sober" government-official father who, although he remained in the background in most family matters, had opinions which counted ("What will he think of me if I do something wrong?"); and even more to his "dictatorial" mother ("The kind of person other people submit to—even dogs listen to her") who directed everyone in the household, bought all of Hermann's socks and underwear until he was twenty-two years old, and created an atmosphere within the home which ensured "that things must be done in a way that mother is pleased."

In his schooling he worked actively to please his teacher; and during the years afterward, he continued to seek to please others, and avoid contention.

I didn't like to have the teacher angry at me. A driving force was to keep my teacher satisfied. This makes it happier for everyone, for him and for me. . . . I always try to find out what in the other person I could agree with. . . . I don't like people who conjure up big conflicts.

Similarly, he accepted without question the Catholic religion in which he was brought up. He was concerned much less with its dogma than with the loyalties which he felt to its moral principles, and to the family and Church organization around it: "I am the kind of man who must live in some kind of organization or society where I feel the need to do good."

He thrived on the "simple cultured form of life" of the Youth Movement in which he participated, especially by its "clean," Puritanical emphasis, and its single-mindedness: "I like people with strong convictions who stick to them."

But the one area in which he found active self-expression and which became his true "holy of holies," was science:

I am a scientist by conviction. I have been since very early in life. It is as an artist uses his art. I like to use my hands, my equipment, to experiment and to teach others.

He even defied his parents in embarking on this career, as they had a different profession in mind for him; but at the same time, he believed his scientific interests to be an inheritance from his maternal grandfather. He also felt that in his work—in his passion for research, his abilities as a teacher, his originality in constructing apparatus—he was, like his mother, a "leading spirit" whom others sought to follow.

He avoided considerations of philosophy and metaphysics ("The more you think about them, the more confused you are"), and had no concern with politics or with abstract ideological principles of any kind; what mattered to him was the operation of a system:

I am not interested in names—monarchy, democracy, dictatorship. I am interested in how things are actualized—how they work. I do feel there must be a factor of stability.

Coming to China at the invitation of a missionary university, he found conditions very agreeable to him in both his personal and professional lives. He was devoted enough to his strong-minded wife; but he readily tolerated long separations brought about by European medical treatments which her ailments were said to require, as long as another equally forceful woman could be found to run his household. Never too drawn to the sensual side of life, he was passionately involved in his teaching and his research. He thrived upon the difficult working conditions, and especially enjoyed the feeling that his professional skills were indispensable. Moreover, he delighted in the slow pace of Chinese life, and in what he called the "spirit of compromise" of the Chinese people. He found himself readily blending with his environment:

It is very interesting how surroundings influence you. . . . The students had a certain way of eating. I began automatically to eat just like them. . . . I even began to call a dog in the Chinese way.

His evaluation of the political regimes under which he lived depended largely upon those around him. Thus he at first was impressed with the Nationalist Government "because I saw the enthusiasm of the students"; later he shared with them a strong resentment of the Japanese invaders, but then he found "a few Japanese who were not bad people," explaining that "in everyone I can see something good." Mostly, however, he was disinterested in the world about him except as it pertained to his work. He did not care for psychological probing, but "if someone told me something about myself, I always thought, probably he is right—there must be something in it."

He continued his work after the Communists came to power; but when the new regime took over the running of his university, he decided to leave because "I thought I would not fit." Several delays occurred in his getting an exit permit, followed by his unexpected arrest.

His response in prison from the beginning was to confess everything he could about his own past actions, and avoid antagonizing his captors. Compared to Father Luca and Dr. Vincent, the pressures applied to him were relatively mild: no chains, no handcuffs, and none of the persistently extreme accusation which leads to falsification. On his part, he made a consistent effort to adapt himself as well as he could to this difficult environment, rather than concern himself with moral or ideological issues. "It is hard to say how I felt. I cannot judge these things, although I can easily find a concrete course to take."

His personal confession was not too greatly emphasized, and he was quickly exposed to re-education. To the *hsüeh hsi* sessions he brought the approach of a scientist:

I paid close attention. I wanted to find what it was about. Mine was the attitude of research.

His approach was made feasible by his captors' failure to make him, as they did most other Europeans, a special target. "They saw at once that I was harmless. If I talked a little, they didn't expect too much." Moreover, he was ingenious in his ingenuousness.

From the very beginning I said what I thought and this made it easier for me. . . . By nature I am anti-revolutionary. I don't like everything turned upside down. So when the Communists said, "You are anti-revolutionary," they were right and I admitted it. I said, "I am." If you admit things openly, they do not make so much fuss about it, they simply preach to you. But the moment you tell them stories, they get mad.

But his "research" (he was, after all, a participant-observer) led him to accept as valid much of the "data."

I began to understand many things that I did not understand before. . . . It was a logical system in itself—talking about land distribution, why the tenants were poor—about China's losses from the international imperialists—things I've never been interested in before. I saw for the first time how the Chinese themselves felt about these matters. My whole thinking about these problems was enlarged.

Nor could he disentangle himself from the bias of his teachers' jargon, although he recognized it for what it was: "Old China was bad, new China good, and America bad—it is an official kind of language."

He could even begin to accept the Communist point of view about his own criminal guilt, although it was based only upon anti-Communist statements he had previously made: "From the way I talked before, I influenced others against the Communists —so from their point of view I am guilty." But he was never able to develop a strong inner sense of sinfulness, and his cellmates frequently criticized him because he had no "*feeling* of guilt." He thought that such a feeling was "too much to expect from a man, because the world is not a religious order, and their requirements were too high."

He viewed Communism as a religion, a point he made frequently during our interviews, yet at the same time he managed to hold on to the general principles of his own Catholic faith. Here he once more made use of the scientist's approach.

I would emphasize the scientific explanation of the world, saying that there must have been a beginning, and therefore religion has a place. They would say, "This is a scientific religion, and it is all right." Officially, they were just supposed to be against superstition and not against religion.

At the same time, his sense of involvement in the Catholic religion was of profound importance in his holding on to his sense of identity.

I would always figure out whether it was Easter or some other Catholic holy day so that I could stick to their custom. . . . If I had no religious background, it is possible that I would have committed suicide.

He was pleased by the more favorable treatment accorded him as he became increasingly viewed as a "progressive"; but he was disturbed by the moves from one cell to another which this shift in status brought about. "I disliked changing groups. I felt I belonged to a group like a chicken belongs to its flock." Moreover, after a period of time, he found his "research" less and less rewarding:

After I understood the fundamentals, I began to get bored by it all— then the main thing became avoiding trouble. . . . Ten hours a day is too much, you get overfed, and this kills off deeper interests.

But he always retained the strong need to please his captors, as well as an underlying wish to be free of them—reflected in a recurrent dream which he had during his imprisonment.

I would dream I was allowed to go home for an afternoon. I didn't remember whether I was required to return at night or allowed to return the next day. I thought, "You are too stupid—you will do something wrong and the man will be very angry with you."

In his associations to this dream, he relates it to his lifelong pattern of avoiding conflict through submission.

I didn't want to displease the official, I would always give in in order to avoid conflict. . . . It was my duty to ask him when to come back and not to break the rule. . . . I have a feeling that I am this kind of person—who does things wrong and who forgets—this could happen to me. . . . I always must satisfy people.

After his release, his "lost" appearance reflected both his emotional and ideological confusion. Sometimes, like Vincent, he seemed to be longing for the security he had known in prison. At other times he would criticize the unfair practices of the Communists, but then temper his criticism, using the thought reform language: "Of course *the people* know this." Of his former jailers he said: "Objectively speaking they are wrong. But you can't help but have a respect for these men. They work hard and sacrifice and have a certain human value."

In a personal sense, he was very labile in his emotions. He formed quick attachments to people he met in Hong Kong, especially if they had also just been in a Chinese prison. He was quick to weep when one of these friends left the Colony; he also wept just listening to sad music. But he expressed an optimistic note despite his difficulties, recognizing his need to "absorb and repair," comparing himself to a "business which has gone bankrupt and now has to start up again." He seemed on the whole less emotionally disturbed than either Dr. Vincent or Father Luca, and others among my subjects who knew him told me that they felt he had weathered the experience much better than they had.

One of his ways of dealing with his own confusion was to attempt to look at thought reform from a distance, discuss its general principles, its effectiveness, and its economy of manpower. At the same time, he would try to evaluate how useful the experience had been to him; his conclusions were ambivalent, but helpful to him in working out his feelings.

A few months would have been worth it—but not three years. . . . I am not converted so much that I go one hundred percent to their way —but what I have seen and learned is worth something.

He sought to maintain a fatalistic attitude toward his imprisonment: "It can't be helped—like breaking a leg. . . . It was a revolution, and they had the guns and not I." And to remain critical of both worlds: "I can't say that it was justice, but I can't say that there is justice here in Hong Kong either."

During the course of his stay in Hong Kong, however, he began to be more critical of Communists, questioning much of what they had taught him, and especially condemning their police methods.

A person you know must tell all about you—they want to check everything. I dislike this police element of the state. I had the attitude of old China—that the best government is one that you don't see or feel at all. . . . There, from the time you get up in the morning until the time you go to bed at night, they control you.

During our last talk together, his words were again conciliatory rather than critical. About his own experience he said:

I don't like it; I have lost too much. But when you go to a country like that, you must expect that these things can happen. . . . Who can I blame? The whole of China because it is so backward? The KMT [Nationalists] because it was so corrupt? The Communists because they could gain victory?

And about Communism in general:

Communism is good for the Chinese—for countries with primitive economic conditions—but I cannot imagine it for the West. . . . But if it makes the West more conscious of the need for social reform, then it has done some good.

He began to make active efforts to rearrange his personal life, seeking a new teaching position in the Far East, again in association with a Catholic missionary group. He realized that his concerns about ideological questions would become much less important to him once he got back to work: "When I find another job, things will be fixed up—then I won't talk about these other things any more."

The patterns of Professor Castorp's early life, imprisonment, and post-release period suggest the identity of the submissive scientist. He had been consistently submissive in his attempts to please parents, teachers, Western and Chinese associates, his wife, prison officials, friends in Hong Kong who had shared his experience, and, during our interviews, me. Beginning with his parents, he could feel sure of love and protection only insofar as he complied with other people's wishes; compliance meant being open to their influence. Consequently, he was deeply influenced by thought reform, and he retained more of its ideology than had either Dr. Vincent or Father Luca.

This is an apparent contradiction: a man most submissive and open to influence seems to be in the end least emotionally affected by thought reform. The contradiction disappears, however, if we recognize that people like Professor Castorp have the ability to hold on to what is most important, while seeming to surrender so much of themselves. Once he had become a scientist—his solution to the identity crisis of adolescence—this identity became the most precious and the most creative part of his being. Science had for him some of the mystical appeal which medicine had for Dr. Vincent and the priesthood for Father Luca, because it enabled him to channel his energies and find his individual form of self-realization. It was the one area in which he could show defiance (whether to parents, wife, or existing intellectual principles), become a leader of men, and find a passionate meaning in life.

On the other hand, although being a scientist was the one thing that was specifically *his*, it also had deep connections with his early family identifications. He felt the scientist in him to be part of his maternal heritage, and he associated this powerful part of himself with his mother. Whatever their demands, his parents had transmitted to him a strong sense of commitment to family, religion, and nationality (the last more cultural than political). This sense of commitment contained the single-mindedness which he admired; and this single-mindedness—enhanced by a repressed sexuality—he brought to his own scientific work. Thus, when under fire, he could call upon both his Catholic religion and his scientific research attitude [2] for strength; it was not the dogma of either which mattered, but rather the sense of affirmation and the survival techniques which both could supply.

Professor Castorp was also fortunate in the high status accorded the scientist in the thought reform environment. Indeed, the identity of the scientist was one which Communist theorists always claimed for themselves. Thus, as long as he submitted on questions of ideology (which had never had great importance to him), they permitted him to retain what he held most sacred. He could remain the empiricist, and keep his gaze on the *system*, rather than look deeply into himself. To be sure, he could hardly maintain complete scientific accuracy in dealing with thought reform material. Nobody could. But by keeping relatively intact that part of himself dedicated to precision and truth, he could at least maintain a check upon the most gross distortions, and bring into play immediately following his release an unusually effective reality-testing mechanism.

The importance of the mild treatment which Professor Castorp received should not be overlooked. Less bludgeoned—physically and mentally—he did not experience guilt and shame as deeply as did both Dr. Vincent and Father Luca. Had his reformers been more severe, they might have tapped a good deal more guilt and shame in him, too: mild-mannered men like Professor Castorp are likely to feel guilty about the hostilities which they tend to repress. His post-release identity crisis was that of a dependent man deprived of his props, a single-minded man deprived of his *raison d'être*, a creative and a plodding man deprived of his materials and of his routine. Although his emotional balance had been disturbed, and although he had experienced more of a sense of evil than he realized, his basic identity structure had not been overturned. His tendency was clearly to return to his scientific work and let the ideologies take care of themselves.

General Patterns

There were, then, many different responses among the obviously confused. Most of the prisoners fell in this category, and its elements of confusion and search were present in some degree in everyone who experienced thought reform. But the obviously confused Westerners were distinguished by the fact that their confusion and search were conscious, and therefore openly dealt with, while the reactions of the apparent converts and the apparent resisters were more rigid and hidden. Yet even in this group, much of the reform experience —as well as the older emotions which it revived—had to be quickly repressed.

When I saw most of these people, they had set themselves the task of returning to what was essentially their previous identity while trying to come to grips with, rather than totally accept or totally reject, the influences they had just experienced. One expression of this task was the conviction of most of them that certain reforms were necessary and desirable in the non-Communist world, if only to meet the Communist challenge. As Professor Castorp put it:

If there is rivalry between the Communists and the West for social reform, that is very good. . . . Maybe Communism's mission is, by its push and impact, to give special strength to social reform. I have the impression that the West should do this. If Western Germany raises the living standard, East Germany will die a natural death.

And a businessman, although committed to private enterprise, expressed similar sentiments:

I am in favor of a gradual evolution of social reform rather than Communist revolution. . . . But some means must come about in which the rich will be less rich and the poor less poor. . . . It may take hundreds of years.

These men had to express such broad convictions to buttress their personal reintegration into the Western world, to give some meaning to their escape from the thought reform influence. Having been made painfully aware of the West's (in many cases all too real) shortcomings, each required a sense of alternative to Communism which would include correction of some of these shortcomings. The stress they put upon economic reform may have been in part a use of the prison idiom; but their even greater stress upon the need to maintain personal freedom while accomplishing these reforms was certainly a rejection of the ideas of thought reform and an affirmation of their Western heritage. (It is perhaps unnecessary to add that my emphasis of underlying psychological factors is not meant to imply that such attitudes toward the West are inappropriate.[3])

For all of these reasons, the obviously confused Westerners tended to suffer post-release identity crises which were visibly severe— partly because they had been emotionally stranded between the two worlds, and partly because they had brought to the surface emotions which in others remain buried.

CHAPTER 7

VARIETIES OF RESPONSE:
APPARENT CONVERTS

Apparent converts were those who made newspaper headlines, who emerged from prison in a state loudly proclaimed as "brainwashed." However one may deplore journalistic sensationalism, there is no doubt that these people did undergo a startling personal change in their view of the world. To talk with one of them immediately after his arrival in Hong Kong was, to say the least, an impressive experience. They seemed to speak only in clichés, parroting the Communist stock phrases, and defending the Communist position at every point.

During my stay in Hong Kong, three such people appeared. One of them was a Jesuit priest, who will be discussed in Chapter 11; for reasons involving both his colleagues and himself, I was not able to meet him then. The other two were introduced to me, but the suspicious and defensive emotions engendered by their reform made them wary of talking with a psychiatrist, especially an American psychiatrist, and both refused to discuss their experiences with me. From my brief encounters with them, however, and from what others—journalists and old friends from China living in Hong Kong—told me about them, I was able to obtain certain impressions about their behavior.

One of them repeated his stock phrases in an agitated manner, proclaiming his "shame and remorse for the harm I have done to the Chinese people," and praising the "real democracy of China" and the "free discussion" within the prison. But his extreme tension, as well as his need to protest too much—to repeat the clichés even when not asked—made me feel that he had serious, if unconscious, doubts about his position, and that the structure of his new identity was brittle. This judgment was borne out later on.

The other, a young woman, was quite different, and much more convincing. Rather than nervousness, she exhibited the euphoric calm of a religious convert. In quiet tones she told a friend that should her family and other people in America reject her and fail to understand her views, it would then be necessary for her to take her life, because "this would at least tell the people of the world about my being persecuted and reveal the truth to them." (One might speculate that her use of the word "persecuted" was an unconscious reference to her prison experience, but there was no doubt that she was at the time giving expression to an urge to martyrdom, and referring to the hostility which she anticipated —and sought—from the people at home.)

After meeting these two people, I wondered what psychological mechanisms were responsible for their being so much more affected by the reform process than anyone else I had seen. I learned more about the problem later, not from them, but from two others I interviewed after their return to the West: the Jesuit just mentioned, whom I met three-and-a-half years after his release (my contact with him was thus both a first evaluation and a follow-up study); and another young woman I interviewed in Canada three months after her release, whose case is described below.

Jane Darrow: The Missionary's Daughter

A young Canadian teacher had emerged from more than four years of imprisonment with strong praise for her captors. She told reporters that the Communists had been justified in arresting her, that she had "passed information" to Western diplomats, and that she had confessed these crimes fully during her imprisonment. She admitted (rather reluctantly) that she had been in chains; but she said that her failure to confess the truth justified it. She spoke of the prison as a "place of hope" where "new people are made," at the same time denouncing the "war-mongering" and "germ warfare" of the Americans. A diplomat expressed the sentiments of most Westerners who met her when he described Miss Darrow as "badly brainwashed."

Even back in Canada, three months later, Miss Darrow had reservations about talking with me, and our meeting was arranged only through the efforts of mutual friends. She was a rather attractive young woman in her midthirties, alert, tense, and unusually articulate. She was immediately friendly, but at the same time suspicious, and inquired in some detail about who I was and what my purpose was in talking with her. She was also, however, eager to plunge into her story. This was the first time she had told it from beginning to end, and she obviously derived much emotional benefit both from the telling itself, and from the opportunity to discuss her complicated feelings with another person who knew something about her experience. During the ten hours we spent together, she remained enthusiastically absorbed in her detailed description.

She quickly expressed the opinion that her "Chinese" background had a great deal to do with her response. Born in China of Canadian Protestant missionary parents, she had spent more than half of her life there. She looked back very critically on her childhood attitudes toward the Chinese people: "I don't think I had any real feeling for them *per se*. . . . I liked living in China because life was comfortable"; and she emphasized the "satisfying sense of superiority," and the "gunboat psychology" which she, as a Westerner in China, had known. Yet this attitude was far from the whole story, since a little later she told me of her deep affection for these same Chinese people: "I loved them tremendously." When she was sent to Canada for her secondary school and university education, however, she avoided mentioning her Chinese past, and tried to "hide from my background" in order to find "identity [the word was hers] with the group there." But whether the foreigner in China or the "Chinese" girl in Canada, she felt she was different from those around her, and when later she returned to China as a teacher, and a student of Chinese culture, she began to be uncomfortably aware of her "lack of roots."

She spoke of "serious tensions" in her family life; she usually found herself allied with her strong-willed and opinionated mother in a mutual impatience with her well-meaning, but ineffectual father. She had, early in life, rebelled against austere and dogmatic Protestant religious teachings. She always had difficulty coming to terms with the "iron-clad honesty" which her parents demanded, believing herself to fall far short of this ideal: "I bordered on cheating and was not above the use of a lie." Her legacy of susceptibility to guilt was, as one might expect, a strong and painful one; "I have always been very quick to feel guilty." This reached the point where she let letters from her parents lie unopened for several months, because "every letter was a stab . . . and I did not want to read the reprimands."

Always bright and much interested in the world about her, Jane became deeply concerned with social reform in both China and the West. She felt that missionary influences, as well as lifelong financial difficulties, affected her militant liberalism.

With my missionary background, I've always felt that something should be done to better the world. . . . My lack of economic security has been a driving force in my life. . . . I thought that society was man-made, and should be regulated in the interests of man.

When she returned to China as a teacher after the war, she was highly critical of the Nationalist regime, but at the same time had "an anti-Communist orientation." She shared these views with Western and Chinese friends, and was in fact more comfortable in such intellectual and ideological matters than in purely social situations. She felt that a tendency to be too outspoken and critical had interfered with many friendships. In her relationships with men, in particular, she believed her forceful intellect to be a disadvantage, and sometimes wished she were "more of a powderpuff." Always restrained in sexual matters, she was long aware of both discomfort and unfulfilled longing in her response to masculine overtures.

During the period preceding her imprisonment she found herself—along with a few other Westerners—leading a beleaguered existence. Increasingly cut off from Chinese friends, she was aware her movements were being observed, and she was not completely surprised when her arrest finally occurred.

Miss Darrow's prison treatment was virtually identical with that described for men. At the beginning she was subjected to the physical and emotional pressures of prolonged interrogations, incessant "struggles," chains and handcuffs, and enforced standing for as long as thirty-six hours. She resisted for a while, and made up a false story which was not accepted; but within a few days she had produced an "espionage" confession which was a distorted reinterpretation of her actual behavior. She did not at the time inwardly accept its validity, but did feel extremely troubled ("I hated myself!") for having so quickly made this confession and for having supplied detailed information about Chinese acquaintances.

This sense of shame and guilt was heightened by her experiences among other women in her cell. A well-educated, Westernized Chinese girl, with whom she closely identified herself, came to the cell apparently fully convinced of the Communist position, and critical of Miss Darrow for her "backwardness." Cell relationships were highly charged and highly personal; she referred repeatedly to a hated cell chief as "the bitch" and another person as "the fiery woman."

During these early stages, she felt a number of conflicting emotions: initial resentment; embarrassment at being a prisoner and at being in such a low-level all-Chinese environment; guilt ("I had curious regrets at not having written the family"); a "grim curiosity"; a sense of opportunity ("I thought it might be grist for my mill and that I would write a book about it"); and perhaps most important, a sense of surrendering herself to the inevitable ("You have the feeling that you are being pushed through something you can't control. . . . it breeds a sort of lightheadedness").

But at the same time, she applied herself to the study of the "rhythms" of her environment, and soon concluded that "everything I believed about the world was not acceptable." Then, during a self-examination, she was surprised at the extremely enthusiastic acceptance of her statement that she had been leading a "parasitic life." Thus encouraged, she continued to express this kind of highly critical judgment on her entire past—an approach which she found came quite naturally to "a guilt-ridden person like myself." In this and in her general views, she "tried to put on a convincing act of being progressive. . . . and a good show of being honest." But this "act" became extremely uncomfortable for her, not only because her "veneer" and "lack of sincerity" were criticized by the others, but primarily because she herself found it difficult to tolerate her own "dishonesty."

I was a cracked bowl. I didn't ring true. . . . I was inferior to people who really tried to reform . . . they really felt guilty. I was superficial. . . . And I respond to the ideal of being good.

As she felt worse and worse about the "double game" which she was playing (or thought she was playing), she began to look upon herself in general with ever-increasing contempt:

I realized that my professed feeling for liberals was not very deep. I was a scheming, small person . . . with a basically opportunistic philosophy. . . . When I reached the bottom, there was nothing more.

She began to not only *say*, but really *feel*, that she had been, and was then, evil: in her attitude of "superiority" toward Chinese, and in her "recognition" that she had (despite economic difficulties) really been a member of the "upper class," and had unfairly enjoyed all of its advantages. More and more her "tactic"—"I was always trying to establish the fact that I was sincere"—became her reality.

Her change was furthered by much that she saw and "learned": the "proof" of American use of germ warfare—especially when this was "confirmed" by the report of a missionary whom she felt must be reliable, because "I know my father would not tell a lie"; the United Nations "procrastinations" in the truce negotiations of the Korean War; and the progress of the "completely planned" Chinese society ("social and economic accomplishments and getting things done that other governments had promised but never delivered.") She was especially struck by the realization that what was happening to her was related to the broad Chinese scene: "I had viewed thought reform as a punishment—restricted to prisoners—but here was the reform of all society." All of this made her feel more comfortable, as "it gave me the intellectual basis for some things I had already accepted on an emotional basis."

Yet over the years of her reform, and despite her continuing "progress," she could not get herself to believe fully in her confessed "espionage" activities. "I never accepted this as *me*." She found it always necessary to make a distinction between her "personal predicament" and "the broad social facts." While conscious that "there was a discrepancy," she sought to get around it by giving less importance to her own situation: "I did more thinking about society than about myself. . . . I worked from outward-inward rather than inward-outward." Using this device, she could begin to accept "the general logic of their position" in viewing her "passing of information" to people who could use it in a way harmful to the Communist regime as "espionage."

As with other prisoners, her relations with the government during the last month of her imprisonment were characterized by mutual frankness and co-operation. Miss Darrow found herself able to admit that she could not completely view herself as a spy, and after so doing was praised for her honesty. Transferred to a new cell where her "dark past" was unknown, she had what she considered to be a new opportunity to "make good." She was even briefly appointed as cell chief, in her view a mixed blessing: "I didn't want it because I was afraid of muffing it, but I was flattered because I had come up from the bottom." She retained the job long enough to "help" a new prisoner (one with a background of missionary education) to her confession; but because she found herself "feeling guilty" in carrying out the duties of the cell chief, she was unable to be decisive with other prisoners and was finally, at her own request, replaced.

At this time, she was also impressed by the dedication of many of the prison officials (both male and female), by their willingness to extend themselves to solve all problems, their readiness to admit past mistakes, and their "growth as human beings"—which she felt she could recognize over the course of her imprisonment. She was especially influenced by one male prisoner-official assigned to her case, a highly cultivated Westernized Chinese with whom she felt much in common—and who reminded her of a man she had once been fond of.

She was struck by the kindness and patience with which young prisoners were treated after the general improvement in prison conditions, and by the consideration for children, some of whom lived for periods of time with their mothers in the cells. She was grateful for special rations of hot water for the women to wash their hair, and for the issue of new uniforms; she noted the officials' concern with the prisoners' diet and medical care and felt that there was a great effort made to "permit us a sense of dignity." Finally, Miss Darrow rounded out her re-education through extensive reading of Marxist texts, some of which she had asked for as her interest developed.

Shortly before her release, she struggled with the problem of whether or not she wished to remain in China. She considered staying (or trying to stay) both because of her admiration for the new regime and her love for China:

Lots of things made me generally in admiration of this society. I felt very warmly toward it and couldn't bear the thought that I would always be cut off from it. . . . It seemed right, the way of the future. . . . And after all, I had lived there most of my life, and I adored Peking.

She also felt closer to the Chinese people than ever before: "I had found the real person." And she believed that, should she remain, the years spent in prison "would count" and she would be appreciated ("in that society you don't have to be apologetic about having ideas")—while at the same time she felt certain that she would be "out of step" back in the West.

On the other hand, she also thought frequently of her parents and of an older woman who had been like a parent to her. "If my mother and father were dead I would not have come home—but when I thought of the three of them, I decided I would return." She also remembered things like Christmas in Canada, and in the end it was the West and family ties which prevailed.

At the time of her trial, she could not rid her mind of the feeling that it was all "rigged," and felt greatly embarrassed at being seen as a "spy" by the Chinese spectators, because "I didn't want them to feel this about me." She was "amazed" at the "light" sentence (expulsion rather than additional time in prison), and at the same time was concerned about the problems of the future. In a last "moving" discussion with her judge, the difficulties of returning were frankly discussed; the judge expressed the hope that she would retain a "realization of what the world was about," and pointed to the example set by a friend of hers, another Westerner who had taken a strong "stand" in favor of his re-education after his release. Prison officials had kept them informed about each other, and this information about his "stand" impressed Miss Darrow very greatly.

It made me feel that I could be as good as he. We felt it together—he put across his case—I could too.

Upon her arrival in Hong Kong, she was aware of the ordeal she had been put through; but her allegiance to her captors was so great that she was determined to present only their position, and to suppress any material which would undermine it. Her attitude was reinforced by a letter she was handed when she crossed the border, written by the friend who had been previously released, offering advice and encouragement. Her anticipation of difficulty with the press only increased her resolve.

I didn't want to say anything to a hostile press against a group getting such a fine deal for a large section of humanity. . . . I had made up my mind I would not mention the chaining. . . . This showed my identification with the Communists. . . . I asked myself how much they would want me to say.

The more her words were questioned, the more she defended her captors ("I was like a fighting lion"); but the entire experience was deeply disturbing to her ("It was hell!").

Feeling uncomfortable with consular officials who met her, she elected to stay with old missionary associates of her family in Hong Kong, a decision she had thought about before her release. There she was made comfortable, was not challenged, and felt "reassured." In thinking about her situation in this more relaxed setting, she began to feel that what she had said at the press conference might not have been completely accurate, and she determined "to put the facts on the table with no distortions." But she did nothing to carry out this resolve, and when some of the missionaries asked her how she had been treated, her answer was, "Perfectly well." Moreover, she even felt guilty for considering such a change of policy, viewing it again through the eyes of the prison officials: "I felt that this was my first retreat—the first thing I would have to explain to them . . . if I were to go back."

When she arrived home and faced the conflicted emotions of her family relationships, she was unable to discuss her imprisonment with her parents; but she did talk about it at great length with two friends. These discussions were sometimes very helpful to her, and at other times confusing, since her feelings about her reform varied greatly and depended largely on which friend she was talking to.

Her closest friend—the older woman whom she recognized as

a substitute for her mother—exerted the greater influence; she lived in the same city, and spent many hours listening sympathetically to Miss Darrow's story. She was never judging or critical; but as an anti-Communist liberal close to Miss Darrow's former position, she would occasionally gently point out some of the Communist inconsistencies and abuses. This relationship was of immense importance to Miss Darrow, and her friend's words had great impact on her. However, her more infrequent visits with the other friend —the man who had emerged from a Communist prison with an even more completely reformed attitude and a more rigid adherence to the Communist position—left her disturbed: "I felt guilty because I thought that maybe he was better than I was." At the same time, she shared many opinions with him about their experiences.

She began to read a great deal, saw many liberal friends whose sympathy affected her, and became increasingly willing to question her experience: "Certain doubts have been allowed to arise." In her personal relations, always difficult for her in the past, she felt "easier, more in control of myself"; she retained certain fears and taboos in her relationships with men, but fewer than before, and she looked toward marriage in her quest for "emotional security." She returned to secondary school teaching, and at the same time maintained her strong interest in China.

She remained greatly troubled and preoccupied with her personal sense of guilt. She felt guilty toward Communist prison officials and toward their entire society whenever she expressed (or even felt) anything critical about them; toward her own government because she still held views in some ways favorable to Communism, although this guilt was mixed with feelings of gratitude toward Canadian officials for negotiating her release; and toward her parents because of her inability to be more warm to them. As she summed it up: "I am full of guilt complexes. . . . I feel guilty almost about the rain."

Near the end of our talks, she asked me questions about guilt feelings, and began to recognize the important part these had played in her own imprisonment: "Your attitude is a creature of your own guilt." But she continued to speak contemptuously of herself as she described her inner struggle between "the urge to adapt" (to her own culture) and "the compulsion to hold on" (to the Communist views), ever ready to denounce her own "selfishness" and "opportunism." As far as her political beliefs were concerned, she predicted to me that she would revert to being a "left-wing liberal," at the same time expressing the opinion that intellectual seeking had its limitations in finding the truth, and that one had to combine it with an "intuitive" approach as well.

Miss Darrow, unlike those people in the obviously confused category, continued, after she had crossed the border into Hong Kong, to present herself to the world as a reformed person. Dr. Vincent, Professor Castorp, and a large number of other subjects had so presented themselves to their captors; but for them the change from the Communist to the non-Communist world was a signal for the portions of themselves which had remained apart from thought reform influence to reappear. In Miss Darrow's case, it was as if nothing but her thought reform identity survived the experience—and herein lay her "conversion." But the "as if" is important; the contending elements were very much there, even if temporarily stilled, and this is why I refer to her conversion as "apparent."

Still, we must ask ourselves, why did Miss Darrow experience such a conversion, even an incomplete one? What strikes us immediately is the Communists' manipulation of her conflicts over honesty and goodness, and over incomplete "Chineseness." These are once again problems of identity and guilt; and Miss Darrow's background encompasses many such problems in relationship to religion, ideology, and cultural conflict, and to historical, racial, and personal sensitivities.

Miss Darrow's early and tenacious identity of the missionary's daughter included a near-absolute approach to good and evil, to guilt and sin. Her parents, and especially her mother, as individual carriers of the Protestant tradition sought to make their daughter "iron-clad," a bastion of honesty and goodness impregnable to the dishonesty and evil ever threatening from both without and within herself.

In her rebellion against her origin, Miss Darrow struggled to find a more moderate course—a compromise identity which would neither violate the "ideal of being good" of her missionary background nor perpetuate the narrowness which she came to see in it.

In becoming the militant liberal (both in her character and her policies), she achieved a compromise which enabled her to swim with some of the most respected ideological currents around her. This, her most positive identity, embodied her accomplishments as an energetic but open-minded reformer, a member of a China-born intellectual and cultural élite, and an experienced cosmopolite conversant with both East and West.

But from the beginning, her struggle was accompanied by many disruptive forces which shaped a negative identity of unusually large dimensions. On both a personal and an ideological level, her parents' inordinate stress upon "iron-clad honesty" produced in Miss Darrow—as it inevitably does—an attraction to honesty's opposite, to beating the game through the hidden maneuver, or the "use of the lie." This attraction had limited importance as a mode of action, for Miss Darrow could bring to bear upon it the powerful conscience of the missionary's daughter: but for this attraction she was forced to pay a terrible price in guilt. At the same time, the tyrannical judgments of her conscience ("negative conscience," as Erikson has called it) [1] could at any moment so magnify this pattern of guilt and self-condemnation that she would see herself as *nothing but* a "selfish person," a "cheat" and a "liar."

These personal sensitivities were fed by her historical situation, about which she was also guilt-prone: a privileged Westerner, who owed her position to imperialistic policies of questionable moral standing, living among poverty-stricken Chinese peasants and articulately resentful Chinese intellectuals. Closely related to this historical guilt was her racial guilt, a sense of evil which the more egalitarian representatives of any dominant race experience in relationship to any ambivalent feelings they may hold toward members of the dominated race. The stronger one's libertarian conscience, the greater the guilt. Miss Darrow could believe herself evil and insincere because she perceived her own sense of repulsion (itself partly a product of guilt) at the idea of becoming a Chinese and having to share personally the disadvantages of an oppressed race. The problem is insoluble as long as situations of racial discrimination or dominance persist, since guilt begets resentment, which in turn begets guilt; both emotions then cause suffering, as they did in Miss Darrow, in direct proportion to the amount of love felt for certain members (if not for the more abstract whole) of the dominated race. And everything is magnified when the problem occurs in the oppressed race's native environment.

Miss Darrow's identification with China had still deeper identity dimensions as well. Part of her did want to become entirely Chinese, to achieve complete union with the country of her birth— just as another part of her wished to be completely Western. She was a cultural outsider, belonging entirely to neither world, feeling guilty about both. She was part of the Chinese landscape, surrounded by Chinese people, and yet separated by special schools and special status, and ultimately by her face and the color of her skin. She faced similar problems as a Westerner: biologically she belonged, but she was separated by the most profound differences of background experience. Her identity as the China-born Westerner was a compromise; but in any crisis, the feeling of being a cultural outsider could reappear and further feed her negative identity.

In the face of this broad negative spectrum, it is not surprising that the usual problems of guilt about parents and biological identity were intensified. Unable to open letters from home because of the guilt they stimulated, Miss Darrow found herself preoccupied with her "badness" as a daughter. Burdened at so many levels, she felt conflict about her identity as a woman. The "bad daughter" and the "inadequate woman" thus joined the array of her negative identities formed from a combination of early susceptibilities to guilt, later difficulties in the control of anger, and— perhaps most important of all—a fear of and desire for total submission.

For an element of totalism [2]—a tendency toward all-or-nothing emotional alignments—seems ever-present in Miss Darrow, working against the more moderate aspirations of her liberalism. It began with the ethos of absolute honesty and goodness bequeathed to her by her parents. It again appeared in her efforts to solve her adolescent identity crisis by becoming, at the expense of her complex cultural background, totally the Canadian girl. And at the onset of thought reform, the girl who had placed great emphasis upon controlling so much of her own behavior experienced a not entirely unpleasant "light headedness" at the moment of giving herself up to a force assuming complete power over her. To be sure, she fought against this tendency during the thought reform struggle; but hers was the type of vulnerability which can lead to the total plunge of the convert.

And this is what happened—or almost happened. Thought reform exploited each of these aspects of her negative identity, made conscious what was previously latent, and built into grotesque dimensions what had previously been held in balance. The core of her negative identity, the self-image of the "schemer," was a crucial factor in depriving her of a more moderate response to thought reform. Most of my subjects could think themselves reasonably clever and ingenious in playing the double game of acting "progressive" while retaining old beliefs, but Miss Darrow could only castigate herself for being a "cracked bowl." She could not permit herself the usual form of adaptation without experiencing the most derogatory view of herself, since in so adapting an inner voice would accuse her of being "the schemer" which in early life she had been warned against becoming.

Thus deprived of the usual defense against thought reform, she was at the mercy of her own totalism. As a response to her historical and racial guilt feelings, she saw herself as having lived not only a "parasitic" life, but a totally parasitic one. Similarly, she came to think herself totally removed from and unconcerned about the Chinese people, rather than maintaining (as did Father Luca, for instance) a more moderate view of a complex situation. On all of these issues, the reformers' totalism made contact with her own, as well as with the other features of her negative identity.

Once the affirmative elements within her liberal identity had been undermined, she could be made to feel at one with the Communist—and, more importantly, with the Chinese—world. For a person so long and so painfully the cultural outsider, this sense of belonging had a good deal to do with the outcome of thought reform.

When she was ready for rebirth, she was able to see in Communism many of her own liberal aspirations: dedicated people working "to better the world," regulating society "in the interests of man." She felt she was among gentlemanly and humane people, to whom submission would be justified. Their society appeared to offer fewer challenges to her problems of femininity, and more opportunity for her old intellectual and newly-acquired ideological prowess. She emerged more a communist liberal than a true convert.

The element of totalism in her new identification with the Chinese Communists made her misrepresent her own inner feelings, and present only her reformed side. Still afraid of the negative identity of the "schemer," she viewed any criticism of the Communists or any reconciliation with her own society as selfishness and betrayal. These emotions were intensified by the reformed sentiments of her friend, since she was able to share with him one of the few identities left open to her, that of the reformed Westerner. But like everyone else, Miss Darrow felt the pull of old ties and old identities; in Hong Kong she turned to the missionaries for comfort and for an ideological moratorium. Once back in Canada, she felt the old appeal of her liberal identity, an appeal reinforced by those liberal friends who offered emotional security. Her liberal identity turned out to have been much stronger than one might have suspected: within it, the search for truth and careful reality-testing were both possible and necessary. At the time I spoke with Miss Darrow, the emotions of her negative self-image were still supplying fuel for her identity crisis. She gave me the feeling nonetheless that whatever her eventual beliefs, she was emerging from totalism, and reaffirming the more moderate parts of herself.

"Conversion" Trends

In all cases of apparent conversion (the two I studied in detail, the two I met briefly, and two others I heard of) similar emotional factors seemed to be at play: a strong and readily accessible negative identity fed by an unusually great susceptibility to guilt, a tendency toward identity confusion (especially that of the cultural outsider), a profound involvement in a situation productive of historical and racial guilt, and finally, a sizable element of totalism.

It should be stressed, however, that I dealt with a very special group of subjects: any Westerner living in China over many years is likely to have experienced some form of profound identity search, and many had missionary ties which enhanced their susceptibility to guilt. This deep involvement with China makes the conversion as much cultural as political.

In Miss Darrow's case, her apparent conversion was associated with the identity struggles of the liberal. But an apparent conversion can also occur in a more authoritarian person. Guilt, identity conflict, and especially totalism are the important psychological factors, and these are not confined to any one kind of character structure.

It is also important to keep in mind that individual traits, although immensely important, are just one side of the coin; the circumstances of imprisonment are the other. These were essentially similar in all cases; but the length of time which people were held and the intensity with which the Communists pursued their reform measures varied. Since vulnerabilities to conversion are to some extent present in everyone (no one is free from susceptibility to guilt, confusion over identity, and some degree of totalism), the variations in the circumstances of imprisonment have a special significance.

There is a good deal of evidence—and European subjects frequently expressed this opinion to me—that American prisoners have been subjected to more severe pressures because of the international political situation. There is no doubt that they have been held longer than other Westerners. If there is a slightly higher percentage of apparent converts among American prisoners than among Europeans (this was not true for my subjects, but there have been some well-publicized cases of Americans who did fall into this group), these particularly difficult circumstances may have played an important part. Released Americans, when they return home, also face very great pressure to abandon their reform identities—although this pressure has acted on some as an incentive to hold on to their reform.

In any case, underneath any apparent conversion there is likely to be (as there was with Miss Darrow) an identity search no less profound, if not nearly as overt, as occurs among the obviously confused. The search is all the more difficult because so much of it must be hidden—from other people, and, to some extent, from the prisoner himself. Yet hidden doubts are very likely, after a period of time, to come to the surface, as they did with Miss Darrow; and at this point, the apparent convert comes close to joining the ranks of the obviously confused. In becoming apparent converts in the first place, however, these people experience the most profound personal upheavals of any of the three groups.

CHAPTER 8

VARIETIES OF RESPONSE: APPARENT RESISTERS

Apparent resisters are the people who cross the border denouncing the cruelties of prison thought reform. At first encounter, many of them appear to be little affected by their ordeal, other than showing a certain amount of physical and mental strain; ideologically, they are bitterly anti-Communist, if anything, more so than they had been before imprisonment. They are received by the Western world with both admiration and relief —admiration for their strength, and relief for the proof which they convey that "brainwashing" can be resisted after all.

In talking with them, I too was impressed with their courage and endurance. As I probed more deeply, however, I found that their inner resistance was not nearly so complete as their external expression suggested. Eight of the people I interviewed fell into this category. The following case best illustrates the diverse psychological factors which influence resistance, the complicated meanings behind the later condemnation of the Communists, and the way in which reform influences come to the surface at unexpected moments.

Hans Barker: Priest, Doctor, Soldier

One of the first subjects I interviewed was an elderly, goateed Belgian Bishop, a man who had lived in the interior of China for more than forty years prior to his three years of imprisonment. When I first saw him, he had already been in Hong Kong for three months, but he was still deeply preoccupied with his three-year reform experience. He immediately launched into his own analysis of the Communist approach, describing it in fundamentalist Catholic theological language. The evil and the power of the Communist behavior could only be explained, he felt, through the influence of demons—the evil counterpart of angels who have equally great power. His explanation, enthusiastically rendered, combined Biblical and modern history:

The Old Testament says that the demons are the murderers of mankind. The Communists have killed off fantastic numbers of people. The demons seek to further the idea of people without God, as do the Communists. Both try to make the human being happy without God and against God. The demons are the mortal enemies of mankind. The demons make use of the Communists in order to kill as many human beings as is possible. . . . Therefore, in the long run, it is a religious question, only thoroughly understood through religion.

Born in a predominantly Catholic community, Bishop Barker was brought up under the strong influence of his deeply religious mother. But even in these surroundings, his response to the Church was unusual: at the age of four he attempted to "convert" one of his brothers to a more religious life; at the age of five he became fascinated with the lives of the saints and particularly those who had been martyred; at the age of seven he was impressed by the story of Daniel in the lion's den. During these early years he donated his spare money to Church collections for missionary work "to redeem the heathen child." And by the time he was eight years old, he had already determined to do missionary work in China. He was influenced in part by an older brother who was studying for the priesthood, and even more strongly by the stories he had read and heard about saints and martyrs in China: "The Chinese were one of the peoples in the world who could make you a martyr . . . there I could have great hope to become a martyr."

He was a weak and sickly child, but in children's games he loved to play the part of the military officer: "I liked to show bravery, in contrast with my body, because I was so weak." Although he never wavered from his early ambition to become a priest and missionary, his childhood imaginings included the wish to be a doctor and a military hero as well; and, as he proudly explained to me, he had managed in his work in China to be all of these.

During his primary and secondary school days, from about the age of eleven through seventeen, his path was not easy. He had difficulty sleeping at night ("I could never have soft, deep sleep") and was troubled by disturbing dreams in which "I was not free. . . . I could not do as I liked. . . . I was hindered even in the dreams." During the day he would often feel weak and tired; he would fall asleep in class during lessons, and in chapel during prayers. He remembers being told that he had "circulatory difficulties," although their exact nature was never made clear. But he remained active, a leader among other children; and as far as his infirmity was concerned, "I tried to ignore it, to do the same work as the strong." These difficulties subsided somewhat during the long years of seminary training, but they never disappeared completely.

In China, he called forth great energies for his missionary work: he studied Chinese music and religious rituals in order to incorporate some of them into his Catholic services; he dispensed medicine, treated wounds, and offered assistance during the famines, droughts, floods, and civil wars; he arranged special meetings with bandit chiefs in order to safeguard "my Christians," in return serving as a guarantor and go-between for the bandits in their negotiations with the government. He often suffered from fatigue and insomnia, and on one occasion, after a brief visit to Europe, he requested that he be transferred to a different area (a request which was granted) in order to avoid the "nervous strain" of the negotiations. But he otherwise carried on his work without interruption, avoiding any outward show of weakness, and refusing many opportunities for periods of rest and temporary replacement. He became widely known in his inland province, according to other Westerners, as a colorful, courageous, able, and dogmatic representative of the Catholic faith.

Bishop Barker divided his imprisonment into two main phases:

the first six weeks of pressures, directed at "personal factors"; and the remaining time, "when I realized that the Communist program was not against me, but against my religion." During the first phase, his captors emphasized "real facts." These included: a description of Communist policies in his mission area which he had written at the request of an American officer (while he was strongly anti-Communist, much of what he described in this report had been far from unfavorable, and he felt that it would have been better for him if the Communists had actually seen the report rather than just hearing about it); and his presence at a meeting organized by Japanese occupiers in their attempt to obtain co-operation from the missionaries (his sympathies were always with the Chinese, and he emphasized the many risks he had taken in helping them against the Japanese). Although he felt that these incidents were misinterpreted and distorted, he nonetheless regretted the two actions greatly, and they contributed to a strong personal sense of guilt.

He also took the next step, and began to view himself in relationship to the Communist doctrine:

I said that imperialism is the parent of pride and acquisitiveness, and that I would fight it. I thought that maybe there was imperialism in me.

But during the second phase, as he began to get a better grasp of the prison world (he had known very little about Communist doctrine or reform methods), he realized that his captors were indicting his mission society and his Church as part of an "espionage network." At this point the trend was reversed, and "I mobilized all of my strength for resistance." As he "learned what play was going on," he consciously substituted within his mind the Catholic religious equivalents of the subjects under discussion:

This saving thought came to me: for the state I substitute God; for the people, my Christians; the imperialists' failings, greed and pride, are aptly represented by uncharitable self-love and love of pleasure, and the "helping" more than takes the place of fraternal admonition. . . . It was necessary for me to find the proper standpoint in relationship to God.

He began to view his imprisonment as a personal religious trial:

I suffered . . . because my self-love had to give way to the love of God. . . . One time when the warden spit in my face, I felt pain, but it was instantly suppressed. The pain meant I still had self-love . . . when you lose self-love, there is almost instant disappearance of pain. . . . In the struggle between the selfish I and God, the selfish I causes pain, uncertainty, insecurity, and a troubled heart. When you are wholly relying on God, you calm down and there is a quietude and peace that you feel. . . . When this happened I could feel my inner happiness increasing. . . . I was thankful to them for a rare occasion to live my religion.

Meditating whenever he could, he thought of the early Roman martyrs and of Christ himself on the Cross, reconstructing in his own way the New Testament passage which applied to his situation:

You will be persecuted. People will kill you like a dog, but do not be afraid. They can kill your body but not your soul. When they press you with arguments . . . give them the answer. The Holy Spirit will give you the answer.

He sought to retain this reversal in symbols throughout his imprisonment: "I would agree to personal shortcomings because I had many shortcomings regarding God."

At the same time, he attempted to avoid involvement in the re-education program as much as he could, pleading poor eyesight (his glasses had been broken soon after his imprisonment and were never replaced), difficulty in hearing (also partially true), and an incomplete knowledge of written Chinese.

He also tried to maintain his sense of the humorous and the human, as the following incidents suggest. Once an intelligent fellow-prisoner, after subjecting Bishop Barker to a grueling individual session of "informal help" shook his head and said, quoting a Chinese proverb, "Talking to you is like playing a violin before a cow." Back in the group, Bishop Barker was asked about the session, and whimsically reported, "He has been playing music to a horse"—stimulating in his helper the response which he had hoped it would bring out—"I must be making some progress." For, as Bishop Barker explained to me, "A horse is more sensitive to music than a cow."

Similarly, he reported on the efforts of a cellmate with a strong but brief argument: "He played a big drum, but he ran away." And at a lighter moment, his cellmates temporarily joined the game and asked him "Which instrument?" another less forceful cellmate had "played," to which Bishop Barker replied, "He played a small drum."

When pressed for his "thoughts," his humor was tinged with the poignancy of the prisoner's position: "I am a man who does not exist. I cannot have any thoughts." And frequently, when he was being abused by his cellmates, he would appeal to their sense of personal ethics: "I can endure this, but I wonder how you can endure it. Does your conscience allow this evil treatment?" This last approach especially would sometimes bring at least temporary relief. Bishop Barker also felt that his advanced age was responsible for a certain amount of moderation, sometimes expressed in the backhanded prison vernacular as an admonishment for his stubbornness: "You have no pity for your old bones."

The occasional presence of other Westerners, including priests, was also of great importance to him, although he had little opportunity for direct exchange with them. Once, however, after a particularly difficult day, he recited a German poem to a fellow-European in the cell: "The day was hot, the battle was fierce, the evening quiet—it will be cool in the night." This poem helped him to express his feelings and rally his strength; but since he was overheard, it also resulted in severe criticism for "cursing us in a foreign tongue."

Despite his friendly, personal approach to other prisoners, Bishop Barker was careful to avoid real intimacy with them:

They would say, "This Number Four is not a good comrade. He remains separate from us. It must be because of his imperialist pride." They wanted me to sit down with the other prisoners and to have them as comrades. But I was afraid that if I did this, my resistance would grow weaker.

Although he made many concessions, his imprisonment—contrary to most cases—ended on a note of resistance. During his last five months, he received his most severe treatment, including handcuffs and chains—which he referred to as "decorations"—directed toward extracting a final "espionage" confession: "my repentance and witness letter." He doggedly refused to follow the judge's suggested version, insisting that untrue accusations involving his colleagues and his Church be left out; he finally agreed to a compromise version consisting only of "facts"—somewhat exaggerated, but mainly concerned with his own behavior. The prison officials, rather than hold him longer to extract a more desirable confession, were apparently determined to release him at this time for reasons of their own. He left with the feeling that he had forced the government to back down and had successfully defended the integrity of the Church.

He arrived in Hong Kong, gaunt but confident, expressing to his friends the conviction that he had successfully met a severe trial. He experienced much less fear and suspiciousness than most, and the physician who first examined him described him as a "superior person," much more composed than others he had examined immediately after the same ordeal.

When he spoke to me three months later, he retained this expressed feeling of victory: "In the long run, I have won." He was strongly critical of the "diabolical" Communist world he had seen, and specifically condemned its manipulation of people:

The Communists drop a net all over the country, closing the frontiers. Then the net is dropped over an individual person, and he loses his freedom of movement and must follow their wishes.

But as we talked more, it became clear that he had some inner doubts about the completeness of his victory. He spoke whimsically of being "almost converted" during the early period of imprisonment, criticized himself for having then gone "too far," and gave me the general impression that he felt very uncomfortable about whatever concessions he had made.

This impression was confirmed when he showed me a summary of his prison experiences which he had prepared. In attempting to convey, in characteristic tongue-in-cheek style, the full impact of Communist arguments upon missionaries, he revealed perhaps more than he meant to:

And now, like a monster from out of the abyss, the most fearful realization dawned: you, a missionary, the herald of the Gospel, are not you a messenger of the imperialistic conquerors, their pioneer, on account of your ethnological and industrial reports on your mission land? And after the occupation of your mission land, you go on rendering the conquerors many different services. And take your mission work as a whole: does it not now prove to be a big, long, and heavy sin? And the question whether your mission activity has been of more harm or good to the people answers itself. But because you grew up in imperialistic ideologies, it has never until now occurred to you how much you have been of help in the enslaving and the exploitation of a people which formerly enjoyed liberty. Yes, the scope of your corrupting activities is enlarged: what you do, your colleagues do. Thus you cannot escape the fact that your society and your mission ought to be regarded as spy centers, sending out reports to both headquarters, and that Rome becomes the world center, from where imperialist governments draw their perverting information. . . . as proof that you now condemn this process, you must at once give full information about the spy activities of your society, of your mission, as of Rome. By doing this you acquire the mentality of the new regime, which alone will make you realize the sins of your past life, and those of your comrades. Only this mentality will give you true guidance for your future work.

Even as he condemned the Communists, he was deeply impressed with their power and energy, and compared these favorably to the shortcomings of the West in general and of the Catholic Church in particular:

The Communists have tremendous enthusiasm in their outright devotion to their doctrine. . . . What they believe, they do. . . . We are divided between doctrine and practice. . . . There is a discrepancy between religious life and doctrine. Therefore we are weak. . . . They are superior to us in carrying out their actions. . . . They have dialectic and a strange use of their proofs. . . . They have a keen instinct for finding out what each man may be doing against his own creed and his work. . . . I don't know where human beings can find such proofs.

In resorting to the demonology of Catholic theology for his analysis of Communist strength, he expressed very little personal bitterness toward his former captors. Rather, he emphasized their antireligious (and therefore "unnatural") character as a cause of their ultimate failure:

Communists' faces are hard, reflecting cultivated hatred, insecurity with each other, and irritations. They are unsatisfied regarding human nature . . . because the essential relationship between the Creator and man is unsatisfied. . . . Their leaders have the greatest authority ever filled by human beings, but they obtained this authority by taking it themselves, without the authority of God. . . . They are hanging in air without foundation, and the frame is too large for the image. . . . Although they aim to make people satisfied and happy by work and sacrifice, in the long run they destroy this goal. . . . They rely only on nature without God or any spiritual forces, but they do so many things against nature.

But despite all of this, he was struck by the similarity ("the identical methods, the identical terminology") between these Communist conversion techniques and those of his own Catholic Church. He also emphasized, however, what was for him the crucial difference between the two: "The state demands such a complete change and turnover of mind as we only allow God to demand." He summed up his admiration-tinged condemnation of the Communists in the simple statement, "They lie so truly."

He extended his analysis to the sources of his own courage and resistance, dividing these into the religious, the ethical ("for others") and the personal. He felt he was weakest in the last category, and for this he felt a certain amount of guilt and shame; but he believed that this "natural defect" was compensated for by his strength in the other two areas, and particularly by the necessary strengthening of his "religious motive": "I had to become more religious or else give way to the Communists." As a consequence, he felt that the entire experience had left him "more separated from the outside world than before," because of his "deeper religious life." Always important in his evaluation of his personal experience was the theological significance he attributed to it. "In my whole life, I have always given suffering a higher meaning. . . . always recalling, 'the blood of the martyrs is the seed of new Christians'."

These religious preoccupations did not diminish his lively responses to life around him. His enthusiasm for China and for the Chinese was always evident, and he was greatly affected by a short trip he took to a neighboring island whose landscape reminded him of the interior of China. He enjoyed wine with his meals, and was quick with a spirited metaphor at any time. He was impatient with clerical colleagues who were either dull or overly propagandistic. He criticized American women, both on moral grounds ("They show to everyone what only their husbands should see"), and for an implied defect in sensuality ("They are like a lukewarm shower bath"). He always welcomed psychological interpretations from me: "You are better in the natural. I am better in the supernatural," and asked for names of books from which he might learn the principles of psychiatric interviewing, which he thought would be useful for his religious work. At the same time, he repeatedly urged me in my future work to encourage my patients to deepen themselves in their religion, whatever it might be; and he was not above a delicate pursuit of my own soul—recommending to me, and then producing the next day, a book written by a psychiatrist describing his spiritual journey from Judaism to psychoanalysis to Catholicism.[1]

Toward the end of our talks, he summed up his feelings about his experience once more in an affirmative way: "My constant feeling is I have done good. . . . I have nothing to forget." But once more I felt that while part of him believed this, another part of him required its expression in order to quiet guilty doubts. At that time, his prescription for the future was essentially a spiritual one: "I am convinced that we can resist Communism only if we are one hundred per cent adherents to God."

I also saw him six months later, about ten months after his release, when he was passing through Hong Kong after a period of rest and travel, and after having lectured and given sermons on his experience. Then he spoke in a different key. He talked of the inevitability of war, implying that we might as well "risk it now"; and he severely attacked the alternative path of negotiation and moderation: "You do not sit down with the Devil to discuss how to save your soul." In developing this point of view, his explanation took a strange turn to economics: "America has lost many of her overseas markets—so something will happen—and this war must result anyway." In his activities, he continued to dedicate himself to what he called the "spiritual mobilization of Christians."

To what extent did Bishop Barker resist thought reform? Certainly, he was impressively successful in accomplishing what every imprisoned Catholic priest attempted to do (and what priests have always attempted in these circumstances): to maintain a sense of inner theological experience rather than surrender to the influence of those who would change him. His emotional strength upon release, his clear preservation of his own ideals and his condemnation of those of the Communists, his capacity to place his entire experience within the framework of his own theological idiom—all were very real demonstrations of strength and of resistance.

Nonetheless, there was clear evidence that his theological structure had also been penetrated by significant thought reform influences. His repeated need to affirm his "victory" had some of the quality of whistling in the dark, especially in the light of his awe and even admiration for the Communists' single-mindedness and "superhuman" (even if demonic) energies. His own written "fearful realization" statement expressed the depth to which one part of him had entered into the Communist idiom, the extent to which he had been made to feel guilty on *their* terms. His preparation of this statement was in fact his way of attempting to purge himself of this unwanted reform influence. Finally, there is his remarkable statement about economics a few months later—an extreme anti-Communist view, to be sure, but at the same time an orthodox Marxist analysis undoubtedly derived from his prison experience.

Bishop Barker—in his exposure to Communist indoctrination, and in his long life before this—had struggled with inner demons of his own. On the one hand, his life is a remarkable study in continuity. From the age of three to seventy, the direction of his life and of his view of the world never changed, only expanded. Moreover, he was one of those fortunate men who could achieve the unachievable, and live out fully during his adult life the imaginative fantasies of his childhood—which may not be, as Freud claimed, the *only* form of true happiness, but which is certainly one of the best paths to self-realization. His was undoubtedly an identity of great strength and consistency, combining fundamentalist absolutism with a well-developed worldliness and a taste for the human drama.

What, then, were his demons? They were his feelings of weakness, of being unable to accomplish what he so wished to do, his self-doubts (and possibly even lapses of faith), and the sense of guilt and shame which accompany such doubt. They were, in short, his negative identity.

His adolescent identity crisis was specifically his struggle with these demons, and he overcame them through subordination of self to the greater authority of Church and God. Like Vincent and Luca, he found his solution in an absorbing profession; in terms of belief and ideology, it was attained more by rigorous reinforcement of what already consciously existed than by the use of some new principle from the outside or of something long-buried within.

Although this ideological solution was certainly a successful one, the demons frequently re-emerged and gave rise, in later life, to anxiety, fatigue, and despair; and in a man as sensual as Bishop Barker, probably to considerable sexual temptation as well. Men are perhaps at their most heroic when fighting such inner demons, however, and Bishop Barker never succumbed. Instead, he used his form of totalism—his urge toward absolute surrender to an all-powerful supernatural force—as a means of taming them. Totalism was not, as it was with Miss Darrow, a threat to his self-affirmation. Quite the reverse; it was the power behind his most cherished self-image, the emotional counterpart of his ideal of martyrdom.

But the Communists would not meet him on this ground. By focusing upon personal weaknesses, and by creating a situation in which martyrdom was impossible, they denied him his strongest inner support. His early susceptibility to their influence was due to their circumventing his totalism and making contact with his personal demons of guilt and self-doubt. And I believe this is what Bishop Barker really meant when he spoke of the alliance between the Communists and the demons: he was expressing in theological symbols what he knew from profound psychological experience— the alliance between the undermining pressures of thought reform and his own negative identity, for him a particularly dangerous entente. It created an inroad for thought reform influence; and with his degree of totalism, the emotional extremes of Communist ideology and behavior held a seductive appeal. The process was, of course, enhanced by his painful awareness of having committed actions (the report for the American officer, and the attendance at the Japanese-run meetings) which violated both Communist law and his own moral standards.

He could protect himself from seduction only by reaffirming his tie to the Church, by reclaiming his totalism as a source of defensive strength. This was possible for him once he felt that the Church itself was under attack. Then he was able, as he always had been, to bring his inner demons under control, even make them work for him. By placing his negative identity squarely within the Catholic perspective, he could denounce his selfishness to his heart's content, as a prisoner was supposed to do, and through the denunciations move closer to the Catholic Church and create distance between himself and the Communists. At the same time he could also call upon that humane and flexible part of himself which had always lived side-by-side with his Catholic fundamentalism and totalism, and which had contributed so much to his stature as a human being.

He was still in the midst of this reclaiming process when I saw him, simultaneously accentuating his totalism, and re-emphasizing its alignment with his Catholic supernatural identity. The thought reform seduction remained a constant threat and gave several evidences of its unconscious presence. Yet despite Bishop Barker's inner doubts about his "victory," it was by no means entirely a hollow one. He had resisted thought reform's disruptive pressures more effectively than most.

Methods of Resistance

Bishop Barker illustrates dramatically the psychological strengths and weaknesses of the apparent resisters. The same factors are present to some extent in all prisoners, but in the apparent resisters these strengths are most effective and the weaknesses most dangerous. These methods of resistance (for that is what both the strengths and weaknesses are) may be classified under five main headings:

The first form of resistance is the acquisition of a sense of understanding, a theory about what is going on, an awareness of being manipulated. In Bishop Barker's case, this understanding was not immediate; and in a man of his intellectual and psychological breadth, we may assume that it was his "demons" which were responsible for the delay. But once he began to grasp "which play was on" it could become for him just that—something of a contrived drama, by no means completely artificial, but one in which he could do his "acting" while keeping in touch with his own spiritual tradition. In his explanation, he undoubtedly oversimplified the importance of this understanding, but it was important nonetheless. Each of my subjects formulated his own psychological, theological, or philosophical concepts to explain the experience to himself, even while he was going through it. These theories offered protection: they gave each prisoner a capacity to predict what was coming next, a sense of anticipation; [2] and they provided him one of the rewards of knowledge, a sense of control. This understanding, always partial at best, cannot offer complete immunization; but as

Bishop Barker and many others demonstrated, a grasp of the techniques being used and the emotions being called forth helps to dispel the terrifying fear of the unknown and the sense of complete helplessness—two great stimulators of human anxiety upon which thought reform depends. The prisoner is thus enabled to mobilize his defenses and bring into play the other methods of resistance.

The second important resistance technique is the avoidance of emotional participation; in other words, the prisoner remains as much as possible outside the communication system of thought reform. Bishop Barker was doing this when he emphasized his difficulties in sight and hearing, and his limited knowledge of written Chinese. Others, who had lived for shorter periods of time in China, managed to resist learning even spoken Chinese while in prison; still others, at their own request, were allowed to study Marxist writings or Russian, and thereby avoided more intense personal involvement in confession and re-education. Bishop Barker went even further. In his human relationships he steered clear of the kind of intimacy which would have drawn him more deeply into the group structure of the cell and integrated him more firmly into the prison world. This in turn enabled him to do what was most important of all—to maintain a private inner world of values, judgments, and symbols, and thereby keep a measure of independence from the ever-pressing environment.[3]

Since a prisoner could never fully avoid participation, the next best form of resistance was to adopt a neutralizing attitude, one which deflated rather than contested, and which thereby took the sting out of the assaults. Hostile rejoinders gained a prisoner little, and in fact brought about even more devastating pressures. But humor or humane stoicism (both of which Bishop Barker demonstrated) put officials and cellmates in a difficult psychological position.

A show of humor had the effect of breaking the general tension and dissipating the anxiety and guilt which hung heavy in the environment. As one subject expressed it, "Since the judge is a tragedian before you, if you keep a smile this protects you, because the impressiveness of the tragedy is avoided." This was not often possible, as the same subject was quick to add. But when it was possible to use it, humor was a way to express a tone contrary to thought reform's self-righteousness, an implication that the intense doings of the moment could be made fun of because they were merely a speck on the great human canvas. Since humor is a shared emotion, it can create a bond of sympathy (as it did for Bishop Barker) independent of and frequently antithetical to the world of reform.

Humane stoicism, the turning of the other cheek in the face of abuse, is, as Bishop Barker made clear, an attitude extremely difficult to maintain in the prison environment. It is a form of passive resistance in the Gandhian tradition; but a prisoner can never flaunt the resistance, and even his passivity, or lack of enthusiasm in any direction, is highly suspect. Moreover, it requires unusual dedication to a supernatural or humanitarian ideal. Yet it may produce startling effects, even to the extent of so dominating the cell for a moment that harsh behavior suddenly seems shameful in everyone's eyes. It is not long, of course, before there is a return to the usual prison standards; but the impact of this stoicism outlasts the brief moment of its effectiveness. It reaffirms—in the eyes of the stoic prisoner and his cellmates—a moral position superior to the grandiose moral claims of thought reform.

The steadfastness of humane stoicism is related to the fourth and generally most important resistance technique, that of identity reinforcement. Bishop Barker's major way of resisting thought reform was to make it a Catholic theological struggle, rather than a Communist remolding. He sought always to maintain himself as a priest struggling against his selfishness, rather than as a stubborn imperialist spy. To do this, he needed a continuous awareness of his own world of prayer, Catholic ritual, missionary experience and Western cultural heritage; with nothing around him to encourage it, this awareness could come only from within. His behavior resembled Father Luca's conscious recollection of the people and places which had special meaning for him. This kind of identity reinforcement was for any prisoner the essence of self-protection, both against reform influence and against always-threatening psychological disintegration.

One priest expressed this very succinctly:

To resist . . . you must affirm your personality whenever there is the opportunity. . . . When I was obliged to speak my views about the government, I would each time begin, "I am a priest. I believe in religion." I said it strongly every time.

This statement was perhaps a retrospective exaggeration of his self-assertion, but there was no doubt that so personal a reminder served him well.

A European professor used a more creative approach. He somehow managed during moments when pressures were relatively relaxed to make a series of drawings representing precious moments in his past: a mother and baby, a boy before a Christmas tree, a university city, a young man on a romantic stroll with his fiancée. He also wrote a brief, idealized account of the incident in his life each drawing represented. He worked on both the drawings and the essays during moments when he was off by himself in a corner of the cell or with other Westerners; and they became so precious to him that he smuggled them out of the prison at great risk and proudly displayed them to me during our interviews. They re-established for him the world in which he wished to exist: "I could escape the horrible world around me and move in a world whose values I agreed with."

The first four methods of resistance depend upon strength—ego strength, strength of character, strength of identity. Another aspect of Bishop Barker's response may be termed *pseudo strength*, and this method of resistance is a potential psychological danger. I am referring to his inability to come to conscious terms with thought reform influences, and his need instead to make use of the psychological mechanisms of denial and repression in order to keep from himself the recognition of undue "weakness." In this pattern he differed, not only from the obviously confused, but also from the apparent converts (although both of these groups of prisoners, especially the latter, had much of their own to hide from themselves). Bishop Barker shared with other apparent resisters a significant attraction to the reform program; his repeated protestations of resistance and his strong condemnations of Communism expressed his attempts to cast off this attraction. The potential danger of this pseudo strength lies in the effects of a highly unacceptable, and at the same time completely unresolved, set of emotions.

Thus, when Bishop Barker advocated "war now" with the Communists—at the same time justifying his view by Communist theory—he was attempting to eradicate these compelling thought reform influences (his new demons) which so deeply threatened his sense of who he was and what he believed. He was, in effect, saying: "If we can destroy all of the demons in the world, it will eliminate those within me without my having to recognize that they have been there."

The apparent resisters characteristically combine these real and pseudo strengths. Their form of totalism, along with their habitual use of denial and repression, create a paradoxical situation in which those who have been least influenced by thought reform unconsciously feel themselves to be most in danger of being overwhelmed by its influence. They struggle continually against a breakthrough of despair.

Survival and Influence

We have been discussing in this, and in the previous two chapters, problems of individual thought reform experiences, and especially the problems of survival and influence. The two are closely related: for a prisoner to survive—hold on to physical and psychic life—he must avoid being totally overwhelmed by environmental influence. From the standpoint of identity, survival and resistance to influence converge, at least in an absolute sense: one cannot have his deepest feelings about who and what he is totally replaced, and still survive in a nonpsychotic state.

But one can go quite far in permitting his identity to give way to outside influence, and still function adequately, both physically and psychologically. Indeed, in thought reform, a prisoner had to submit to some degree of environmental influence as the price of survival.[4] This was especially clear in the cases of Professor Castorp and Miss Darrow, both of whom were aware that they had bartered the acceptance of reform views for survival. This bargain was also struck by prisoners like Bishop Barker, even though more of the bartering occurred outside of awareness. To survive thought reform and retain absolutely no trace of its influences was an ideal impossible to achieve—whether the ideal was held by the prisoner himself, his colleagues, or the shocked onlookers of the outside world.

This paradoxical relationship between survival and influence allows a better understanding of the Westerners' performances during imprisonment. As far as survival is concerned, these men and women, when put under extreme forms of stress, were able to summon an impressive store of strength and ingenuity. Bishop Barker's use of humor, Dr. Vincent's characterological shift from isolation to "togetherness," even Father Luca's delusions all were methods of survival, as were the confessions and the "reformed" patterns of behavior elicited during imprisonment from every prisoner.

Thought reform succeeded with all Westerners in the first of its aims, the extraction of an incriminating personal confession, because it made this confession a requirement for survival. It fell far short of its more ambitious goal of converting Westerners into enthusiastic Communist adherents; for although none could avoid being profoundly influenced, virtually all prisoners showed a general tendency to revert to what they had been before prison, or at least to a modified version of their previous identity. The barter of influence for survival which Western prisoners made with their reformers turned out to be reasonable enough; only the unreasonable demands of their inner voice of conscience made some of these Westerners feel that their bargain had been a Faustian one.

One very important question remains: granted the variations in external reform pressures, what factors in individual character structure are responsible for the differing susceptibilities to thought reform influence? I found that it is not so much the specific *type* of character structure which is important, as is the degree of balance and integration; not so much who one is as how well one is put together. To speak, for instance, of "hysterical" or "obsessive" character types does not help us, since these characterological tendencies appear among people in all three categories. Distinguishing "authoritarian" from "liberal" character traits [5] is a bit more useful; but it does not explain why one apparent convert (Miss Darrow) falls into the liberal category, and another (Father Simon, discussed in Chapter 11) into the authoritarian.

Rather, each tended to be influenced to the degree that his identity, whatever it may have been, could be undermined through the self-deprecating effects of guilt and shame. This susceptibility in turn depended largely upon his balance between flexibility and totalism, and their special significance for his character structure. Apparent converts shared with apparent resisters a significant amount of totalism; hence both extreme responses.[6] But apparent resisters (Bishop Barker) possessed great strength of identity in contrast to the apparent converts (Miss Darrow) who tended to show identity diffusion. Those among the obviously confused were able to be more flexible in experimenting with identity alternatives, without feeling the need to totally accept or reject the new influence. This is not to say that they were without elements of totalism, any more than the apparent resisters were completely devoid of flexibility; every character structure has both. It was more a question of degree and of lifelong pattern.[7] Some individual cases (Dr. Vincent) defy even these broad patterns: his totalism was predominant throughout his life and during reform itself, but his idiosyncratic identity strength and flexibility were responsible for his ending up in the most moderate of the three categories.

Each of the three styles of response had its own psychological advantages and disadvantages, as well as its variations. None held a monopoly on human limitation, strength, or courage.

CHAPTER 9

GROUP REFORM:
DOUBLE-EDGED
LEADERSHIP

A consistent feature of all the cases discussed so far has been the isolation of the Western prisoner. Even when physically part of a cell group, he was completely removed from it—emotionally, culturally, and ideologically—until he "changed" and adopted its standards. Never did the group support him as an individual, or help him to resist the onslaughts of thought reform; rather, the group was the agent of thought reform, the conveyor of its message.

There was just one exception to this pattern among my Western subjects. One all-European group was permitted to reform itself; it developed in the process a remarkable series of resistance ploys, and at the same time an incomplete immunity to the reform effects of these ploys. This group showed a poignant combination of solidarity and antagonism, of tortured and tender behavior; its story is one of a struggle to maintain group autonomy in an environment specifically geared to prevent the appearance of any such autonomy.

This unusual Western group functioned for two-and-one-half years, and conducted its thought reform in English. The six men who were its members for most of its existence averaged close to two years of this form of re-education; and each spent at least one year with all five of the others. There were several manipulations and changes in personnel, so that four additional Westerners spent short periods of time in the group; but these men did not play as important roles in the group. The Europeans never constituted an entire cell by themselves, but were always a subgroup within a larger cell which also contained eight Chinese prisoners. A Chinese cell chief was always in charge of both subgroups. All the prisoners involved—Western and Chinese—were completely occupied during these two-and-a-half years with their re-education. Before each Westerner joined the group, he had been in prison for at least a few months; each had already made some concession to the government's demands, some form of incriminating personal confession.

The Europeans were brought into the cell one by one, for the apparent purpose of "helping" each other with their confessions and reform. The early pattern was essentially as follows. One European who had achieved some degree of adaptation to his environment by making a satisfactory confession and taking part in the criticism of others would be joined by a second Westerner who was still in acute conflict over how much to submit. The influence of the adjusted upon the conflicted European would inevitably be in the direction of confession and reform, but his motivations for this "progressive" influence were complex and uncertain. Always present, in combinations only partially understood by himself, were a genuine desire to help a fellow Westerner to accept the inevitable; an attempt to demonstrate his own "progressiveness" to the authorities in order to gain "merits" toward release; and the need to justify his own self-surrender through bringing a person similar to himself into the sphere of those who have already surrendered—a way to share guilt, shame, and weakness. All this "helping" preceded the existence of a true group structure, and served as a preliminary softening up for the group re-education process. It also set much of the pattern for the complicated personal relationships which were later maintained within the group.

The particular people involved in this group brought to it additional sources of friction of a very formidable nature. The group eventually included a German physician with ardent Nazi sympathies, a highly-trained French Jesuit philosopher, a Dutch priest of lowly origin, a successful North German merchant, an adventurous South German businessman, and a French Jesuit science teacher. Among such a group, personal, cultural, intellectual, national, political, and religious conflicts were always potentially disruptive, and were particularly apt to emerge at times when things were not going well. The potential conflicts included the German versus the Frenchman, the Nazi versus the anti-Nazi, the priest versus the layman, the Catholic versus the Protestant, the Jesuit priest versus the non-Jesuit, the crude peasant versus the middle-class gentleman, the North German versus the Bavarian, the university graduate versus the man of limited education, the professional man versus the merchant.

As though this were not enough, these men also had conflicts with each other which had existed before imprisonment—some personal and social, some ideological—for instance, disagreements among priests about whether to stand firm against all Communist pressure, or to adapt flexibly to it and accept the Communist-sponsored "independent church" movement in China. Members of these separate families within the group (priests, Germans, professional men, and so on) tended to support each other on many issues, but also found themselves in the most severe personality clashes; these were sometimes so extreme that the mildest statement or action on the part of one automatically became the cause for overwhelming resentment on the part of another, and group members often quoted the maxim: "No one is the other man's devil like one priest together with another."

Could any cohesion at all develop among such contending and unwilling guests? One might easily doubt it. Yet somehow leaders did emerge, along with a rather remarkable *esprit de corps*. In fact, the story of this group is really a study in leadership under stress [1] —leadership not absolute or static, but active and changing. It is also a study of group, rather than individual, resistance patterns. These patterns reveal much about the group process specifically produced by thought reform, as well as something about group process in general; they also tell us something about the interplay among the personal qualities of a leader, the special demands of a milieu, and the behavior of a group.

This group experience can be divided into three phases, each identified by a particular atmosphere, and by the domination of one man. To be sure, what happened in one phase also occurred to some extent in the others; but the following descriptions record what was most characteristic of each phase.

The Academic Phase

When Dr. Bauer, the German physician, arrived in the cell, he found there three other Westerners, each struggling to recover from severe personal pressures, and all living in an atmosphere of great fear.

The first, Mr. Weber, the businessman from Bavaria, had just a short time before made an attempt to kill himself, and had also experienced delusions and hallucinations; with the help of the other two, he was in the process of recovering his faculties. A man of extremes, he had lived a life of great heroism and of alcoholic excess, always in conflict between his very demanding internal ethics, and his intense need to act out his rebellion. In prison, this pattern continued: he was at times absolutely unyielding in his resistance, at other moments unduly "progressive." Inclined to be petulant and moody, he was leaning heavily upon the other two men.

The second, Mr. Kallmann, the North German merchant, had also attempted to take his own life a few months before in the midst of a severe depression with psychotic features. He had been given more time and opportunity to recover, and he had learned a "progressive" stance which he tried to convey to Mr. Weber. Mr. Kallmann possessed what the others described as "typically German" traits—loyalty, reliability, sentimentality, irascibility. At this point, his great fear was expressed in an attitude of extreme submissiveness: "I was so submissive that when going to the water closet, they told me I was bending my head too much, and that I might run into something."

The third, Father Émile, the French Jesuit scientist, had been a great comfort to both of the other two men. He impressed them with his outward calm and with his religious devotion, and had exerted a particularly strong influence upon Mr. Weber in reviving within him the will to live. Father Émile was slow, deliberate, and was regarded by the others as "the most sober of us mentally." He managed to remain cheerful, even to interject an occasional humorous monologue or bawdy story. But he did not possess either great intellectual breadth or quick tactical responses; and he was still under great personal pressure because much in his case was considered to be "unsolved."

Dr. Bauer's arrival heralded a change in fortune for this oppressed trio. Having been subjected to relatively minor pressures, his attitude was still one of confidence, and his entry was an injection of strength. As Mr. Weber expressed it: "He arrived like a breath of fresh air . . . He still had guts."

Very soon after his arrival the four men were instructed to study together in English, since none of them had an extensive knowledge of spoken or written Chinese. They were to follow the usual procedure—reading from Communist documents, criticism, and analytic self-criticism—under the general direction of the English-speaking Chinese cell chief. Thus the Westerners' group re-education began.

For the first three months, the pressures from above were relatively mild. The prison officials had apparently not yet fully worked out a system for the foreigners to follow, and the cell chief himself was notably easygoing, almost friendly. Although he met daily with prison officials, he did not seem to be greatly pressed about the behavior of the Europeans. Thus he demanded of them only that they maintain an attitude of study—without exercising any great control over what it was they were studying.

The four Westerners took advantage of this situation, and began to organize their resistance. ("It was then that our group opinion formed.") They went through the motions of reading and discussing Communist material for just a few minutes at the beginning of each study period. Then, still maintaining a strict outer decorum, they made use of their varied intellectual backgrounds to discuss principles of philosophy, religion, science, and business practice. Further, they pooled their knowledge to evolve a critique of the Communist position. As Dr. Bauer explained: "We developed the concept that modern science completely disproved Marxist materialism, and that modern science was forced to recognize a divine being."

No one among the four Westerners had any official status as leader, but Dr. Bauer soon assumed unofficial hegemony. His intact emotional state was a big factor in his doing so, but his intellectual and psychological equipment specifically suited him for this role. He was by far the most knowledgeable of the group, possessing a great fund of information in the natural and social sciences which far transcended his medical training. He put his extraordinary memory to good use in bringing facts and principles to the group discussions. His unusual didactic skill enabled him to command the interest of the other group members over prolonged periods of time. Further, he was happiest when dominating and teaching others, since this helped him to reinforce his tight control over his own anxiety, and over his repressed moral conflicts and self-doubts. His general psychological integration, and hard core of personal and national identity (including the exaggerated German nationalism of the expatriate) enabled him to articulate his firm convictions with great persuasive force. His tendency toward romantic nostalgia frequently led to enjoyable group discussions of childhood memories and idealized past experience. During most of his life, he had been quick to view anyone who disagreed with him as a personal "enemy"; in prison he was much more flexible in adapting himself to other Westerners against the "common enemy."

His influence largely shaped most of the group practices—and his influence was overwhelmingly in the direction of resistance. Throughout the group's existence he was considered the most "reactionary" of the Western prisoners. He repeatedly expressed to the group his opinions that the imprisonment was essentially a "police action" in which the Communists sought to obtain maximum information from everyone, that the officials were not unrealistic enough to expect genuine conversions from Westerners, and that their release would have nothing to do with their "progress" in reform. He illustrated his point of view by drawing a carrot-and-donkey cartoon in which the Communist rider holds out on a stick the promise of release (carrot) before the ever-struggling prisoner (donkey). He agreed with the others that it was necessary to tell everything about one's self that could be politically incriminating, and to make only statements acceptable to the Communist point of view when on public display. But he insisted that the small group of Westerners counteract the reform process by continually discussing with each other their true beliefs and their tactical maneuvers. "After following the correct platform for a while, taking notes, admitting our faults, and so on, we would say, 'Enough, boys,' and then talk frankly."

Dr. Bauer's influence in the group did not go completely un-resisted. The others were fearful that the group might be broken up, and each Westerner individually forced to confess to the decep-tion—a gamble which Dr. Bauer felt was worth taking. Mr. Kall-mann feared that "they might use drugs or special treatments to get out from us what was really in our hearts"; he tended to be more cautious and "progressive," even when he was with other Westerners, and he was critical of Dr. Bauer because "he did not understand the fundamental need to submit." Mr. Weber also had doubts, feeling it was necessary to "put your cards on the table," and was at times unwilling, and other times unable, to maintain the subterfuge. Father Émile, although willing to go along, was at times slow to grasp the method.

Group members had other, more personal criticisms of Bauer: of his overbearing manner and need to be all-knowing ("I couldn't understand why, because if I knew as much as he knew, I wouldn't worry about not knowing something occasionally"); of his attitude of superiority, especially on a racial (Nazi) basis toward the Chinese ("He has a brilliant brain, but in regard to tactfulness there is space for improvement"); of his demand for special privileges—extra blankets and added space in the cell, officially condoned because of the "cardiac condition" which his medical knowledge enabled him to feign. His Western fellow-prisoners, from whom he also kept this subterfuge, could not object to the situation, but they did resent the arrogant fashion in which he demanded these rights. Of even more concern to the other three Westerners was Bauer's "care-lessness" and "rascal spirit"; his tendency to take what were, in their eyes, unnecessary chances out of sheer bravado. They exerted great pressure upon him to change his ways, and they succeeded in con-vincing him to behave more moderately for the sake of the group.

Despite his shortcomings, they found Bauer to be a very "good comrade," unusually patient and skillful in aiding them individually, and "a man whom you can rely on in very difficult circumstances." They admired his intellect, and they greatly valued the calming and strengthening effect which they all acknowledged he had upon their previously beleaguered group. This first phase was by far the most untroubled and unthreatening. The group was under no great pressure from without; and the potential sources of friction within did not often materialize because all recognized the importance of making small personal concessions in order to maintain the group structure which they had come to treasure.

Bauer's controversial but effective presence had made this cohesion possible; and he in turn drew much of his personal strength from his alternative mystique of Nazism. He was a strong leader, if not always for the right reasons. In the light of what followed, the Westerners looked back over these three "academic" months as near-idyllic.

Phase of Reform

The dramatic entrance of Father Benét, the Jesuit philosopher, ushered in a new and disturbing series of events. He had been transferred from another cell, in what was for him a demotion, as he had previously been a cell chief. He was under fire partly for disciplinary violations, which were always dealt with firmly, as well as for an offense considered much more serious. A Chinese Catholic prisoner had tricked Benét into hearing a religious confession in the cell, and then had denounced him, since this form of religious practice was strictly prohibited in the prison. The struggle to which he was subjected upon reaching the new cell was aimed at making him do what for a Catholic priest is unthinkable—reveal the details of this religious confession. Chinese prisoners led the attack, but the Westerners had to take part. Bauer describes the scene which followed:

They manhandled him . . . pulled his beard, and kicked him in the chest. He screamed to the man who accused him, "You know I am not allowed to tell. You tell it yourself." But the other man was silent. . . . It was difficult for us, too. We were in a rage. Kallmann was close to tears. Émile clenched his fists. I was the same.

A way out was finally achieved when Father Benét, after much insisting, succeeded in obtaining a release from the Chinese prisoner to reveal the contents of the confession. But after this incident the Westerners never returned to the relative calm of their academic phase. Life in their cell had changed.

Pressures from above dictated a more intense program of personal reform, and a new cell chief, much more observant and vindictive than his predecessor (he had a great deal in the way of "reactionary" past affiliations to live down himself), was brought in to enforce this policy change. Father Benét was put through a series of severe struggles and "thought examinations" during the next few weeks; at the same time he was made "study leader" of the small Western group—a post for which he qualified because of his fluency in written and spoken Chinese, and his previous standing as a leading Western "progressive." Now the foreigners "studied" sometimes as a separate five-man group, sometimes with their eight Chinese cellmates. In either case, the new cell chief kept a close eye on their activities. Benét assumed a position of great responsibility, interpreting all of the study materials from Chinese to English for his Western fellow-prisoners, and answering to the authorities for what went on among them.

He brought to this task a form of leadership completely different from Bauer's approach, startling in its demands and its performance. He expressed to the other Westerners his firm conviction that the only way for them to earn their release was to throw themselves energetically into the reform process. This meant stopping at nothing to convince the officials of the extent of personal reform. He set an impressive example with his own behavior—histrionic gestures and expressions of guilt, repentance, and self-deprecation. He went to such extremes as describing intimate details of his own sexual life, including self-stimulation and affairs with women. His Western cellmates were themselves unsure of the truth of these sexual "confessions"; some suspected that Benét derived a good deal of satisfaction in their telling, and all were aware of the effect they had of damaging his relationship to the Catholic priesthood. At times, however, his lurid stories of personal misbehavior were clearly fabricated, intended—as were his expressions of opinions he knew to be "incorrect"—to supply more sins to repent, additional material for his demonstrative confessions. As one of the other Westerners said:

He confessed everything, exaggerated everything. He admitted all blame with an empty heart. He was very submissive, fully and deeply recognizing faults, showing himself a repentant sinner. He had a lively face, lots of grimaces. He was a marvelous actor.

He expected similar behavior from the Westerners under his direction, and exerted great pressure upon them in the form of criticisms and sharply-worded rebukes. Not only did he insist upon the prerogatives of his official position, but he also felt that as a priest it was his duty to do everything possible to help others in the cell. With religious procedures strictly forbidden, this help had to take other forms—and the ironic situation arose in which a Jesuit saw as his priestly duty the need to "help" others along the path to Communist reform. To be sure, Benét initially presented his approach as a technique, a means of obtaining early release and thereby preserving values. But his extreme behavior—and particularly his insistence that the Westerners maintain their "progressive" enthusiasms and pro-Communist sentiments even among themselves—obscured this original purpose. The distinction between real and make-believe was soon lost—certainly to the other Westerners in the group, and apparently to Benét himself.

Despite this "progressive" approach, Benét was severely treated by the cell chief, and constantly accused of "shielding" his fellow Westerners. And indeed, according to the Europeans, he did on many occasions absorb great punishment himself rather than expose them. But their admiration for his courage in protecting them was offset by their gradual realization that he seemed to make little effort to avoid difficulties with the authorities, and even appeared to court them. He derived a certain amount of pleasure from his own humiliation; or, as one of his European cellmates explained, "He asked for trouble, got beatings, and was then satisfied." Benét also had a penchant for bringing up highly controversial subjects when he need not have done so—for instance, the possible reconciliation of Catholicism with Communist materialism. He enjoyed these flirtations with danger and the opportunities they afforded for displaying his intellectual brilliance and his extensive knowledge of Communist theory—a practice they called "skating on thin ice."

An even more serious problem was his tendency to be domineering, and he was frequently told by his Western cellmates that he would have made a "good Prussian corporal." What particularly disturbed them was the vehemence with which he denounced fellow-prisoners:

He fell too easily into beating on one . . . making a man afraid . . . scolding him for hours . . . if he won't come out with something . . . forcing him to dig deeper . . . he rather enjoyed doing such things.

After being pressured from above, he invariably increased his demands upon the other Europeans; wary of his approach, they frequently offered resistance, but they could not avoid completely the effects of his powerful influence.

Gradually the group moved in a "progressive" direction. Under Benét's direction, it studied Communist theory and practice, legal codes and policy documents, and particularly case histories—of "big criminals" who had been successfully re-educated, treated leniently, and accepted into Communist society, and of lesser offenders whose unwillingness to confess and reform resulted in their being shot. In his zeal, Benét was far from precise in his translations, and frequently slanted them in the direction of his own point of view: "Sometimes he did not translate at all, but just told us what he wanted us to hear." The net result was a feeling, on the part of both the officials and the prisoners themselves, that the Westerners had "raised" their (Communist-style) "political level."

But such "progress" had to be at the expense of group solidarity. No longer pulling together in a protective effort, the Westerners' potential sources of friction became open antagonisms. Differences of opinion about how to behave were inextricably merged with the irritations of close confinement, as each of the men experienced his own special set of resentments.

Kallmann (the "typical German") describes this from his own experience:

Lots of antagonism developed between us. I myself suffered particularly. I developed a hatred at times against more or less all of them . . . hundreds of minor ridiculous things.

Kallmann sometimes viewed these differences as petty irritations, such as his impatience with Weber's voice ("loud and like a trumpet"). At other times he interpreted them through the idiom of the environment, seeing in Bauer's egotism "a typical example of an imperialist." He could, however, recognize that much of the trouble came from within himself: "I developed a horrible psychosis. . . . I knew my irritabilities were particularly great."

Émile (the scientist-priest) and Weber (the businessman-adventurer), were still close to each other, and had a common problem. Neither of them as intellectually quick as the others, both of them stubborn, they were frequently made the "scapegoats" (so-called by themselves and the others) of the group controversies. Émile (his humor and goodwill notwithstanding) was resented for his unwillingness to compromise when the group thought it necessary. Weber's position was much more painful. Impetuous and outspoken, he had immense difficulty in adjusting to group discipline, both to the general prison discipline and to the particular discipline imposed by the other Westerners. He was frequently guilty of such offenses as breaking dishes (a very serious matter), for which he was severely criticized by both the Chinese and Westerners.

More important, Weber insisted upon maintaining a separate, personal approach, an attitude of "absolute sincerity"; he deeply resented attempts by anyone to "force me to act differently from what I felt." He neither accepted nor fully understood the tactics used by the other Westerners. They in turn criticized him sharply, feeling this criticism to be necessary from the standpoint of group survival. But he remained convinced that the others were picking on him in order to rid themselves of their own tensions.

Weber also was the center of an especially bizarre and disturbing situation. The group of foreigners was required to denounce the wife of one of its members, who was being held in the woman's section of the same prison. The denunciation became a very important issue, because refusal to participate meant questioning the infallibility of the government. Each of the other foreigners, including the husband, denounced her as a tactical maneuver—but Weber refused to do so, despite the insistence of the husband himself. In this matter Weber's attitude elicited respect and caused the others shame as well as anger.

Even when the group was functioning smoothly, Weber felt uncomfortable with its policies; but during the turmoil of Benét's leadership, the pressures became so unbearable to him that he longed to be transferred to another cell—the only member of the group who at any time preferred to be separated from it prior to release.

My mental suffering was the limit of what I could endure . . . my main suffering came from these foreigners . . . not so much with the inspectors who I felt tried to be human. . . . Whatever I did I was always in the wrong. . . . I felt like a kind of prey in a cage. . . . I often thought it would be a pleasure to be transferred and to get away from this mental pressure. . . . I couldn't trust my friends or myself!

No one escaped experiencing hostility toward each of the others, nor did anyone fully avoid becoming the target of the others' resentment. Now it was Bauer's aggressive and superior manner, now Kallmann's intransigent "progressivism," now Weber's shift from Kallmann to Bauer for guidance and support—and all these seemed most disrupting during this chaotic time.

But the central focus of group dissension was Benét himself. Here everyone had strong feelings, since Benét's character and policies so forcibly affected the minute-to-minute existence of each. The sentiment was mainly negative; most of the other Westerners were highly resentful of his egotism, his instability, and his extreme behavior. They were by no means united, however, in their attitudes toward him. Countering their resentment was their awareness of his courage in shielding them. Kallmann was the group member who felt this most keenly, and was for some time Benét's closest collaborator and most staunch defender. His affection for him had begun when the two men had been together in a different cell before the formation of the Western group. At that time, when Kallmann was near-psychotic and overwhelmed by fear after his unsuccessful attempt at suicide, Benét had been compassionate, patient, and very helpful in teaching him how to deal with the officials. Kallmann had become convinced of the validity of Benét's approach, and believed it to be based on a superior understanding of Communism. Moreover, Kallmann's strong fears led him to the conviction that "we must work their mentalities into ourselves and really feel the guilt"—because "only when I get to the stage where I can genuinely feel the guilt can I genuinely convince them."

For a long time he felt only gratitude toward Benét:

For the first months they could only approach us through him, and he took all of the struggles. If he criticized us, we beat him back. He was like a cushion, pressed from both sides. . . . I cautioned the others that this was a great strain for him. He was the person who best served as a teacher in how to behave with the Communists . . . he shielded us . . . he was kind-hearted, and we took advantage of it. . . . He did as much for us as any comrade could do.

But after a few more months, even Kallmann resisted Benét's "exaggerations," and criticized much of his domineering and aggressive behavior. The others in the group were less impressed by

Benét's shielding of them, and more consistent in their resentment. Bauer especially was constantly antagonistic to Benét ("When I look at you, I realize why Martin Luther reformed the Catholic Church"), strongly opposed his policies, and attempted to offset his influence in the group whenever possible. Émile was in conflict with him over statements and attitudes about the Catholic Church, and on several occasions flew into a rage because of Benét's behavior. To Weber, Benét was a "proper charlatan."

The result of this conflict was an intragroup struggle for power and influence, something like the Communist intraparty struggle, rather than a harmonious, mutually-nourishing interplay. To be sure, even during this period the Europeans made strong attempts to preserve some degree of unity. Kallmann, for instance, recognizing his growing hostilities, pleaded with the group for assistance, and got some, at least temporarily.

I confessed it to my comrades and asked them to help me out of it— not to allow me to isolate myself . . . and they helped me. . . . Our antagonisms were not easy to overcome.

But the trend was one of disruption. As confusion between, as one man expressed it, "playing the game and reality" mounted, the protection of a united group was lost.

What was behind Father Benét's rather strange approach, and where did it lead? This was not the first group with which he had come in conflict. The statements of others who knew him well —both in and out of prison—(and I have to rely on these, since he was the only one of this six-man group I did not have the opportunity to interview) indicate he had always been a man of great learning, erratic behavior, and seething inner rebellion. Colleagues who worked with him described him as an opinionated, outspoken person, perpetually involved in disputes. He was always very sensitive to criticism from others, and one friend felt that he had a "weak paranoia." Despite this, he had had a brilliant and vigorous career as a Jesuit missionary in China.

Originally torn between the French and German cultural influences present in the border area in which he grew up, he found a new cultural home in China: he participated energetically in Chinese life, he learned a great deal about the civilization, and translated many religious works into Chinese. His identification with his mission-land was so strong that he had, during the course of his work, taken out Chinese citizenship; a tradition had been established for this by earlier missionaries, but it was nonetheless a highly unusual step. Later, under the Communists, he had favored the acceptance of the government-sponsored independent church movement, and refrained from joining it only because of orders from his religious superiors.

His colleagues believed that much of his behavior in prison was influenced by his overwhelming desire to remain in China as a missionary. They also cited as another very important influence something that had happened shortly before Benét was arrested. Two Chinese brothers whom Benét knew well were imprisoned by the Communists: one of them "confessed" and was released; the other refused to confess and was shot. This was believed to be crucial in his later conviction that "confession is the only way out." In addition, he had, early in his own imprisonment, experienced what a colleague referred to as "a near-complete breakdown"; and one of his Western cellmates attributed his later behavior to "enormous fear." He also developed the concept that it was necessary to degrade oneself "to convince the Communists that you are with them—and not in grace in the bourgeois world—so that the Communists would feel that you were so degraded in the bourgeois world that you could not go back."

Even in prison he had moments which paralleled the brilliance of his missionary career, and evoked admiration from his Western cellmates. "He was so sparkling. . . . he had a strongly French personality—flexible, elastic, extremely 'intellectual' in a formal way . . . like Voltaire." And there was a certain amount of awe even in their criticisms of him. "He had a satanic, biting humor . . . with his sharp intellect he could criticize everyone, even God." But his prestige and his power within the group soon declined. His penchant for, even joy in, self-humiliation caused the other Westerners to lose respect for him. Further, his extremism led to distrust, both among Westerners and Chinese. It was felt that he was "too convincing"—or, in other words, easily seen through as insincere. Other Westerners referred to him as "the foxy philosopher"; Chinese prisoners called him "the fox." Although he was technically their study leader for more than a year, his influence on the Europeans gradually waned during the last half of this period, and by mutual unspoken consent Benét began to study more and more with the Chinese prisoners. When he was transferred from the cell, after fifteen months with the European group, he was an isolated, bitter, and defeated man:

At the end he didn't want to be with our group, only wanted to study with the Chinese, and went one hundred per cent the Chinese way. . . . When he left he was down and out, fed up with everything, and especially with us—because we wouldn't follow him.

Phase of Adaptation

Father Vechten, the Dutch priest who was the last of the six to join the group, entered the cell while Benét was still in charge. Since he too could speak, read, and write Chinese, the other Europeans began to turn to him as an intermediary between themselves and the officials or their Chinese cellmates. Father Vechten, both in his translations, and in his general approach, was a much more moderate and reliable guide than Benét. Their willingness to be influenced by him undoubtedly was an important factor in the authorities' later decision to make him the official "study leader."

But even before this, other changes from above helped to create an atmosphere in which he could assume informal leadership. Although pressures were still very strong, the extreme struggle atmosphere which had prevailed during Benét's first few months in the cell had gone. The acute assaults required to "raise" the group's political level had given way to longer-term demands for the consolidation of what had been accomplished, and the grinding out of further, day-to-day "progress." The vindictive cell chief was replaced by a conscientious but somewhat less zealous person. And during this period, also, the group benefited from the generally moderating effects of the policy change in the Chinese penal system already referred to in Chapter 4. The extreme exhortation, the one-sided atmosphere, the hysteria of the mass campaigns, the unrelenting criticism were all still very much there. But the Westerners were permitted to settle in, and to experience their reform as a more evolutionary, and less explosive procedure.

What influence did Father Vechten have on the Western group? His personal qualities were in many ways the direct antitheses of those of the man he replaced: a steady intelligence without brilliance, a circumspect and cautious approach, a capacity to instill profound trust in others. Further, he set a high example of personal courage and self-sacrifice, and always backed up his professed principles with his personal actions.

Before he could begin to make his influence felt, however, he had to be personally broken in, initiated into the group pattern through the "raising" of his own personal level of reform to that of the others. (Although he had been through rather severe confession pressures during his previous months of imprisonment, he had not yet experienced a sustained re-education program.) During his first few weeks in the cell, therefore, he was severely struggled, largely about issues dealing with the relationship of church activities to "imperialism."

Nor was his first response to the group completely auspicious. At one point, when he was being treated in a way he considered extremely unjust, he burst into tears in a manner described by a cellmate as "crying with fury." He had already won the sympathy of the other Westerners, but they were "surprised and shocked" at his lack of control. He weathered this episode, greatly helped by the other Europeans; at the same time they persuaded him that he had to make some concessions in order to get along.

For a while he was quite uncomfortable about making these concessions, and disturbed by the confusion in the group under Benét's leadership. But once he became convinced that the other Westerners genuinely wished to assist him, and that there was a possibility of a co-operative group approach, he became increasingly willing to compromise and fall into step. Interestingly enough, it was Bauer's "good fellowship"—despite definite points of conflict between the two men—which did most to persuade Vechten. Once he had achieved some harmony with the group, Vechten's authority was quickly established.

For a brief period, there was a certain amount of infighting among the Westerners, a conflict among them over policy, and an inner struggle for control of the group. Bauer and Kallmann were resisting Benét's authority, which was declining; Vechten agreed more with them than with Benét, and his own leadership developed aided by their support.

Out of the confusion came a definite group policy which replaced chaos with a fair measure of stability. The approach was not completely new, nor the exclusive idea of any one man; but it was Vechten, strongly influenced by Bauer, who did more than anyone else to develop it. The policy consisted of a form of acting —or "window dressing"—in which the Westerners made "big self-accusations backed up by small facts": one would accuse himself, for instance, of being "reactionary" and "backward," because of taking too much time in going to the bathroom.

Even more important, this tactic involved continual emphasis upon "playing the game" rather than losing oneself completely in the reform process. Vechten, for example, might criticize another Westerner harshly, but at the same time he would attempt to get across to him some indication that he was merely going through the necessary motions. This could not usually be done overtly, but semantic tricks were exploited by the Westerners to create a communication system which their Chinese cellmates could not penetrate. They sometimes spoke in French or German; when this was prohibited, they interjected single words or concepts from European languages. They also developed special pronunciations to which they ascribed their own connotations. For instance, they distinguished between *people* in the ordinary meaning and the Communist mystique of "the people," by using an ordinary English pronunciation for the first meaning, and a mock French pronunciation—*pee-púl*—for the second. Similarly, "horse language" became a euphemism for German, and when Vechten would advise some of the others not to use the "horse language," they would know that he meant it "as a friend and not really from the side of the government." Vechten maintained at all times the conviction that "you must conserve your higher values in confession. . . . not let them bring you down."

This new approach was essentially a compromise between the two earlier ones. In its stress upon preservation of individual dignity, it resembled Bauer's method during phase one; but it entailed much more concession to and individual participation in the reform program. In its insistence upon a strongly "progressive" display, it resembled Benét's approach of phase two; but its crucial difference was the distinction it made between public gestures made to placate the government and the private world of resistance maintained among the Europeans.

The policy was logical enough. The difficulty lay in carrying it out. The group not only had to satisfy Chinese officials and cell-mates, it also had to sustain courage and cohesion among the group members. And it was here that Vechten's special genius emerged. He demonstrated an extraordinary capacity to deflate hostilities, dissolve conflicts, and preserve group unity. He invariably accomplished this through a human appeal to the contending or disruptive parties, and always sought to mediate and find something which he could personally share with each of them. Even his replacement of Benét as the actual leader of the group was accomplished with surprisingly little hostility. He approached Benét sympathetically, and made an effort to avoid animosity despite their differences of policy; and at the same time he adopted, as a personal principle, Benét's concept that it was the duty of a Catholic priest to assist others in so stressful a situation. To the other Westerners, he emphasized Benét's personal sacrifices, and defended him in the face of their sharp criticisms. When Benét finally left the group, Vechten was on closer terms with him than was any other Westerner.

In a similar fashion, when Bauer's Nazi and racist views led to friction—Vechten himself had strong inner resentments on this matter since he had lived through the Nazi occupation of Holland, and also identified closely with the Chinese people—he appealed to Bauer's "corps spirit"; he would mention their personal bond—Bauer's mother came from an area close to Vechten's birthplace. In the continuous conflict between Weber and the others in the group, he was a continuous mediator. He sympathized with Weber because of common features in their background, and because both had "rough and good-hearted" characters. He viewed Weber as a man who, because of personal limitations, particularly needed help to get through the experience; and he emphasized this need to the others while at the same time using his influence with Weber to get him to submit to group discipline. With Kallmann, he found common ground in their religious feelings, despite the fact that Kallmann was a Protestant; he also discussed with him what was closest to Kallmann's heart—his wife and family. This sympathy helped Kallmann overcome many of his antagonisms, and also served to dispel occasional differences which arose between Kallmann and Vechten himself over policy and leadership. When Émile came into conflict with the group because of his intransigence,

Vechten appealed to him as a fellow priest, emphasizing the good he could do for others by co-operating.

Vechten's path was not always smooth, however, and he experienced his own personal difficulties. When he was caught between strong pressures from above, and resistance to his policies from below, he would sometimes have outbursts of anger, severe headaches, or tremors. He had moments when he felt that the game he was leading, with its concessions to the Communists, was "dirty," and from the standpoint of a priest, wrong. Therefore, when another European would resist his demands with the accusing statement, "And you a priest—" he became extremely upset. He was also tortured by the feeling that the others in the group did not really like him or fully trust him. But he did not allow these disruptive emotions to persist, and if he could not overcome them himself, he accepted the help of others in the group. Bauer knew best how to render personal assistance to Vechten—reassuring him of the admiration the others had for him, and gently warning him on one occasion that he was becoming too angry in his dealings with the others and that the sides of his mouth were beginning to turn downward. Bauer also took advantage of his medical standing to do something else for Vechten: he told an official that Vechten's headaches, if not checked, could develop into a mental breakdown, hoping thereby to ease the pressures on him and to speed up his release. Kallmann by this time was over his own crisis, and he became strong enough to lend moral support to Vechten and to the others. All saw Vechten's difficulties as understandable sensitivities for which he deserved their help. Everyone had become, to some extent, a therapist for everyone else.

In this way the group gradually evolved enough of an equilibrium among its individual members to function as an effective unit. It was a tenuous equilibrium which could be readily threatened; but a certain balance prevailed. Although no individual member was immune to attack, the group as a whole offered protection, solace, and amelioration. It prevented Bauer from being too bold, Kallmann from being too submissive, Vechten from demanding too many concessions. It listened to and prescribed for emotional problems from any source. When the balance seemed to be giving way in the face of internal conflicts, the group invariably found itself reunited by the immediate threat of new assaults from without. At the same time, the group was ever mindful of the danger that their inner dissension, if not checked, might be exploited by Chinese cellmates or by prison officials.

The group pattern and the double life of its members thus became a means of resistance. The group had reached its highest point of re-education under Benét, and this reform trend continued to some extent during the early months of Vechten's leadership; but after this, the equilibrium worked toward fending off—although by no means completely escaping—Communist influence.

An important aspect of the equilibrium was the relationship of the group to the Chinese prisoners who lived in the same cell. Here Vechten's influence was particularly important, as his affection for Chinese culture and Chinese people became quickly apparent. He was the most popular of the Westerners among the Chinese, and his personal integrity made a strong impression upon them. This compatibility was more than just a convenience; it played an extremely important part in the group's survival. Chinese prisoners tended to become (or at least appeared to become) more quickly and enthusiastically "progressive" than Westerners, and they were likely to express strong political and personal animosities toward Westerners. Much of this hostile feeling had prevailed with this group of Europeans, particularly during Benét's leadership. But Vechten's personal appeal, as well as the improved atmosphere within the Western group, brought about a gradual change in the situation; antagonism from Chinese cellmates gave way to a tolerant, sometimes even friendly, attitude. The Chinese were apparently impressed by much of the Westerners' behavior, and sometimes seemed to be attempting to imitate it themselves. Periodically, they still loosed torrents of criticism upon their European cellmates, but these were not necessarily hateful in tone, and they had a lot of performance in them. Even Bauer's attitude of superiority (which they were aware of, and which he frequently had to confess to) was absorbed. Later on, during the recreation periods afforded by more "lenient treatment," the Europeans found themselves teaching their Chinese cellmates various games, and even social dancing. The Western group had, so to speak, secured its flank; every bit of goodwill from its Chinese cellmates created some measure of insulation from reform pressures.

The qualities in Vechten which meant so much to this group

were not emerging for the first time. As a missionary, he had shown unusual ability and leadership. His special talents for bringing men together, for arbitrating between extremes, for pursuing a steady and moderate approach, had long been prominent. Yet it is interesting to note that from early life he had been subject to severe episodes of uncontrolled anger. As a child he experienced such severe temper tantrums when his will was frustrated that "I would turn red, then blue, and stop breathing, and my brother had to beat me to make me again conscious"; during early adolescence he suffered from almost daily headaches, caused mainly by inner hostility; as a young man he had outbursts of anger or tears. He had painfully conquered these tendencies, largely through his strong emotional bonds with the Catholic religion; and his skills as a moderator were in part the reflection of his highly-developed personal mechanisms of control. They were much more than this, however, because they depended upon an additional quality which was described by Bauer as "*echt*," a term by which he suggested purity and authenticity: "He is not an imitation. He doesn't pretend to be what he is not . . . he is one of the few people I have met in life who at least realizes what he is." What Bauer meant by this statement was Vechten's unusual integrity, his ability to live the life to which he claimed to aspire. At moments when Vechten felt himself overwhelmed by anger, guilt, and doubt, he would draw upon an unusual blend of the supernatural and the human: "Praying brings you back to the reality of what you are. Talking with the group of foreigners [Europeans], had a similar effect."

The full impact of Vechten's prison behavior can only be understood through the effect it had on his Western cellmates. His leadership, once assumed, was never questioned; his influence increased steadily over the two years he was in the cell, until the eventual breakup of the group through the sentencing and release of the Western prisoners. He was the only person among the Europeans whose stature completely overshadowed the complicated hostilities and weaknesses which thought reform engenders—the one most warmly and unreservedly praised by all of the others. Every one of them felt that it was his influence, more than anything else, that kept the group intact, which in turn preserved the values and stability of each of them. Kallmann perhaps summed up their feelings best:

He made the most impressive showing of all of us—human and spiritual. He never really lowered himself . . . he taught us how to do the necessary and still keep our own.

Epilogue

To what extent was the group successful? Did it really protect the psychological health and the private beliefs of its members? We can answer this by taking a brief look at each of the men immediately after his release.

The first of the six to arrive in Hong Kong was Father Benét. I was not able to interview him (either because of his resistance, or that of his Church colleagues, or both), but I was able to talk with several people very close to him. Benét claimed that his relatively early release proved that his policy had been the best one after all; but there was much question about this, since he was released simultaneously with a number of other French priests, apparently for political reasons. He had spent almost another year in a different cell after his transfer from the group. At some point, his attitude (or at least his tactics) dramatically changed: not only did he become a good deal less "progressive" himself, but he encouraged resistance in others; and a Westerner who had known him in both cells described him as "completely different." When he arrived in Hong Kong, his old friends felt that his prison experience had left him "not much changed"—still brilliantly outspoken and erratic as ever. They were struck, however, by his combination of bitter criticism of the Communists and his impression of their immense power, their near-invincibility. Unusually fearful during the post-release period, Benét had apparently undergone a great emotional upset rather than an ideological change. His form of totalism had carried him from his initial stance of the apparent convert to the opposite (and clearly related) category of the apparent resister. Yet like Bishop Barker and others in this latter category, his sharp condemnation of Communism was in part a defensive device for denying the profound reform influences he had clearly absorbed. I will say more about his peculiar form of leadership later on.

Dr. Bauer was the next to arrive; and since he had been considered the most reactionary, his belief that the date of a prisoner's release had little to do with the extent of his "progress" was confirmed. He was, as might be expected, the most adamant in his denunciation of the Communists, and the most personally removed from the Communist communication system. Although not without fear, he was very quick to regain sufficient composure and detachment to launch into a comprehensive analysis of Communist methods. More than any of the others, he emphasized the absolute effectiveness of the group—even to the point of idealization: "We played theatre with them day in and day out." When discussing the other group members, he spoke in a similar vein, stressing the "comradeship" of each, and carefully controlling his own hostilities wherever they existed—except in the case of his feelings toward Benét, which were admittedly bitter. He was an archetype of the apparent resister, and he exhibited clearly the oppositional attitudes, the totalism in his character, and the use of repression and denial to ward off reform influences. Yet he did impress me as being one of the least affected ideologically of all of my Western subjects. He had tenaciously held on to his alternative Nazi ideology (although disclaiming of course its excesses); but he emphasized even more his frank devotion to "bourgeois" family life, and always maintained a controlled charm and friendliness with me and with whomever he met in Hong Kong. His identity had stood firm.

Father Émile, whom I met next, was somewhat confused and agitated when he arrived, but he still managed to express himself with a good deal of gaiety and humor, as he had when in prison. He was critical of the Communists, but less interested in discussing ideological matters than in the sequence of his own experiences and their religious implications; he frequently mentioned St. Paul. He referred to the group sympathetically ("Foreigners tried to protect each other") but did not speak of it with especially strong emotion. He had spent just one year in the group, less time than most of the others, and had for the last few months of his imprisonment been permitted to perform technical work under much less intensive psychological pressure. His colleagues felt that he had greatly matured through his prison experience, that he had attained more self-mastery, and greater inner peace, and that he was not as "overly active" as they felt he had been before.

Mr. Kallmann emerged with a strong need to discuss his experiences in great detail as a means of conquering his remaining fear.

Sensitive to psychological currents, he spoke with a striking combination of insight and confusion. He stated that he had "studied hard," learned a great deal, and now wished to "continue his studies" through extensive readings in non-Communist political literature; he felt that he could never become an adherent of the Communist world, but had come to realize the grave shortcomings of the capitalist world. He spoke enthusiastically of his experiences in the group: "They were all marvelous comrades . . . we always felt we were mentally holding our own," although he also talked of the difficulties and the painful personal irritabilities. He remained Benét's staunchest defender. While he was certainly among the obviously confused, he believed that he had been protected from Communist indoctrination by the values he had absorbed from the German youth movement: "*Erlebnis* . . . the value in life of the natural experience . . . the sensation of the eternal beauty of what God creates." It was to this earlier ideology that he wished to return.

Mr. Weber too had signs of obvious confusion when I met him in Hong Kong. He felt that his condition had been greatly improved by a period of skilled manual labor in which he had participated after his transfer from the group. Vehemently critical of the Communists, he nonetheless had become convinced during his imprisonment that "evolutionary socialism rather than revolution" was desirable; and he also felt that the technique of self-criticism could be a useful personal device. Concerning the group and its function, he was more critical than any of the others, and emphasized the suffering it caused him and his relief at being separated from it. Yet in the next breath, he would unwittingly praise it, pointing out that "we foreigners used self-criticism in a fair way," in contrast to the cruel and "reckless manner of the Communists." Moreover, the behavior of Émile and Vechten had so deeply impressed him that he wished to return to his own active Catholic religious practice. He managed his mixed feelings about the group with outward good humor: "I guess we were all a bit crazy in there." On the whole, he wanted to leave his prison experience behind him and be "through with politics."

Father Vechten, even after his arrival in Hong Kong, remained the group's leader and guardian. Still speaking as if responsible for it, he gave the most thoughtful and comprehensive picture of its function. He was in fact remarkably balanced in all of his expressed opinions, and yet he too spoke of feeling confused about many issues. Rather than seeing himself as the hero which the others thought him to be, he was deeply troubled that "maybe I was too progressive." He seemed mildly depressed, torn by feelings of shame and guilt; and he minimized his own accomplishments at every turn. He did feel that the "corps spirit" of the group had been very helpful to everyone, including himself, and he recognized that he had been "better than the others" in holding the group together; but he also stated that "all of us could have very easily been enemies. . . . except for the fact that we all had a greater enemy." Deeply aware of the magnitude of individual antagonisms, he tended, if anything, to understate the group's accomplishments. He was critical of Communist theory and practice, and much concerned (like Father Luca) about the future of the Catholic Church in China. He felt that he had done his Church a great disservice in making certain confessions about religion. After a few weeks in Hong Kong, his psychological state seemed a bit improved, but he still stressed that he had much to think about in the future.

In assessing these men after their release, it was not easy to make an over-all judgment of the group's effectiveness. One thing is immediately clear: the experience meant something different to each of its members. For Bauer, the experience was a panacea, although his reaction must be judged in the light of a tendency to idealize many of his relationships as a way to control disruptive forces within himself; for Weber it was painful and humiliating, and yet even he derived emotional benefits from it; for Benét, the group exposure must have been deeply disillusioning; and for the remaining three men, it was, to varying degrees, a source of strength, despite its emotional pitfalls. Moreover, the man whom the others saw as the unifying spirit (Vechten) seemed much less enthusiastic about the group's effectiveness than at least two of the others (Bauer and Kallmann); and many of the very acts of leadership which the others thought heroic were to him shameful evidences of compromise.

I felt, when I interviewed these men in Hong Kong, that the group achievement had been a rather remarkable one. These six men had succeeded in creating a small world of partial independence within the larger threatening universe of the Communist prison. Their independence was never anything like complete, and at times it seemed about to disappear altogether; but its survival created vital alternatives within an otherwise saturated environment. The intellectual alternative—the standing critique of Communist theory —was impressive enough; but even more important was the emotional alternative—the construction through trust and co-operative resistance of a psychological "home" and "family" where each member could find support and spiritual replenishment, and thereby avoid complete dependence upon the offerings of reform. This amounted to the undermining of thought reform's communication network, an impediment to the milieu control which thought reform seeks always to maintain. These six men were not reformed within a closed system of Communist discourse: rather, by pooling their knowledge and the emotions of their individual backgrounds, they created a vital alternative to the Communist system. In the midst of penal thought reform pressures this was no mean accomplishment.

There is little doubt that the group did much to preserve the emotional well-being and the resistance to Communist influence of its individual members. It also, of course, to some extent served as a vehicle for conveying Communist influence to those within it; but it is probably fair to say that, without the group, this influence would have been at least as great and a good deal more painful.

The results of this group achievement were evident in the condition of the five men I interviewed after release. They showed symptoms and attitudes in many ways typical of all of my subjects, but they were quicker than others to overcome confusion and fear and to begin to reconstruct a sense of identity in the non-Communist environment. As far as indoctrination was concerned, I felt that these men had emerged slightly less affected than my average subject. Their distribution among the response categories was not unusual (four obviously confused, one apparent resister, and one apparent convert turned apparent resister); but they were unusual in their capacities to weigh their reform experience not only against what they found in the non-Communist world, but also against the alternative group ethos they had known during their imprisonment.

These judgments were, of course, tenuous. So many factors affected the way in which a man emerged that it was very difficult, in comparing these people with other subjects, to evaluate the part which the group had played. And I had to keep in mind the fact that this group contained two men who had made serious suicidal attempts, the only ones among my twenty-five subjects. Indeed, in the followup studies I made three years later (see Chapter 10), I encountered a number of surprises, including severe emotional difficulties which I had not been able to predict. I concluded then that the group had supplied a good deal of spiritual nourishment and protection during the imprisonment itself, but that this protection could not last sufficiently to avoid profound problems later on. Nonetheless, the psychological and biological strengths which an intimate group structure can evoke were convincingly demonstrated.

Styles of Leadership

What did the history of this group reveal about the relationship among leader, milieu demands, and group behavior? The exaggerated and bizarre quality of the group experience throws into sharp relief principles which are equally operative, if less apparent, in everyday situations.

Three men became official or unofficial leaders of this group of Westerners during the course of its existence, and yet none was the leader during his entire stay with the group. Each of the three men developed a style of leadership which became characteristic for the particular phase which he dominated. What characterized each style, and what produced it?

The first, Bauer's hegemony during the academic phase, was characterized by intellectual leadership and avoidance of participation. The combination which produced this style was: first, a lax milieu, which said, in effect, as long as you keep studying and *seem* to be reforming, you will not be bothered; second, a previously demoralized group of three Westerners ready to respond to any show of strength; and third, the sudden appearance of a confident and emotionally intact European (Bauer) psychologically suited to exert strong influence over others. Bauer's intellectual skills were especially useful at a time when independent study and speculation were allowed; his authoritarian emotional traits served well during a period when maximum self-assertion and resistance were permitted; his human skills (which were considerable) were especially geared to foster individual strength rather than a spirit of compromise in others, which is just what is needed when resistance is possible.

The style of academic resistance which developed had something to offer to everyone: to the officials and the cell chief directing the outer environment, a studious display and a certain amount of reform; to the other Westerners, protection, clear policy, and spellbinding intellectual excursions; to Bauer himself, a means of remaining emotionally intact and avoiding anxiety by guiding and dominating others, as well as egocentric satisfactions derived by the exercise of his superior intellect. This style of leadership was thus nourishing to all of the Westerners, although perhaps most so to Bauer himself; others in the group (especially Kallmann and Weber) had more of a need to submit, and indeed were sometimes at odds with Bauer even during this harmonious time. From the standpoint of group independence, this was the most successful of the three styles of leadership. It was also the easiest of the three to maintain.

The second style (Benét's) involved histrionic exhortation and the splitting of identity. The circumstances were very different: the group had not chosen an unofficial leader, but rather had had an official one thrust upon it. And the style of leadership, although predominant, was never fully accepted by the other group members. In terms of the three factors we have been discussing: the environment had suddenly clamped down—no more of this foolery, we mean business, and you had better reform yourselves or else; the four Westerners, who by this time had learned the ropes, were ready to make concessions where necessary, but were still riding a small private wave of resistance; and a newcomer, Benét, appeared who was a strange blend of fear, brilliance, exhibitionism, and sadomasochism. Benét behaved as he did partly because he believed that extreme progressivism was necessary, and partly because he was so frightened—primarily because the combination of self-flagellating submissiveness and arrogant, pain-inflicting domination of others was his own long-standing mechanism for dealing with anxiety. Yet this mechanism was especially appropriate for the position into which Benét was thrust: any new study leader under these same circumstances would have had to take a good deal of punishment from the officials and cell chief above, and deal in some mutually painful manner with the recalcitrant Westerners below.

As with Bauer's, Benét's leadership offered some service to everyone involved: the officials got their whipping boy, who at the same time effectively conveyed their pressures to the group; Benét himself derived an emotional satisfaction from the pain-and-punishment pattern; and the other Westerners, through Benét's own absorption of punishment, were afforded some degree of protection from the renewed assaults. But such histrionic and chaotic leadership could not be expected to last, and Benét's style soon became universally disturbing: the officials could not trust such an exaggerated performance, especially when they noted his declining influence upon his fellow Europeans; the other Westerners were made hostile and antagonistic to Benét and to each other by the loss of their group independence and solidarity, and—worst of all—by the loss of the capacity to test emotional and intellectual realities; Benét himself began to break down under the strain. All of the Westerners, including Benét, were pressured toward a disintegration of identity and a strong sense of guilt.

On the whole, Benét's style also was more compatible with his own emotional needs than with those of the led. Benét, the "marvelous actor," was able to take a histrionic plunge and still land mostly on his feet, as his later attitudes suggest. But the other Westerners, who lacked this talent, could never trust him sufficiently to be certain that he was truly identified with them in their struggle to preserve values and group cohesion, rather than with his captors' demands for confession and reform. Under these conditions, one can play no "game": the whole thing becomes "real," and personal accusations are a true threat to one's sense of self.

Were these circumstances created by the demanding outer milieu, or by Benét's special character traits? We can only say that the small group became a captive audience for both.

The third style of leadership may be termed flexible adaptation and preservation of identity. This was undoubtedly the most remarkable phase of the group's existence. Still subjected to extremely disruptive pressures, its members somehow managed to achieve a restoration of trust. How did this come about?

An emotional demand for a change in style came from all three directions. The group of Westerners' urge for survival made them cast about for some alternative to the painful confusion of Benét's leadership; the environment slightly toned down its assaults in order to pursue its reform process on a more even keel; and a potential replacement for Benét appeared, a man of unusual humility and integrity—a man who also had the necessary knowledge of Chinese. Vechten brought to his leadership an emphasis upon moderation because this had always been his emphasis; he brought the men together skilfully, emphasizing what they shared, and activating the best in each of them because this had long been his method of dealing with conflict—conflict among others and within himself. His was the gift of the creative man: the capacity to make use of inner struggles to evolve a new form which can both express personal emotions and strike deep chords of feeling in others. In human relations, he was a true artist; and like any artist, his own wellbeing depended upon his continuous creativity. He was inwardly impelled as well as outwardly encouraged to take an active role in guiding the fortunes of the group: his own self-control and his sense of clerical identity demanded it.

Again there were satisfactions to be derived from his leadership for all three elements, but this time, in contrast to the previous two stages, there were more satisfactions for the other Westerners than for either the officials or for the leader himself. The resuscitated Europeans had their group independence restored, and found a means of mutual emotional support. The officials seem to have benefited the least, although from their standpoint, Vechten was still an active enough reformer.

For Vechten himself, the benefits of his leadership were most contradictory. He did derive the satisfaction of doing, and doing well, what inner needs and outer demands required of him. His talent for moderation, however, conflicted with the more immoderate (and totalistic) ideal of martyrdom against which every Catholic priest, when under extreme duress, must in some degree measure himself—a self-judgment likely to be particularly severe in a man for whom complete integrity is essential. In a study leader this conflict is especially intense, because of the continuous compromises he must make. Further, Vechten's give-and-take approach could not permit him to be conveniently absolute in his judgments (in the manner of Bauer or Benét), but rather required him to question continuously his own ideas and to weigh them against the points of view of the others. Finally, the style of deception which he and the other Westerners worked out was more complicated than either the academic iconoclasm of Bauer or the all-or-none submersion of Benét. It is no surprise that under these circumstances, earlier problems of feeling unloved, inferior, and overwhelmed by his own anger once more emerged. And any problem for Vechten immediately became a problem for the entire group, which had, after all, never rid itself of its antagonisms. Vechten's preservation of autonomy, both of the group and of the individual, under conditions such as these was one of the most unusual human achievements I met with during the course of this study.

In evaluating these three patterns of leadership (and I have made them, for purposes of clarity, perhaps a bit more sharply defined than they really were), I have tried to make it clear that neither the milieu, the leader, nor the led were solely responsible for producing a particular style of behavior. Rather, each phase is an example of the principle (as valid for psychology as for physics and medicine) of multiple causation. It would be wrong to say, for instance, that Vechten's emergence as a leader was entirely due to his character traits, although it is probable that, because of his outstanding qualities, he would become a leader of most groups in most situations. The point is that he was a particularly appropriate leader of *this* group at *this* time. It may well be that Bauer's intellectual attainments would have kept him the leader, even if Vechten had been present, during the lax early phase, and that Benét's "progressive" histrionics would have made him the most likely leader during the time when political levels had to be "raised." Also, leadership styles may vary in the same man. Had Bauer experienced stronger personal pressures before he came into the group, his leadership could have been a good deal less firm; had Benét been less fearful, his leadership might have been less extreme. Leadership leaves a good deal of room for heroism; but this heroism is intimately related to the peculiar demands which prevail in a particular environment at a given time.

This group experience also suggests that we re-examine and expand our concepts (and stereotypes) of "The Leader." [2] Father Vechten's impressive performance demonstrates the leadership potential of the man who can mediate with integrity, who can set an example which helps other men retain their identity and adapt with dignity. It may be that during our age of ideological excess, it is he, rather than his more flamboyant and charismatic counterpart, who is needed.

CHAPTER 10

FOLLOW-UP VISITS

What happened to these twenty-five people in the years after their thought reform experiences? When I saw most of them in Hong Kong, they were in what was clearly a transitional state, a brief period of stocktaking before their return to a permanent, non-Communist, Western way of life. I felt then that many were about to meet emotional challenges almost as difficult as those they had just faced. Some of these psychological problems were inherent in their strong sense of guilt and shame, and in conflicts over where they stood in relationship to their professions, to their sacred personal commitments, and to themselves. Of course I could not predict exactly what was in store for them; I was, however, very much interested in finding out. And my efforts were further stimulated by comments of colleagues and friends: "What you say about thought reform is all very well—but what about the long-term effects? Do these people undergo a new course of 'brainwashing' in the environment to which they return?"

I kept in touch with many of my subjects by mail: some wrote to me on their own, wishing to continue our relationship, and others responded to a follow-up questionnaire which I sent out when I returned to America. But my real opportunity for learning about the residual effects of thought reform came during the summer of 1958, when I was scheduled to spend two months in Japan in connection with another psychiatric study. I decided to go by way of

Europe in order to revisit some of my subjects in their Western settings; and I also arranged to meet one of them in South Asia where he had returned to do missionary work.

I was able to obtain information about twenty-one of my twenty-five subjects. I especially sought personal interviews with those people with whom I had worked intensively in Hong Kong; and in meeting them once more, I was struck by how different they looked to me, as well as by the strange combinations of emotions which they expressed. I felt they had personally served as battlegrounds for the conflicting ideologies of our time, and had been victims of the many kinds of alienation peculiar to the twentieth century.

I will start with the members of the Western group, and then return to the others who were discussed in earlier chapters.

Father Vechten

Father Vechten wrote to me several times in the four years between our meetings. Still the group's central figure, he kept in touch with all the others, and sent me some of their latest addresses. He had also informed me of a tragic motorbike accident in which he nearly lost his life three weeks after his arrival in Holland. From his hospital bed, he had written of his feeling of shame "for my moral, human, mental, ideological defects which I have suffered in prison. . . . For having been weak, without principle, even harming others in co-operating with Communism." And he described his great longing for the chance to "continue my mission-work among the Chinese."

When we were seated across a table in his austere room, in his small seminary in the Dutch farmlands, I was struck by the remoteness and quiet of his new environment, so different from the sense of urgency and involvement which had existed during our interviews in Hong Kong. Father Vechten had to some extent blended with this milieu: as he talked of such things as "moral faults" (while puffing on a large cigar), he seemed more the returned Dutch priest than the "Chinese" missionary and group leader I had known in Hong Kong. But it was not long before he began to express the more profound emotions he had experienced since his return; and as he described those first few weeks, the events seemed to follow with the psychological inevitability of Greek tragedy.

Vechten had stopped briefly in Rome on his way home. It was a visit of the deepest significance for him, at once magnifying his pain, symbolizing his complete return to the embrace of the Church, and accelerating his new changes in attitude.

When I arrived in Rome, things became more urgent for me. . . . When I entered St. Peter's, I shed tears just before the chair of Peter. I had suffered. I was much impressed. . . . My way of thinking and judging became more that which I had formerly.

In Rome he made a detailed confession in which he told of all he had said and done in prison which could be considered against the Church's interests. He told his confessor of his embarrassment at being considered a hero, and asked whether he was required to tell others of the extent of his co-operation and "weakness"; he was relieved by the confessor's reassurance that he was not obliged to talk about shortcomings, and should feel "no need to humiliate yourself."

Arriving in Holland he felt "rather serene" because "there was no more feeling that I had not made things right." He was, however, struck by the contrast between his own and others' views of his prison experiences:

When I was asked to speak on the radio, I did not know what to say. The superior asked me: "Were you always in a cell?" I said, "Sure, for one-and-one-half years I was not out of the cell." He considered this terrible, so I told it over the radio. I hadn't realized it was so bad. I considered it normal. People were astonished and I was astonished that the people were astonished.

The warmth of the greetings which he received from family, fellow priests, and villagers affected him greatly: "Contact with people . . . with love for each other . . . who admired and didn't ask about faults . . . was of great importance. . . . If I had not been so well received, I should have been a broken man and useless in society."

But he was nonetheless troubled by recurrent anxiety dreams, in one of which he was in a Chinese Communist prison for a second time, again preoccupied with "trying to escape from difficulties for myself and for the group." In this dream he also asked himself,

"Why have you been so foolish as to go back to China?" In his waking life, too, he experienced a similar fear, so that when he requested he be returned to a Chinese area, he also asked that he be permitted to leave before any Communist occupation, should this occur: "I thought, 'Never a second time'."

And his sense of shame and guilt could not be stilled. He kept thinking that if he had been physically tortured, as some other priests had, his concessions might have been justified. "But I had not been tortured. Why have I come to such deeds?" During this early period, it was almost impossible for him to talk about his prison experiences. He did, on one occasion, tell a colleague a few of the things he confessed; but when the latter gave evidence of surprise, Vechten felt deeply upset. On the other hand, he condemned himself for holding back this information: "I thought to myself that it was a lack of humility, because you don't like other people to consider you so weak." He could find no relief from his suffering, despite considerate, and often psychologically sensitive attitudes on the part of his fellow-priests.

Nor could he permit himself to rest as others suggested that he do; he felt almost immediately an urge to be active. "I had one strong idea; I had lost three years of working time, and I had to make up for it, to work more and be as busy as possible." In response to invitations, he preached and lectured repeatedly, less about his imprisonment than about Catholic activities in China.

He also, soon after his return, became fascinated with the new motorbikes, never having seen this type before. He immediately decided to buy one, despite warnings from family and friends who —possibly sensing his agitation and his adjustment difficulties— told him that it might be dangerous for him to ride one. These warnings had little effect upon him because of his sense of invulnerability ("I felt that nothing could happen to me"), and his conviction that, with increased mobility, "I would be free."

He decided to use his new motorbike to travel part of the way to a nearby conference of Catholic missionaries who had been recently released from Chinese prisons. The conference was emotionally loaded for him: he was pleased at being invited by a group of distinguished colleagues, but apprehensive about meeting one of them who had been together with him in a cell for a brief period during which time Vechten had exerted a slightly "progressive" influence. When he was returning a few days later, he started to turn off on a back road not far from his home, only to find that the road had been closed during his absence. As he crossed the main highway to reroute himself, he was struck from behind by a car, and suffered severe head and leg injuries; he spent the next two years in hospitals, undergoing a long series of difficult operations. It was significant that he was told by others (he did not remember himself) that in a semiconscious state soon after the accident he answered a policeman's questions in a manner which placed all the blame upon himself.

Despite his concern with his physical state, he told me that he "enjoyed" his hospital experience. Not only was it a relief from his immediate struggles, but it seemed to answer a deep longing:

Sometimes when I was in prison I thought, "Some day you will come back to Holland, to a clean bed, and people will take care of you." In the hospital it happened exactly as I had imagined.

This period of hospitalization also served as a useful interlude during which he was able to prepare himself for life in the Western world. "In the beginning I said that I never will succeed in adapting myself to Holland as it is now. . . . But in the hospital I began to understand the Dutch way of thinking, to read and study. . . . It did me a lot of good to have a long rest in the hospital."

I was convinced that Vechten's emotional conflicts had played a very important role in bringing about his accident. His experience in Rome had symbolized a return to a more "pure" Catholic identity; it had also intensified his sense of guilt and shame about his prison behavior, guilt and shame which not even his religious confession could erase. Physical torture in prison might have offered inner justification, as well as more concrete punishment, for his compromises; his accident supplied the punishment which he unconsciously sought. It also satisfied his strong desire to lie back and be cared for, a passive longing which reflected the human tendency to regress to earlier forms of emotional satisfaction when under great duress. In addition, the accident fulfilled his need to withdraw from his outer environment—now inappropriately viewed as accusatory—in order to come to better terms with his inner self. His exaggerated activity had been largely a form of compensation, an unsuccessful attempt to master the situation through external action rather than introspection, and—as it turned out—a round-about route to the more passive goal.[1] Caught between painful and unresolved conflicts in both his prison and his Catholic identities, he found his solution through a third and more transitional identity, that of the hospital patient.

Father Vechten later recognized that his injuries had served as a substitute expression for a psychological condition and that his hospitalization offered him an opportunity for psychological recovery.

It benefited me very much in a spiritual sense. . . . Other people told me that before I had looked so wild, so restless. Afterwards in the hospital, little by little, I became normal once more. . . . If I didn't have the accident, something else would have happened—perhaps a mental breakdown.

He become "normal" by bringing into the open and coming to better terms with his feelings about thought reform and about China; these problems were, for Father Vechten, unusually compelling.

Indeed, he began to unburden himself (once more he could not remember having done so) when still in a semiconscious state: "After the accident, they could not speak to me about anything but China, the nurses told me." A few months later, he discussed with a senior Church official his feeling that his behavior had not been justified because he had not been physically tortured; and he was much relieved by his colleague's reassurance that those who had been so tortured had been in a situation no more difficult than his, and that he had been no less brave than they. Vechten considered these words a turning point in his recovery. They had the effect of a valid and reassuring psychotherapeutic interpretation, made at a time when the patient is ready to receive it. After that Vechten felt encouraged to talk more about his experiences, and he also read everything he could find on the general subject of brainwashing or thought reform: "It was the one subject which could captivate my imagination." He has since continued these explorations: "I am always looking to find an explanation, especially one which could give me more assurance." Gradually, after leaving the hospital, he began to write and speak about his own experiences, and to formulate his own analysis of the process. In the continuing struggle for mastery, he had gained much ground.

His difficulties over being separated from China were greatly eased by a professional assignment which involved translating Chinese documents. Moreover, during his hospital stay, he was able to discuss China to his heart's content with other patients and staff members—while at the same time absorbing, in small and relatively painless doses, the Dutch Catholic environment from which he was protectively shielded by the hospital itself. Nor had he severed his ties with China even after he left the hospital. He still made an effort to meet with other China missionaries; they would sometimes speak in Chinese and call each other by their Chinese names. And in talking to ordinary colleagues, he found it necessary to check himself constantly to avoid "always talking about China." Despite his fear of again falling into Communist hands, he was still trying to arrange to return to a Chinese cultural area to work. He had by no means cast off his "Chinese" self, but he had come to better terms with it. "There remains my great love for China and all that is Chinese; but now I should be able to accustom myself to the Dutch way too."

During the years after his release, Vechten's ideological position regarding Communism hardened:

Before being in prison I was much opposed to the Communists because I regarded them as enemies of religion. . . . Now my opposition is greater and I hate them because they are opposed to humanity. . . . I see now the enormous danger to the human person to be under Communism—more even than just its opposition to religion.

He had also become more critical of socialist movements in his own country which favored more government controls. He advocated the "co-operative" form of social welfare described in official Catholic sociology as an alternative to the Communist class struggle. In all expressions of political opinion, he combined these personal and official approaches.

Toward the end of my two-day visit with Vechten, we discussed some of the long-range effects of thought reform upon his personal character. He described an "increased guilt consciousness" which included not only a highly critical attitude toward himself, but an insistence that others maintain it toward themselves as well. When a colleague, for instance, during a game of table tennis placed the blame for a bad shot on the racket, Vechten replied—whimsically but meaningfully—"You don't recognize your own faults. You should be put in prison in China and then you would be taught what is really your fault and what is due to other things." He was defending by this remark the general importance of personal guilt and responsibility; and yet it was significant that he chose to use thought reform as a specific (and affirmative) example. Even among priests, he was considered "too guilt-conscious."

As I have already noted, Vechten's tendency toward guilt did not originate with thought reform. In discussing it, he recalled that between the ages of eighteen and twenty-two he had been preoccupied with avoiding sin, and with a fear that he was, as much as he tried, not telling all during confession. He retained a similar attitude toward revealing in full detail his prison "sins"; he was more aware of consciously holding back, but he always felt guilty about doing so. He also gave a classical description of his sense of shame: "I am ashamed I could not be as strong as others supposed I should be." But like many such descriptions, it was incomplete: he suffered not so much from failing to live up to others' standards as from having internalized these standards (however unrealizable), so that he became his own worst critic in matters of shame as well as of guilt.

He felt, however, that both the shame and guilt were becoming attenuated because of his gradual acquisition of the distance from, understanding of, and perspective on the thought reform process which he had so lacked when he had arrived in Europe: "These feelings are diminishing a lot, because I can better see the whole impact of brainwashing. I can explain now why, with my full consent, I have come to such things as I now consider not good." He emphasized that my talks with him in Hong Kong had been of some help; and at that time I did have the impression that he was beginning to come to grips with his prison experiences. His subsequent difficulties, however, suggest that he had actually been a long way from any genuine insight; and his experience confirmed the psychiatric truism that insight is not a thing of the moment, but is rather a continuous and repetitious form of inner recognition which is always contested by antagonistic emotions.

Apart from this "increased guilt-consciousness," about whose value Father Vechten had mixed feelings, he described a series of more indirect effects which were more clearly positive. He said that he had become "more optimistic about people" because of observing other prisoners' impressive behavior. He felt more confident about meeting people of higher standing, and less apt to believe himself unworthy of their presence. He had retained the "Chinese way" of avoiding direct refusal, preferring to say "Yes, I will" to requests for his services even when he knew he would not be able to do what was asked. He felt "more able to make jokes about things that are difficult"—about his return to "normality" after the prison experience, about the results of his accident, about future problems; and he found himself advising his students to face their difficulties with a sense of humor. Without attempting to speculate extensively about the meaning of all of these effects, we can summarize them as: 1) an intensification of old traits: susceptibility to guilt and shame, and a strong conciliatory tendency, now with a Chinese flavor; and 2) a general expansion of his emotional horizons, leading to an increased receptivity to his own feelings and those of others. Father Vechten had spent four years overcoming an inappropriate sense of defeat; the problem was still with him, but he was making psychological use of it to emerge as a more developed human being.

I have described Father Vechten's experiences in some detail because they shed light not only on his personal struggle, but on the general psychological patterns typical of most Western subjects. Before summarizing these patterns (see Chapter 12), I will first discuss briefly the other group members. Of those I had met in Hong Kong, two (Kallmann and Émile) were available for follow-up visits. The other two were geographically inaccessible to me, but I was able to learn something about them, and about Benét, from the three group members I did interview, as well as from correspondence.

The Kallmanns

When I met Mr. Kallmann in his modest but attractive apartment in a small West German city, he presented many-sided views of the world and of himself. He had followed through in the intention he had expressed in Hong Kong, and had returned to the ideals of his youth. Condemning the postwar tendency "not to believe in anything," he sought out many old friends from his youth movement days, and not only tried to maintain close relations with them, but also established with them a youth group for their children. This gave him some satisfaction, but it did not produce the ideological absorption for which he had hoped.

He was, in fact, caught up in the very pattern which he complained about. Rather than believing in "nothing," he believed in, and felt some part of himself to be, practically *everything*—which is almost the same thing. He alternated between being an outspoken critic of Communism, who found the Communist world "just utterly unacceptable. . . . beyond human dignity" and who became angry when visiting dignitaries "naively" accepted Communist propaganda during trips to China; an explainer and to some extent a justifier of Chinese Communism—he wrote me, "In spite of my very adverse experiences, I take a positive view towards the things in China," and when I saw him he emphasized the regime's accomplishments and his willingness to "give credit" and extend himself to be fair in his judgments; a moderator between East and West, who stressed his love for the Chinese people and imagined the possibility of being invited to China by Mao Tse-tung to help bring together the opposing camps; an "Old China Hand," who remembered his life in the Far East fondly, and who set his expert personal knowledge against the ignorance of those who had not been there; a German bourgeois merchant, struggling to re-establish his business and deeply concerned with the welfare of his family; a nostalgic Nazi, who quoted the opinion of friends that the movement "could have succeeded"—he had himself been a Nazi when in China, and although he was very critical of many of its features, he nonetheless felt it had been a "genuine people's movement"; and a new believer in democracy, who had read a number of books on the subject, favored his country's postwar democratic methods, and tried diligently to indoctrinate his family with the principles of freedom and responsibility which he considered to be the basis of democracy.

He maintained an extremely active interest in China, Chinese Communism, and thought reform; and he lectured, wrote, and sought out prominent people he wished to influence with his views.

In attempting to achieve what he termed "*résonance*" with his audiences, he was reversing the thought reform situation (*he* was now exerting the influence) as well as expressing his desire for human intimacy.

Although he emphasized to me the depth of his suffering under thought reform, he had tried to adopt one of its main features—a planned program of criticism and self-criticism—within his own family. He claimed he was using it to instill democracy, and his slogan was "The Democratic Family." He had organized family gatherings at which children and parents were to criticize themselves and each other, but this program was something less than a glowing success. His young children, ignorant of adult techniques for playing the game, at first frankly confessed their sins: one would reveal that he had been bad at school, while another would admit that he had stayed on the toilet a particularly long time in order to avoid the chore of drying dishes. They soon caught on, however, and began to find themselves having "too much homework" whenever the time for the evening sessions arrived. Nor did they welcome the opportunity to criticize their parents; they made it clear that equality was not what they wanted, and that they preferred their mother and father to take over. Kallmann himself began to see the program's limitation: "It was as if I had lined them up and had them all undressed." He had not given up the idea entirely, but he had come to the conclusion that "even children want to have some sphere of privacy."

Kallmann's path was not easy. He tried to look upon thought reform as "something that has passed," but he found that the experience had left him "more sensitive" in many ways. Since his return, he had experienced phobic symptoms (fear of policemen, of crowds, of large cities), periods of profound anxiety sometimes related to family and business problems, rather severe physical illness, and episodes of moderate depression. These had diminished; but he did mention that he would still at times feel envious of those who, through death, no longer had to face the struggles of existence. Some (and perhaps all) of these symptom patterns had been present during crises in his life prior to imprisonment. I felt that he was having great difficulty establishing a new sense of identity after having hit rock bottom during his reform. He was genuinely pursuing the ideological ideal of democracy which he had adopted; yet the extreme diffusion of his multiple identities made it difficult for him to develop a coherent pattern, whether of self or of belief. While he denied conscious feelings of guilt, he had clearly been unable to divest himself of thought reform's humiliation, and of the compounded shame and guilt which this included. Because of his diffuse self-image, he remained extremely vulnerable to others' attitudes, easily hurt by criticism, encouraged by praise. Withal, he remained loyal to the Western group experience and retained his warm attitudes toward the other men; he had been able to arrange to see most of them, and was still Father Benét's staunchest defender.

Mrs. Kallman's response made an interesting contrast to her husband's. She had also been in prison in China, and arrangements had been made for them to leave the country together. She described to me their dramatically silent jeep ride to the pier (still in police custody, they were forbidden to talk), their silence long after the Communist guard had left them alone in their cabin on the European-owned ship, while both of them looked up at the ventilators fearing that they might be overheard; and finally, their speaking to each other only when they were certain that they were out of Chinese waters.

Her responses after prison were simpler and a good deal less ambivalent than her husband's. She hated the Communists for what they had done to her husband and herself. She disapproved of her husband's lectures because she feared that they might cause him trouble in the future. She and her husband had discussed their prison experiences at great length; now she wished to forget about them and devote her energies to her family. She did not escape aftereffects—recurrent dreams and a certain amount of physical and psychosomatic illness—and we may assume that she was not entirely free of inner doubts. But she remained the stronger of the two, offering continual emotional support to her husband. She also felt that, in their marriage, thought reform had made them both more conciliatory. She was very "female" in her entirely personal and nonideological judgments, although, as we have seen with Miss Darrow, such a response was by no means characteristic of every woman who experienced thought reform.

Father Émile

I visited Father Émile at a mission house in southern France. Robust, confident, and energetic, he bore little resemblance to the tense and confused man I had seen in Hong Kong. In characteristic fashion, he opened our talk with several humorous anecdotes about his experiences during and after imprisonment. Indeed, his sense of humor was his mainstay in his recovery ("I took it lightly, not tragically"), so much so that he was concerned lest he deal with these matters "too much as a joke." Like other priests, he had experienced a certain amount of remorse about things he had said and done which might hurt the Church. He was especially concerned about a Chinese priest who might have been endangered by his words, and extended this concern to all Chinese priests: "Now I suffer about Chinese fathers. . . . I am afraid they might feel we betrayed them." Most foreign priests shared these sentiments about imprisoned Chinese colleagues, but Émile carried it to the point of insisting upon sleeping on a wooden bed without a mattress—much as he did in jail—"to show my sympathy for them."

He too had retained his passion for China, and looked all over France for friends he had known there. When asked if he wished to take up missionary activities in another part of the world, his answer was: "I have been married to China—and I am faithful to my first wife." So intense was his interest in speaking and writing about thought reform and other aspects of Chinese Communism that he neglected his first teaching assignment; he was then transferred to a new position which allowed him contact with Chinese missionary activities. During this period he became extremely interested in supplying detailed information to an international group which was investigating forced labor practices throughout the world. He much preferred this form of activity to concentrating upon his new French surroundings; after two decades in China, Europe seemed so alien to him that "I thought I needed another re-education."

When I saw him in France, his anti-Communist position was firm ("They don't even consider elementary human rights"), and more outspoken than it had been in Hong Kong, although perhaps a bit less vehement than it had been one year after his return—in a letter to me then he spoke of the "mixture of threats, wheedling, and blackmail" characteristic of thought reform. He had also become more accustomed to life in France, and had achieved a balance between his continuing interest in China and his involvement in his immediate environment.

Father Émile still conceded that the thought reform method had "some good" in its ability to get to the "root of the bad thought." He also believed the Communist stress upon communal co-operation was valuable. He had remained on good, though not intimate, terms with the other group members. He tended to avoid extensive introspection concerning his experience, preferring to deal with it in an "active way," and characterizing himself as "dynamic rather than speculative." His recovery was, on the whole, quite impressive. He had (in contrast to Father Vechten) been able to deal effectively and promptly with his guilt and shame within the idiom of the Catholic priesthood. This accomplished, he was free to make good use of humor and activity as a means of further detoxifying these dangerous post-release emotions, and creating distance between himself and the prison experience.

What about the other three men?

Mr. Weber (the businessman-adventurer) paid a warm visit to Father Vechten almost immediately after their return to Europe, during which he received the sacraments from his previous cellmate in a formal resumption of Catholic religious life. But almost immediately afterward he apparently went back to his former style of existence: active engagement in commerce and adventure in an underdeveloped country, supported by a liberal indulgence in alcohol. Most of the others in the group retained an affectionate, if not fully admiring, feeling for Weber, and believed this resumption of his previous pattern to be inevitable because of his "instability."

Dr. Bauer had lived up to his impressive Hong Kong performance. He had been able to resume medical practice almost immediately, and had re-established his family in a European-inhabited area far from Europe itself. In letters to me, he denied psychological difficulties of any variety, described his continuing antagonism to Communism ("I feel hot under the collar about it in general"), and considered himself to be "a scientific witness of unpleasant experiments." On this basis he had lectured extensively during the months after his return. He continued to make friendly overtures toward other group members, to which they were not unresponsive; but most of the others experienced mixed feelings toward him, remembering with admiration his courage and support during imprisonment, but at the same time being unable to reconcile antagonisms related to his Nazi background, racist views, and to certain of his personal traits.

Father Benét's readjustment was apparently a bit more stormy, as might be expected. According to a colleague who accompanied him, Benét had experienced "a kind of crisis" during the boat trip back to Europe which was apparently related to his overwhelming fear—no longer fear of the Communists, but rather of his own Church superiors because of his behavior during imprisonment. But it was not long before he too was able to resume his professional activities. When he did, however, and began to give talks about his prison experiences, he emphasized (as he explained in a letter to one of the others) how the missionaries had deceived themselves, how much they had been humiliated, how close they had been brought to complete breakdown. He thus still maintained a histrionic posture of exhibitionism and masochism. As one colleague expressed it, "He is still playing a game—now on the other side." Moreover, Benét claimed that the man to whom he wrote the letter mentioned above had been "near a nervous breakdown" himself—a part of this posture, and at the same time a means of projecting his own state on to someone else. The other group members maintained many of the critical feelings toward him they had expressed upon their release; but these had, on the whole, tended to soften over the years.

Of those prisoners discussed in earlier chapters, I have follow-up information about all but one, Dr. Vincent. I was not surprised when he failed to respond to my letters, and I was unable to obtain any definite information about him. An acquaintance of his told me that Vincent had been trying to arrange to return to medical work in another part of Asia; since this was consistent with the plans Vincent had described to me, it is probably what happened. We may also assume that he regained his exaggerated possession of his "insides" and reverted to his distinctive identity of the mystical healer.

Father Luca

About Father Luca, I have more definite knowledge. When I visited him at his family home in a medium-sized Italian city, I encountered a man different from the driven, restless, and probing missionary I had met in Hong Kong. He was a friendly and forceful priest, lively and definite in his discussion of everything Chinese, and at the same time quite at home in his middle-class European surroundings. He was now physically healthy—he had recovered from his back injuries and gained a good deal of weight—and emotionally assertive rather than self-questioning.

He had not found Europe too difficult to get used to—he had not been away nearly as long as many of the others—but he had experienced the painful inner struggle which, from our talks in Hong Kong, I knew he could not escape. He was deeply moved by his reunion with family members and colleagues; but he found himself troubled by feelings of confusion and sadness. He related these to his separation from China and from his Chinese friends, and to his uncertain physical condition, thus tending to minimize his sense of guilt. He came to crave useful activity, and chafed under his physician's prescription of extended rest. He achieved an active solution similar to the one utilized by many of my other subjects. He prepared an extensive evaluation of Communist reform practices for the group investigating concentration camps and forced labor, an evaluation which included opinions about both the reformers and the reformed. When this was completed, he began, on his own initiative, a much more ambitious piece of work: a detailed study and analysis of the life and letters of the founder of his society, an outstanding figure among modern missionaries to China. As he proceeded with this study, Father Luca compared his own religious experiences, in Europe as well as in China, with those of a man who had long served as his ideal, and this project helped him greatly in his continual struggle to define himself in relationship to the Church and to China. Moreover, he was able to work on both these tasks during a time when his physical activities were restricted.

Soon after, he began to make strong efforts to educate others about the realities of Communist China—by briefing people preparing for visits, writing magazine articles, and appearing at public debates. His voice rose as he described to me the "naiveté of some people who refuse to recognize that persecutions exist in Communist China." His sense of personal integrity was clearly involved in these matters—so much so, that on one occasion he sought out the leader of an official group of Communist Chinese visitors, described the brutality he had experienced in prison, and urged this man to request his government to admit (making use, if necessary, of some face-saving maneuver) that the "people it said were guilty were really not guilty." Luca also continued to advocate a liberal course in future missionary activities, recommending more self-expression and local authority among indigenous groups. He could still admit that the Chinese Communists were "right" about some things, and that the missionaries had made mistakes; but his general tone when he referred to the present regime, as compared to his attitude in Hong Kong, had become more militantly critical and more consistently hostile.

He had remained concerned about the possible harm some of the statements in his confession might have caused to the Church and its representatives. He was especially troubled about the letter he had written under duress to a young Chinese Catholic girl denouncing his own organizational activities, and he had gone so far as to send a gift to the girl through a countryman visiting China in order to rectify the situation. He felt hurt when the gift was refused, although he knew that the refusal was based on the girl's concern for her own safety. Nor was he free of his old nemeses: he still had trouble managing his emotions whenever he wished to oppose a superior, and he had to maintain his vigilance against ever-recurring sexual desires. But in all of these matters, I felt, his conflicts were under much better control than when I had last seen him. Like so many of the other imprisoned Westerners, Father Luca believed he had become more spontaneous and more fluent in his self-expression as a result of his thought reform: "I am more free in my behavior. . . . I speak more easily in public and with other people." His spiritual life, he felt, had become more routine and "plain," in contrast to its precious intensity during imprisonment: "then I had to seek an opportunity."

When I asked him, near the end of our three-hour talk, whether any of the ideas of thought reform remained with him, he replied: "They come to mind, sometimes to be taken into account, sometimes to be contradicted, sometimes to be accepted." He elaborated upon those ideas which he at least partially accepted:

I agree that a way for the peasants to escape the moneylender when they needed credit was necessary. . . . Sometimes I have a feeling that a system of co-operatives can solve some of these problems. . . . Not necessarily the whole Marxist system. . . . I had already a theoretical idea of this before, but I have a more sensitive idea of it now.

In these ideas, as in all of his emotions, Father Luca was attempting to reconcile influences he felt he could not ignore with older respected values. He had found it necessary to repress much that was painful, especially those things related to feelings of guilt; and he had taken on some of the aspects of a conventional priest expressing the accepted ideas of the Church. Yet beneath, he fought a continuous struggle with his own most negative images of himself, and continuously searched for a personal synthesis. He had not been spared anxiety, but he had managed to make an effective recovery without undue self-damage (had his prison injuries made this unnecessary?) or excessive inner distortion.

Professor Castorp

At the time of my trip to Europe, Professor Castorp, the submissive scientist, was well established in a teaching position in another part of Asia. He had, in fact, begun to make these new arrangements within weeks after his release. He wrote me a long and humorous letter describing his experiences since leaving Hong Kong. He mentioned family matters, but focused mainly upon problems of resuming his work—which to him meant resuming his existence as a self-respecting human being. He too wrote a report of his prison experiences; but after he had completed this, he looked forward to returning to teaching and research in his more usual scientific areas.

Professor Castorp at first was impeded by physical difficulties with his teeth, gums, and hearing, poor memory, easy fatigue, and worst of all, the loss of his former "pleasure and delight in solving somewhat complicated problems." But gradually his enthusiasms returned, and he was able to look at his diminishing difficulties with his usual acceptance and detachment: "It may be . . . that a racehorse just has to race to keep fit, and if you put him in a stable for a long time, he does not race well any more in spite of good food." He was apparently following his long-standing pattern of blending with his new surroundings in his individualistic and somewhat withdrawn manner, and had already become an expert in the local geography. He retained his interest in thought reform and in problems of imprisonment; he also continued to feel some apprehension about the possibility of being captured again by the Communists. Characteristically, he made no mention of ideological issues; rather, he was concerned with practical matters. The letter, on the whole, confirmed my earlier impression of good recovery, and suggested that Professor Castorp had quickly and actively resumed his pre-thought reform identity.

Bishop Barker

I saw Bishop Barker (the elderly Belgian "priest, doctor, soldier") at an unusual but not inappropriate site—the Catholic shrine at Lourdes. He had led a pilgrimage there, and he suggested it as the most convenient place to meet, a suggestion which I welcomed. Now about seventy, he was an impressive figure in bishop's purple, his eyes alert, his movements quick, and his goatee pure white. In some ways he seemed more removed from other people (he explained this as a continuation of his deepening religious sense), but at the same time he clearly enjoyed the adulation he received everywhere he went in Lourdes. As I observed him one day, taking part in a large Church processional, marching among other high Church officials in the privileged place behind the Holy Sacrament —his step slow and dignified, his lips moving in prayer—I thought that he had indeed come far from the deep humiliation of his thought reform.

During the years since I had first seen him, Bishop Barker had continued his two crusades: his personal attempt to direct all of his emotions into a continuing Catholic religious experience, and his broader effort to spread his message about Chinese Communism and about reform techniques. He had spoken before many groups, always bent upon "stirring up the audience to reform their inner life." He would stress both the power of the Communists and the need for sacrifice in order to "overcome" them. At the same time he emphasized that he was still "using the material of thought reform to deepen my own religious sense."

His ideological interests—and in fact his major life interests—had become limited to Communism and Catholicism, and he concerned himself with political questions only when they were related to one or both of these. He had retained his strongly anti-Communist position; he admired John Foster Dulles and Konrad Adenauer as the two men "best against Communism." There was, at the same time, some suggestion of ambivalence toward Americans: when I told him that my spoken French was far from fluent, he immediately replied, "No matter—your dollars speak for you all over the world." This was not a remarkable statement, of course, but it must be viewed in relationship to Bishop Barker's previous tendency to express unconsciously retained reform influences. His interest in thought reform continued only so long as he could discuss it in his own crusading Catholic idiom. When I questioned him about specific post-release feelings related to guilt and shame, he became evasive and suggested to me that the conversation was becoming a strain. He did tell me that if he were to be imprisoned again, he would "not give in at all," since the Communists distort any admission a prisoner makes. He had carried this attitude a step further, however, and he implied (and almost believed) that he *had not* given in at all during his actual prison experience.

Thus, another one of my subjects was astounded to hear Barker say, during a brief meeting, that he had "not confessed anything." The Bishop did not say this to me, but he did limit his prison references to stories of outwitting his jailers and frustrating their intentions. After relating one of these anecdotes, he would quickly change the subject to his varied experiences during his long stay in China, again presenting himself in a heroic light and only occasionally permitting himself an admission of fear or nervousness.

He also delighted in telling me of his Catholic religious life—of his greeting his guardian angel the first thing every morning, and of his feeling that in prison he needed an additional guardian angel and his calling upon the archangel Raphael. He asked me to attend one of his Masses; and—with minimal encouragement—he launched into long discussions of theological symbolism. At the same time he enjoyed bringing up questions of morality and sexual behavior, presenting always a conventional Catholic viewpoint, but curious about a psychiatrist's opinions as well.

I had the impression that Bishop Barker, keenly aware he was living in his declining years, was attempting to assume a final identity stance which would permit him to feel that his life had had value and meaning. In struggling to maintain the self-image of the hero—to which he had aspired since early childhood—he was still fighting off the inner voice which accused him instead of being the weakling. This underlying threat of despair made him much more comfortable in reaching for others' souls than in probing the psychological conflicts of his own. In dealing with thought reform experiences, he had not only intensified his tendency to repress and to deny: he had taken the next step, that of confabulation. Certainly, during thought reform and in the rest of his life, as well, he had in many ways come close to realizing his heroic self-image; yet to believe this and to maintain a sense of self-esteem, he had to resort to grossly distorted reconstructions.

Miss Darrow

This leaves only Miss Darrow (the missionary's daughter) whose apparent conversion had, when I last saw her, already begun to wear off. From occasional correspondence, as well as from contacts with people who knew her, I learned that her pattern had continued to be very similar to the one she had shown when I interviewed her; but since these interviews had taken place in Canada three months after her release, they were able—much more clearly than the Hong Kong encounters—to indicate long-range tendencies. She was continuing her gradual adaptation to Canadian life, and also continuing her painful and guilt-ridden reality testing. She remained much more sympathetic to the Chinese Communist regime than most other subjects, but she was able to be increasingly critical of its distortion and its oppression. She was indeed realizing her (self-fulfilling) prophecy of becoming the "left-wing liberal"—willing to co-operate with various groups and individuals interested in studying thought reform but strongly opposed to right-wing propagandistic exploitation. In her personal and professional life, she impressed friends and colleagues with her unusual intelligence and perceptiveness. She still suffered from the sense of being the "betrayer" when she was critical of the Chinese Communists, especially when she contrasted her change in view with the still uncompromisingly "reformed" ideas of her male friend. Her older and closer female friend had continued to offer much emotional support, and an interlude of physical illness had supplied a helpful moratorium; but Miss Darrow continued with her step-by-step search, still plagued by her ever-present susceptibilities to guilt.

CHAPTER 11

FATHER SIMON:
THE CONVERTED JESUIT

In the course of my follow-up visits, I was introduced to a priest who had experienced prison thought
reform, but who had not been a subject of my original Hong Kong
study. A French Jesuit, he was teaching science at a small Catholic
school near the Franco-German border. My interview with him was
not, strictly speaking, a follow-up visit; but it proved to be an unusually interesting encounter. This Catholic Father, three-and-a-
half years after his release, was still seeing the world almost entirely
through "reformed" eyes. He had come closer to a true conversion
experience than had any of my original subjects.

The interplay between Father Simon and the colleague of his
(also a subject of mine) who introduced us was a good indication
of what was to follow. This other priest explained to Simon that
I had tried to meet him in Hong Kong, but had been told that he
(Simon) did not wish to see me. Simon irately denied this, insisting that he had never been approached, and accusing his clerical
colleagues in Hong Kong of preventing a meeting between us because they were embarrassed by his views. (Actually, it is difficult
to say just who had prevented me from seeing Father Simon in Hong
Kong; it is quite probable that neither he nor his fellow priests felt
very enthusiastic about my interviewing him.)

In Europe, however, Simon was clearly interested in talking with me. A thin, tense man in his late fifties, he quickly gave me the impression that he had a great deal to say about matters which he did not feel free to discuss too openly in his present environment. Indeed, his first words were pointed expressions of criticism directed at fellow priests who published strongly anti-Communist writings or presented what were in his opinion distorted views of prison thought reform. And when I asked him how he felt about his imprisonment, he answered without hesitation: "It was one of the best periods of my life." Then he explained that thought reform was valid *because it was effective:* "People claim that the Communists tried to introduce false points of view into your brain—but this could never work; it is only because they introduced true things . . . that it works." He went on to say that, "As for freedom of speech, I had more . . . in jail than I have right here," explaining that while he was in prison, "I accepted all of their points of view—political and economic, everything," then adding as something of an afterthought, "except for a deadlock on the religious point of view."

Father Simon wasted no time in making it clear just where he stood. I could not help feeling amazement during these first few minutes of our interview, as I heard this Jesuit priest express only praise for Communism and only criticism for the actions of his Catholic colleagues. Although I knew the general principles of thought reform, I wondered just how this had been accomplished.

Father Simon was brought up in a hardworking middle-class family in a French provincial town. Since his father owned a small business enterprise, he now felt that "I was born on the wrong side of the fence. . . . My education was entirely on the capitalistic side." He had learned in prison that "I lived from a salary taken from workmen," but defended his parents as having done the best they could, limited as they were by "the ideas of their surroundings." Simon described the religious influences in his family as very strong: two sisters trained as nuns, and two uncles became missionaries. A conscientious boy who always "had the feeling that life was something serious," he had wished to become a priest from the age of eleven, and had made his definite decision when he was fifteen. He attributed his religious inclinations to his mother's influence; his father—an austere, distant, and highly-respected figure—had originally opposed his decision to enter the priesthood. As in the case of Father Luca, his mother's intercession helped him to carry it through.

He received extensive training in science, philosophy, and theology. This work included three years of study in the United States during his early thirties, and it is significant that he returned to Europe something of a convert to the American way of life, so much so that he sometimes irked his colleagues (several of whom I had spoken to) with his expression of his new allegiance, and his insistence that French science was nothing compared to advanced American developments. He had retained these sentiments over the twenty years he spent teaching science in China; but they were soon overshadowed by his enormous attachment to China itself. Although a distant and reserved man, he sought always to enter deeply into Chinese life. He organized scientific trips during which he traveled and camped outdoors with a small group from his university. "For two or three weeks . . . I lived entirely among students. . . . It made life more human . . . and the students found me as a man they did not know before."

In other ways too, he tended to be different from and sometimes at odds with his colleagues. One described him as "very independent in judgments . . . liked to be against things . . . enthusiasms strong but changeable . . . apparently cold, but really passionate."

He was at the same time extremely diligent in his work, and utterly conscientious in his religious life. As one friend expressed it, "I often broke rules, but Simon never did."

Thus, before his contact with the Communists, he was a man strongly susceptible to some forms of environmental influence, and at the same time capable of stubbornly resisting others. He possessed a powerful conscience and an accompanying susceptibility to guilt, both related to early family struggles; and much of Simon's life was involved with which influence he should follow as the "good" one, and which he should resist as the "bad." In his various experiments with identity, however, it was his sense of being the conscientious enthusiast which prevailed over each of a number of different enthusiasms.

During the early years of Communist rule, he was proud of being the only foreigner permitted to integrate his scientific work with the government program. At the same time, he was extremely critical of the Communist movement, and strongly opposed the regime's attempts to spread its influence within his university. He expected to be arrested because he had been accused with others (falsely) of using a radio for espionage purposes.

Simon admitted to me that the early period of his imprisonment was "hard." But he avoided any mention of specific brutality and claimed that he had been deprived of sleep for only one night. He preferred to "explain" the Communist approach ("According to their method they take advantage of the first shock"), and implied that their techniques were necessary because he had so extremely opposed them at the beginning. I was able to learn some of the missing details, however, from another European who had shared the same cell with Simon for a while: "Simon had been interrogated three days without sleep. They said he hadn't been giving any information. The inspector, when alone with him, spat in his face ten times." This same informant said that Simon had been unusually stubborn in his resistance: "a daredevil." In both versions, however, it was clear that Simon was extremely fearful of being shot.

He went then from extreme resistance to complete compliance, and his own story makes clear the psychological features of this reversal. Even after he no longer feared death, his desire to remain in China profoundly influenced his behavior:

I thought that I was one of those with the best chance to stay. I had received instructions from my superior to try to stay. I realized that if I did not change my mind, I would have no chance at all to stay. I decided I would try to see what was right, and if doubtful, I could try to adopt the Communist point of view.

Simon was helped along this path by a fellow Jesuit in the same cell who taught him how to begin his confession.

But he recognized that his own sense of guilt had played the most important part: "My position changed when I said, 'I am guilty'." While unconscious guilt was undoubtedly present all along, his sense of being criminally guilty developed after about one year, and was accompanied by a strong compulsion to confess. "I made a list in French . . . for my own use of ten points which I should never mention. . . . Six months later I had told everything. . . . I was then ready to tell everything about myself and anyone else."

His list had, of course, been his unconscious preparation for what was to come. When he made it he decided that "if I put together all these faults I had been accused of . . . I could say I was guilty."

When I asked him what he had to feel guilty about, he first answered evasively, "We had plenty of things." And then he did describe one of them—an occasion soon after World War II when Catholic chaplains from the American Army brought an intelligence officer to see Simon and some of his colleagues, "and then we told them plenty of things." But, as if realizing that this might not be in itself so damning, he added, "What we did any foreigner would have done, but we should have been more careful." Then, as if to justify further his guilt, he explained that "In jail we didn't accuse only our crimes, but rather the intention of our crimes"; he went on to describe how he had contemplated (but had never carried out) telling an American missionary who was leaving details about Communist work on an airfield, realizing that this information might be passed on to an official American group.

I had no way of knowing whether this idea had really occurred to Simon before his imprisonment, or whether it was a product of the guilt-stimulating pressures of imprisonment itself. Either way, it was part of his need to find evidence of both wrongdoing and wrong-thinking so he could rationalize, in thought reform terms, his own psychological state: "Every time I found a crime I had committed, I was glad to find it." But among a myriad of trivial self-accusations, the encounter with an American intelligence officer was undoubtedly a true source of psychological guilt, as it violated Simon's deepest sense of what a missionary should do and be.

His guilt established in his own mind, Simon moved on to the next step—complete enthusiasm and complete trust:

One of the prisoners suggested writing diaries—only about our change of mind. . . . Every day we gave the cell chief our diary. We had the feeling we were living in a glass house—but we had no bad feelings at all. Our souls were entirely open. It was complete confidence. We could trust the government.

Simon's attainment of mutual trust and harmony with the Chinese realized a long-desired goal, a goal which he felt had before this always eluded him: "I never had a good chance to live among the Chinese except the last three years in jail." During this period he held nothing back from his colleagues and cellmates ("I was glad to get rid of all I had on my mind and to speak very frankly"), and his statements included extensive denunciations of the behavior of many of his colleagues, both in and out of jail.

He was transferred during his last year to a jail where he was permitted to do manual labor. His guilt had led to a feeling of tranquility: "I was more quiet. I thought I am guilty and deserve it." Once he was happy in jail, his main fear was that he would soon be released. He knew that jail was a safer place for him than life in China on the outside; and contact with his own colleagues in Europe seemed least safe of all:

When I was in labor camp during the last year, I was glad to be there. I was afraid to be out, because if allowed to stay in China I would have much trouble. If I came out, there would be trouble with my Order. . . . When I received my sentence, I wrote immediately to the head of the court, "I do not ask for a reduction in the sentence, but I would like you to cross out the clause about being kicked out of the country."

By this time, he was, more than any of my subjects, identifying himself with his reformers. He took pride in bringing others around: "There was one fellow we worked on for two full days. At first we couldn't get to him . . . but finally we did." Much impressed with individual Communists, he set them up as his standard, and always compared himself unfavorably to them: "We worked hard—but could not beat them. . . . They worked all of the days, and had meetings at night. . . . And they were very enthusiastic about their work." He could justify in his mind even their curbs upon religion: "They said that outside of jail there is religious freedom, inside no. . . . That was tough on us, but we had to follow regulations"; and he was grateful for a slight relaxation in this area: "At the end, for instance, I was allowed to say my breviary."

He emphasized that in all this he had become increasingly impressed with the sincerity of the Communist officials, and illustrated this with their attitude toward their false accusation about the radio:

At the beginning, I thought that this was a pretext to arrest me. They wanted to take over our university and used this as their pretext. Later I found they really believed it. They were in good faith. . . . Then they dropped it, and they believed me.

Thus he had, during the course of his imprisonment, run the gamut from opposition to merger: "When they called me at the beginning, it was a fight—at the end it was a chat with a friend."

Simon related this story to me in a simple, straightforward manner, impressing me both with his conscientiousness and his naiveté. At times he seemed totally unaware of the degree to which he had been manipulated. But at other times, I felt that awareness of this manipulation—as well as of the inconsistencies of the Communist position—had intruded upon his consciousness, and that he was hard put to fend it off. This inner struggle became more evident as he told me of his experiences after his release.

Tense and agitated upon his arrival in Hong Kong, Simon had found himself in total disagreement with everyone and everything around him. His situation was aggravated by his compulsion to express these antagonistic feelings:

I couldn't control myself . . . when I was in jail, I could read Chinese newspapers for an entire month with no reaction, but when I came out, after every paragraph, I jumped . . . when someone told me something I thought was wrong, I had to speak.

At that time, he was convinced that because of his "change of ideas" he would not be able to remain in the Jesuit Order: "I don't mean I thought I would leave, but that I might be kicked out." He thought he might have to become a secular priest (one who belongs to no special order) and "find a bishop who would take me."

His Jesuit colleagues, however, felt differently. Appalled at his behavior and attitudes, but for the most part sympathetic to him as a person, they were intent upon tiding him over what they considered to be a crisis and winning him back to a more acceptable set of views. One of them with whom I had talked in Hong Kong had even asked my advice about the problem. He had decided—partly in response to pressures from other colleagues and partly because of his own convictions—to apply to Simon what he called "shock therapy." By this he meant confronting him with the disparaging material that had been published about him in Chinese Communist newspapers and magazines, including accusations and confessions of heterosexual and homosexual behavior. (Simon had been accused of committing a "sexual crime" [homosexual act] during his imprisonment; although this was probably a false accusation, it could well have touched off latent fears and impulses and stimulated a good deal of confession material.) Simon's Jesuit friend had hesitated to use his "shock" approach because he had noted that on the few occasions when he had attempted to bring up the subject of prison confessions, Simon had become silent and fearful. felt he had good reason to hesitate, and advised him against the "shock therapy." However, influenced by the fact that Simon was leaving for Europe in a few days, and believing that others in the Church might be less understanding about the whole problem than he was, the Jesuit had disregarded my advice and gone ahead with his direct but gently-administered confrontation.

He felt at the time that his shock therapy had been effective since Simon had responded with surprise and a certain amount of anger directed at the Communists. But like many therapists, shock or otherwise, he had been premature in his evaluation; for soon Simon overcame his resentment toward the Communists through a rationalized analysis of the situation, which he also gave to me:

The Communists have two different departments, justice and propaganda. Justice wants to know the truth. Propaganda wants to amplify everything. . . . For justice, I still have the document of condemnation . . . based on the true facts. . . . Some expressions are rather ambiguous, but what they charged me of, I have admitted. . . . What they wrote in the newspapers [for propaganda] is entirely different.

It is possible, however, that this incident did play a part in Simon's gradual realization that the Communists were not completely truthful:

That's one point on which I have changed a little. Then [when in prison] I had the feeling that the Communists never lied. I feel now that although there are more lies on the other side, the Communists also lie—although they are more clever and more skillful. . . . If the Communists only told the truth, it would be awful for us.

Despite this small concession, he remained acutely at odds with his fellow priests. He looked upon them as "reactionary," and they tended to view him as one who had been convinced (and deceived) by the Communists because he was "doctrinally unsound" in his Catholic theology. One priest used him to illustrate the point that it is the "technicians" among Catholic priests who are likely to be most affected by thought reform, rather than those who are more strongly grounded philosophically. Another, who had been de-nounced in prison by Simon, referred to the latter's behavior as a "twist of conscience. . . . He is a very conscientious man, and when he reported against me he was being very conscientious in another way."

The Jesuit organization seemed to have more tolerance for his point of view than Simon had anticipated; but he felt that in re-assigning him to a teaching position, they had expected him even-tually to "become normal again." He made a point of expressing his Communist sympathies clearly to his superiors, and he finally reached a *modus vivendi* with them in which they accepted his right to hold any beliefs he pleased as long as he did not proclaim them too loudly to the outside world. He accepted this restriction as part of the principle (emphasized by both the Communists and the Catholics) that an individual priest cannot separate his actions from his responsibilities to his order; at the same time he indicated that he would like to express his views publicly through writing or speak-ing "if I were free."

He was—emotionally and intellectually—much more distant from his colleagues than before. He had always viewed himself as "rather cold toward other people," and this isolation was increased "because I live with people who don't share the same idea." When I asked him if he had been influenced by any of his colleagues since his return, he replied, "There couldn't be much influence because their ideas are so contradictory to mine."

He was so much alone with his thoughts that his only oppor-tunities to express himself came during long automobile trips he made to preach in outlying areas. These trips were arranged by a local organization, and on them he found release in talking to the driver, usually a businessman volunteer: "I know they don't share my opinions, but it is very enjoyable for me." Sometimes his com-panion, when he first heard that Simon had been through interest-ing experiences in China, would enthusiastically invite him to speak before a local club—to which Simon would reply, "Let us talk together for a few more minutes and then see whether you still wish me to speak before your group." The invitation was never repeated. Simon concluded that "they don't want their members to hear that kind of stuff."

Toward the end of our three-hour talk, he described to me his attempts to achieve an inner synthesis between his older Catholic and newer Communist ideologies. He claimed that this attempt had begun even before he was imprisoned, when he had envisioned a political party "entirely Communist but with Christian principles" (although at the time he supported his fellow priests against the encroachments of the Communist regime). Like other priests among my subjects, he felt that he had reinforced his own spiritual life through his imprisonment: "The fact of feeling guilty is good Christian humility." But unlike the others, he believed that the Communists themselves possessed the Christian virtues ("I feel that most of the Communists are humble"), a strong expression of praise from a Catholic priest.

He claimed that through his experience he felt himself closer to the Catholic religion "because, in one way I am nearer the truth." His facial expression became animated and enthusiastic as he described to me the way in which he had improved his inner life:

I have had more experience with introspection. With all of the methods of criticism we go very deep into the subconscious. I remember in jail . . . everyone told their faults against the discipline, then we decided to get deep into the reasons. Then others would say, "This and this is the reason." We would say, "No, no, no—that's not it." Then at night you would think they are right, and as soon as you realized this, the fault was corrected at once. . . . This is very important for the religious life. . . . A very powerful tool.

I felt his alternation in this statement between first person singular and plural, and the second and third persons, was more than a matter of a European speaking English (his English was, in fact, fluent), and really reflected his alternating images of himself as a member of the Communist-oriented group, as the target of its criticism, and as a spiritually-active European Catholic. He in fact emphasized that it was not possible to use this kind of group criticism in his present circumstances, and that he was forced to apply this "tool" himself—and so, in effect, assume simultaneously all three identities. He believed that Communism and Catholicism should maintain their interchange of techniques and that Catholicism should seek to benefit from the Communist improvements "Lenin borrowed many things from religious orders, but amplified them a lot. . . . If we can get them back from Lenin, that is all right."

Yet he could not avoid recognizing his inevitable conflict, as a Catholic priest, with the Communist creed. When I asked, for instance, if he were troubled by the problem of materialism—a point of bitter controversy, at least theoretically, between Communism and Catholicism—he replied, "No, but it means I can never be a Communist," and went on to say:

My conflict with the Communists came when I said, "For me religion is first, Communism is second." If I had been able to write a blank check and say that anything the Communists do about religion is OK, then I could have stayed. That much I could not have done. . . . I trusted them very much, but not that much. . . . If not for this problem of religion I would have followed the Communist Party entirely, without any restriction.

He added that during his last month in jail he wondered, "Do I not go too far?" and then decided, "I shall never have an unconditional surrender. I shall never sign a blank check." Now he concluded, not without some sadness, that because of this unwillingness, "for the Communists I am still an enemy . . . since if you don't accept them entirely, they consider you an enemy."

When I asked him whether he would consider such a black-and-white judgment on the part of the Communists to be at all unfair, his answer was what could be expected—but its implications were nonetheless striking:

No. To understand Communism you must compare it with Catholic belief. If with Catholic belief, you don't accept one article of faith, you are not a Catholic. If you don't sign a blank check, you are not a Catholic.

Simon had no objection to the demand itself. When I asked him whether he was willing to make this "unconditional surrender" to Catholicism, he replied:

Of course. . . . I like Communism and Catholicism, but Catholicism always comes first. In case of conflict, I will stay with Catholicism.

World politics were, of course, another matter. As far as Communist activities in general were concerned, Simon said, "I am not even against a revolution—of course as mild as possible, but you cannot always do anything about that." And about the return of

General de Gaulle to power during 1958, he offered a remarkabl
candid opinion:

Well, give him a chance. See what he can do. I was rather against hir
at first because I thought he was reactionary. Then someone said tha
Moscow was not against him because they thought he would brea
NATO. Since then I have not been so much against him because Mo
cow had that opinion. If Moscow stands for de Gaulle, then I am fc
de Gaulle.

But in discussing thought reform, he made a statement far mor
significant than he realized:

The way you look at it depends upon whether you feel that their opin
ions are true or false. If you say they are false, then it is all brainwashin,
stuff. If you think them true, they help you. I saw cases of seriou
offences—even some real crimes—completely changed. . . . With th
habit of introspection you can very quickly see whether someone is tel
ing the truth.

Here Simon, quite unintentionally, let his inner doubts out o
the bag, implying with this slip that he and others like him wer
not guilty of "real crimes," but of something else that must be dis
tinguished from them.

He ended the interview—just as he began it—with praise for th
"very powerful" and "wonderful" thought reform methods, anc
denunciation of those Catholic priests who he felt had presentec
distorted views of Communist China.

Why did Father Simon go so far that his conversion strains the
meaning of *apparent?* It is interesting to compare him with ou
other apparent convert, Miss Darrow. The two are very differen
kinds of people; and yet there are striking similarities in their emo
tional reactions. Both responded very strongly to the opportunity
to merge with the Chinese people; both experienced an unusually
strong sense of guilt, and a strong need to be *absolutely sincere*
with their captors; both eventually achieved a greater harmony
with their prison environment than with any they had previously
known, and were loath to surrender it for the anticipated pain o
"freedom." This authoritarian priest shared with the liberal mis
sionary's daughter psychological traits characteristic for the ap
parent convert: strong susceptibility to guilt, confusion of identity,

and most important of all, a long-standing pattern of totalism.

Simon's totalism had in fact always been much more prominent than Miss Darrow's. As the conscientious enthusiast, he had shown a tendency to embrace totally a series of influences—Catholicism, American know-how, Chinese life, and then Chinese Communism. Unlike Miss Darrow, he had not rebelled from the religious influences which helped to shape this totalism during his early life. He did not seek a liberal alternative; rather, in his "unconditional surrender" to Catholicism he was attracted toward the most authoritarian and uncompromising elements within a many-sided (but always potentially authoritarian) ideology.

But within his identity of conscientious enthusiast were two vying elements, the convert and the defier. As the former, he sought, and as the latter feared, total unity with an all-powerful force. He required a pattern of defiance in order to ward off the strong attractions to continuous influences around him. Sometimes he would defy one first and convert to it later, sometimes convert to it first and then defy it; or on still other occasions, defy one strong influence while converting to another. Thus he defied his father to convert to the priesthood (it would be interesting to know whether he had originally been at all defiant in his attitude toward religion), defied French influence in his conversion to America and Western influence in his conversion to China, defied both Catholic and American influences in his conversion to Communism, and then continued to defy Catholic pressures as a means of maintaining this conversion. Whether defying or converting, his was an all-or-none approach. This is symbolized in his repeated use of the term "blank check": for one who issues a "blank check" to another may be offering either everything or nothing, without specifying how much of himself he gives and how much he insists upon retaining.

As a conscientious Catholic priest and scientist, his total dedication to missionary work, credal purity, truthfulness, and sincerity were basic to his affirmative self-image. But both the defier and the convert within him could interfere and become part of his negative identity; for underneath both of them was a profound inability to trust or to become intimate with other human beings. Each conversion was a quest for the trust and intimacy that had long eluded him; unable to experience them in ordinary human doses, he sought trust and intimacy on absolute terms. For him, both conversion and defiance were attempts to ward off inner feelings of aloneness, weakness, and helplessness.

In prison, he was first the defier (an unusually courageous one), and then the convert (an unusually loyal one). In both identities, his conscientiousness was outstanding; but his behavior also revealed the basic contradiction within his convert-defier pattern. His ideal of "unconditional surrender" was not fully attainable. He could not, after all, sign the "blank check." He tells us that this was because he could not submit simultaneously and totally to two masters; and this is true enough. But it is also true that he could not—either then or before—submit totally to *any* master. Ultimately, the "unconditional surrender" and the "blank check" were unrealizable ideals, as they so often are for those who seek them. For Simon, they had been an inspiring myth; but defiance, doubt, and mistrust eventually interfered in relation to both Catholicism and Communism.

In his post-prison years, Simon—despite his outward assurance—was inwardly walking an emotional tightrope. Whatever his denials, he did continue to serve two emotional masters, and this is a considerable strain. Even more subject to totalism than Miss Darrow, he remained truer than she to his thought reform conversion. Three-and-a-half years after his release he was still unable to come to terms with the actualities of his experience: he felt the need to reconstruct thought reform events to make them more congenial and less brutal, and to emphasize his compliance rather than his resistance. He had to avoid the recognition of having been manipulated, or else minimize the manipulation and justify its usage.

Obviously all was not well with this last—and perhaps most profound—of Simon's conversions. He was not, after all, immune from the Catholic influences around him, nor from the forces of reality testing, nor from the voice of his own doubts. Evidence for this lies in his slightly more critical (though hardly very critical) attitude toward Communism, in his slips of the tongue, in his overstated protestations. As with all true believers, his doubts were not easy to tolerate, since unconsciously he tended to see them as a lack of total sincerity on his part. Yet his doubts were constantly stimulated by the presence of his other (Catholic) master—that is, by Church officials and Catholic ideas. This accounts for some of the vehemence with which he criticized his fellow clergymen; he was calling his defiant self into play in order to purge the doubts which threatened to "betray" his thought reform experience, and consequently overstating his praise for Communism.

It may be that in the long run he, too, will backslide. But the tenacity with which this Jesuit priest had held on to his Chinese Communist conversion was as impressive a reform result as any I witnessed, particularly since there was no environmental reinforcement for his thought reform views. To be sure, the unanimity of his colleagues' opposition served as a stimulus to his defiance of them; and some reinforcement was available, even if from a distance, in the constant information about the Communist world reaching him through newspapers, magazines, and casual conversations. But even after all of this has been said, Father Simon's case leaves one with a renewed respect for the emotional power of thought reform.

CHAPTER 12

RECOVERY AND RENEWAL: A SUMMING UP

We have described in the last two chapters the emotional trials of Westerners during their first few post-thought reform years. These were never easy, and they took many different personal forms, but the common pattern was one of recovery and renewal. There were certain basic tasks which they all faced, psychological principles to which they were all subject. Their common problems were mainly the result of the thought reform emotions they had shared; but they were also related to another heritage common to all these men, that of the Westerner in China.

Mastery and Integrity

When the Westerners returned home, typically they found themselves compelled to be active, preoccupied with thought reform in particular and with China in general, and unable to become immediately interested in their Western environments. It was as if they had some piece of psychological business to attend to before they could permit themselves the luxury of rest or could assume the responsibility of new involvements. This unrest represented the psychological need to re-enact a highly disturbing experience, and is related to what Freud called the "repetition compulsion."[1] It is an effort at mastery in which, as Erikson has described, "The individual unconsciously arranges for variations of an original theme which he has not learned either to overcome or to live with," and deals with the stressful situation by "meeting it repeatedly and of his own accord."[2]

As is also true of people put through many other kinds of painful experiences, these subjects were reliving their thought reform as a means of coming to terms with it. Their experience involved special emphasis upon problems of shame and guilt, and it was these emotions which they had in some measure to overcome. Otherwise they would be unable either to overcome or to live with their thought reform, and unable to recover their self-esteem. We may therefore describe their psychological task as *mastery through restoration of integrity*.

Lecturing and writing about thought reform were particularly effective ways of achieving this mastery. By these acts the subject was in effect saying: "I am no longer the passive, helpless criminal and betrayer. I am an active, strong authority on a manipulative process which could affect any of you in my audience or reading public." Such retelling is the former prisoner's means of declaring his identity shift, his beginning disengagement from his own experience.

However, after any great adventure, or even a commonplace occurrence, the reconstruction can never reproduce exactly the experience itself. The changed inner and outer circumstances and the passage of time must induce distortions. Truth is at best an approximation, and for these men the need for altered reconstruction is likely to be great. The direction and the degree of distortion depended upon the Westerner's way of responding to thought reform, his developing relationship with his new environment, and his long-standing psychological techniques for dealing with threats to his sense of integrity.

Bishop Barker's reconstruction, for instance, was the story of a clever and heroic man who made no concessions and who outwitted his reformers at every turn. I said of him that he had extended his use of the mechanism of denial to the point of confabulation, because I knew that his reconstruction was inaccurate both in terms of actual events and attitudes towards those events.

Such a distortion in self-representation was characteristic for apparent resisters: in order to maintain a sense of integrity, over the years they would build upon the heroic self-image, and "forget" events and emotions associated with their having been weak or deceived. While Bishop Barker was by no means completely free of inner doubts about his heroic self-image, he had been able to master the thought reform experience sufficiently to carry through his distortion rather effectively.

But there were apparent resisters to whom these patterns of denial and repression were dangerous. Another priest whom I saw in follow-up (he was not mentioned earlier) had, like Bishop Barker used denial and repression to reinforce the heroic image which others were ready to confer upon him. He too gave many crusading speeches, and impressed both his audiences and his colleagues with his strength, energy, and stature. Yet when I saw him, I noticed that his eyes expressed fear and agitation. His gaze resembled the "thousand-mile stare" characteristic of prisoners immediately after their release—and he was the only one of my subjects who looked this way three years later. For almost two hours this priest described his flawless adjustment to European life, denied emotional difficulties of any kind, and spoke of the enthusiasm which he was able to arouse during his lectures on thought reform. Then, in a suddenly lowered voice, he made this admission:

But one thing was strange. . . . For months after I came out, each time I saw a stairway in a house, I thought, "What a wonderful place to jump . . . to commit suicide."

Underneath the show of strength he was a deeply troubled man who could not fully believe his own self-representation. His obsessive thoughts of suicide and his outer signs of fear revealed underlying patterns of depression and anxiety. His efforts at mastery could not still his inner self-accusations, and his need to idealize his behavior prevented him from coming to terms with his strong feelings of guilt. Although he demonstrated strength and effectiveness in many areas, he was having great difficulty restoring his sense of integrity.

Father Simon made use of similar mechanisms, but his distortions were in the opposite direction. His need was to justify his conversion to Communism and live up to his identity of the conscientious enthusiast. This involved denial of brutality during his imprisonment, repression of antagonisms toward the Communists and of recent doubts, and rationalization to justify and explain Communist behavior. Like all apparent converts, his sense of integrity required that he idealize the Communists and deprecate himself, and he reconstructed, in this light, not only his prison experience, but his entire life history. The identity of the apparent convert (and this was true of Miss Darrow as well) puts one in a masochistic stance, the paradoxical situation of being able to maintain self-esteem only by continuous self-flagellation.

The same thing was true of Father Benét. Although he had run the gamut from apparent convert to apparent resister, his approach to mastery required that he continually focus upon thought reform's capacity to humiliate and to make men betray themselves. His distortion was in the direction of exaggerating both thought reform's power and the human weakness of those put through it. This "analysis" was partly a reflection of his own experience, and partly a means of restating the sado-masochistic self-representation which he needed for his sense of integrity.

Father Vechten required a serious "accident" to interrupt his compensatory overactivity and permit him the opportunity to deal with his inner conflicts. As one of the obviously confused, he had not resorted to the gross distortions which were characteristic for (although by no means limited to) apparent resisters and apparent converts. He in fact went to the opposite extreme, and his inability to permit himself the slightest amount of poetic license was a large factor in his difficulties. His approach to integrity demanded that he spare no details of his own "misbehavior" in his reconstruction; on the other hand, his intensified shame and guilt, and his fear of not finding acceptance within his European Catholic environment, prevented him from sharing this accurate version with his colleagues and as a result, he had no way to express his inner preoccupations. His integrity could not be restored until the "accident" broke this impasse.

The struggle for mastery is most intense immediately following thought reform, and during the first weeks and months after release emotional crises center around it. In most of my Western subjects, it tended to subside a great deal after a year, as distance and perspective were gradually achieved, and the Westerners became able to formulate an explanation of their behavior. This reconstruction is the subject's new psychological truth, his means of coming to terms with both his thought reform and his Western environment. A subject was likely to have difficulty with his reconstruction when it was so distorted that he found it hard to support his own belief in it, or when it was so literal and unsparing that he was unable to express it. In any event, each subject's struggle for mastery probably will continue indefinitely, whether or not he is consciously aware of the struggle.

Separation

A second major emotional conflict for these men and women was the problem of separation. At first I was surprised when Western subjects, almost without exception, put as much emphasis on their sadness at being separated from China as on their conflicts over thought reform, and wondered if their doing so was a means of avoiding more disturbing emotions. This was the situation to some extent in a few; but the continued longing for China which most of them expressed years later convinced me that separation was a profound problem in itself. They were clearly experiencing a "grief" reaction. But what were they mourning?

Some were mourning the loss of the very special intimacy of the thought reform group—the delight in total exposure and sharing. As was true of Dr. Vincent, this delight can be keenly felt if one has never before known it; and Father Simon still retained the effects of this loss years later. Others, like Father Émile, mourned for those (in his case, Chinese Catholic priests) who were left behind to suffer. As a Western missionary, he felt that because he had helped introduce the alien religion now being persecuted, he was responsible for the suffering. This emotion is not unlike that of a man who has lost a wife, parent, or, perhaps more appropriately, brother or son by death; he remembers all the ways in which he had caused his loved one suffering, to the point where (at least unconsciously) he feels he is responsible for the death itself. This type of reaction is intensified by any pre-existing hostility which the mourner might have had for the mourned, since this makes the assumption of a sense of responsibility for the death or suffering all the easier.

Others among my subjects—Father Luca is a notable example—suffered from the realization that they were being separated permanently from their life in China. They would have no more contact with the special combination of human beings and landscape which had nourished them during important adult years. This more generalized grief at separation from China includes and transcends the first two reactions. In fact, the fear of separation, and the anticipated grief could render a prisoner susceptible to thought reform, as was clearly true of Father Simon. When this separation does occur, finally and irrevocably, the Westerner must experience true mourning: he temporarily intensifies his identification with China, preoccupies himself with reminders of his past existence there, and then bit-by-bit works through the process of detaching himself from what has been lost.[3]

All these Westerners mourned the loss of something which involved their most profound emotions; we may say that each mourned a lost part of himself. Moreover, this symbolic splitting of identity was forced upon these men under the most dishonorable conditions: they were expelled from China as criminals and spies. This separation with dishonor at the same time robbed them of that part of their identities they most treasured, and imposed on them the shameful and guilt-laden thought reform elements.

The problem of separation becomes most acute when a Westerner arrives in Europe or America: at that time he becomes aware of having been totally removed from the Chinese environment. He will then seek to return to a Chinese environment, or to maintain contact with others who are in one, in order to recapture what has been lost of himself, to reverse the separation process. Much depends, of course, upon the degree of involvement with China; but among my subjects, there were few for whom the problem of separation is not a lingering source of pain.

Expatriate's Return

The return to Europe or America confronts the Westerner with still another difficult psychological issue, that of the expatriate's return. (None was literally an expatriate; the term is used here symbolically.) Long residence in China had created in many of them a sense of alienation from their own countries, an alienation which thought reform greatly intensified; and almost all felt themselves emotionally removed from those around them who had not shared their Chinese experiences. They themselves created and perpetuated this emotional distance, partly because of their need for a personal moratorium which would help them solve problems of mastery and separation. This moratorium also allowed them to postpone their confrontation with the Western milieu.

Most of my subjects found the Western world strange and hard to get used to. And indeed, for those who had been in China for several decades, the changes that had occurred in the Western environment during that time, as well as in its people, must have been striking. Yet the problem was not so much strangeness as it was familiarity. Father Vechten's visit to Rome (the center and the spiritual *patria* for all Catholic priests) confronted him with beliefs, behavioral codes, and a world view which had always been part of him, but which had, during his years in China—and especially during his imprisonment—become in some ways modified, combined with other influences, and less clearly present in his moment-to-moment consciousness. This confrontation did not have the effect of something new; rather, he felt an uneasy revival within him of a "way of thinking and judging . . . more that which I had formerly." The same kind of revival also occurred, usually in a more insidious fashion, with all of my Western subjects, whether in matters religious, cultural, or specifically personal.

The expatriate's return then is a confrontation with elements of one's identity which one has long denied, repressed, or modified beyond easy recognition. The Westerners had originally become expatriates only in relation to their own identity: the emotions which led them to choose careers in China included a need to deny or repress, at least temporarily, portions of their heritage in the search for a newer synthesis. Each man's early self had been further undermined by the imposed judgments of thought reform. Back home, they were brought in contact—sometimes critically, sometimes with psychological sensitivity, but always with full impact—with these archaic parts of themselves, reminded of them by the physical surroundings they encountered and by the people they met. Having to face their roots in this manner was both nourishing and disturbing: they could feel strengthened by being brought back to what they had been, and at the same time feel threatened by partisan and provincial emotions and ideas which they thought they had long discarded in their cosmopolitan existence. This experience of outward journey and inward return is not characteristic only of the temporary exile or expatriate; it occurs with anyone who risks the slightest deviation from the life patterns originally assigned him.[4] For these subjects, either their years of work in China or the thought reform experience alone would have made this problem a profound one. Together, the two exposures produced one of the most difficult forms of expatriate's return imaginable.

Renewal of Identity

The overriding task for these men—a task which included and went beyond problems of mastery, separation, and return—was that of renewal of identity. To renew, one must look to what has gone before; and it was no accident that so many of these men approached the problem historically, in both a personal and a broader sense.

Sometimes, as in the case of Mr. Kallmann, this historical orientation led to a good deal of confusion: unable to trust sufficiently any one among many identity elements, he clung tenaciously and somewhat uncritically to a number of antithetical sides of himself, relating to Communism and anti-Communism, Nazism and anti-Nazism, authoritarian and libertarian emotions, China and the West, and a general sense of being "all things to all men" in mediating among men. In other cases the historical search had a careful, almost academic pattern, although no less emotionally involved: when Father Luca, for example, studied the life of a great modern missionary, he was also immersing himself in the historical problems of all Western missionaries in China. To understand this process of renewal, we must make a brief excursion into some of these historical aspects of the identity of the Westerner in China.

We may begin with the most painful of Western identities— that of the imperialist. The Communists built a highly personalized image around this term; a non-Communist Westerner was *per se* an "imperialist" (one spoke in prison of "the People" and "the Imperialists"); he was greedy, demanding, intrusive, and unscrupulous; he sought to further his own interests by taking from others what was rightfully theirs. And only a Westerner could be an imperialist; Chinese might be "bourgeois" or "reactionary"—even "lackeys" of the imperialists—but never imperialists themselves. In ideological terms derived from Lenin's theory of imperialism, they considered the imperialist the agent of military, political, economic, and cultural subversion, and the destroyer of all that was good and noble in Chinese civilization.

The Westerners who had this version of the imperialist identity drummed into them during imprisonment began to dislodge themselves from it during the years after release; but each remained troubled by the kernel of truth around which the identity is built. It is mainly to decide how much of this guilt they should personally assume that so many of them made investigations of what the Westerner in China had really been. Each discovered what he had already known, that the heritage was mixed: schools and gunboats, industrial techniques and exploitation, enlightenment and dogmatism.

At best, Chinese attitudes toward Westerners have always been ambivalent. They have always viewed Westerners with an ethnocentric eye, and during four centuries of contact there have been periodic waves of persecution and anti-foreign outbreaks. Many times before, they have accused the foreigner (with his strange, non-Confucian doctrines) of being dangerous and "subversive." Conflicts magnified during the latter part of the nineteenth and the early part of the twentieth centuries, the era of the West's most vigorous military penetration of China. Then all individual Westerners became party to the special arrangements and privileges of the "unequal treaties" so much resented by the Chinese. This was as true for the missionaries as for anyone else—perhaps even truer for them because of their influence on Chinese subjects:

> . . . the treaties placed not only the missionaries but Chinese Christians under the aegis of the foreign powers. . . . The provision . . . tended to remove Chinese Christians from the jurisdiction of their government and to make of Christian communities *imperia in imperio*, widely scattered enclaves under the defense of aliens. . . . The Church had become a partner in Western imperialism and could not well disavow some responsibility for the consequences.[5]

These are not the words of Chinese Communists, but the well-considered opinions of Kenneth Latourette, a distinguished American historian of China, and himself part of the Protestant missionary movement.

Some missionaries welcomed this "partnership" with imperialism, viewing the military operations and treaties which followed as "God's way of opening up the country to his servants." [6] But an increasing number of both Catholics and Protestants came to regard the situation as not only highly "un-Christian" but potentially dangerous. In terms of identity, these two groups may be divided roughly into *pure proselytizers* and *spiritual mediators*; one of these two patterns predominated in every Western missionary who came to the Middle Kingdom from the sixteenth to the twentieth centuries.

The spiritual mediator approached China with respect for (or at least recognition of) its traditions; he sought to establish common cultural ground, so that Chinese could become Christians and still retain their identity as Chinese. The missionary himself also had to undergo some shift in his own identity before he could move toward this common ground. Matteo Ricci (1552–1610), one of the first and greatest of Catholic missionaries in China and a spiritual mediator *par excellence*, found that the best way to approach the Chinese was through the literati, and the best way to approach the literati was to blend with the Chinese scene—to become proficient in the Chinese language, wear the clothes of a mandarin, adopt completely the complex honorifics of literati speech and writing. He gained the respect of his hosts by demonstrating his scholarship, and by teaching them the latest (Renaissance) Western ideas in mathematics, natural sciences, astronomy, and geography. But even in this teaching he and his colleagues were careful to make concessions to Chinese ethnocentricity: on a map of the world which they prepared, China was located at the center—it was hard enough for the Chinese to accept the idea that great geographical and cultural areas existed at all among the "barbarians" outside the Chinese sphere.

Ricci went further: he made a detailed study of classical Chinese philosophical texts, finding much to admire in Confucian beliefs, and always stressing whatever similarities he could find between the words of the Sage and the Christian doctrine. He made a special point of his conviction that a man could embrace the beliefs and customs of both without doing injustice to either. Ricci and his colleagues were known as "preaching literati." Their early Jesuit successors became important figures at court; some of them were given titles as scholar-officials, and received financial and moral support from the Emperor himself. Their learning, and especially their cultural flexibility, carried them far. As one historian has put it, "The Jesuits largely fulfilled traditional Chinese expectations as to the likely course of intelligent barbarians in Chinese society." They were "culturally conciliatory" and quick to realize that in the stable and self-confident Chinese society of that day, "they would receive a hearing more or less as candidates for membership or not at all." [7]

Not all Catholic missionaries approached China with such a light touch. The early Franciscans and Dominicans were contemporaries of the Jesuits, and they—rather than Renaissance-influenced scholars—were the "simple friars" [8] who brought with them to China attitudes of purified medieval Christianity. They were pure proselytizers; and their approach to missionary work was "going headlong at it." Thus, in 1579, a Franciscan expedition on its way to Japan "took possession of China in the name of Christ by offering mass on the 24th of June in Canton." [9]

The Jesuits were cautious about displaying the crucifix because they realized that it "horrified" many Chinese; but the Franciscans, in their evangelizing, would "march openly through the streets dressed in their outlandish habit, cross in hand." [10] Similarly, one Dominican "set about overthrowing idols wherever he could lay his hands on them" until "the Mandarins . . . laid their hands on him and he was speedily ejected." [11] A great Dominican hero of this period was Francis Capellas who, during a persecution, was taken into custody and put to death. Before achieving martyrdom, he is reported to have said: "I have no other house than the wide world, no other bed than the ground, no other food than what Providence provides from day to day, and no occupation other than that of laboring and suffering for the glory of Jesus Christ and the eternal happiness of those who believe in Him." His death was witnessed by some of his own recently arrived Dominican colleagues, and its news was received in Spanish Catholic circles throughout the world "not . . . with mourning but with great joy." [12]

Conflict between spiritual mediators and pure proselytizers soon developed. The Jesuits were appalled by what they considered the

crude approach of the Dominicans, and feared that it would en-
danger their own patiently constructed accomplishments. The
Dominicans—at least many of them—regarded the Jesuits as too
loose in their methods and too tolerant toward paganism, and as
threats to the purity of Christianity. Their battle was the celebrated
"Rites Controversy" of the late seventeenth and early eighteenth
centuries, fought over the question of how much of customary
Chinese practice the Christian convert could be permitted to retain. The Jesuits favored Ricci's approach of conveying the Christian concept of God through the use of the classical Chinese terms
for "Heaven" (*T'ien* and *Shang Ti*), claiming that these words
originally had a theistic significance, and were in any case necessary
to explain the new faith in a familiar idiom. The Dominicans held
that these Chinese terms connoted a material heaven or sky; that
much "superstition" had grown up around them in the Chinese
mind; and that therefore they should not be used.

Again following Ricci, the Jesuits favored allowing Chinese
Christians to continue to honor Confucius and their ancestors, on
the ground that these observances were a tradition of the Chinese
empire, with a civil rather than a religious significance. The Dominicans considered the observances "pagan" and "superstitious,"
and therefore not permissible. The Dominican position was upheld
by Papal decrees in 1704, 1710, 1715, and 1742, much to the detri-
ment of Catholic missionary efforts. The decision injured Chinese
sensibilities in a variety of ways—the Emperor K'ang Hsi had expressed his support of the Jesuit position, and felt that the Pope
was contesting his authority—and a century of persecutions followed. These persecutions had complex causes and were by no
means simply a result of the Rites Controversy: but the outcome
of this controversy and the events which followed were in psychological and cultural senses, a major triumph for purist, extremist forces—and a major defeat for the mediators on both sides.
Not until 1939, 235 years after the initial decree, did Rome finally
reverse its decision.

Much more can be said about the political, religious, and cultural issues of the Rites Controversy; but this outline is enough to
indicate the importance of these two conflicting identity stances
for the Westerner in China, and for relations in general between
China and the West.[13] The examples cited were from early Catholic

experience, but these two identities were equally present in later Protestant missionaries: the pure proselytizers were the Fundamentalist preachers who with their message of hellfire and brimstone had little regard for Chinese cultural traditions; the spiritual mediators were those more liberal and socially-oriented missionaries who tried to understand and to enter into Chinese life while building their churches, universities, and hospitals.

Even secular Western residents—businessmen, diplomats, non-missionary teachers, students, and free-lance Sinophiles—were not entirely free from this dilemma. They had not come to China to propagate Christianity, but they too had the problem of how much of the West to sell to the Chinese (or at least to hold onto themselves) versus how "Chinese" to become. The treaty-port businessman, that prototype of the "old China hand," could be something of a proselytizer of Western business methods; or he could relax comfortably into his surroundings, accepting his privileged position as his due, and regarding the Chinese around him with "patronizing affection." [14] The true spiritual expatriates were the "Peking Men," a unique group of scholars, writers, and assorted individualists so thoroughly absorbed by China (even if they lived in its past glory) that the rest of the world seemed to them virtually uninhabitable, and everything after Peking anticlimactic. Those among the Peking Men who had the special subidentity of the "China-born" often (like Miss Darrow) struggled hard in their adult lives to establish an intimacy with China which they felt had been denied to them by the segregated patterns of their missionary upbringing; at the same time they tried to recapture and embellish an idealized childhood memory.

My Western subjects had also found that confronted with China over a period of time, one's identity could not, so to speak, stand still. Most, spiritual mediators more than anything else, gradually slipped into a "Chinese" pattern. They usually made an elaborate identity compromise, rather than completely "going native"; the compromise offered many creative satisfactions, but there was always the danger, whether or not a Westerner was aware of it, of his old identities becoming obscured and his sense of commitment confused. Yet the same man could also identify a part of himself as uncompromisingly Western, and feel stirrings of the pure proselytizer. The psychological rewards for so doing were those of imposing on others one's own creed and thereby exerting influence over others; the dangers (in a sense interchangeable with the rewards) were those of arousing antagonism and persecution, and of becoming isolated from Chinese life. What is more, these subjects found that historical circumstances generated increasing tension between the mediator and the proselytizer within them. China, in its quest for modernization, both sought and resented various forms of proselytizing. Western institutions which sent people to China became more sensitive to the need for mediating, but these increasing sensitivities opened the way for the kind of historical and racial guilt I have already described.

These conflicts were especially great for the priests among my subjects. Their education and characters bore the stamp of modern liberalism; they tended strongly to become cultural mediators, and play down the pure proselytizer within themselves. Even so, the conflict between these two aspects of their identity was ever-present: Father Luca was torn between his liberalism and his urge to martyrdom; Father Vechten's deep commitment to spiritual mediating was certainly undermined by his confrontation in Rome with a more pure proselytizing attitude. All these men experienced with unusual intensity the inner struggle between liberal and authoritarian emotions which any modern Catholic priest faces. Many tried to resolve the struggle by using the approach of Father Vincent Lebbe, considered by many to be a modern counterpart of Father Ricci. One of the most articulate of modern mediators, he had condemned Western imperialism, refused the protection of his own consul, and advocated love for and intimate identification with the host country; he had set a personal example by taking out Chinese citizenship and forming a stretcher-bearing battalion during the Japanese war.[15] But whatever the approach, the tension between these two elements had to remain, since they are both part of the identity of any missionary anywhere: the urge to proselytize takes him to the mission land in the first place; and the mediator within him makes his work possible.

The Communists—themselves pure proselytizers in the extreme—were quick to make the association between missionary proselytizing and imperialism, an association not too difficult to establish. It was a bit harder for them to cast a spiritual mediator as an imperialist, but they accomplished this also with two approaches: they held him responsible for the behavior of his less liberal colleagues, and called his flexible adjustment a tactical maneuver to deceive people and obscure ultimate goals. Moreover, although Father Lebbe himself was a spiritual mediator, some of the priests (including close colleagues of my subjects) who had followed his lead in aiding China's defense efforts against the Japanese had gone on to co-operate with Nationalist forces in their struggle against the Communists—thus giving the reformers a good reason to label them imperialists.

The Communists thus used actual historical events to exploit already-existing identity strains of the Westerner in China, simplifying the complex elements involved into the single pure image of the evil imperialist. They then did everything possible to make the man fit the image.

During the years after their release, my subjects were preoccupied with extricating themselves from this pure image, and finding a version of what they had been (and still were) which was both reasonably accurate and morally justifiable. Some form of reconstruction was necessary, and the degree of distortion paralleled that of the thought reform experience itself. Thus Fathers Luca and Vechten could be critical of much of their Church's behavior and at the same time reject exaggerated Communist charges; while Bishop Barker brought his characteristic all-or-nothing fundamentalist judgments to bear upon both the Church and the Communists.

These men and women were aware that their prison thought reform marked the end of an era for the non-Communist Westerner in China, as well as for them as individuals. They had to achieve a new relationship with Western institutions to overcome the guilt associated with the imperialist label. What they sought during the years after imprisonment, and what many of them attained, was nothing short of another rebirth.

Long-term Effects

What can be said about the long-range success or failure of prison thought reform as applied to Westerners? From the standpoint of winning them over to a Communist view of the world, the program must certainly be judged a failure. Only one (Father

Simon) among my twenty-five subjects (and only one or possibly two more from among the scores of others I heard about) could be regarded as a truly successful convert. Follow-up information confirmed what I had begun to observe when I interviewed these subjects in Hong Kong: a general movement away from the reform ethos toward a more critical view of Chinese Communist behavior. Three or four years after their release, most of them expressed sentiments much more harsh toward Communism than those they had felt before being imprisoned. They looked not to Communism, but to the forces in the West they had known earlier, and to an inner synthesis of their own, for answers to the world's great ideological questions. This conscious disavowal of their reform was by no means the entire psychological picture; but conscious opinions are, after all, not unimportant.

Whatever success thought reform had with most of the Westerners lay in the unconscious influences which they retained from it. These influences are basic to an understanding of what really happened, even though they can be easily overlooked. Despite the years that had passed since their imprisonment, these men and women were still grappling with the powerful emotions and ideas implanted by the Chinese Communists. Most had succeeded in neutralizing them; but the implant had been compelling enough to defy easy excision. For once a man has been put through prison thought reform, he never completely casts off its picture of the world and of himself.

Inner tension between the reformed and nonreformed elements of a person can be itself imprisoning; or lead toward expanding horizons. Most people felt something of each, but the ratio between the two varied greatly. Father Luca and Father Vechten, for example, had suffered and continued to suffer from a compulsive weighing of the influences of thought reform; yet both had broadened their personal vistas and enlarged their sense of identity as a result of their prison experiences. Father Simon and Bishop Barker, on the other hand, seemed to have narrowed their focus, constantly protecting themselves against too broad an exposure lest this upset their singlemindedness. It was generally true that those who, like Father Simon and Bishop Barker, were either apparent converts or apparent resisters, had to live on this constricted level if they were to maintain their extreme position; while the obviously confused reaped both pain and creative benefit from their confusion. Those who, like Miss Darrow, gradually gave up an extreme position, were opened to the same pitfalls and opportunities as they surrendered both their constriction and the reassuring certainties it had offered. One other position is possible: one can, like Mr. Kallmann, become so "broad" in his horizons that the inner substance of identity and commitment can scarcely take shape.

And this brings up the nonideological residua present in all Westerners, whose effects were also mixed. Four years after the experience, my subjects still bore marks of both fear and relief. The fear was related to the basic fear mentioned earlier, the fear of total annihilation; it is an unconscious memory not easily lost. Some people may equate it with the experience of having felt totally controlled and dangerously threatened by a powerful parent; but whatever its associations, all dread the possibility of risking its recurrence through re-exposure to total control. Along with this dread, however, some entertain a deeply repressed desire for just such a repetition as a means of atoning for a troubling sense of guilt. I need not again emphasize the importance of this guilt, except to say that it joins with the residual fear to form the most destructive of thought reform's bequests.

Nonetheless, thought reform can also produce a genuinely therapeutic effect. Western subjects consistently reported a sense of having been benefited and emotionally strengthened, of having become more sensitive to their own and others' inner feelings, and more flexible and confident in human relationships. These beneficial effects occurred in subjects with all three reactions, although it is difficult to say just what produced them. The best explanation is perhaps that these people had had the experience of testing their emotional limits. They had undergone the ultimate in physical and spiritual pain, and had yet survived; they had been forced to hit rock bottom in their imposed negative self-analysis, and yet had emerged with some measure of self-respect. Each had thus gone farther than ever before in realizing his human potential. Their consequent feeling of having been benefited is analogous to the sense of well-being which has been observed in people after they have experienced severe stress of almost any kind, including that of prolonged sensory deprivation.[16] When the stress is brief, the wellbeing may be limited to a rebound euphoria. But after an experience as totally disintegrating as prison thought reform, the relief at being put together again is more basic and more enduring. In the experience itself, and in the process of recovery and renewal which followed it, these men and women gained access to parts of themselves they had never known existed.

PART THREE

THOUGHT REFORM OF CHINESE INTELLECTUALS

We must be engineers of the human soul.

V. I. Lenin

The cultivation of the person depends upon recti-
fying the mind.

Confucius

CHAPTER 13

THE ENCOUNTER

In turning from imprisoned Westerners to "free" Chinese intellectuals, we arrive at the ideological center of the thought reform movement. Instead of being directed at alleged criminals and "imperialists," reform is used to manipulate the passions of the most enlightened members of Chinese society. Chinese intellectuals experience thought reform in their own country's educational institutions, under the direction of countrymen not too different from themselves. They are asked to undergo it as an act of patriotism, as an expression of personal and national rejuvenation.

Their thought reform is not entirely different from the prison program applied to Westerners. Indeed, as I alternated between Western and Chinese subjects during the study, I was often struck by the similarities in the emotional experiences reported by two such divergent groups. But the contrasts were also impressive—contrasts in thought reform settings and pressures, in life experiences and character traits, and in differing relationships to Chinese Communism—so much so that I sometimes felt as if I were conducting two separate research projects.

An exploration of these differences takes us inevitably into matters Chinese, into a consideration of influences derived from traditional Chinese culture and from the modern, antitraditional Chinese cultural rebellion. Only these patterns can account for China's unique way of dealing with imported Communist principles. I shall retain my emphasis upon individual emotions and the sense of inner identity, and move from the individual outward as I attempt to explain his experience in the light of his own and his country's history and culture. This approach also requires an examination of thought reform's origins, both its actual history, and its use of psychological themes derived from Soviet Russian and traditional Chinese models. After that, I shall summarize the general principles derived from my study of both subject groups—principles which apply to any culture and have significance far beyond that of thought reform itself.

Who are the "Chinese intellectuals"? The term is a loose one and is often applied to anyone in China with a secondary school education, although the Communists themselves distinguish between "higher intellectuals" and "general intellectuals." It includes, of course, scholars, teachers, artists, writers, scientists, advanced students, physicians, and other professional people—all of whom make up a very small but particularly influential segment of the Chinese population. As a group, they are the spiritual if not lineal descendants of the Confucian literati, the celebrated class of scholar-officials who in the past set the cultural standards and administered the political structure for whatever dynasty they served. Nowhere was learning more honored than in traditional China, and nowhere was a body of knowledge more necessary for personal advancement; until the beginning of the twentieth century, the main path to wealth and prestige was the state examination based entirely upon the Confucian classics.

But during the last fifty years, the intellectuals, influenced by the West, have led the revolutionary movements to cast off the decaying traditional social structure. Much of their identity was transformed in the process, and the rebellion was costly to them in an emotional as well as a material sense. Yet even when most beleaguered, they have always retained their aura of a learned élite and a sharp sense of separation from the rest of the mostly illiterate population.

Like the dynasties before them (and like Communist parties everywhere) the Chinese Communists recognized the importance of winning over and putting to effective use this precious intellectual talent. Indeed, their thought reform program has gone far beyond anything either their dynastic predecessors or their Russian Communist mentors ever attempted. They called for a personal conversion (or for something very closely resembling one) from every Chinese intellectual, surely an excessively ambitious program. Yet during the period immediately after they assumed power, many circumstances favored their efforts.

The Communists were then in the full flush of triumph. Their discipline and their confidence could not fail to impress a population which had been spiritually sapped by decades of civil war, foreign encroachments, and political corruption. Well before this a sizable number of intellectuals had been attracted to the Communist movement, many of whom had been introduced to it during their student days. By 1949, intellectuals as a group—including those with no particular ideological commitment—seemed more prone to welcome than to oppose the Communist victory. This was the impression of many observers and scholars, and one also clearly conveyed to me by my Chinese subjects and by friends in Hong Kong. Most intellectuals and students regarded the Nationalist regime with bitter hostility. They resented what they felt were police-state methods without the compensation of police-state efficiency. If one can speak of a class despair—a despair born of disillusionment, emotional confusion, repeated frustration, and economic suffering accompanying runaway inflation—one may certainly say it of the Chinese intellectuals during the years before the Communist takeover. In this condition, many of them were receptive not only to change, but to methods of being changed which they might otherwise have abhorred.[1]

Some Chinese intellectuals (although by no means all) had an opportunity to acquaint themselves gradually with Communist reform measures through small "political study" and "mutual aid" groups organized where they lived, worked, or studied. These were dogmatic, but relatively mild compared with what followed. By late 1951, all intellectuals were swept up in a year-long Thought Reform Campaign primarily aimed at them as a group—the first of China's national outbreaks of soul-searching. One Chinese commentator, writing from Hong Kong, described this campaign as "one of the most spectacular events in human history." [2] Other equally spectacular campaigns were to come; but this one set the precedent, and its sequence of top-to-bottom manipulations—typical for all national campaigns—is worth describing.[3]

First came the mandate from Mao Tse-tung himself: "Ideological reform, first of all the ideological reform of the intellectuals, is one of the most important conditions for a country's all-out complete democratic reform and industrialization." Next, the central ministry of education called together three thousand leading university professors and academic administrators of the Peking-Tientsin area to launch a "study campaign" aimed at "the reform of the teachers' ideology and of higher education." Premier Chou En-lai addressed this group for five hours, spelling out in detail a program for transforming the university into a genuinely "progressive" institution, and stressing such personal reform issues as "standpoint," "attitude," "whom we serve," "problems of thought," "problems of knowledge," "problems of democracy," and "criticism and self-criticism." (One of the educators present reported that Chou set a personal example with a self-criticism of his own "social relations.") Then, under Communist guidance, study groups were formed. At the same time, the campaign was given wide publicity in newspapers, magazines, and radio broadcasts; and through organizational work, it spread from the capital city outward, to all universities and intellectual communities throughout China.

Centered in universities (but including all intellectuals, whatever their affiliations), the campaign included everyone from the elderly college president to the newly-admitted freshman student, as "tens of thousands of intellectuals . . . [were] brought to their knees, accusing themselves relentlessly at tens of thousands of meetings and in tens of millions of written words." [4] This was the campaign's harvest: a flood of self-castigation from China's most learned men, public confessions which became a prominent feature in the country's press during the next few months, and on repeated occasions from then on. Combining personal anecdote, philosophical sophistication, and stereotyped jargon, the confessions followed a consistent pattern: first, the denunciation of one's past—of personal immorality and erroneous views; then a description of the way in which one was changing all of this under Communist guidance; and finally, a humble expression of remaining defects and a pledge to work hard at overcoming them with the help of progressive colleagues and Party members.

Distinguished scholars denounced careers that had brought them international fame, and expressed the desire to begin over again in their work and in their lives. One prominent feature (also present in the case histories) was the professor's public humiliation before his own students: a professor of law, for instance, in making his confession before a large meeting of undergraduates, addressed them as "fellow students," went on to thank them for their suggestions and to promise to adhere to these "in the most minute detail so that I can improve myself," then closed with the pledge "to be your pupil and to learn from you." (These confessions must be read to appreciate their full flavor; the published confession of a Harvard-trained professor of philosophy, made at a leading university in Peking, appears in the Appendix, page 473.) While much of the content of these documents seems ritualistic and unconvincing, my Western subjects made it clear that even such expressions are by no means free of emotional involvement, and reflect pressures of immense magnitude. Students outdid their professors in reform enthusiasms.

During the two years of Communist rule before this official campaign began, however, many intellectuals underwent their thought reform in special centers called "revolutionary universities" or "revolutionary colleges." These institutions provided the most concentrated of programs, sealed-in worlds in which thought reform existed in its own pure culture. The revolutionary university was directly derived from Party schools in which (see Chapter 20) the reform program for Chinese intellectuals had been developed years before; these schools were quietly conducted prototypes for the later, more flamboyant public displays.

Set up in every area of China almost in the wake of the victorious Communist armies, revolutionary universities were most active during the regime's first few years; by 1952, many had been converted into more conventional cadre-training centers. One of their purposes was to meet an emergency need for trained personnel; the course was usually only six months long, at most eight or twelve months, and the student body was by no means exclusive. It included such groups as former officials of the Nationalist regime, professors from ordinary universities in a particular area; "returned" students from the West, some who had just come back and others who had been to Europe or America as long as thirty or forty years before; and arbitrarily selected groups of young university instructors, recent graduates, and even undergraduates. There were also Communist party members and affiliates, some of whom had demonstrated significant "errors" in their work or thoughts, and others who had merely spent enough time in Kuomintang areas to be considered contaminated by the exposure.

Many came to revolutionary universities in response to thinly-veiled coercion—the strong "suggestion" that they attend. But others actively sought admission because they wished to adapt themselves to the new regime, or at least to find out what was expected of them; they believed, moreover, that a diploma from one of these centers would be a big help in the New China. And, as the first Chinese case history demonstrates, some sought admission to solve personal problems in their relationships to the Communist regime.

I soon became aware that the programs at both regular universities and revolutionary universities had maximum importance for Chinese intellectuals and maximum psychological interest for my research. Twelve of my fifteen subjects underwent their reforms at one or the other, and the four case histories I shall describe are equally divided between them. I have given the revolutionary college the most detailed attention, because I believe it represents the hard core of the entire Chinese thought reform movement. But before we attempt to penetrate this core, I must say a bit more about my Chinese subjects, and the nature of my work with them.

As a group, they could not show as wide a spectrum of responses to thought reform as the Westerners whom I interviewed, for they were all essentially thought reform failures. They belonged to that small minority of Chinese intellectuals who had elected to leave the mainland and remain in Hong Kong as refugees from the Communist regime. They are therefore in no sense typical of Chinese intellectuals in general. But neither are their reactions unrelated to those of the larger body of intellectuals who remained: even as thought reform failures, they had some positive responses which can help us understand the program's successes; and their negative reactions, although stronger than those of the majority of intellectuals, can help us to appreciate some of the stumbling blocks thought reform ran into with China's intellectuals. Moreover, the nature of the reform process—its stress on close contact and on the psychological exposé—enabled my subjects to make telling observations about others who responded quite differently from themselves.

Chinese subjects, of course, could not avoid the psychological and financial strains of their refugee status. Sometimes one of them would attempt to use an interview with me as a forum to attack, not the Communists or the Nationalists, but a rival refugee organization. Most were living under conditions which were, at best, tenuous, and they tended to look upon their participation in the research as a potential means of sooner or later bettering their lot. This attitude was in keeping with Chinese views of reciprocity; as L. S. Yang has pointed out, when a Chinese acts, he anticipates a response: "Favors done for others are often considered what may be termed 'social investments,' for which handsome returns are expected." [5] A Chinese subject, understandably enough, usually wanted material rather than psychological assistance from me; and some of the "handsome returns" expected (or at least hoped for) included my recommending a particular refugee organization to an American group whose assistance was desired, my helping a man to obtain a job with a Western organization in Hong Kong, or my supporting a man's efforts to enter the United States.

I decided that financial remuneration in some form was in order, both because these people badly needed money, and because it could serve as my reciprocal response in place of other expectations, which usually were impossible (if not inadvisable) for me to meet. But I felt that paying by the interview would not be a good idea, since it might create an incentive for a subject to hold back material in order to prolong the financial opportunity, and also because it might have conveyed the undesirable suggestion that I was paying for information. I hit upon a compromise arrangement which worked so well that I used it throughout the study. I had the subject prepare written materials useful to my work, most often a near verbatim reconstruction of the final thought summary originally composed during thought reform itself; and for this I paid the standard Hong Kong publication rate for an article of approximately that length. If my relationship with a subject was prolonged, I simply repeated the procedure after a certain number of interviews, and asked the subject to contribute additional autobiographical information that was of special significance in his case. This arrangement proved to be highly beneficial and face-saving for both of us.

My interpreters were also refugee intellectuals, and this too created problems. Subjects often felt more uneasy about revealing themselves, especially their political convictions, to fellow Chinese refugees than they did to me. I was a relatively harmless American; but who could tell what my interpreter's affiliations might be? Sometimes a subject required that a friend of his serve as interpreter, an arrangement I accepted only when I also knew the person suggested and thought he was suitable. And even then, I usually tried to replace him with one of my own interpreters for some portion of the work. Other subjects cultivated the interpreter after hours, hoping to win his support for a favor from me. For all of these reasons, I considered it extremely important that the interpreter strongly identify himself with me and with the research. The two men I regularly worked with were personal friends who more than met my requirements.

These considerations were important because my interpreters were required to do a good deal more than simply translate back and forth during the interviews: as Westernized Chinese, they were a bridge between the relatively un-Westernized Chinese subject and the (also relatively) un-Sinicized Western interviewer. David Riesman has called this "tandem interviewing": the interpreter served as an acculturating force in both directions, making it possible for the subject and myself—between whom there was no common language and much cultural distance—to converse with one another. There had to be a certain amount of compromise: the subject had to adapt himself to my Western approach and I had to bend slightly in a Chinese direction. This included, on my part, serving tea with each interview, the unconscious development of a bit more reserve than usual, and the conscious development of an indirect (or circular) approach to the more sensitive topics discussed.

I have emphasized the difficulties I encountered owing to the Chineseness and the refugee status of this subject group (the latter condition perhaps created more problems than did the former); but once the three of us had surmounted these early barriers, a three-way team enthusiasm often developed. All of us directed our full energies toward illuminating the nuances of the subject's emotions and then conveying these to me as the final common pathway;

and all of us shared in the excitement of achieving a deepening understanding of thought reform. These interviews were often quite grueling, and required at least twice as much time as ordinary interviews to cover the same ground; but they had a special fascination. After months of work, a significant therapeutic relationship often developed in both interpreted and direct (English language) interviews with Chinese subjects. This usually did not have the same cathartic intensity as with Westerners (although with one English-speaking girl it did); rather there was a gradual shift from my probing to the subject's raising questions on his own about past and present emotions which had troubled him.

On the whole, my Chinese subject group was young, with a heavy student representation. I did not intentionally seek young subjects; their preponderance was due to a number of reasons. They were available to me through the refugee publishing organizations to which they belonged; and younger people could more easily leave Communist China after intensive thought reform, both with and without official permission: they had fewer family responsibilities, greater anonymity, and better excuses (visiting parents in Hong Kong during university vacations for example) to cross the border. This accidental emphasis upon youth turned out to be a great advantage. It helped me to achieve better understanding of the phenomenal role which young people have played in revolutionary twentieth-century China, and it shed light upon psychological questions relating to identity and change. The subject group did not lack diversity, however; it included college students in their late teens and early twenties, seasoned revolutionaries in their thirties, and experienced government officials close to middle age. My subjects came from all parts of China, and from such diverse backgrounds as middle-class urban merchant families, rural gentry, and, rarely, rural peasantry.

The Chinese subject group may be broken down as follows: total —fifteen; locale of thought reform experience—seven in regular universities, five in revolutionary colleges, two in military settings, and one in a business group; occupation at time of thought reform —seven students, two displaced students, two government officials (both of whom had done some university teaching), one university instructor, two soldiers, and one businessman (in the Hong Kong environment, thirteen of the subjects were in an ill-defined group of students-teachers-writers, and the other two were in business); geographical distribution—seven from the Hunan-Hupei-Anhui area (South Central China); four from the Peking area (North Central China); and four from the Canton area (South China); sex—twelve male, three female; age—from nineteen to forty-nine, mostly between twenty and thirty-five.

Chinese subjects were on the whole more removed in time from their thought reform than the Western group, most having experienced it one to four years before our interviews. This time lapse increased the possibility of retrospective distortion, which I had always to keep in mind. To get underneath any such distortion, I encouraged each subject to try to recapture during our interviews the actual emotions of his reform, rather than merely talk about them from a distance. I eventually got most of them to do this to a considerable extent, because there is something about the reform process which causes it to retain an unusually high degree of emotional vividness for the former participant. Only after extensive efforts of this kind—including much focused questioning and re-checking of responses, as well as an over-all estimation of a man's reliability of recall—did I attempt to reconstruct an individual case.

As I participated in the subject's recapturing process, I often felt that I was listening to a Gulliver telling of his travels in a very strange land. That strange land was not so much China as it was thought reform—especially the alien realm of the revolutionary university.

CHAPTER 14

THE REVOLUTIONARY
UNIVERSITY: MR. HU

Early in my stay in Hong Kong I was introduced to
Mr. Hu Wei-han, a native of Hupeh province in
Central China, and a graduate of North China University, a large
revolutionary university [1] situated just outside of Peking. I met
him in the customary fashion, through intermediaries: a Chinese acquaintance of mine was working closely with him in a
"third force" (critical of both Communists and Nationalists) press
service. Mr. Hu was then thirty, tall and thin, erect and dignified,
if a bit rigid, in his bearing. Courteous and formal in the fashion
of an upper-class Chinese, he spoke in quiet, measured tones, always with intensity. I soon noticed that he rarely smiled; his facial
expression was invariably serious, not infrequently sullen, never
really relaxed. At the same time, he maintained throughout our
sessions an unusual degree of enthusiasm and stamina.

Although he had left Communist China four years before, he
was still cautious about interview arrangements. For a while, he
preferred to meet at his own office, although later he came regularly to my apartment. He insisted that the friend who had introduced us serve as interpreter (although months later, after a falling
out with his friend, he welcomed the substitution of one of my
regular interpreters). And at first he wondered whether I wasn't

"something more than a psychiatrist." But over the course of sixteen months of interviews (twenty-five meetings totalling about eighty hours), he became increasingly open and spontaneous. Indeed, after a few all-day sessions during the first weeks of our work together, we got to know each other quite well.

At the time Hu began his thought reform, he was no stranger to the Communist movement. He had been sympathetic to it since his middle-school days, and as a student leader at the University of Nanking he had worked closely with the Communist underground for several years. Just after the takeover, however, he became involved in a controversy with Communist officials which eventually led to his admission to North China University. Appointed to a special committee set up at the University of Nanking, he had spoken strongly in favor of keeping the University in session, in opposition to the Communist representatives who wanted it temporarily closed down. Not only was he overruled, he was "tricked into accepting their point of view." Deeply upset by this experience ("My views . . . were widely known. . . . Now I considered myself a failure. I had no face to see my fellow students"), he decided to leave Nanking. Hoping that things might be better in the north, he went to Peking and sought, through well-situated friends, some position within the Communist movement. Meeting with little success, he expressed his disappointment to one of these friends, who in reply offered the following advice:

Your thoughts are still those of the bourgeoisie. You must change for the great period ahead. You should go to North China University for ideological reform and they will help you to make the change.

Still wishing to find a place in the new regime, Hu accepted the idea that a change in his thoughts might be necessary. He took his friend's words seriously, and hearing that a class was about to begin, embarked on the short trip to the revolutionary university. A letter of recommendation which he had obtained from a high-ranking Communist official served as his admission credentials.

The Great Togetherness: Group Identification

Hu found himself in an atmosphere that was austere but friendly: an open area with low wooden buildings which served as living quarters and places of study; old students (who had arrived

a week or two before) and Communist cadres warm in their greetings, helpful in their orienting tours, and enthusiastic in their talk
about the revolutionary university, the Communist movement, the
new hope for the future. He was assigned to a small group of nine
other young intellectuals much like himself. Because of his superior
knowledge of Marxism he was elected by this group to be its leader,
which thus thrust him directly into the organizational hierarchy.

He discovered that the revolutionary university was a huge establishment, tightly organized along Communist principles of "democratic centralism." It contained four large sections each with more
than a thousand students. His section consisted of miscellaneous
young intellectuals and was the largest; he estimated that it included
about three thousand men and women. The other three were made
up of "cultural workers" (writers and artists), older professors and
former government officials (a well-publicized invitation to the
school had been extended to many such prominent figures), and
teachers in training. The nominal head of the institution, who gave
the official welcoming speech and presided over other ritual occasions, was an elderly educator formerly associated with the KMT;
real authority was in the hands of the four section heads, who were
Party members, and the subsection heads and class heads who
worked under them. Each class head was responsible for the reform of one hundred students (ten small groups), and had at his
disposal three special assistants.

These three assistants, who acted as links between the faculty and
students, were the *cadres*. (This term is used for Communist "organization men"—lower-level officials, usually but not necessarily
Party members, whose lives are inseparable from Party activity, and
who express at all times the Party point of view.) The three cadres
performed the day-to-day legwork of reform. They knew the procedure well, not only because they had guided previous classes
through it, but also because they had experienced it themselves as
part of their training.[2] Each of the cadres had a designated function:
the "executive cadre" was concerned with courses of study, reports,
and records; the "organizing cadre" was most intimately involved
with group activities and with the attitudes of individual students;
the "advisory cadre" (the only one of the three who might be a
woman) concerned himself with the students' personal affairs and
reading habits, and offered counsel on ideological problems. Hu

noticed that the three cadres assigned to his class worked as a unit; they were approachable separately, but always united in policy, and even made many of their public appearances together.

During the first days at the university, the cadres were rarely in evidence: the students were left to themselves in complete freedom, and told to "just get to know each other." To Hu and to most of the others, the atmosphere was exhilarating. Initial reserve quickly gave way, and students began to reveal to one another details of their backgrounds, and of their frustrations, beliefs, and future aspirations. Forgetting his recent conflict with the Communists, Hu was caught up in the general enthusiasm and the high *esprit de corps*:

> The revolutionary university seemed to be a place which brought together young people from all over with a great deal in common. We ate, slept and talked together, all of us eager to make new friends. The ten of us were at first strangers, but we quickly developed a strong bond. . . . I had very warm feelings toward the group and toward the school. I felt I was being treated well in a very free atmosphere. I was happy and thought that I was on my way to a new life.

Only one incident, which occurred about ten days after Hu's arrival, marred an otherwise perfect honeymoon period—an incident which revealed much about Hu, and initiated a pattern in his relationship to school authorities which persisted throughout his six months at the revolutionary university. While taking an after-dinner stroll, he came upon an informal gathering of about one hundred students and three cadres. He listened as one of the cadres explained that Marxism was an "everlasting truth of society"; but during the discussion which followed, he got up and politely but definitely disagreed with this statement, asserting that Marxism was no more than a "guiding principle of a certain period" which would probably be replaced by a new doctrine once the transition from capitalism to socialism had been accomplished. Hu recalled the incident (possibly exaggerating it in retrospect) in dramatic terms:

> It was late at night, and there was no electric light. We had only an oil lamp and it was dim with shadows. When the discussion reached its climax . . . many of the students agreed with me. . . . and I was in a more powerful position than the cadres. . . . Someone started applause and it spread to most of the group. Rarely could an idea in such opposition to the cadres gain such a response.

Hu felt that this incident gained him respect among the other students, but that his outspoken behavior had caused the authorities to begin to regard him as an "individualist" and a man to be watched. Soon after this the same cadre began to criticize Hu strongly, to a degree that Hu felt was above and beyond the call of thought reform duty. He attributed this to his having caused the cadre a public loss of face, and gave a clear explanation of what he meant by this: "He was supposed to be the most distinguished person among us; by opposing him openly and gaining public support during the discussion. . . . I disgraced him in a Chinese sense."

After two weeks of this shared informality, all the students in Hu's class were called together for "thought mobilization" meetings at which the philosophy of the program was forcefully presented. Individual thought reform was to be a part of the over-all reform of Chinese society. Just as past social evils had to be swept away, so did one have to remedy one's personal evil if he wished to take his place in this great renaissance. For a Chinese intellectual, reform was a particularly pressing matter: his talents were urgently needed by "the people," and yet his class background had so "poisoned" him that until he was reformed, he was unable to serve them.

Next came the beginning of formal courses, the first of which was entitled the History of the Development of Society. This course was followed by: Lenin—The State; Materialistic Dialectics; History of the Chinese Revolution; Theory of the New Democracy—Maoism; and Field Study—visits to old Communist workshops and industrial centers. A leading Communist theorist came from Peking to deliver the opening lecture (there was just one lecture for each course). This talk was a memorable one: for more than five hours the distinguished visitor presented a carefully-documented exposition of Marxist views on organic evolution (the emergence of man from lower primates by means of labor, or as a popular pamphlet put it: "From monkey to man, through labor"), and on social evolution (the development of human society from its primitive communist stage through subsequent "slave," "feudal," "capitalist," "socialist," and inevitable "Communist" stages). The thousand students in the audience listened carefully, and took copious notes. There were no interruptions and no questions at the end.

Rather, the students quickly reassembled in their small groups to discuss the lecture material. And from then on, these *hsüeh hsi* sessions continued virtually all day, every day, until they were interrupted for another marathon lecture introducing a new course. A major national event, such as a speech by Mao Tse-tung, might also be the occasion for larger gatherings, and a temporary change in the subject matter of the small group sessions as well.

As group leader, Hu guided the *hsüeh hsi* discussions, and tried to clarify the lecture material for the other students. He and the other nine group leaders of his class held daily (sometimes twice daily) meetings with a cadre, during which each gave a rundown on the attitude and progress of the individual members of his group. The other students knew about these reports, but seemed, on the whole, to accept them as regular organizational procedure. Hu was instructed by the cadre to take a "relatively neutral" attitude in his group, and to encourage free and lively discussion. He enjoyed both his teaching and his organizational responsibilities. He shared with the other students a sense of pulling together toward a common goal in a spirit of crusade.

The Closing In: Conflict and "Struggle"

After a few weeks of this study, however, Hu noticed a gradual change. The cadre receiving his daily reports demanded more detailed analyses of the other students' behavior; less stress was put on Marxist theory and more on individual attitudes. Hu was no longer enjoying the role he was asked to play: "My intention was to help the students to study about Communism, but I soon began to realize that the Communists were more interested in my helping them to study the students." At the same time, it was made clear to him that he was to be no longer neutral in his attitude, but was instead (in Mao's phrase) to "lean to one side," to support the "progressive elements," and to apply stronger pressures to the others in the direction of reform.

Matters came to a head at the time of the first "thought summary"; each student prepared one of these at the end of every course. The cadres passed along information—via group leaders and informal contacts in such places as the dining room—about the form these summaries should take: they were mainly to discuss the influence of the first course upon the student's previous views of society. A two-day period was devoted to writing the summary; then each of these students was required to read his to the other group members, each of whom offered criticisms. Some of the students, still influenced by the easy-going atmosphere of the honeymoon period, took the matter lightly and dashed off their summaries without much thought; but Hu noticed that the cadres took it very seriously, and that they made a practice of sitting in on some of the summary readings to make sure that the criticisms were thorough and penetrating.

Criticisms gave rise to countercriticisms, and group harmony gave way to tense antagonisms. The descriptions of past and present attitudes which students had so freely offered each other during the first days now came back to haunt them. Previously quiet students suddenly became "activists," stepping up the pace of criticism and intensifying the emotional tone within the group. Some of these activists identified themselves as members of the Communist Youth Corps or of the Communist Party itself, thus emerging from an underground status. Their regular attendance at Party and Youth Corps meetings gave them a channel to the school hierarchy which, in terms of real power, superseded Hu's authority as group leader. When Hu realized this, he became increasingly uncomfortable—aware that he was being informed on, but never quite sure just when and by whom. He also noted that the authorities had begun to shift students about from one group to another in order to make most effective use of activists, always keeping in his group one or two who could exert strong influence. And his experience with his own thought summary increased his apprehension. Although it was fully orthodox in form and content, he had made it somewhat terse. He was strongly criticized by an activist who accused him of concealing details, and the interested presence of all three cadres convinced him that the faculty was showing special concern about his personal progress.

From this point on, pressures steadily mounted, and Hu lived in an atmosphere of criticism, self-criticism, and confession much like the prison environment of the Western subjects. Not only ideas, but underlying motivations were carefully scrutinized. Students were taken to task for failure to achieve the correct "materialistic viewpoint," "proletarian (or "people's") standpoint," and "dialectical methodology"—and the reasons for these failures were analyzed even more carefully than in prison reform. As a group leader, Hu helped to promote this orthodoxy; as a student, he was himself sometimes rebuked for failing to live up to it.

His advanced theoretical knowledge of Communism served him well, but it did not render him immune from the array of standard criticisms which in the revolutionary college covered an even broader spectrum than in the prison. The prisoner was attacked for his associations with imperialism and for his own "imperialistic traits"; the student at the revolutionary university was mainly under fire for his "individualism." As interpreted from Mao's writings by cadres, activists, and the student rank and file, this term was extended to include any tendency to follow personal inclinations rather than the path charted out by the Party. Since this meant "placing one's own interests above those of 'the people,'" individualism was considered highly immoral. And so were the other faults for which the students were repeatedly criticized and for which they criticized others: "subjectivism"—applying to a problem a personal viewpoint rather than a "scientific" Marxist approach; "objectivism"—undue detachment, viewing oneself "above class distinction," or "posing as a spectator of the new China"; "sentimentalism"—allowing one's attachments to family or friends to interfere with reform needs, and therefore "carrying about an ideological burden" (usually a reluctance to denounce the objects of one's sentimentalism); as well as "deviationism," "opportunism," "dogmatism," "reflecting exploiting class ideology," "overly technical viewpoints," "bureaucratism," "individual heroism," "revisionism," "departmentalism," "sectarianism," and (neither last nor least) "pro-American outlook."

Hu, in the eyes of cadres and fellow-students, was clearly an individualist. His unsolicited public debate with the cadre had given him this status at the onset, and his subsequent behavior did little to dispel it. Even though he conducted himself in an exemplary fashion—"progressive" in attitude, circumspect in manner, conscientious in carrying out his responsibilities as a group leader—it was clear to everyone that he was holding much of himself back. He did not join in group enthusiasms, and kept to himself as much as he could in such an environment. In his reports to the cadre as group leader, he maintained a correct standard of Communist-style analysis, but at the same time tried always to say as little as possible, and to avoid making damaging assessments of other students. These reports were a source of great inner conflict to him: he hated the idea of informing upon others, yet he could not fully dissociate himself from the cadres' claim that these evaluations served a moral purpose in "helping" backward students; in any case, he felt compelled—as a means of adapting to pressures brought to bear upon him—to offer some degree of compliance.

When criticized, he would admit his shortcomings, and even go on to make the proper self-criticism in attributing them to "ruling class" and "bourgeois" influences in his family and educational background. But there was something perfunctory in his manner of doing so, and the cadres sensed his inner resistance. Often one or more of them would make a friendly approach to him, suggesting that he seemed troubled by "ideological problems," asking him to "talk things over." They would go on to tell him that they considered him a man of great promise, the type needed by the Party, one who would go far in the organization. They even described other cases of similar young men, also highly individualistic at the time of their thought reform, who had, after ridding themselves of this deficiency, become high-ranking Communist officials.

Hu did not respond to these overtures. Instead he felt his inner opposition steadily mounting ("I was becoming more and more sick of the process"), and his inability to discuss his true sentiments with anyone an increasing strain:

I could never have a chance to talk about these things or about what I considered to be right. I had to restrain myself constantly, to be patient, to avoid offending the cadres or the activists. I always had to conceal what was on my mind. . . . I could never feel easy.

Hu began to sense that the cadres were antagonistic to him, and he feared that, should he make one false move, they might well label him a "reactionary"—a dangerous accusation for anyone. He found himself in the paradoxical position of still retaining his general faith in the Chinese Communist movement, while feeling increasingly trapped in his personal thought reform experience.

His dilemma increased as the moralistic tone of the criticism and self-criticism process extended into every aspect of his daily existence. As in the prison setting (but in a "native" rather than "imperialist" frame) students were criticized for such "bourgeois" or "ruling class" characteristics as pride, conceit, greed, competitiveness, dishonesty, boastfulness, and rudeness. And when liaisons between the sexes developed (the revolutionary university was co-educational, although living quarters for men and women were completely separate) these were discussed within the small groups and evaluated solely in terms of their effect on the reform progress of the two people involved. If a "backward" girl friend was thought to be impeding a student's progress, he was advised to break off the relationship; but if both were "progressive," or if one were thought to be aiding the other's progress, the group would give its approval. One female activist gave evidence of a romantic interest in Hu, but he was unresponsive and highly suspicious (probably with justification) of her motives. Sexual unions were, on the whole, discouraged, as it was felt that they drained energies from the thought reform process. The opportunity for romance was limited anyway, since the days were taken up almost completely by *hsüeh hsi*, and the evenings by additional meetings and by reading. Sunday, although nominally a day of rest, was frequently devoted to self-examinations that had not been completed during the week; and such entertainments as there were—movies, plays, group singing, and dancing—were invariably tied in with some aspect of the Communist ideological message. Students in Hu's section were not expected to leave the grounds of the revolutionary university unless they had some special reason.

As in prisons, the atmosphere became saturated with individual confessions. Instead of criminal activities, each student was expected to reveal everything about past affiliations with "reactionary" groups (usually the KMT regime or its student organizations). Each course became a vehicle for exposing more of his own self, for condemning more of the evil in his character. Each student developed a running confession, compounded of self-criticisms, thought summaries, and extracurricular self-examinations; this was a major indicator of his progress in reform. Taking shape both orally and in writing, its content became known to other students and to cadres and class heads. One's eagerness to reveal himself seemed to be more important than any specific thing revealed.

Like the Western prisoners, students vied to outdo each other in the frankness, completeness, and luridness of their individual confessions: one group would issue a challenge to another to match its collective confessions; personal confession became the major topic of discussion in small group meetings, large student gatherings, informal talks with cadres, articles posted upon bulletin boards, and "wall newspapers." Hu had the feeling that everywhere he went, he encountered the question, "Have you made your full confession?"

In his case, he had little in his past to conceal; indeed, his "progressive" record, though he stated it with restraint, was a mark of distinction. What troubled him was a "secret" of the immediate present, and its consequences for his Communist future. For he was becoming obsessed with his own inner antagonism, and the dangerous rebel within him—the formulator of these obsessive thoughts—threatened always to expose the rest of him:

The intensity of my anti-Communist thoughts greatly increased. I developed a terrible fear that these thoughts would come out and be known to all. But I was determined to prevent this. I tried to appear calm, but I was in great inner turmoil. I knew that if I kept quiet no one could know this secret which I had not confessed. But people were always talking about secrets . . . saying that it was wrong to keep secrets, that one had to confess everything. Sometimes during an ordinary conversation the cadre or a student would mention secrets, and I would feel very disturbed. . . . Or we would be called suddenly to an informal meeting, and someone would get up and say, "There are still some students in the university who remain 'antiorganization'." I knew that no one else was thinking of me, but I couldn't help feeling very upset. . . . The secret was always something that was trying to escape from me.

Part of Hu's "secret" was his growing disillusionment and despair:

I had thought that by entering the revolutionary university I could make a new start. Instead of this it had brought me mainly the loss of personal liberty. . . . I felt disappointed . . . infuriated and disgusted. . . . I had little hope for the future.

Observing the other students around him, Hu felt that all were tense and agitated, without necessarily sharing his own response. In fact, many of the younger ones—those in their teens and early twenties—seemed to be throwing themselves fully, even ecstatically, into the reform process, thriving upon their activist frenzy. Others a bit older made a great public display of their progressiveness in what Hu considered an opportunist fashion, some of them seeking to compensate for incriminating ties with the old regime in the past. But Hu felt that almost everyone in his section who was over twenty-five was in conflict about how much of himself to surrender to the process.

Students' attitudes toward one another had changed greatly from the idyllic togetherness of the earliest days. The sense of common purpose had by no means completely disappeared; but the pressures which everyone was experiencing had converted the small group sessions into a complicated blend of eager analysis, cautious orthodoxy, covert personal antagonism, and beleaguered co-operation.

Hu's own position grew steadily worse. His suppressed resentment was always just beneath the surface, and on one occasion, when he intervened on behalf of a female student in an argument with school guards, this resentment exploded openly. Hu was then required to make a special self-examination to condemn his misconduct, his lack of full faith in the Party's representatives, and the "individualism" at the bottom of it all. Cadres were no longer gentle and therapeutic in their approach to him, but made it clear that they considered him stubborn and unco-operative. One of them (his old nemesis) began to make indirect threats, implying that if his attitude did not improve, his case would be dealt with at a public gathering. Hu knew well what this meant; he had witnessed three such mass meetings. Two of these had been revivalist-like gatherings at which a student with a particularly evil past had been given a dramatic (and well-staged) opportunity to redeem himself. Before an audience of 3,000 fellow students, this offender gave a lurid description of his misdeeds—political work with the Nationalists, spying for the Japanese, anti-Communist activity, stealing money from his company, violating his neighbor's daughter —followed by an expression of relief at "washing away all of my sins" and of gratitude to the government for "helping me to become a new man." The effect of the meetings had been an intensification of confession pressures and a widespread feeling that whatever one had done was mild by comparison and might as well be revealed.

Aware that he was not a likely candidate for this type of display, Hu worried about another kind of public exposure: the ultimate humiliation of the mass "struggle." He had seen a student considered to be a hopelessly "backward element" face an equally large audience to be denounced rather than redeemed; faculty members, cadres, and fellow students had embellished upon his "reactionary tendencies," his stubborn refusal to change his ways, his failure to respond to repeated offers of "help" which all claimed to have made. It had been made quite clear that this young man's future in Communist China was quite precarious, and the ceremony had been a grim warning to Hu and other students of questionable standing.

Hu received one additional warning. A Youth Corps member personally sympathetic to him told him that his case had been critically discussed by cadres at Youth Corps meetings, and that he had better be more careful in the future. Hu was moved by this show of compassion, realizing that the other student had acted at considerable personal risk.

He did become more cautious, and tried to make a better reform showing. One of the ways he did this, at the same time finding some escape, was to spend as much time as possible alone in the library, immersing himself in the only reading material available—Communist literature. What he learned gave him added authority in the group; and the cadre's threats of public exposure were never carried out. Hu felt he had also been protected by his progressive past, his letter of recommendation from a high Communist official, his favorable standing among many of the students, his knowledge of Communism, and, perhaps most important, something in his character which made the cadres feel that he might be still salvaged as an effective Communist worker.

But his added readings, especially of Lenin's works, were also a source of anxiety. For he began to realize that what he was experiencing in thought reform was not, as he had preferred to believe, a misapplication of Communist principles, but was in every respect consistent with Leninist teachings. He found himself questioning the entire Communist structure. He achieved better external control; but his inner feelings of hostility, suffocation, and confusion were more intolerable than ever:

I had a very strong hatred for the Communists and for the whole system. But it was a general kind of feeling and I wasn't sure of its exact source. It wasn't directed exclusively against the Communists—but was rather vague and diffuse. I was very unhappy about the surroundings; everything from all directions was pressing upon me. I couldn't stand this pressure and wanted only to get rid of it. It was not a feeling of resistance—I just wanted to escape. I felt persecuted and depressed.

He began to have nightmares and thought he was talking in his sleep; he would wake up anxiously, fearing that he might have revealed his "secret." He was also greatly upset by a suicide which occurred during this stage of the reform program (a young student had apparently jumped into a well); this student had been a Youth Corps member and outwardly an activist, and his death led Hu to believe that "he too must have had some hidden secret." Two other students had to be sent to mental hospitals, having apparently become psychotic. Many other students (Hu estimated their number as high as one-third of the student body) by this time had visible psychological or psychosomatic symptoms—fatigue, insomnia, loss of appetite, vague aches and pains, and upper respiratory or gastrointestinal symptoms.[3] Hu himself suffered from fatigue and general malaise. He visited the school doctor, who gave him a reform-oriented and psychologically sophisticated diagnosis: "There's nothing wrong with your body. It must be your thoughts that are sick. You will feel better when you have solved your problems and completed your reform." And indeed, he shared with many other students a state of painful inner conflict. Yet the contagious cacophony of enthusiasm, tension, and fear was still, after five months, very much in crescendo.

Final Thought Summary:
Submission and the New Harmony

The announcement that it was time to begin work on the overall thought summary (or final confession) implied that relief was in sight, but it also made clear that this last effort would be the crucial one. At a mass meeting, faculty members emphasized the importance of the summary as the crystallization of the entire reform experience, the final opportunity for each student to resolve his thought problems. For the next two days, small group sessions were devoted almost entirely to discussions of the form of the summary. It was to be a life history, beginning two generations back and extending through the thought reform experience, describing, candidly and thoroughly, the development of one's thoughts and the relationship of these to actions. It was also to analyze the personal effects of thought reform, on one's character as well as one's view of the world, including but going beyond what had already been written and discussed in previous thought summaries. It would require anywhere from five to twenty-five thousand Chinese characters (roughly equivalent to the same number of English words); but content was much more important than length. And each man's summary had to be approved before he could graduate. Rumors circulated among the students of "backward elements" having been asked to repeat the entire thought reform course, and of "reactionaries" or "enemies of the people" sent to prison for reform by labor.

After a ten-day writing period, students read their summaries to the small group. They encountered even more prolonged and penetrating criticism than before, since everyone was now required to sign each confession read, to signify his approval and his responsibility for letting it pass. In Hu's group, some students were kept under critical fire for several days and wrote many revisions. As usual, the students themselves worked upon each other, but cadres and faculty members had the final say; they later added their own evaluative comments to the thought summaries. The final document then became a permanent part of the student's personal record, and (in the possession of his superiors) accompanied him throughout his future career.

Hu, determined to surmount this final hurdle, concentrated upon using his theoretical knowledge to produce an acceptable final confession. He knew that two special emphases were required. The first, an analysis of class origin, gave him little difficulty: he could readily place his family in the "landlord" or "rural ruling class" category, and attribute to this circumstance his own evil character traits and false ideas. He called himself an "exploiter," and accused himself of "having adopted a stand diametrically opposed to that of the people," and having been in the past "actually . . . an enemy of the people."

But the second requirement was not quite as simple, for it was the denunciation of his father, both as an individual and as a representative of the old order. This was the ultimate symbolic act in the thought reform of young Chinese, and many found it to be extremely painful. A cadre noticed that Hu was particularly reluctant to criticize his father, and began to prod him about it at every opportunity: "He said that the most important part of the reform of an intellectual was the denunciation of his father—since the intellectual almost invariably comes from a wealthy family which must have been anti-Communist, and if he does not denounce his father he cannot be a faithful citizen of the new regime." Hu tried to beg off, claiming that he had retained no clear impressions because he and his father had been separated during much of his childhood. The cadre insisted however that "the father is a hero to every small boy," and demanded that Hu take a stand for or against him.

Two letters which Hu received from his family home at about this time suddenly gave the problem a new tragic dimension. The first letter, written by his uncle, carried the disturbing news that his father had been publicly "struggled" and then imprisoned during the land reform campaign in Hupeh, and asked Hu to use his influence with the Communists to secure his father's release. A day or two later, Hu received a second letter, from his father, telling that he had been released from prison, but that all of the family holdings had been taken from him, and that the family situation was still very dangerous. Hu had difficulty describing to me his feelings at this time, which were compounded of shock, guilt, and anger. At the beginning of land reform, Hu had written to his father to urge him to surrender voluntarily most of his land holdings to the surrounding peasants, and to co-operate fully with the Communists in the manner of an "enlightened landlord." The father had followed his son's advice; and now Hu felt that they both had been deceived. He recalled his last meeting with his father, when he had refused to follow his father's advice. He had decided to enter the distant University of Nanking, contrary to his father's wishes that he choose an institution closer to home; now he kept hearing the words of his father's parting admonition:

You young people no longer think of the older generation. Your affections towards us must be very light. You do not understand how an old man feels about his son. Our affection for you is beyond your comprehension.

We shall see later that these words were less than fair; but this did not save Hu from his sense of remorse, and from castigating himself for disobeying his father and for not remaining close enough to him to be a help in a time of crisis. He began to imagine —from descriptions he had heard of land-reform "struggle" meetings in the north—the picture of his father being insulted, spat upon, beaten, and stoned at the hands of a "people's court." He pictured his father imprisoned in chains; he remembered a sordid prison he had visited years before, and even more vividly his own experience of having been briefly imprisoned by the Nationalists because of his anti-government activities as a university student: "I relived all of my sufferings through this vision of my father meeting the same fate." Soon grief gave way to resentment: "I overcame my sorrow with my desire for vengeance." He identified himself closely with his father, and saw in both their maltreatment evidence of basic Communist hypocrisy and evil:

I began to feel that my father and I, each of us in his own way, were enemies to the Communists. My father was old and useless, and was therefore persecuted by them. I was young and useful and so the Communists were still trying to win me. . . . I was considered by the other students to be an able man. My father enjoyed great respect among the peasants of the countryside, and was always generous to them in time of need, never the greedy, cruel, heartless landlord, which the Communists always spoke about. . . . Both my father and I had tried very hard to work with the new regime; yet both of us were being victimized. I realized that the Communists had no sense of fairness or justice. They insisted upon beating down any person who held prestige among those around him outside of Party circles, and they would do whatever they thought necessary to accomplish this, no matter how "enlightened" such people might be concerning Communism. . . . I thought of the old model I had developed in my mind in the past of a Communist ideal state which would give land to the poor, and offer a new solution for a corrupt society. But I realized that Communism did not fit this ideal, and that the Communist is a very cruel man who uses the poor and their resentment against the rich for the purpose of furthering his own power.

As he told me these things (and especially when he referred to his father) Hu lost his usual composure, sometimes turning troubled eyes to the floor, at other times pacing restlessly about the room. He seemed more anxious than at any other time during our interviews; and at the next session I was told that he had remained agitated after our meeting and had insisted upon spending several hours alone with the interpreter discussing these same experiences.

Hu said nothing about the two letters to anyone around him in the revolutionary university. He found a compromise solution to the cadre's demand that he denounce his father by using a tortuous form of Communist reasoning: after mentioning his father's benevolence to the peasants, he went on to condemn his acts as "even more reactionary than the ruthless abuse . . . by the vicious landlords" because "these good deeds helped to render the position of the ruling class even more unassailable" (a statement which echoes Father Luca's remark that, "What you do that is good— is bad—precisely because it is good!").

In presenting his own life history, Hu was careful to play down his leftist student activities, and even related them critically to the "individualism" which was a central theme of the document. Only later did he realize how much an expression of personal submission this summary was:

It is a report very much against my own will. If you put this final thought summary before me now, I could write a new summary contradictory to it in each sentence. If it isn't fear, what else could push one to do something so completely against his own will? If I had not been so fearful I should have refused to write something like this.

He could not tell me how much of the summary he believed at that time. It included ideas which he did not believe even then, others which he believed then but subsequently discarded, and still others—as he explains in an eloquent testimony to the power of language—so enmeshed in Communist patterns of thought and speech as to defy evaluation:

Using the pattern of words for so long, you are so accustomed to them that you feel chained. If you make a mistake, you make a mistake within the pattern. Although you don't admit that you have adopted this kind of ideology, you are actually using it subconsciously, almost automatically. . . . At that time I believed in certain aspects of their principles and theories. But such was the state of confusion in my own mind that I couldn't tell or make out what were the things that I did believe in.

Hu noticed that after the thought summaries were completed (all in his group, and apparently in the other groups as well, were eventually accepted), most of the students seemed to experience a great sense of relief. They had passed through their trial and made their symbolic submission; and many—especially among the young—seemed to feel that a closer bond had been established between themselves and the government.

But for Hu there was no great relief and little or any feeling of bond. Still depressed and disappointed, his strongest desire was to leave the environment as soon as possible. He had previously decided to return to Nanking—the past scene of happy and successful days—and seek a job and a way of life (possibly as a school teacher) outside the main currents of politics. He had already written friends there who had sent him money for the journey. Therefore, when students were given cards to fill out to state their job preference, Hu paid little attention, and left his card blank—preferring to make his own arrangements. His action was considered an unfriendly one; it would have been quite different if he had indicated no choice and had added a note, as some students did, saying that he left the matter entirely up to the government's discretion. A cadre called him in for a talk, and when he defended his action on the basis of wishing to become a schoolteacher in Nanking, he was told, "We can assign you to a schoolteacher's job, but it would do you good to work in the countryside. You have been too long in the big cities, and maybe that is why you have not been so activist."

When the job assignment did come through, however, it was as a political worker and teacher in an obscure North China military area —a kind of assignment generally considered highly undesirable. No one was required to accept the job offered him, although most students had little choice, since they were unlikely to find an alternative position and they knew that a job refusal would not look well on their records. But Hu, without too much logical consideration, did decide to refuse the assignment—at least at first. Three days later, after constant visits from cadres and activists, he reversed himself and once more succumbed to the wishes of the authorities. He could not say just why he did this, but the implication was clear that he wished to make one last effort to fit in with the new regime, and hoped that life outside of the revolutionary university might be less oppressive. He also stated that the idea of actively fighting Communism in the future was already taking shape in his mind, and that he considered the job a good opportunity to obtain greater firsthand knowledge of Communist procedures. While this second reason might well have been an attempt to justify that which he felt emotionally impelled to do, it is quite possible that, confused and fearful as he was, ideas of adapting himself to Communism and of fighting Communism existed simultaneously within him.

All that was left was the graduation ceremony. The first part of this was devoted to an admission ritual for new Party members: facing a huge photograph of Mao, nine faculty cadres solemnly took their oaths, suggesting to the 3,000 students in the audience (according to Hu) "the honor, the great difficulty, and the importance of becoming a Party member." Hu felt that the students were almost forgotten in the excitement surrounding the new Party members, although faculty representatives and visiting officials (there to recruit personnel from among the graduates) did congratulate the students upon the completion of their thought reform, and urge them to continue to follow its principles in their future work.

When Hu arrived at his assignment in North China, he was required to undergo a two-month training period whose routine, except for more rigorous physical training, was not too different from that of the revolutionary university. At the end of this training, when he was faced with the prospect of accepting a permanent assignment with the army, Hu was unwilling to go through with it and requested that he be permitted to leave. He had been no happier there than at the revolutionary university; he had, in fact, found the new cadres under whom he worked to be, if less devious, more crude and unpleasant than those he had dealt with during his reform. The antagonisms he had observed between older and younger cadres, and between the military authorities and the rural peasant population, had confirmed his critical feelings toward the regime. In addition, he feared the possible outbreak of war with the West, and believed that should this happen his own position would become much more dangerous. But most important of all perhaps was his reluctance to become involved in any commitment to the regime that would make it impossible for him to get away in the future.

Communist authorities made strong attempts to get Hu to change his mind, but he pleaded failing health and inability, as a southerner, to tolerate the extreme cold (from which he actually did suffer). He was finally permitted to depart, although he was given virtually no travel credentials. He headed for Nanking, selling some of his belongings to finance the trip. There he found only a few positions available, all of which he felt would involve him too closely with the regime. He wished to visit his father in Hupeh; but from all he could learn, he decided that it would be much too dangerous. After a few weeks in Nanking, he was called for questioning by the police because of his idleness; and he felt it was unsafe to remain there. Through friends with whom he was staying he discovered that it was possible to leave China by way of the Hong Kong border (during early 1950, such travel was still not too difficult). He quickly decided to do this; and even an expression of affection from a girl he met in Canton (of whom he had been very fond during his middle-school days) could not deter him from leaving his country and entering the British Crown Colony.

CHAPTER 15

A CHINESE ODYSSEY

Many of Hu's emotional experiences have a familiar ring, since the psychological pressures at a revolutionary university closely resemble those in a prison. There is the assault upon identity, although without any physical brutality; the establishment of guilt and shame; a form of self-betrayal; alternating leniency and harshness; a compulsion to confess; the logical dishonoring of re-education; a final confession, elaborate and inclusive rather than terse; and an even greater emphasis upon the experience of personal rebirth. There are also important differences, such as the development of group intimacy ("the great togetherness") before the emotional pressures. But these differences, significant as they are, do not warrant a new step-by-step analysis.

To get at more basic contrasts and more basic underlying principles, we must, as with the Westerners, turn from the process to the individual, and follow Hu beyond his thought reform, first back over his early years and then through his Hong Kong life. Although the program which Hu encountered at the revolutionary university was typical enough (the other fourteen Chinese subjects, especially those four who had attended a revolutionary university, confirmed this), his responses were obviously unusual. Why was this so? What was there in his background and his character which led him to feel as he did? What can his experiences teach us of the reform conflicts and life struggles of Chinese intellectuals in general?

Childhood and Youth: Background for Reform

Symbolically enough, Hu's life began in exile. His father had been a high-ranking Nationalist official during the early years of the Chinese Revolution, and had spent many years in distant assignments or in flight from his enemies. One of these flights (from the forces of Yuan Shi-k'ai, a powerful general who sought to restore the monarchy and place himself on the throne) took him to Kansu, a remote province in the northwest. There he married Hu's mother, a relatively uneducated woman of undistinguished family background; and it was there that Hu was born and spent the first four years of his life. His only memories of that period were of the frightening folk tales which his maternal grandmother told him (of owls who carried off bad little boys, and of devils disguised as men who, simply by looking at little boys, caused them to disappear) and of that same grandmother's unhappiness when Hu and his parents left their Kansu home. The themes of fear and unhappiness which appeared first in these recollections recurred frequently throughout his reconstruction of his childhood.

When Hu was six years old (the family had spent two years in more or less temporary dwellings) Hu was moved to his father's family home in Hupeh Province, and he remained there or nearby for the next thirteen years. But this move, rather than uniting the family, marked the beginning of long separations; his father was away most of the time, appearing only on rare occasions, and then briefly and often unannounced. Hu senior belonged to a faction of the Kuomintang (Nationalist Party) which had come into active conflict with Chiang Kai-shek, so that he was almost a fugitive.

Hu held a special position in this fatherless household (there was an uncle nearby but not in the same compound). He was the "young master" being groomed for family leadership, the only direct male heir (an older brother and one or two sisters had died in infancy). Moreover, Hu's father too had been an oldest son, and this placed Hu in the main line of family authority. His family's long prominence in the area (his paternal grandfather had been an important provincial official during the Ch'ing dynasty), its heritage of scholarly attainment, the importance of preserving the "family name"—all this was impressed upon him. It was a situation which in every way encouraged the development within him of precocious self-assertion.

But this celebrated little boy (and no culture has ever made a greater fuss over its male children) had a strange rival for power within the family: a woman two generations his senior. This "step-grandmother" was the *bête noire* of his childhood, and indeed of much of his life. Originally his paternal grandfather's second wife (she was not a concubine, as his first wife had died before she came into the family), she was the only surviving member of her generation. Possessing seniority as well as the ability and will to rule, she took full advantage of the family's power vacuum and full charge of its affairs. Yet her leadership placed her in a complicated position (nothing is ever simple in a Chinese family)—because she was a woman, and, more important, because she was unrelated by blood to any of the other family members, which, as Hu explained, made them regard her as little more than a concubine. She had borne a male child—always a matter of great prestige for a Chinese woman—who had been kidnapped by bandits and never returned. This, according to Hu, was another source of tension, as she had become embittered by this incident, and resented "the family" for not making strong enough efforts (possibly not paying a large enough ransom) to get the child back. Hu felt that she extracted her revenge through her tyrannical reign over the household, to the point where she became "a saboteur of the family." Although the others chafed under her domination, she was acting within Chinese tradition, and no one had the courage or the sanction to contest her. Indeed, Hu's uncle (his father's younger brother), the only person around who might have offered resistance, preferred to move out from her control at the time of his marriage rather than follow the more conventional pattern of bringing his bride back to the main family home.

Hu believed that, as the "young master," he was the special target of her abuse. She became for him a symbol of the "old," and a special object of his hatred, a hatred which was not, however, devoid of respect:

She was a woman of the old China. She was tall, very tall and impressive looking. She had bound feet. She was a very able and intelligent woman. . . . She could be very eloquent, convincing to others, but she was stubborn and couldn't be talked into anything herself. . . .

She never liked me, and was very jealous of my position in the family. I could always feel her antagonism in the atmosphere, but she was much too shrewd to mistreat me in a direct manner. She never beat me physically. . . . It was in a glance or a phrase directed at me that I could feel it. . . . I hated her so much that at times I felt that I could not stand her.

The conflict between the old woman and the boy reached its climax when he was ten years old through what began as a seemingly inconsequential incident but grew into an event of major proportions:

One day someone was telling a story before a gathering of our family members. The story was very unfavorable to the head of the household. It described how he had misused family funds and cheated the other members of the family. After listening for a while I said, "That man is a thief!" My grandmother then spoke up with great emotion and said, "He is saying this about me, that I am not honest, that I am corrupt." She immediately called all the family members into the hall of the ancestors, the family shrine, and in a very dramatic fashion she lit up all of the candles that were in the room. Then she said, "The young master has accused me of being dishonest. I will pray to my ancestors to be more honest." Other relatives attempted to calm her down, saying that I was only a boy and that she should accept an apology from me. But she refused to do this, saying, "No, I am not worthy of his apology. I am just a poor old servant of the family." She maintained this attitude very stubbornly, and nothing that anybody said to her could convince her to change her mind.

Her actions, in effect, forced Hu to leave the family home, since this kind of conflict within a Chinese family cannot remain openly unresolved. As Hu explained:

This was really a skillful way to squeeze me out of the household. With her refusal to accept my apology, my only recourse was to leave. But it was done so cleverly within the framework of tradition that no one could accuse her of acting wrongly. . . . She was not treating me as a grandson or as a little boy, but rather as the legal heir, as if she were dealing with my father.

It is quite possible, of course, that Hu did more to provoke these actions than his version of the story suggests. Or even if he did not, it is likely that the step-grandmother accurately perceived that Hu was expressing indirect hostility toward her. In any case, his outburst could have been considered a sign of disrespect for his elders.

In most situations like this, an apology from the youthful offender would have ended the matter—and Hu is right in perceiving that his step-grandmother's show of humility was really a highly-charged form of aggressiveness. Although cleverly correct in her forms, however, she could have been criticized for a lack of spirit of compromise, an important virtue in traditional Chinese culture. Such bitter animosity, kept well beneath the surface, occurred in many Chinese families.

In Hu's family, external forms were still maintained. Although he went to live in his uncle's house nearby and visited his family home infrequently, it was still necessary for him to appear on special occasions—for instance, the Chinese New Year celebration —to pay his respects to his step-grandmother through the traditional symbol of submissive reverence, the *k'o-t'ou*. He dreaded these visits long in advance, but it was made clear to him that he had no choice in the matter because "if I did not, I would be condemned by all society." His step-grandmother, on each such occasion, maintained her "humility" and perpetuated the conflict by declaring herself "unworthy" of the salutation.

Hu's mother, rather than offering him protection against the step-grandmother, was herself another victim. Cowed and powerless before her elder, she was so looked down on as a "common woman" from a backward province, that even the servants treated her badly. Sickly, nervous, and resentful of her husband's continued absence, she often had to turn over her son's care to others. Hu remembers her with some fondness, but also recalls that she sometimes took her frustrations out on him and subjected him to beatings. She died when Hu was fourteen years old, and was in many ways an even more distant figure ("I never experienced the intimacy of a mother with her") than his absent father.

For to Hu, his father soon became the center of a lasting personal myth—that of the all-powerful father who suddenly materializes and rescues his son from an otherwise invincible oppressor:

I found myself always thinking of him. . . . To me he was the most dignified and impressive man in the world. . . . I felt that one day my father would return and all of my troubles would be over.

Nor could repeated evidence to the contrary dispel this myth: the family lost touch with his father for periods of years, and when he did visit, the step-grandmother and he observed all proper forms (he too had to be filial) and things remained as they had been. Hu was never too happy at his uncle's house, where he felt he was being cared for more out of obligation than love, and he went on hoping; when he got tired of this his thoughts turned toward revenge, and toward the day when he would be big enough and smart enough to be able to deal with his arch-enemy. Her death, which occurred shortly after that of his mother, and his father's continued absence caused him to avoid the family home, which he then considered haunted.

Hu's erratic pattern of education exposed him to the full chaos of the Chinese cultural and political scene. From the ages of eight to twelve, he studied with private tutors employed by his and neighboring families; in the traditional fashion, he learned how to read and write from simplified versions of the Confucian classics. He did not like the stern discipline of the tutor, and was frequently punished for misbehavior; but he was impressed with Confucian teachings of filial piety and loyalty to family and country, as yet unaware of the inconsistencies between these theoretical virtues and the realities of the life around him.

Next, he spent two years studying and boarding at a new-style upper primary school not too far from his home. There he was surprised to encounter classmates who were mostly adults or near-adults, prospective employees of the local government who had come to take advantage of the school's "modern" curriculum, in keeping with a new regulation that officials have some Western education. As the youngest pupil in the school, Hu deeply resented the teasing and bullying he received from the others, some of them two or three times his age—especially when they told him that "a little boy is not supposed to lose his temper with his elders." He no doubt stimulated many of these antagonisms, since by this time he had become a rebellious, outspoken child. Again made aware of his helplessness in the face of superior power, he once more dreamed of the day when he could outwit his tormentors; he partially realized this goal in demonstrating his quicker ability to grasp the Western subjects in the academic curriculum.

After his graduation, his uncle planned to send him to a junior middle school in a nearby city. Just when Hu was about to leave for the new school, his father suddenly appeared, and Hu took advantage of the occasion to express many of his grievances. His father was angered by the boy's story. As a man of the world, he disapproved of the provincial way in which Hu was dressed, and of the undistinguished school which had been selected for him. As usual, Hu senior stayed only briefly, but before he left he canceled the existing plans and promised to return soon to take the boy to a better school in a larger city. For the next three years, however, nothing more was heard from him; and between the ages of thirteen and sixteen Hu remained idle, receiving no formal education.

These years were the most lonely interlude of a life in which loneliness had already become a regular feature. Hu felt estranged from his uncle as well as his father, since the uncle resented both the boy and the father for undermining what he considered to be a reasonable discharge of his responsibilities. Hu became more embittered than ever—angry at his uncle for allowing family conflicts to interfere with his education, and even having doubts about his father and wondering whether he was really in hiding or had "just forgotten about the family." But he clung tenaciously to his father-return myth, and even when he was telling me about these events, he could admit no resentment toward his mythical hero. Feeling at home nowhere, thinking a great deal about running away, but unable to decide where to go, he described his general emotion as "fatalistic anger" (the kind of hostility which is temporarily held in abeyance until an opportunity arises to express it).

Finally dismissing the entire problem from his mind, Hu began to interest himself in other things—taking long walks through the neighboring countryside, and reading voraciously the traditional Chinese *chien-hsia* novels. The *chien-hsia* is a superhuman hero who combines physical strength and magical powers in punishing evil and helping the oppressed, always acting outside of and frequently in opposition to vested authority; so great is the *chien-hsia's* imaginative impact that one Chinese colleague—possibly with a certain amount of cultural chauvinism—described him to me as "a combination of the Western knight errant and Robin Hood, only much more skillful and ingenious." Imagining himself a *chien-hsia* was an ideal antidote to Hu's sense of loneliness and helplessness. His period of inactivity came to an end only through the chance appearance of an old family friend who prevailed upon the uncle to send Hu back to school (respected outsiders have frequently been the best mediators in severe Chinese intrafamily disputes).

Hu was then sent to a middle school sponsored by the Kuomintang Youth Corps. He spent just one semester there, but it was an experience which had great significance in shaping his political emotions. He had chosen the school himself, for even in his isolation he had been caught up in the wave of patriotism which swept the country at the time of the outbreak of the Sino-Japanese War. But he was horrified by what he found there. Hastily put together, the school had enrolled many more students than the small faculty could handle; the academic program was practically nonexistent, and most of the time was devoted to military training. Discipline was not only strict, but needlessly vindictive, and severe whippings were administered for minor infractions. Hu was from the beginning critical of the school and suspicious of its attempts to mobilize student emotions—so much so that he was among the very few who did not, in the initial burst of patriotic fervor, join the KMT Youth Corps. He later told me that his restraint might have been due to memories of his father's tribulations within the KMT. Students soon became united in their resentment of the school and so rebellious that the atmosphere began to resemble that of an armed camp; none of the twenty youths from Hu's area returned the following semester. While there, Hu, developed his talent for rebellion a bit further: he became an expert at forging the signature of the chief military trainer on passes (he proudly demonstrated his technique to me during our interview). The experience left him with the feeling that the KMT Youth Corps was "disappointing and silly . . . brutal and irrational." His "disgust and hatred" was soon extended to the entire KMT Party and Government, and it later developed into the predominating passion of his youth.

The county junior middle school to which he transferred seemed a great improvement. He did well academically, and quickly became a leader among the students. In addition, he held a specially privileged status among the faculty because the president of the school was Hu's uncle's "adopted son"—that is, the uncle, as a prominent person in the area, sponsored the school official's career and exercised considerable influence over it. This made things particularly complicated for Hu when, just a few months after his arrival, he came into direct conflict with this same school president.

For when the students began to notice that their meals seemed meager, and suspected some form of corruption in connection with the school's rice supply, they turned to Hu to direct an investigation. This was an extremely serious situation: the rice kept in the school storehouse represented the institution's capital, since rice was the only stable currency available; students' tuition fees and teachers' salaries were both paid in it, and it was used to buy other foods and supplies. Since teachers were badly underpaid, irregularities were not infrequent, and sometimes were even considered customary.

Before long, Hu had organized a special committee of students to keep a close watch over every grain of rice brought to or taken from the storehouse. The system worked admirably: corruption apparently ended, and meals improved. But the school president was angered by the students' assumption of authority, and especially resented Hu as their ringleader. Matters came to a climax when an old school servant, despite official permission from the school accountant, was refused rice for a late meal upon returning from a trip; the student committee members insisted that he first had to get Hu's personal approval. Hu soon became involved in a power struggle with the school president, which he described to me with some relish; it was eventually resolved through a tacit compromise in which the students continued their vigilance, but did so as quietly as possible in order to cause minimal embarrassment to the authorities.

Hu's sense of victory was eventually reinforced by his uncle's grudging praise. The latter was at first enraged when informed of Hu's activities by the school president; but after a short time, his respect for Hu became apparent, and he referred to him as a "straight-boned boy"—an expression suggesting strength, courage, and integrity. The only unfavorable repercussion came about a year later when, despite having announced that Hu had won the prize for the outstanding student of the semester, the faculty members "forgot" to present the award to him. He became angered, ceased making his best efforts, and concluded that "people never get what they deserve."

His personal struggles with authority thus found effective social expression in the turbulent Chinese student world. His rebellious urges were constantly fed by real injustice, until

I developed the conviction that any authority held over me was irrational. I transferred from school to school. . . . As soon as I would meet the head of a new school, I would automatically think: "This man must be an irrational authority." And I would invariably find out that this was true.

There was another rice incident at the provincial upper middle school which Hu next attended. This time he was in danger of being expelled, until the approaching Japanese armies interrupted his personal battle. Hu fled to Free China in the interior, as all students were urged to do. His uncle sent him off with these words: "When the whole society is so corrupt, what can you, just an individual person, do about it?"—an attitude of resignation which Hu strongly contested at the time, but one which he was never to stop wondering about.

Arriving in Chungking, where students were instructed to report for reassignment, Hu got into an argument with an arrogant official who reprimanded him for not having the correct papers. He later felt that this dispute caused him extra months of waiting and resulted in his receiving an undesirable school placement to a poorly-organized agricultural institution.

Now he became extremely discouraged. He had sustained himself through a difficult trip to Chungking with the belief that "everything would be all right when I got there," but found instead that "it was only the beginning of my troubles." Out of touch with his family, financially destitute (and cheated when he sold his only valuable possession, a gold ring), feeling awkward in imposing upon family contacts for temporary shelter, Hu found solace in a new friendship. A sympathetic middle-aged scholar and former government official from his own village area offered him the first meaningful explanation of his sufferings, and became his first political mentor:

He was a man about the age of my father, an extremely eloquent person who quickly became my hero. He told me how he had worked with the KMT during its real revolutionary days, but was now being discriminated against because of his leftist views. I too had felt discriminated against as a child and he told me that this was due to the evils of the old society. I could see little hope for the future, but then he described the Communist program as a solution for China and a way to a bright future. . . . He was kind and encouraging. I visited him frequently and soon adopted his views.

Hu's new beliefs gave him further confidence in his participation in student agitation about corruption in the food supply as well as other issues at the agricultural school. And for the first time he became involved in a dangerous predicament: Nationalist secret police arrested some of the students, and Hu was accused by school authorities of being a Communist although he had no such affiliation at the time other than his beginning sympathies. Since he had heard stories of cruelty and torture inflicted by this division of the KMT, and of special "training" to which alleged offenders had been submitted, he decided to flee rather than risk arrest.

Having no place to go, and wishing to contribute to China's war effort, he enlisted in a special student military unit then being formed. There he found temporary sanctuary, but was once more deeply disturbed by the enormous corruption and inefficiency regarding payrolls, allocation of weapons, and training arrangements. These things were not unique at the time, but the student unit apparently became something of a national scandal. At this time his father and uncle succeeded in getting in touch with him again and were horrified to find he was in the army; they wrote that they had sent him to the interior to become a scholar, not a soldier, and that, as the only male of his generation in the family, he had no right to take such liberties with his person. Their attitude can be summed up in the popular Chinese proverb which Hu himself quoted to me: "Good iron is not used for nails; good men do not become soldiers." Hu resigned after six months of service when he was given the chance; he had come to the conclusion that "there could be no hope for the Nationalist government."

A veteran enthusiast-cynic at nineteen, Hu's fortunes now finally changed. He managed through friends to gain admission to a much-respected high school primarily for overseas Chinese from southeast Asia, but which took some students in Hu's displaced circumstances. When the school had to disband because of a new Japanese penetration, Hu accompanied a group of students and faculty members to Szechwan Province where it was re-established in combination with another school. Hu encountered here, despite the limited physical facilities, an atmosphere unique in his experience: complete absence of corruption, great intellectual stimulation, an intimate group life among students, informal relations with faculty, and a generally shared hope for future reforms which could cure China's ills. In an inspiring history teacher, Hu found his second political (and Marxist) mentor:

I already had an emotional sympathy for the Communists. I now began to read about the materialist interpretation of history, the history of the development of society, and Ai Ssu-ch'i's popular philosophy.[1] When I had difficulty understanding some of these principles I went to this history teacher for help. He was always friendly and patient, and seemed to answer my questions logically. I acquired the theoretical background to go along with my emotional sympathy. . . . From that time on I developed the idea in my mind that Communism was the inevitable outcome of history. . . . It seemed to be the only way out for young people.

He emphasized the importance of his resentment of the old regime in bringing about this new view of the world.

My main feeling then was hatred for the KMT. All that I had seen and experienced was wrong. This hatred was the active side of my being; my feeling for Communism was a more passive side. Before I could understand the true meaning of their writing I accepted them because I was predisposed to do so. . . . I was at first excited by their solution to China's problems. Then I had more of the feeling that it was all settled: the KMT was out of the question, of no use, and Communism was the right way.

This was for Hu, "the happiest period of my life," the only time he can remember—perhaps with some retrospective glorification —being free of disturbing conflicts: "I no longer thought of any of my troubles. . . . I just forgot about the family." Graduating near the top of his class at the age of twenty-one, he left for his home shortly after the Japanese surrender.

But when he arrived in Hupeh, he found his father, at sixty, "a defeated, frustrated, lonely old man, disillusioned with world events." Hu senior had by this time become convinced that man's earthly efforts were futile, and (following a frequent Chinese life pattern) wished to spend his declining years in Buddhist meditation. Hu found his father surprisingly approachable and affectionate, and the two became closer than at any previous time. There was just one conflict between them—the old sore spot of Hu's education. His father, drawing upon his own experience, even went so far as to discourage university studies: "I have studied and tried to serve my country all my life and what did it lead to?" This failing, he urged Hu to attend a nearby university. But Hu recalled his past frustrations over his father's failure to keep his word about arrangements for study, and at that moment "the old resentment returned." He refused his father's request and entered the University of Nanking, where he felt he could get a better education.

Majoring in law and government, he found the atmosphere not conducive to study. Students and faculty members were vehemently denouncing the postwar KMT government, especially its failure to curb inflation and its repressive methods in attempting to stamp out opposition. Before long Hu assumed a leading role in student agitation, working closely with Communist Party members who did much of the behind-the-scenes organizing. During his junior year, he was arrested by the KMT police as part of a general roundup of student "activists." Most were soon released, but a small group, including Hu, were taken to a country house just outside of Nanking where they were told they were to be secretly executed. Imprisoned for several months, Hu claimed that a spirit of group dedication protected him from fear. In fact, his description of the experience—even if the words are not taken at complete face value —implies a genuine exhilaration:

We were there together and had no horror of death. We always tried to encourage each other. . . . We felt that we were being sacrificed for a great cause, that our deaths would have a purpose. . . . Some of us felt that we were so young and our greatest regret was that we could not do more work for China. . . . I did feel grief and sorrow at night when I would think of my parents and my family. Then I would think of the meaning of our sacrifice, and I would forget about my sorrow.

All agreed that the meaning of their sacrifice was its contribution to China's future, but Hu recalls a certain amount of disagreement among the imprisoned students concerning just what that future should be. Hu and a few of the others believed that China's civil war would be best resolved through a coalition government including the more enlightened Nationalist leaders (who had just replaced Chiang Kai-shek) as well as Communists; but the Communist students in the group insisted that there must be nothing short of a complete Communist victory. Their position made Hu wonder whether these students "had greater loyalties to the Communist party than to China itself," although not until later did he recognize the significance of this disagreement. Hu was not too excited (there was a suggestion that one side of him might even have been disappointed) when a general amnesty for political prisoners led to their release. His main preoccupation at the time was that of smuggling out his handcuffs in order to retain them as evidence of his mistreatment at the hands of the KMT. When he returned to the campus, he was greeted as a hero, and he remained active until the Communist entry a few months later.

Evaluation and Follow-up

Hu brought to thought reform an extraordinary capacity for anger and indignation; indeed, these had long before become the leitmotif of his existence. More than merely expressing them himself, he excelled at mobilizing similar emotions among others in his immediate environment. In this ability lay his capacity for leadership and the core of his youthful identity as an activist student leader. Behind his indignation and his leadership was an unusual degree of totalism—an all-or-nothing quality which pervaded his emotional life.

Hu's character in some ways was more reminiscent of the spirit of the young Martin Luther than of that of Confucius. Like Luther's (and like many figures in the Old Testament), Hu's totalism demanded both full authority over those he led, and absolute self-surrender to a higher authority. Hu also possessed a conscience of terrifying proportions. This kind of conscience can serve the creative function of inspiring total sincerity and absolute integrity—of making men mean what they say; it also, in its uncompromising judgments, contains the potential for the most extreme form of destructiveness, including self-destructiveness.[2]

We could consider Hu a psychological misfit, a compulsive rebel who goes into battle at the mere sight of authority, any authority. We could also see him as one of those exceptional young leaders who learn early in life to harness their own emotions in such a way that they make sensitive contact with yearnings of less intense people around them. Both of these judgments are true; either one alone distorts the picture. We can certainly say that Hu had little of the spirit of compromise and moderation so long valued in Chinese character structure; rather, he was an extremist who grew up in a series of environments conducive to extremism. This made him no less Chinese, but Chinese in a twentieth-century fashion. To understand the complexities of his character and of his response to thought reform, we must examine the strengths and the underlying conflicts in an identity shaped against a background of chaos and change.

Whatever his struggles, Hu carried with him from early life a strong sense of himself as an aristocrat and a potential leader. As a young master within Chinese tradition, he was a little adult groomed for authority almost from birth. Moving from his family out into society, he maintained the conviction that it was his destiny to speak and act on behalf of others, and he developed an early talent for doing so. As with any talent, one must avoid oversimplified cause-and-effect explanations of origin (hereditary factors are probably of great importance); but once this talent had been combined with the identity of the aristocratic leader, a pattern of strength and bold self-expression emerged which was crucial for what Hu would do and be in any situation. His development into a straight-boned boy (the last honorable confirmation he received within the idiom of traditional Chinese culture) expressed a similar self-image, matured to the point where he had become a youth with a cause. Both the youth and the cause continued to evolve until Hu became the activist student leader. This élite identity sequence supplied Hu with a sense of inner continuity, even when he turned against the traditional Chinese culture which had originally nurtured it. He used the strength of his family heritage—his identification with his father and his grandfather—to do battle with that same heritage, or at least with its remnants.

At the same time, Hu had always to fight off a profound sense of despair growing out of his personal, social, and historical predicament. Hu's environment had imposed on him a series of painful inner contradictions. To be a young master had its advantages; but it also involved him in a premature power struggle from which no child could emerge unscarred. It was, moreover, an archaic identity, one which was based upon a system of values in human relationships which was rapidly breaking down. Indeed, the extremes of behavior in Hu's family (especially that of his step-grandmother) were desperate attempts to hold on to what was already slipping away. Hu's childhood environment was thus a caricature of Chinese family life, an expression of traditionalism rather than tradition.

A young master was also expected to be a filial son—obedient and proper not from coercion but love. Yet, so lacking in love and trust was his family environment that any such an identity had to be more pseudo than real. Hu's step-grandmother's indirect aggressiveness, his mother's harassed nervousness, his uncle's petulance —and perhaps something inherent in Hu which made him difficult to love—all contributed to this contradictory atmosphere. These circumstances were both partly created and strongly intensified by historical and political currents: his father's fugitive status brought about a marriage with inevitable class strains, and was also responsible for the step-grandmother's being permitted to abuse her matriarchal power. Hu had no choice but to go through the filial motions; and even though he faltered at an early age (in the family shrine incident, for instance), he submitted to his step-grandmother more than he could comfortably admit to me.

This submission to his hated adversary had a lasting symbolic meaning for Hu: it established within him an exaggerated sensitivity toward being controlled or dominated by anyone. It also contributed to his later yearning for the very thing he was always fighting off: total domination, if not by a strong individual, at least by a mystical force. Children subjected to unusually controlling family authority can come to depend upon and even find pleasure in being so controlled; their subsequent struggle against new, would-be controllers becomes an inner battle between fear and desire. In Hu's case, the controlling person (his grandmother) became a symbol of both "irrational authority" and "the past," so that the two became equated in his mind. This is a frequent association for a youth in any culture, but is especially strong when he grows up in the midst of crumbling institutions and abused family prerogatives. Yet, ironically enough, this step-grandmother also supplied Hu with a model for his own later domineering tendencies, and initiated a response by which Hu came to view almost every relationship as essentially a power struggle.

Rather than the filial son, Hu regarded himself as the abandoned and betrayed victim of the most gross injustice. Whom did he blame for this injustice? He made clear that he focused most of his conscious hostility on his step-grandmother; and she thus served a useful function for him as the first of his total villains, acceptable outlets for his hatred against whom he could rally real or imagined action. But Hu also experienced resentment toward another person, for whom such resentment was entirely unacceptable: his father. He could not quite suppress the hostility which accompanied his sense of having been abandoned; and hostility toward one's father is, by traditional Chinese cultural standards, the most *unfilial* emotion a child can experience. These resentful feelings were Hu's first painful secret. Certainly his desire for revenge against his step-grandmother was real enough; but it was intensified by his need to purge his mind of similar feelings toward his father, and possibly his mother as well. His sense of himself as the unfilial son (to both father and grandmother), as the abandoned and betrayed victim, and as the avenger made up a formidable negative identity complex. Each of these elements was something against which his culture and family had warned him, and each was something he could not avoid becoming, despite and partly because of this warning; in lasting combination, they had the destructive effect of maintaining within him the bitterness and guilt which gave his rebellion its desperate and compulsive character.

To bring all these aspects of himself—positive and negative—into effective combination, Hu resorted to two personal, utopian myths. (The term *personal myth* is used here to suggest a recurrently-imagined sequence of events which supply purpose and momentum to an individual's existence.) The first myth, involving his father's return, was mostly passive—a longing for a golden age which had never existed. The second, the myth of himself as the hero (or *chien hsia*), was more active, and for a time he lived it out quite effectively. These two myths assumed tremendous importance in Hu's life, for they were the antidote for his despair: the first offered hope eternal, the second a bold life of self-sacrifice and redemption. At the same time they generated strong emotional forces which, once initiated, had a staying power of their own. His quests for some form of golden age and for perpetual heroic expression [3] came to influence Hu's every action. They also reinforced his already well-developed totalism: for so deep had been his despair, so strong his sense of personal oppression, so extreme the social chaos, and so dramatic the contemporary historical events, that Hu began very early to seek all-embracing personal and political solutions.

As an activist student leader in a turbulent student movement, Hu found an ideal métier for acting upon his personal myths and giving expression to his talents and his emotional urges. Embracing a Communist ideology which promised a universal golden age, he could remain sufficiently independent to follow a hero's path of individual leadership, and almost martyrdom.

He required a new total villain, a role for which the KMT was admirably suited. It was "old"; and—on the basis of his own experience, beginning with the Youth Corps school—its authority was "irrational." These judgments were by no means simply the product of Hu's own emotional urges (the KMT's inept and repressive policies have been widely documented): but Hu—like many others of his generation—found in this regime a focus for all of the bitterness, anger, and frustration which had built up during his young life.

Hu was helped to make the short step from hatred of the KMT to sympathy for the Communists (and the feeling he had found something "new" and "rational") by the two fatherly men he encountered. One may say that they were, at least temporarily, fathers regained; but their attraction for Hu lay in the contrasts between them and his real father: they were *there*, they were consistent, they had time for him, and they explained things. Indeed, they did what mentors and healers (religious, political, academic, or psychological) so often do; they made it possible for Hu to unite his personal myths with more sweeping social and historical myths, and pointed out to him a way to a relationship with mankind. This new ideology was as totalistic as he could wish it to be; and his most vengeful feelings could be justified within a framework of an apocalyptic cause.

Once Communism became the prevailing authority, however, Hu was bound to be troubled by the manipulations of its cadres. First at the university, and then during thought reform itself, he experienced a profound sense of humiliation at being forced to submit to suffocating domination. And as in the past, much of his emotional energy was taken up with fighting off his own urge to surrender himself totally to the force imposing this domination. His entering the revolutionary university was in itself a partial admission that something in his attitude should be changed; during the first days of reform he seemed to be giving himself completely to the process, and recapturing that golden age of total sincerity and harmony which he had known just once before at his last high school. But as much as part of him longed for total emotional immersion, he was, in the long run, incapable of it. As with Father Simon (the converted Jesuit), the defier in Hu could never allow the convert in him to gain the upper hand; he could not trust any environment, even a Communist one, sufficiently to permit himself the absolute merger toward which his totalism constantly drove him.

Hu's means of dealing with this conflict was to cling tenaciously to a sense of autonomy, and the only kind of autonomy he knew was that of the leader or hero. Hence his unsolicited debate with the cadre, and his view of himself as both a teacher and a defender of his fellow students. His heroic self-image required him to maintain high standards of integrity (even if he violated these more than he admits); and it gave a dramatic quality to his every action, a sense that all he did or said had significance not only for himself but for the world at large. It was thus of great help in maintaining his self-respect and his autonomy, and in preserving a certain amount of independence from the bizarre thought-reform morality. But in the face of thought reform's consistent antipathy to heroes—to anyone who might exert a strong influence over others which was different from the immediate thought reform message—this self-image also imposed an extremely heavy psychological burden.

The greatest threat to Hu's emotional balance, however, was his "secret"—the bitter hatred toward the Communist reformers which welled up within him. Contained within this secret were all of his negative identity elements, which now had a confused relationship to the Communist authorities. That is, Hu felt himself to be unfilial to a movement he had long embraced and to an all-powerful authority which would brook no disloyalty; to be the abandoned and betrayed victim of that same Communist authority; and to be a potential avenger who would some day smite down his persecutors. These sentiments not only would have placed him in considerable personal danger had they become known; but their unacceptability —to the environment and to Hu himself—stimulated strong feelings of guilt, just as his secret resentment of his father had earlier in his life. This guilt was partly responsible for Hu's unconscious urge to reveal his secret ("The secret was something which was always trying to escape from me"). But also contributing to this urge was his strong inner drive toward total self-surrender, since revealing the extent of his hostility would have been the first step in a genuine Communist-style reform. As is so often the case in totalitarian confession and reform procedures, Hu's secret was almost his undoing.

The news of his father's imprisonment caused him to revert suddenly to traditional self-judgments, and to revive his long-standing negative self-image of the unfilial son. He experienced the terrible guilt of the son who had defied and, by participating in the Communist movement, had overthrown—had symbolically demolished —his father. After this, the requirement that he denounce his father in the final summary added salt to his wounds. What is puzzling is not that he made this denunciation, since it was a requirement which no one could escape, but that he subsequently decided to accept the Communist job assignment and give up his plan to flee to Nanking. He did this despite having closely identified with his father as a victim of Communist persecution, and having become, if possible, even more resentful toward the new regime. I believe the explanation lies in what I have called the bond of betrayal between reformers and reformed. With so strong a sense of having betrayed his own filial heritage (a heritage of immense emotional power, whatever its inconsistencies, and however long his defiance of it), he was all the more involved with those who had brought about the betrayal, and there was no turning back. Not until he actually found himself in the job situation, and had perhaps recovered from the shock and depression which had accompanied the news of his father's imprisonment, did he realize he was incapable of even the minimal amount of submission necessary to survive within the Communist environment.

Why did Hu leave China? Should his defection be attributed to courageous resistance to coercion, to psychological conflict, or to chance? Certainly all three factors were important. The chance lay in the opportunity he found to leave the country, an opportunity which, to be sure, he had done much to create. His bloodhound's nose for coercion made him especially sensitive to the manipulative aspects of thought reform. His heroic self-image contributed to the strength of his resistance. At the same time, his overwhelming psychological conflicts had produced an urgent need to escape. To put it another way, he left because he perceived an incompatibility between his personal character structure and the Communist environment around him. For him, thought reform had a reverse effect: before it he had been an avowed (if somewhat disgruntled) sympathizer; soon after, he became a bitterly disenchanted opponent.

As for Hu's experiences in Hong Kong, he tried to establish himself there as an anti-Communist writer. From what we know about him, and about Hong Kong, it would have been predictable that he would not have had an easy time. At the age of twenty-six, he had not been able to establish any workable adult life pattern; he was still in the midst of an action-oriented search, a continuous identity crisis, which had begun at the age of sixteen. We would expect him to experiment, as most refugee Chinese intellectuals did, with new identities and new ideologies. And we would expect his experiments to be consuming in their intensity, heroic in their proportions, and devastating in their potential for disillusionment. This is essentially what did happen—but it is not the whole story, for as tenacious as these patterns were within Hu, he was not entirely incapable of change.

The first great shock he had to sustain was the news of his father's death—probably at the hands of a new "People's Court"—which he heard within a few months after his arrival. His emotions were similar to those he had experienced at hearing about his father's first imprisonment, but this time they were much more severe. He had the same visions of mob terrorism, similar feelings of guilt and responsibility, and an even greater preoccupation with his failure to be filial: "I regretted very much that I could not be there. . . . It is a strong Chinese tradition that a son should be present at the time of his father's death. It is part of filial piety." Even before this news, he had begun to be discouraged about his difficulty in locating an anti-Communist group with whom he could work, about the unconcerned attitude of Hong Kong people toward Communist China, and about his dependency upon a friend's kindness for support. Discouragement gave way to depression, and for several weeks he had little hope.

Then a few articles he had written for Hong Kong periodicals caught the attention of the leaders of a newly-formed "third force" youth group, and he was asked to join them. Before long he was playing a prominent role in the group's activities, enjoying living and working with its members, and contributing to their sense of enthusiasm. The organization became more recognized and began to receive American subsidies; however, he noted that the co-operative atmosphere began to give way to intrigue and a struggle for power. Soon he came into sharp conflict with the other leaders over their dismissal of some of his colleagues, and he decided that he had no alternative but to resign. Disillusioned and despairing, he bitterly resented his adversaries; but he was not without some tendency to place part of the blame upon himself. "I left with the feeling I had personally failed. . . . I was disappointed and frustrated, and I had no more 'heart'." Some time later the same pattern repeated itself: active involvement with a new anti-Communist press organization, severe personal conflicts, then resignation from the group. The second experience revealed Hu's panic at the threat of being dominated by one of the other leaders. "Although he never came to dominate me, I resented the fact that he had been planning ways to do this. . . . I couldn't concentrate on anything else. . . . Just thinking how to stop this person's domination." At one point in this conflict, Hu became aware of his own excitability, and commented to his close friend (our interpreter) that there must be something wrong with him, and that perhaps he was in need of a woman. (He later told me, however, that he had never had sexual relations because he feared that "once I gave myself to it, I might lose all control"—a statement which reflected a fear of his own hostile urges, as well as his feelings of attraction and repulsion for any total experience.) According to the interpreter, others in the press group admitted that Hu's rival had attempted to dominate all of the members; but they felt that Hu was oversensitive and impulsive, and that he still retained Communist-like tendencies to view every situation as a struggle for power.

After each of these episodes, Hu retreated into a quiet rural life —long walks, swimming, and lonely meditation upon his personal plight, a habit he kept from early adolescence. When he was calmer and felt less pressured, he began to accept some of the judgments of others, even judgments about his own character. He realized that he had unwittingly favored Communist-like organization within both the press groups, and determined to "lead myself away from this old Communist way of thinking." He also began to change his estimate of human character. "I had always felt that when suppressed, people could fight for their ideals and sacrifice everything. . . . I came to understand that what friends had told me was true—that there is a lust for power in the human mind, and that those who failed to understand this get into all kinds of trouble."

And like many other refugee Chinese intellectuals, he gravitated —because of his need and its availability—toward Christianity. He again came to a new ideology through a kind and parental mentor, this time a woman: a middle-aged American Lutheran missionary who had worked for many years in a province near his home and was able to talk to him in a dialect which reminded him of his childhood. In addition to these geographical and emotional associations, so important for Chinese, he was moved by her affection for him. "When I went to see her I had a feeling that her concern for me was something I badly needed. You might say she had a kind of maternal feeling for me." He felt that she and her colleagues were among the few people he had ever encountered who were "concerned with the welfare of human beings as such without hoping to get something out of them."

He also found a spirit of humility and compromise among the members of this group; he thought this spirit was Christianity's contribution to Western democracy, and he wished to emulate it, realizing that he lacked it in his own character. "My old attitude was that when I thought myself in the right, I must stick strictly to my views and never give in or compromise. . . . This caused me much suffering in the past." He attributed his intransigence to Chinese tradition: "The word *compromise* had an undesirable flavor in old Chinese society." Although this view slighted his own cultural heritage (Confucianism actually emphasizes a spirit of compromise) and perhaps was naïvely uncritical of Lutheran Christianity (in which uncompromising credal purity has often been a prominent feature), it did have validity for Hu's own experience.

Equally important was Hu's discovery that the Christian concepts of guilt and sin offered a meaningful interpretation of all of the evils he had seen, as well as a way to deal with his own angers:

When I was on the mainland, I was influenced by Confucian teaching, ideas that human nature was basically good, and that people can do good if they wish to. . . . I could not reconcile this belief with the evils I observed in the KMT, the Communist, and the refugee organizations in Hong Kong. . . . In my own mind there was turmoil, and I was troubled by feelings of hatred for certain people. . . . But from reading the Scriptures, I learned that evils exist in every human being, including myself, and that the only way to remove these evils is to forgive them.

Although Hu's antagonisms scarcely disappeared, his association with the Lutherans did seem to agree with him. They found a place for him to stay near them, and offered him a job as secretary and translator. This happened concurrently with our interviews; and after living among the Lutherans for a few months Hu gained weight, and seemed much more relaxed and content than I had ever seen him. He described leading a "quiet, pleasant life," and said he was increasingly interested in Christian teachings.

At the same time (six years after his thought reform) he discussed with me some of his lingering preoccupations with his escape from Communism, and the terrifying images of the Communist cadres which remained with him. He still had nightmares, although not as frequently as he did earlier in his Hong Kong stay, in which he was fleeing Communist cadres, resisting capture, even shooting and killing a pursuer; sometimes he dreamt he was hunted as a criminal, sometimes helped by a kind friend, but never quite escaping. The cadre appeared as an all-powerful apparition which his eyes were forced to behold.

. . . a big terrible monster whose face and body-build I cannot see clearly. He does not actually appear to be a substantial person. What I see is only the Communist uniform. . . . It is as if there is nothing specifically to force me to see him, but I am compelled to see him of my own volition. I don't wish to but I have to. . . . I am so full of fear I cannot consider refusing.

He went on to give a subjective analysis of the sources of the cadre's effectiveness; using machine images, he came to conclusions similar to those of others who have studied the Communist cadre.

A Communist cadre is an apparatus rather than an individual. His knowledge, ability, emotion, every part of his body, is dedicated to the utilization of this piece of apparatus. That is why he has no real emotion toward you, no real feeling. That is why he is so terrible. . . . In action, a Communist cadre is more effective than an ordinary man because where an ordinary man would quit a job and say that he has done his best, a Communist cadre would go on and finish it. He is always responsible for what he has done because there is a deliberate system behind him such that he may be considered responsible for something he had done ten years before. He must check and check again, as when he finishes a job and hands in his work, there is no way of escape. He is not working for himself, but for the glory of the Party.[4]

Hu was still troubled by guilty, fearful secrets which he had kept from the Communists:

I have a feeling of guilt—not to my own conscience—but because I had a secret with them as one who came from among them. . . . When I decided to leave the mainland, I did not tell them that I had been a student at North China University or that I had been in the People's Revolutionary Army. If I had told them this, they would not have let me go. . . . If they knew that I were here working against them and they caught me, they would show no mercy. . . . It is like being a member of an underground gang somewhere, deciding that this is not decent, and then leaving. The fear that the gang would catch up with you would still be in your heart.

He expressed a feeling of helplessness toward Communism, and made it clear that its control over him had been the most thorough and the most frightening he had ever known. When he compared it with previous authorities in his life, even his step-grandmother seemed less forbidding: "She could compel me to do things that I was not willing to do, but she could never make me say that they were good things." And so did the KMT:

The KMT could bore me, make me disgusted, bitter and angry at them —but even when they arrested me and I thought that I was being shot, they could not frighten me. It was the Communists who really made me fearful. Now I have no way to protect myself against them. If I face a Communist cadre he can do anything he wants to me and I can do nothing to him.

He began to ask me many questions about human emotions, perhaps the most significant of which was, "How is it possible for a man to hate—to be irreconcilable in this hatred—but to actually submit to the person or group which he hates?" He was speaking of his general conflicts relating to hatred and submission, but his associations also suggested that he was indirectly referring to a feeling of being still partly under the Communists' intellectual and emotional control, a control which he was always fighting off within himself. This interpretation was confirmed by a second question, asked in ostensible reference to someone else: "Why is it that some people who have suffered persecution and oppression at the hands of the Communists remain enthusiastic about them?"

As he became more introspective, Hu expressed a basic insight about the relationship of his character to the Communist movement, and about his own quest for selfhood:

I now realized why the Communists tried so hard to gain me over. . . . When I believe in something I can forget myself completely while throwing myself into the cause. It was for this reason that I could be so unusually persistent in maintaining my own opinion in opposition to that of the Communists. For this is also a standard characteristic of the Communist cadre, to be so determined because he had no self, and the Communists knew that I could be a very good cadre. . . . I was proud of these characteristics within myself before. But now I understand that if I could preserve some of my individual interest, some individuality, I would be less like the Communists. . . . My life would be more balanced and I would not go to such extremes as I used to.

Hu was beginning to recognize his own totalism, and understand its affinity for Communism and its usefulness in preserving his identity against Communist pressures. The recognition itself suggested that he was making a dent in this totalism, as did his identification with Western Protestant individualism. He had (at least temporarily) traded heroic action for introspection, leadership for discipleship.

This may have been just another lull in Hu's lifelong emotional storm, but perhaps it was something more as well. I was not surprised when he told me during a follow-up visit to Hong Kong I made years later that he had become dissatisfied with Lutheranism and Lutherans (although he had been baptized), that he no longer felt comforted by religion, and that most of the missionaries were "not truly religious." He also attributed their failure to support him more actively for an American visa to his disinclination to pursue a religious career. Whatever truth there was in this last assertion, his critical attitudes were part of his old pattern, reflections of a still-viable totalism forever seeking and never finding its ideal of sincerity. On the other hand, there had been no explosive break with the missionaries, and after an association of almost eight years Hu was still living and working among them. As always, he was imposing severe discipline upon himself, but his cause had finally become one of self-interest: he rose at six in the morning to study English and mathematics to prepare himself for the possibility of further education in America. And he was no longer alone; he had met a girl he wanted to marry and bring to America with him.

I do not know what the outcome of Hu's personal struggles will be; I do know that in his own exaggerated way, he had lived through and described to me most of the major emotional dilemmas of his generation of Chinese intellectuals.

CHAPTER 16

THE OLDER GENERATION:
ROBERT CHAO

As much as Hu's story does reveal about the thought reform of intellectuals and about their background environments, it cannot tell us everything. Others differed from him in their identity patterns and their responses to reform. Some of these differences—as we shall observe in the three case histories which follow—were a matter of personal variation, and others of group trends.

The age at which one undergoes reform has great significance: a revolutionary university reform experience at forty-five cannot be the same as one at twenty-five. The next life story, that of an older intellectual, has an emotional flavor quite distinct from Hu's.

Robert Chao had been a Nationalist official for almost twenty years when he was "invited" (in effect, ordered) to attend a revolutionary university set up soon after the takeover especially for affiliates of the old regime. When I met him in Hong Kong three years later (we had been introduced by a common acquaintance), he was working as a translator for a Western business concern. A stocky and ruddy-faced man who had studied for several years in America, he was unusually articulate and his English was fluent.

I soon gained the impression, however, that he had mixed feelings about talking with me. He was overly courteous (too proper even for a Chinese), and he rarely looked at me directly. I sensed in his guarded manner a fear that should he permit himself to relax, his exaggerated self-control might give way and permit disturbing feelings to emerge. And this is what frequently happened during the course of our interviews: after cautious platitudes and detached statements of general principles, where he felt on safe ground, something would set off in him a brief, tense outburst in which the frustration and pain of his emotional life would be revealed. Our sessions did not become any easier for him as the work progressed, and for this reason we spent just nine hours together— enough time only to discuss the main currents of his experiences.

Brought up in a rural area of Hunan Province during the early years of the twentieth century, Mr. Chao's first memory was of weird supernatural fear, from which he still does not feel free:

It was New Years Day. . . . I was about four years old. . . . I was brought out by a maternal uncle to the Temple of the City God. And in front of the Temple, under a wooden shed, there were two statues made of clay. There was an image of a man attending a horse. . . . Somehow I got scared—very scared—and very ill, because he looked at me as though smiling at me. . . . I was very sick after this for a few weeks. It was a serious illness and nothing would cure me—no medicine would help me until my relatives suggested that they get a Taoist priest to say incantations. And actually this had the effect of curing me. . . . I was generally superstitious—and later read a lot of superstitious books. It was a different world from now. . . . These things can be scarey. I can still be scared by them. . . . Superstition influences me even now.

The only child in a family of small landowners, he was still in his infancy when his father died. He later heard tales of his father's adventurous career as a local civil servant during the Ch'ing dynasty, adventurous because of the presence of bandits and the frequent social and natural upheavals. He and his mother lived with different groups of relatives, but it was she—a little-educated, yet strong-minded and intelligent country woman—who took on the roles of both parents, and devoted her major life energies to the boy's future. Chao spoke of his mother and of her sacrifices for him in glowing terms:

She was a very affectionate woman. As a young widow, I was her only child and this made her treasure me. . . . The only son is very spoiled in China. . . . She was kindhearted and generous—very open-minded and modern for her age. She was progressive and believed in change. . . . She was very clever and knew the importance of education. . . . She made great personal sacrifices to get me a complete education . . . which was not ordinarily available to a person of my background.

Mother and son combined forces to overcome financial and social difficulties and obtain this education, which included a special tutor in Chinese classics, the best primary and secondary school training available in the region, and later a university degree and graduate study abroad.

As a youngster, Chao spent most of his time at home with his mother, had few friends, and focused his attention mainly on his studies. He was extremely competitive, frequently transferring from one school to another when his superior grades made this possible. His mother moved with him, first to a large provincial city for his secondary school training, and then to Peking for his university education; she sold the small amount of remaining family land to get money for them to live upon.

Together they planned out Chao's future, always calculating carefully how best to use their resources, how best to carry out the steps necessary to attain worldly success. During the early years she contributed what she could from her own knowledge, teaching him to read and write, and telling him the historical anecdotes, legends, and romances which were part of her heritage. When he began to attend boarding schools, and to move beyond her intellectual capability, she lived apart from him and saw him on weekends. Their efforts were rewarded: Chao obtained a government scholarship which included his undergraduate university work in China as well as advanced studies in the United States financed by Boxer indemnity funds.

From the time of his arrival in America, Chao (now Robert) began for the first time to encounter difficulties, both external and internal. He was extremely uncomfortable about his social status, highly sensitive to slights of any kind and especially to possible suggestions of racial discrimination. During our talks, it was still difficult for him to come to terms with his own feelings about these problems:

I think the Americans have a justification because I can see clearly the racial situation in America. . . . They have such a large Negro population, so many alien people from Eastern Europe. . . . And besides, I was very proud myself—I didn't want to mix with them either. . . . I didn't go with any coeds—and in a way it was disconcerting—but I never had the courage. Once I felt the Americans looked down on the Chinese, I was too proud to make approaches.

He found, as did many Chinese in the West, that his friends were limited to other Chinese students, or to members of minority groups: "I had American friends, but I discovered that most of them were Jews. It was commiseration." Only after we had discussed these matters at some length did he begin to express his hostilities, and even then he checked himself in the midst of his brief outburst:

I think the Americans have a superiority complex. In a way they are narrow-minded, not interested in knowing foreign things and foreign people. . . . Of course as a human being I could not be free from resentment. . . . But then I was never insulted during my experience in America. I felt that the Americans showed indifference rather than discrimination. Those people who showed too much interest in the Chinese were too patronizing and not spontaneous.

He also experienced a certain amount of indecision about his course of study, switching from journalism to history, starting at one large midwestern university where he found that "life was too lonely," and then changing to another. In the end, he used only four of the five years allotted by his scholarship for study in America. He brought back to China a Chinese-American bride, as well as considerable admiration for American confidence and self-reliance: "I noticed that Americans, in making their own efforts, are sure of their destiny."

He described his experiences in his own country during the next twenty years as "a sad story—a story of frustrations." Working for various government departments as administrator, publicist, and diplomat, occasionally engaging in brief periods of teaching—many of these jobs being held during the confusion of wartime—he was perpetually disappointed, and in his view, unappreciated.

Sometimes he blamed himself:

The trouble is I haven't stuck to any line. If I had stayed in the foreign service, I could have risen and become an ambassador. . . . I had friends high up, but I didn't follow one particular man or faction. I was often offered jobs which I thought were below me.

Sometimes he blamed the ingratitude of friends and political associates:

I knew everybody in Chinese government—from the generals down many were my close friends. But although I had helped them plenty, they have never given me help. . . . Frequently in a foreign office, people didn't want you under them because your qualifications were better than theirs.

But he was always highly critical of the entire government structure of which he was a part. "There was absolutely no security if you didn't accumulate money. . . . Everyone was out for himself."

Therefore, at the time of the change in regimes, he felt neither sympathy for the victorious Communists nor loyalty to the defeated Nationalists:

I knew nothing about Chinese Communism, but from contacts with the Russians during the war, I did not like Russian Communism, as I thought there was no freedom. But on the other hand, I did not feel that I had an obligation to flee with the Nationalists. They were going nowhere, and we did not think that they could hold Taiwan.

When he was sent for his thought reform, he was "tense" about not knowing what to expect, but at the same time he anticipated from the experience an opportunity to "fit in better" with the Communists. From the beginning, he tried to remain emotionally detached, to adopt a practical wait-and-see attitude, and to judge the program on the basis of the material rewards it might offer him. His cautious and pliable approach—also that of many fellow "students" much like him—was a far cry from the youthful enthusiasms of Hu's group:

I entered into the situation without knowing exactly what it would be. I wanted to see results. . . . We felt that if it suited our interests, then it would be successful. If I were to get the kind of job that I wanted, it would be successful. If I did not get a desirable job, it would have the opposite kind of result. . . . At the beginning, we discussed the best way to go about it, which we decided was . . . not to be too progressive and not to be reactionary. . . . There was nothing idealistic, we had no emotional abandon. . . . But most of us wanted to get on the good side of the Communists. . . . Often the sessions were sterile because everybody followed the Party line.

But when the reformers began to demand that the participants deepen their self-analyses, Chao found that it became increasingly difficult, even for such a wary group, to maintain its detachment:

We were always baffled because we did not know how to link theory with practice. . . . To link up personal experience with the question being discussed. . . . They were always asking us for examples. This was difficult.

And as the participants revealed more of themselves, they found that detachment gave way to genuine involvement:

Everybody began to know a great deal about everybody else. . . . Everything was public—money, crime, past sins, and so on. We developed a kind of esprit de corps.

Nor could Chao and his fellow students avoid the usual group hostilities, especially when individual people overplayed their "progressive" roles:

Although we wanted to increase our solidarity, in practice often the opposite occurred. Men didn't like to be criticized, and they would regard those who criticized them as an enemy—as in bourgeois psychology. This caused bad feelings in the group. . . . Sometimes a man was not sincere and would try to put something over. . . . Being not really progressive he would falsify his thought and pretend to be more progressive than the others. Everyone was acting to a certain extent, but there was no need in trying to be extra progressive. . . . Such a man would be ostracized by the group. . . . Even the Communists don't want this.

In dealing with the problem of guilt, the men continued their efforts to go through the proper motions:

It was taken for granted that every man from the old society was a bad man—guilty of all kinds of crimes—that anyone connected with the Nationalist regime was really unpatriotic. . . . In discussing this, everybody tried to put himself in a favorable light. Even when someone admitted guilt, it was with the intention of showing everyone how much he had improved.

Again Chao and the others found themselves unable to remain detached, for their past experiences made them especially susceptible to a genuine sense of guilt—which offered an avenue of entry for thought reform influences:

I knew that in the past I had done things without purpose—whereas the Communists said everything should be done with the idea of serving the people. . . . The important question was whether you considered what you did in the past really wrong. . . . I admitted that certain criticisms of me were valid—having a self-seeking approach and not considering the masses. . . . And when you put things down on paper, you believe them more than when you just say them. . . . You really feel them to be shortcomings. . . . We all fell for the phrase, "working for the people." We couldn't answer it.

This acceptance extended to much of the Communist message: "You begin to believe a great deal of it . . . and all of us believed that the Communists were better than the Nationalists."

But when Chao summed up the effects of thought reform for me, he presented two alternative, almost contradictory views. The first was a strongly negative statement, based upon a return to a detached and calculating judgment: the Communists had not come through with a good job offer and therefore the "reform" did not succeed:

After thought reform, they offered us low clerical jobs in the farming areas. . . . The indoctrination failed because we did not like the jobs assigned. We became more reactionary. . . . Now I am more critical of them. They allow no personal freedom, and no freedom of silence. . . . They are liars and I do not believe them.

The second view was one of moderate praise, and a recognition of personal gain from thought reform.

Any Communist indoctrination, well taken, must leave some effects. It is not entirely bad. . . . A man who has been indoctrinated will always think differently as compared with those who have not been indoctrinated—at least in certain respects. For instance, I might have been very haughty to my servants before, but now I would never treat servants as some of the Hong Kong people treat their servants. I think that this emphasis on labor and the respect they pay to labor is a very good idea. . . . Personally I had a great change. Before I had all of the ambitions that other people had. . . . I was egocentric. . . . But now I really realize that the individual is rather insignificant.

He tried to resolve his dilemma by transcending both views and withdrawing from all involvements:

People don't understand me. When they pick a quarrel with me, I don't respond—even if you persecute me. It is because of what I have been through. I am above human emotions.

Yet the circumstances of Mr. Chao's departure from Communist China reveal he was susceptible to human emotions after all: he ran off with a Western woman who was leaving for Hong Kong. The affair dissolved after their arrival, and just at that time, travel between China and Hong Kong became much more difficult. He felt that if he returned to China, as he had more or less planned to do when he left (his wife, mother, and children were still there), he would not again have the chance to leave, and would also be regarded with suspicion. His eventual decision to stay had little to do with ideological considerations:

I left only because of this woman. If I felt that I could move in and out freely I would have gone back. I wasn't too decided. . . . I could have been very useful to them [the Communists]—one of their propagandists in the foreign office or something.

In his contemplative moments, Chao took a somewhat Taoist or Buddhist view of his life, emphasizing its pointlessness and its nothingness. He expressed this view in one of his responses to the Thematic Apperception Test, when he was shown a blank card and asked to make up a story: [1]

On this piece of cardboard all I can see just now is empty whiteness. But if I look at it more intently I can imagine things which crowd into a life of many years. These things were the happenings in a man's career. When one came into this world he was just like a piece of white cardboard. There was no image, nothing engraved on it. Pretty soon when he got into contact with worldly things he carried out his own destiny and he could have painted many pictures of many kinds—some gay and some sad, some successful, some failures, some permanent, some ephemeral. And this seems to be what happened to me. In my life I have gone through all of the stages, but in a moment of self-complacency, it would seem to me that everything vanishes again into this original piece of cardboard, without picture, without color, and without emotions.

This passive resignation—real as it was for Chao—did not prevent him from calling into play the more active side of his character. He showed extraordinary energy and effectiveness in finding work in Hong Kong, arranging for his wife and his children to leave Communist China, and then utilizing his Western contacts to set up employment for himself and residence for his family in England. There he will probably carry on ably, if without clear purpose.

Chao's life story (even more than Hu's) indicates something of the vast emotional journey which many of his generation were required to make from the "old China" of their youth to the Communist reform of their middle years. Taking into account the personal, cultural, and political obstacles they faced, their accomplishments were often impressive; but each of these accomplishments was apt to be paid for with an increasing sense of anomie—with profound personal and social dislocation and unrelatedness.

Chao's oldest identities (oldest in the history of both his culture and his own life) were those of the fearful rural mystic and the "mother-directed" filial son. The first identity, which included both an awe of the supernatural and an imaginative richness, was his bond with generations of people from his local area. It formed a basic underlying identity upon which later more worldly ones were grafted, and it contributed to his inability to ever feel truly at home in the modern, urban world. Many Chinese intellectuals (including Hu) possessed similar elements of rural mysticism, however suppressed by the rational demands of both Confucian and Western teachings; but Chao reveals the strong staying power of this rural self, which made it both a refuge and an embarrassment.

Chao's relationship with his mother supplied him with something of a conveyor identity, and allowed him to remain filial and at the same time move beyond the narrow world of filialism. It was not unusual in Chao's generation, especially if one's beginnings were rather humble, for a parent like this—rooted in tradition, but possessing the capacity to imagine a modern future—to help a child make this great emotional leap; nor is such a phenomenon confined to Chinese society. In Chao's case, more conflict was involved than he cared to reveal: he made clear his early dependency upon his mother, as well as his sense of gratitude and of personal debt; but from some of his test responses (descriptions of bitter disagreements between mothers and sons), I learned of his struggle to become independent of her control, and of the guilt and resentment which accompanied this struggle. This mother-son alliance of love and ambition was nonetheless the means by which a rural child of the old China reached the educational channels which transformed him into a sophisticated (if brittle) modern Chinese man.

Chao became immersed in his personal ideology of social accomplishment and recognition, and remained relatively detached from broad ideological movements. Although his developing identity of the detached careerist was a natural outgrowth of his relationship with his mother, it was also an identity very frequently chosen by others during these chaotic years—a means of survival in a society whose moral cohesion was rapidly breaking down.

For Chao's generation, the path to accomplishment was Western learning, and the price of Western learning some degree of Westernization. But by spending his early twenties in America, and by becoming a Westernized Chinese, Chao experienced the beginning of an almost interminable identity crisis. Before he went, he was able—with some difficulty—to handle the continuous adaptations and personal changes necessary for his advance within Chinese society; but the more jarring conflict of feeling both attracted to and repelled by the Western world was almost too much for him. Like many Asian students in the West, he felt himself simultaneously liberated and denigrated. In the midst of newfound possibilities for self-expression, he felt keenly his status as a non-Westerner, an Oriental. Along with the threat to his masculinity—Asian men are apt to look upon American women with trepidation, and American women are likely to treat Asian men in a kindly, sisterly fashion—American society posed a more important threat to his general sense of autonomy: how much of his self would be consumed by this tantalizing new Western influence? Historical events both American and Chinese led Chao to value all that was Western; and men like Chao wavered between taking too great a plunge into Westernization and recoiling defensively into Chineseness. Facing all of these problems while for the first time navigating without his mother's help, Chao never fully recovered from the intense sense of identity diffusion initiated within him by his American experience.

He returned to China much better educated in useful Western ways, but less sure of what he was and where he was going. His sensitivity to, and expectation of, rebuff made him, over the years, a resentful bureaucrat, another identity in which personal conflicts blended with the social realities of a frequently unscrupulous environment. This identity also was common among those Chinese intellectuals who threw in their lot with the Nationalist regime (the academic field was the only major alternative, and this had its own severe strains). What characterized the resentful bureaucrat was a lack of involvement in an ideal beyond himself, a nagging suspiciousness of others, and the kind of deep-seated self-hatred which is the inevitable outcome of losing a battle with one's sense of integrity.

Chao and many of his associates, naturally enough, attempted to carry over their detached attitude to thought reform; older participants in any case tended to be rather cautious. Yet this exaggerated detachment was a liability as well as a strength. It did enable Chao to keep a cool eye out for his self-interest; but it also rendered him susceptible to strong feelings of guilt and shame in response to Communist-style self-analysis. He was most disturbed by the exposure of his detached careerism, most impressed by the Communist program to devote oneself "wholeheartedly" to serving "the people." As was also true for Dr. Vincent, this detached man —always refractory to ideologies—found much that was compelling in the ideology of Communism. The Westernized Chinese in Chao, although he did not verbalize this, was also vulnerable (had he not at times been contemptuous of things Chinese, and susceptible to alien and "subversive" influences?). Confronted with such negative identity elements as his alienation from his own heritage, his uneasy emotional passivity, and his ever-violated integrity, Chao could not fail to respond to thought reform's clear purpose and stringent morality.

But in men of Chao's age, emotional patterns are not easily altered, and in the long run the self-interest of the careerist served as the criterion for his judgments. We can take Chao's word that everything depended upon the job offered at the end of the process; this job assignment had great significance for everyone, for it indicated the way in which the Communists identified a man in their system, as well as the new identity patterns which he would be permitted to develop. Chao's affair with the Western woman thus served two purposes: it permitted him, at a difficult psychological moment, to reassert his Asian manhood where it had been most rebuffed; and it got him out of China. Not only had his old emotional balance been threatened; he was again feeling unappreciated and badly treated. His departure, and especially his failure to return, reflected his awareness (like Hu's) that his character was not compatible with the Communist environment.

In the non-Communist world, Chao attempted to recover his

detachment in the identity of a withdrawn Chinese sage. He combined the sophisticated ennui of one who has experienced everything with a return to early mysticism in the Taoist-Buddhist sense
of the ephemeral nature of worldly experience (very much like
Hu's father). His passions were not to be so easily stilled, but this
at least was his ideal. Moreover, he had become expert in the techniques of personal survival: the extraordinary variety of cultures,
subcultures, and stray environments which he had traversed were
not wasted upon him; and in this adaptability, his character structure is, after all, that of a modern man.[2]

Like Hu, Chao represented something of an extreme: his sensitivities about his background and the extent of his frustration and
withdrawal may well have been exceptional. His detached approach
to the social movements of his time was, of course, just the opposite
of that of Hu. Yet his combination of adaptability and anomie—a
combination so crucial to the outcome of his thought reform—is
another character pattern of great importance for twentieth-century
China.

CHAPTER 17

GEORGE CHEN: THE CON-
VERSIONS OF YOUTH

For those who faced thought reform not as young
or mature adults, but as unformed teenagers, the
process was as much a matter of education as re-education. Their
reform took place in secondary schools and universities.

George Chen, our next Chinese subject, experienced thought
reform on both of these levels: fifteen years old at the time of the
Communist takeover, he was exposed to it first at a boarding school
for two years, and then at a university for two additional years. He
was twenty at the time that I met him, not yet one year out of
Communist China.

He was introduced to me by a first cousin of his who was an
acquaintance of mine. A slim, delicate-looking lad, George had a
quality that was both distant and intense. He was shy and serious,
but by no means reluctant to express himself, and—as became
quickly evident during the interviews—both sensitive and intelligent. We met fourteen times over the course of one year; our
sessions together totalled more than forty hours. At George's request, the cousin who brought us together, and who had done
some work with me before, served as interpreter; but during later
interviews, I used, with George's consent, one of my regular interpreters.

George was born in Canton, the son of a middle-level Nationalist official. He was the fourth of eight children, the third of five boys. Through most of his childhood, he remembers, his mother was "the symbol of the family." She had a more aristocratic background, and in times of difficulty her leadership and her money sustained them all. The close attachment between George and his mother had a crucial bearing upon his later life; but during his earliest years, he was attended to mainly by maids or *amahs*. One of these *amahs* (said to be as strict as she was devoted) took care of him from birth until the age of two-and-a-half; and when she left, George experienced (as he was later told) a true infantile depression: he cried incessantly, called the *amah's* name, refused food, and resisted the efforts of others—including his mother—to take care of him. When he got a bit older, he began to realize that his mother found it very hard to care for her eight children; she was often short of breast milk, and became flustered by minor crises. He came to think of her as possessing "the virtues and the frailties" of womanhood: sentimental, indecisive, kind, easy-going, and generous.

In the face of the Japanese invasion, the family moved to Hong Kong, where George lived from the ages of three to seven. During this period—and for most of his childhood—George remembers seeing his father only infrequently, since distant assignments kept him away from home. George spent a good deal of his time with his two grandmothers, and each of these elderly women had a distinctive impact upon the boy. His paternal grandmother, a garrulous and opinionated lady, was kind to George and the other children; but she conveyed to them in no uncertain terms her moralistic, fundamentalist Protestant beliefs: whoever did evil would be condemned to everlasting suffering in Hell, and only the good would enter Heaven and enjoy eternal happiness. George later learned that she had her own cross to bear: her husband, much to the disgrace of the entire family, chose to ignore them and lived with a concubine in another section of Hong Kong. Quite different was the influence of George's "adopted grandmother," who was the wife of George's great-uncle. (The great-uncle was an elder son, and since he and his wife were childless, they had "adopted" George's father in order to continue the main line of the family.) This grandmother was a gay country woman who imparted to the children her own love of nature, and delighted in taking them on outdoor excursions and in buying them frivolous presents.

George remembers himself as a very weak and sickly youngster, who frequently suffered from indigestion, cough, and nervousness: "Whenever I would get very scared, this would cause me some illness." He was considered not strong enough to play with the other children, and was carried on the back of his *amah* longer than the others; despite the attention he received from his family members, he felt lonely a good deal of the time. Often kept indoors, he would sit on a small balcony and draw pictures of people, automobiles, and steamships he saw below, showing some talent in art and calligraphy. He lived a great deal in the world of his daydreams, imagining himself to be, instead of a weak little boy, a powerful hero, an armed policeman, a soldier, or a man of wealth who would deliver the family from its constant economic difficulties.

Even this small child was made to feel that everything was temporary, that he and the other family members were refugees in a very disturbed world, and that all of them had to somehow survive the indignity of living and dressing in a manner considered beneath the family station. And it was further suggested to him that if the family could only return to its home in Canton, everything would be all right: George's father would be able to join them, their financial status would be better, the errant grandfather would come back and "end the family shame," and the family would be able to hold up its head once more.

Attending school from the ages of five to seven in Hong Kong, George was whisked to and from the building by his *amah*, and mixed little with the other children. Then the family moved to Chungking in central China and became part of a friendly wartime community. During the years he lived in Chungking, George's physical strength greatly improved, and he began to take part in all activities centering around the nearby school. He emerged as an outstanding student. He became interested in Chinese history, particularly in great heroes of the past, and developed the ambition of becoming himself a national hero.

In 1945, when George was ten years old, the war ended. The family made several quick moves, finally returning to Canton. In rapid succession, George was sent to three different boarding schools, two of them run by Protestant missionary groups. These were his first separations from his family; and during one period of three months, his mother was several hundred miles away from him. The homesickness which he experienced was largely a longing for her; he also contrasted his sense of "coldness" at being thrust among strange boys in shabby dormitories with the warmth and recognition he had known in Chungking.

When the family was finally reunited, however, he was faced with still another set of painful emotions, centering around an increasingly critical attitude toward his father. This protector, whose return he had so longed for, began to assume much less heroic proportions at close hand. Not only did George feel that he had been replaced in his father's affections by the younger children; he also began to realize that his father was not too good a family provider. Worse than this, he came to see his father as "not a reasonable man"—and to regard his outbursts of temper and general clumsiness in human relationships as extremely offensive.

In his distress, George turned to the religion offered to him in school. Influenced by his grandmother's earlier teachings and by the example of his older brother, who had become a Christian, George was baptized at the age of twelve, together with a younger brother and cousin. Behind this act, in addition to family influences, was a highly personal quest:

I then felt that life was very fleeting, and that nothing was very sure . . . that when one died, all of his hopes and achievements would perish with him . . . and that religion might be a way to a solution for all of this.

Before long George lost interest in organized religion; but he never lost his concern about man's spiritual needs and the conviction that "life is much more than just its materialistic interpretation."

Whatever emotional help this religious orientation may have supplied him, George did succeed in righting himself, overcoming his youthful despair, and again distinguishing himself academically —this time especially in mathematics and physics. Still preferring literature to athletics, he continued to go his own way: "I was considered by others to be lonesome, although at the time I did not consider myself to be very lonely."

Soon, however, he began to be troubled by sexual urges. He enjoyed the pornographic literature passed around in school as much as the next fellow, but he suffered more than most over his enjoyment. He dealt with the situation by establishing a personal taboo: "I felt very ashamed of myself. . . . I would prevent myself from touching these books even if they were available." He found great relief by reading (at the age of fifteen) a Chinese translation of *Lady Chatterley's Lover*, after which "I no longer felt that sex was evil." But this partial enlightenment by no means eradicated his moralistic condemnation of his self-stimulation nor prevented a developing tendency (as frequent in Chinese culture as in the West) to distinguish sharply between the "nice girls" he knew and the more lascivious objects of his fantasy. "I would imagine the sexual act with some sexy woman, never my wife or fiancée. . . . I never connect physical desire with emotional interest."

He was in the midst of these adolescent conflicts at the time of the national political excitement preceding the Communist take-over. Although he had shared in the wartime patriotism and anti-Japanese sentiment, he was slower than most youths around him to develop sharp political convictions. When he was fourteen, he had criticized his older brother because of the latter's increasing in-volvement with left-wing causes, believing that "young people should not get into these affairs because they cannot do anything about them." As he began to learn more himself, however, he too began to take a stand against the corruption of the Nationalist regime and in favor of far-reaching changes for his country, looking toward a "great leader" to bring them about. He had mixed feelings about the Communists: as a political party antagonistic to the Nationalists, he felt that they might be able to implement some of the necessary changes; but he could not help suspecting that they were "puppets of Soviet Russia."

At this time, his father's activities caused him much resentment. With Communist hegemony imminent, his father—now at home, with little to do—spent hours eating and talking at tea houses, where, according to George, friends would come and flatter him and amateur palm readers would tell him of the brilliant career ahead of him. George bitterly condemned his father's self-indulgence, his eating too much, and his wasting of time and money. But he was even more angered by the futile, last-ditch anti-Communist activi-ties in which his father suddenly became involved, considering them nothing more than an escape from idleness, and potentially harmful to others in the family.

When the Communist armies entered Canton, however, George

realized that he too felt hostile toward them because, although aware of the old regime's shortcomings, "I had always taken the Nationalist government as my mother country." Shortly afterward, when he returned home from school on a visit, he learned that his father had fled to Hong Kong. His mother had been required to quarter Communist soldiers in the family home, and although they were well-behaved, she expressed to George her resentment of the intrusion. She also told her son that the new regime was likely to be no better than the Nationalists, and quoted the Chinese proverb, "Crows everywhere are black."

At his Protestant middle school, he found that students around him varied in their sentiments. Many were enthusiastic about the Communists, and followed the lead of political activists who— even in this age group—identified themselves as former members of the Communist underground. A significant number of students, however (some but not all of whom were Christian), shared George's suspicion of the Communists. But few had much sympathy for the defeated Nationalists, and George "felt foolish" about his own emotional loyalties to them.

Thought reform (or "political study") was soon initiated, but only gradually. Students were told that at the middle school level they were more "ignorant" than "contaminated." Regular political classes were started, as well as small group sessions for criticism and self-criticism; the latter at first took up about two hours a day and were not regularly held. Political instructors were chosen from among the most "progressive" of the old teachers. One of these presented the Communist doctrine in earnest, logical terms and had a profound effect upon George:

I was always moved listening to him. . . . It was under his influence that my thought began to change a few months after the liberation. Emotionally, I was still in favor of the Nationalist Government. All my family and relatives didn't like this new regime, and I myself also felt that the new regime was hostile to us. But rationally I could not oppose it. I thought its way of expression a little too exaggerated, but its principles always right; moreover, morally I should support it, because it represented the people, and it was righteous and justified.

Beyond considerations of logic, George was deeply affected by such emotions as the urge to belong and the need for hope—to the point of experiencing something close to a religious conversion:

How this occurred is a little vague. One night I went back to school alone. On the road to the dormitory in the campus there were only a few dimly-lit road lamps, and the place seemed very lonesome. I suddenly felt very lonely, and had the understanding of what my own situation was. I knew that I had no future, that people like us seemed to have been thrown out. And yet I could not even hate this regime. Then suddenly my thought turned towards the opposite direction. Perhaps this revolution was good for everybody. Perhaps all of us would one day be happy and satisfied just as the Communists had said. If so, why should I feel sorry any more? . . . I once thought that my change in emotion was made by the power of will after my intellectual understanding had changed. But I can see it in retrospect now, that whenever I was bothered emotionally by the thought of having no future and being thrown out politically, I always tried to think toward the opposite direction, and then would feel rather resolved in the new point of view.

Over the next two years, the Communist material presented in lectures, discussions, and reading assignments always appealed to the students' "conscience and compassion" so that "we could not neglect nor turn away from it." Even when the program seemed moderate, George felt that it was "very tense inside." He occasionally experienced doubts, and he once expressed to a cousin the belief that the regime was undemocratic and illiberal. But his cousin disagreed with him, replying, "If you are right about this, what future can we have for our country?" George's doubts were also suppressed by his need to believe: "I thought to myself, 'If the Communists were really malicious and wicked, what would we do?' This problem was too formidable. Everybody preferred the thought that they were righteous and just . . . and everybody was willing to believe this."

Three mass campaigns—"Accuse Japan," "Accuse America," and "Enlist for the Army"—dramatically mobilized student emotions. The first of these campaigns, according to George, was especially effective because the students, young as they were, could recall personal antagonisms toward the Japanese:

Before the Accuse-Japan Meeting was launched, there was an Anti-Japanese-Rearmament Week, and all of the songs we sang during the war against Japanese aggression were played over the radio. This helped the students to remember wartime and to revive the old hatred. Then the Accuse-Japan general meeting took place for three continuous days. At first there were reports of the historical events of Japanese aggression in China, and the hideous plot of the American imperialists to rearm

Japan. Then the students spoke freely about their own experiences, sufferings, and tragedies during the war. The first few speeches were pre-arranged by the Students' League and the New Democratic Youth Corps. . . . The atmosphere was easily achieved. . . . Many students went up to the stage voluntarily, and even those who did not go up had just the same hatred for the Japanese and for the American imperialists.

George was deeply affected by this campaign, and critical of himself for not being even more zealous: "I felt ashamed that I was less full of hate than the others."

Similar passions were aroused during the "Accuse America" meetings, although George thought these less successful because students had less personal animosity toward America. But they did resolve to destroy all of the imported American bluejeans which they owned. In retrospect, George felt this to be "the epidemic spread of a fashion. . . . The fear of being considered lagging behind, and not the genuine change of an idea."

The Enlist for the Army campaign, which lasted for one month, was more a means of eliciting the students' willingness to serve than an actual attempt to obtain military personnel. George described the movement's moral force, and the threat of ostracism to those who resisted:

Progressive students were always there to criticize those who were not willing to enlist, saying that they were just being selfish, since the fear of sacrifice or the consideration of one's own future were only selfishness. . . . The students who enlisted had some special activities together, and everybody wished to participate in these. . . . Those who enlisted called for the others to join them. . . . And those who did not enlist were not as well regarded. . . . To a student who did not enlist, this month was really a kind of persecution. . . . The constant meetings in large and small groups were a way of reproach. . . . You felt yourself all wrong. You found no way out of this. You felt that you could not stand among the enlisted when you met them. . . . The student who had not enlisted had already admitted inside his own mind that he was not right. . . . He felt lonely, and he and others like him did not dare to unite or to encourage each other. Everyone was aware that this disturbance could be resolved by enlisting for the army. . . . I was among the enlisted.

George felt, however (again in retrospect), that there was a tendency in him to resist, and that "if I had a family member to talk to me personally or a girl friend to oppose it," he might not have enlisted. But his faith in Communism, like that of his fellow students, steadily increased.

This faith was then greatly undermined during a visit to his family in Hong Kong over the summer vacation. And this same sequence occurred the following year: reinforcement of his Communist beliefs at school on the mainland, then the emergence of critical views in Hong Kong. He attributed these shifts to the influence of individual family members, as well as to an underlying sympathy for Western democracies. "When I was on the mainland I had to suppress this original affection and favor. . . . But once arriving in Hong Kong, the suppression was relieved and my ideas naturally went back to their original form." In any case, the shifts were rather extreme: "On the mainland I thought the Communist aims to be just, and that I should devote myself to them. . . . In Hong Kong, I thought the Communist aims were but lies, their means too cruel, and that even if we did want to achieve a modern cosmopolitan country we should not follow the Communist way." Whatever his vantage point, he was extremely impressionable: "I was quite inevitably sentimental: on the mainland I was willing to believe the Communists, and in Hong Kong I was willing to oppose them."

He was nonetheless determined to return to the mainland for his university education, having passed his entrance examination for Peking University (China's leading academic center) before his second Hong Kong visit. His parents bitterly opposed this and urged him to remain with them. His father went so far as to issue what is in any culture the ultimate parental threat: "If you insist upon going to Peking, I cannot any longer consider you my son." But George was less affected by this pronouncement than he was by his mother's obvious grief at the time of his departure. His conflict was so great that just after he got on the boat to go back to China, he had a strong urge to run ashore; and even after he arrived at Canton, the first mainland city on the way to Peking, he almost changed his mind again, and was dissuaded from returning to Hong Kong only by friends who urged him to remain for the sake of his education and his future.

At the University of Peking, George found the pattern of thought reform similar to that at middle school, but more intensive: not only did criticism and self-criticism within small groups become more focused and personal, but students were expected to be instigators as well as followers. During the Three Anti Movement —against waste, corruption, and bureaucracy—the first of a series of campaigns on the campus, it was the students who searched out these evils among all university employees, including faculty members. In fact, a student, as local Communist Party secretary, ran the campaign, and for some time virtually ran the university.

The movement followed the usual sequence: an announcement by Mao Tse-tung, editorials in leading newspapers about its purposes and general methods, and then preparation at the university itself. Posters were prominent everywhere, slogans and cartoon caricatures appeared on all the classroom blackboards (called the "blackboard press"), and loudspeakers broadcasted throughout the university—in dining rooms, dormitories, assembly halls, and department buildings. The campaign achieved its greatest intensity during a two-month period devoted entirely to its activities: students were required to remain at the university for what would ordinarily have been a one-month vacation period, and the beginning of the next term's classes was delayed for still another month. George served as a "detention guard," watching over those nonprofessional employees (servants and clerical help) who were detained in special bedrooms or classrooms, each isolated and subjected to a barrage of pressures to confess his past participation in corrupt activities. None of those singled out failed to confess, and some were sent to prison.

For George and the other students, the most impressive events were the public confessions of their professors (here the Three Anti Movement merged with the Thought Reform Campaign). Each faculty member was required to make a "self-examination" before the students of his own department, and criticize his political shortcomings and also his deficiencies in teaching method and outlook. George was impressed by the influence which students could bring to bear upon their professors, especially so in the case of his own department head:

Professor M was the ex-chairman of the Chinese National League of Physicists, a very renowned professor. But the students did not like him too much. He muttered when he spoke, and he was not too sociable a person. . . . All the students were free to give their true opinions about his teaching, their criticism about him. They emphasized with him and with most of the professors that they neglected their teaching and were more interested in research. . . . But his case was especially big because as faculty chairman he was accused about other aspects of university behavior. . . . He got up and accused himself of his previous dealings with the KMT, his friendship with KMT leaders. He also confessed that he had not been very enthusiastic in thought reform, and had not taken a very active part in the political classes among the professors. Then he said that when he had been chairman of the faculty committee, he had not really worked as a true chairman—that he had been only eager to write articles in order to get them published in magazines for his own international fame—and that his work was really for himself, not for his students. . . . The students kept adding criticisms, and he had to criticize himself on four occasions before he was allowed to finish. . . . Practically speaking, almost all of the professors "bowed their heads" in front of the Party. They were approved sooner or later. Some were very tough and stubborn at first, but then to everybody's surprise, they would turn about face and admit that they had been wrong.

George felt that some of these criticisms and self-criticisms were overdone, but thought most of them "reasonable"; for by now he was once more joining with group enthusiasms, and was in general accord with student actions.

During the Honesty and Frankness Movement which followed (also a part of the Thought Reform Campaign), students turned their criticisms upon themselves. They were told that in the past the government had been corrupt and the political system "irrational," so that people were forced to be dishonest; but now, with an enlightened and "rational" government, one could be "honest and frank" about everything. In addition to the usual details about their backgrounds, students were expected to confess such things as "intrigues and wrongs of parents," cheating during examinations, listening to illegal radio broadcasts, and (especially for women) lies about age.

At first, George thought that any denunciation of his family would be immoral: "Prior to these meetings, I did not believe that family affiliation could be a mistake." But group pressures soon led him to the opposite conviction, that it would be immoral *not* to denounce one's family: "The Organization [Party, Youth Corps, and government] kept emphasizing that attachment toward our families was selfish and wrong, since they had been against the welfare of the people. So I began to feel that by loving my family, I was neglecting my duty to my country." Like Hu, George felt guilty over keeping a secret: "I also thought that if each individual kept something secret, something only known to himself, it would certainly have a bad effect upon his work for the government—and for the sake of the people, it was right to ask everyone to tell the truth." And he was greatly influenced by the unanimous confession trend among the forty freshmen physics students in his section: "When I saw others criticizing their family happily, and I contrasted this with my own reluctance, I began to think that this must be due to my own selfishness." By this time, his inner moral conflict had become inextricably merged with fear of external reprisal, so that the only solution he saw was to submit.

I felt very confused and upset. . . . I knew that the matter must be settled—and that if I didn't do it well, the government would discover that I wasn't being frank enough and I would be in for trouble. I felt that if I could once and for all settle the turmoil in my mind, I would calm down and be able to feel that I had done my duty to my country.

In deciding what to confess, George was influenced by others before him ("they set good examples for me") and by his realization that the purpose of the movement was to get people to confess those things they most wished to conceal:

To me the only thing I wanted to conceal was that I had come from a reactionary, bureaucratic family—so this was the thing to confess. . . . I told that my father had been a KMT official, a KMT party member, and had held important KMT positions. I said that he had been a reactionary, a man who worked for the welfare of his class which was against the welfare of the people. . . . and that my attachment for my family was selfish and wrong. . . .

He experienced the relief of one who has carried out his obligations: "I had the feeling that what I did was right, because it was what the government required me to do, and that it was proper behavior." But his family attachments could not be severed, and he could not avoid recurrent guilt:

When I would receive letters from my family, or look through my luggage and see reminders of home, I felt sorry about what I had done. . . . Other students told me that after they had made their confession they considered their relationship with their family ended, and that they felt great relief and did not have to worry any more. . . . I did not feel this way.

George also experienced the full impact of one other campaign —the fabricated Chinese charges about bacteriological warfare.

At a mass meeting there were formal reports given of the proofs available —of American planes having carried leaves with insects and bacteria, pictures of these. . . . Then all of the students went to an open exhibition in Peking of small glass bottles of leaves that carried the germs, as well as insects—also test tubes, and dissected pathological parts of dead people who had died from these germs—everything in great detail . . . cholera and other epidemic diseases to destroy the agriculture of China. It said that some of these germs had been dropped in North Korea, some in Manchuria, and some in other Chinese provinces. . . . At first I was not so sure. . . . But later, when the confessions of American pilots were published [1]—photographs and attached signatures—and there was confirmation of the fact by several famous scientists from various countries, including a Fellow of the Royal Society, I believed it to be true.

Although convinced by this campaign, George found himself once more deficient in hatred, this time because he was unable to evoke the necessary stereotype of the evil American; and once more he considered this to be a moral shortcoming on his part.

I felt resentful against the Americans, and believed that it was very inhuman for a civilized country to commit such an evil deed. . . . But when many students in my class became very angry and made heated accusations against the American imperialists . . . I found that I could not feel as angry as they did. . . . Perhaps it was because I could never experience a bloodthirsty image of an American. I had a bloodthirsty image of a Japanese soldier in my mind. . . . of a cold, able, but inhuman German. But I saw an American—though no longer easygoing, kindhearted and generous—still cheerful, openminded, and innocent. . . . I admitted that germ warfare was a fact, and I tried very hard to model a picture of the fierce American . . . but my impression of the innocent American never quite diminished. . . . But then I was ashamed of myself for not being emotional enough.

Beyond these personal limitations, however, George was impressed with the effectiveness of the germ warfare agitation, not only in stirring up anti-American feeling and in rallying the Chinese people in a greater effort in the Korean war, but also in serving as a stimulus for a nationwide hygiene campaign, a campaign in which the students participated by laboring on improvement of their university sewage and drainage systems.

During George's sophomore year, there were no major movements; but he experienced similar emotions in relationship to a continuing program of less dramatic thought reform measures. He did maintain a certain amount of emotional distance between himself and the Communists: "I never deified the Party. . . . I believed in it, but I never could make myself love it." And especially during those rare moments when he was alone, he wondered whether Communism went too far in curbing personal freedom, or whether it was not being "unscientific" in its exaggeration and its claims of infallibility. But these doubts did not last: "I could not dare to believe that they were wrong and I was right." By the end of his second year at the university—and at the end of four years of Communist student life and reform—the Party had gained his trust and his allegiance: "I was completely confident in their theories. I trusted their program. . . . They seemed invincible. Emotionally speaking, I relied on them." Other students classified him as a "scholastic inactivist"—an outstanding student sufficiently progressive in his views but somewhat "lagging behind" in his enthusiasm and a bit "sentimental" about his family.

When he was summoned to Hong Kong during his vacation because of the death of his grandfather—his first family visit in two years—he thought the trip would be nothing more than an interlude before returning to an exciting future in Communist China, and he planned to be back in Peking at the University well before the next semester began. Indeed, he applied a "reformed" judgment to all that he saw in Hong Kong:

I was hostile to the old society, and I looked upon the people in it with the eyes of an owl. I found myself unaccustomed to the capitalist way of life, and could not bear the vanity, waste, and extravagance of life here. . . . I resented differences and discrimination between rich and poor . . . well-to-do people enslaving their servants. . . . I thought that I could openly and disinterestedly scorn and hate them, for I was so much superior to them.

Yet within a few weeks he had reversed himself completely, this time not only in his point of view, but in his life plans. He decided to give up his university education on the mainland and remain in Hong Kong: again the influence of family members initiated a change of heart. He found his mother in an unhappy and "pitiable" state; he felt "overwhelmed by affection" for her and unwilling to contemplate the pain he would cause her if he returned to the mainland. He also experienced feelings of guilt and responsibility toward a younger brother whom he had sometimes bullied during childhood (one is responsible for one's younger brother in Chinese culture); and since this brother planned to study in Taiwan, George feared that if he returned to Peking he might never see him again. George described these family influences as "not rational, but rather emotional."

Moreover, his older brother, to whom he had often looked for guidance in the past, was able to bring to bear upon him intellectual pressures as well. As an editor of an anti-Communist press service in Hong Kong, he made available to George a large number of books dealing with Western political theory, and presenting critical views of Russian Communism; these included a political biography of Lenin and a study of forced labor in the Soviet Union. George spent all of his waking hours reading; he was impressed by the works of Bertrand Russell, Arthur Lovejoy, and C. E. M. Joad, and was strongly affected by George Orwell's 1984: "I could compare this with my own experience on the mainland, and see that this was the logical eventual result of life under Communism."

He developed a critical attitude toward Soviet Russia, and then a sense of mistrust for Chinese Communism, together with a more sympathetic view of the Western democratic tradition.

While on the mainland, I had considered democracy as an age-old idea, outmoded—the capitalist world a corrupt and decadent one which must be historically eliminated within a short period. . . . But now I began to feel that things in the capitalist system were not as hopeless as the Communists said . . . that some form of socialism might be a desirable goal . . . but that in any case, we should not follow the road set by Communism—a road of revolution, violence, and killing. . . . I re-evaluated my ideas about humanity, and the importance of liberalism. I also felt that the humanism derived from the tradition of the Italian Renaissance, and its skeptical spirit were much in contrast to the Communists and their fatalism. Their ideas about dialectical materialism seemed quite opposed to the scientific method and spirit.

Similarly, he began to feel that the uncertain future of life in Hong Kong—with the possible hope of some day studying in America—was more desirable than completing his university education and accepting a job assignment in Communist China. Having tasted a certain amount of this kind of exploration in ideas, he concluded that this was what he wanted, and had in fact always wanted:

The whole atmosphere on the mainland did not encourage clear thinking. But when I came out, I was able to read books, and permitted to think about things to a logical conclusion. I began to feel that I had no future in a society without this freedom. . . . I concluded that I had always been latently hostile to the Communists and now my hostility could come out.

As might be expected, George went through a period of painful doubt and indecision, "a conflict of the two understandings." He also feared that the Communists might take over Hong Kong and force him to "face the consequences of my desertion." And even after making a formal promise to his parents that he would remain, he was unable to quiet the turmoil which emanated from his unconscious mind as a series of dreams:

In those ten days right after I had decided to remain here, I often—six or seven times—dreamed of getting back to the mainland. In the dreams, I was living with my classmates and talking with them as things used to be. In one dream I was at that very moment at the boundary of Hong Kong and China. I hoped to get back and something was preventing me from doing so. Suddenly I discovered that I had no document of admittance and I was in despair. Then I awoke. . . . In another dream, I was back on the mainland, talking to several schoolmates, close friends, as we always did. Suddenly a thought came to me: what a narrow escape I had had in Hong Kong. I almost did not go back, and I was relieved to realize that I was back on the mainland. . . . Each time, before going to sleep, and on waking up in the morning, my decision to remain was definite. I was sure that I was here and that I wasn't going back. But in the dreams I lacked this understanding . . . and my thoughts were just like those that I had when I was really on the mainland.

In associating to these dreams, George spoke of happy moments on the mainland—friendly talks with fellow students, visits to record stalls to listen to classical music. He also revealed the resentment which he felt toward his parents for their role in influencing his decision.

When I awoke after one of these dreams, I actually resented my family a little. Going back to the mainland still at that moment seemed very desirable. . . . Then I thought of the promise I made to them that I would stay. I made it first to my mother. . . . But with my father also —he is a very stubborn man—and once you promise him something, if you break it you have a very hard time. . . . I felt then that the family would not let me break the promise—which was made originally because of their request. . . . I felt it was giving me some kind of restriction, holding me back, causing me to lose my opportunity to study. . . . I usually felt the resentment toward my father.

George even admitted that he had been happier on the mainland than he was in Hong Kong "because of my friends there and the absence of financial worry."

But before long, George settled into Hong Kong life, busying himself with studies at a local college, with editing and writing for an anti-Communist press organization, and with work on a novel about his life in Communist China. Although he was convinced that he had made the correct decision, he was still disturbed by letters from friends on the mainland which criticized his action and referred to the exciting future for young men in Communist China. He was especially troubled by letters from one former classmate with whom George had previously shared doubts about some Communist actions; this boy now wrote to him in a vein not uncritical of Communism, yet he still found fault with George for staying in Hong Kong.

One year later, during the course of our interviews, George underwent still another period of painful indecision, and another sudden reversal of his plans. Having received little encouragement from American universities in response to his inquiries about scholarships, he decided to take advantage of an opportunity to study medicine in Taiwan, and achieved very high grades on an entrance examination he took in Hong Kong. But after booking his boat ticket, he spent two or three sleepless nights before the scheduled departure, tortured by fear and doubt. He felt completely unable to undertake the trip. A family conference was called, and it was decided that since he was so fearful, he should cancel his plans. It was mainly the Communists whom he feared.

The more I thought about going, the more fear I felt. . . . There was the fear of leaving my parents, but I realized that it wasn't this alone that led to my decision. I also feared the political situation on Taiwan . . . that it might be dangerous for someone who had been so long on the mainland to go there. . . . And I feared that the Communists may stop the ship and kidnap passengers as they did once on a ferry between Hong Kong and Macao. I feared that the Communists may come and take the island. . . . I knew that my father's contacts could help if I were in trouble with the KMT—but with the Communists nothing could help. . . . If they should come I had the feeling that I would lose all of my freedom and safety and might never see my family again. . . . This fear of the Communists was by far the most important factor in my decision.

Once he and his family had decided he would not go, his sense of relief was immediate. He then weathered a certain amount of criticism from his father, who accused him of being "indecisive," continued with his life in Hong Kong, and renewed his efforts to arrange study in America. In discussing this incident with me, he emphasized that he had never experienced this kind of fear of the Communists during the years that he actually lived under them.

Toward the end of our meetings, George talked freely of the development of his personal philosophy and his quest for the meaning of life. He described his earliest convictions—derived from his own childhood experiences, and from reading the tragic love poetry from the T'ang and Sung dynasties—of the "futility of life"; its replacement by a religious belief that "the meaning of life could be the glorification of God"; and after having been disillusioned with this, finding very compelling the Communist claim that "the purpose of life is to serve the people." After his break with Communism, he remained concerned with this problem, but came to look upon it in terms of man's relationship to his individual existence:

In all these previous concepts I thought that the purpose of life was something definite that you could grasp. Now I know that this is not so. I am inclined to believe that the purpose of life has to do with what degree you have carried out your aims and ideals . . . your responsibilities to your own thoughts and feelings.

He illustrated his personal change through his altered idea of the hero:

If I had daydreams now, they would still be different from that of my childhood. Then it was a person of great heroic grandeur; now I think of perfection of ability and of moral sentiments . . . unselfishness, disinterestedness, honesty to others and to oneself.

George retained his emphasis upon the inner man, contrasting this with the Communist ethos as he saw it:

In their opinion there is nothing beyond the material. They have no recognition of spirit. They think there is no need for artistic search and for beauty. I cannot agree with this. . . . I believe that human beings need all kinds of satisfaction, of material feelings and of spirit. When you eat something you are satisfied. But when it is over and you think of the act of eating, there is no more satisfaction. But if you have emotional satisfaction or emotional sympathy for something, then even on reflection you still feel that satisfaction or sympathy. All of the satisfaction that can be retained by reflection in retrospect belongs to your inner feelings, and these are most valuable.

George was critical of Communist attitudes toward family relationships, especially that between mother and son:

They said that even the relationship of a mother and son is a relationship of economic interest . . . that when a mother was very fond of her son who was rich, after he was broke, she would treat him badly. . . . My own experience didn't lead me to think of such economic factors between mother and son. . . . I had doubts about their theory, but I could not then fully disagree with them. . . . Now I realize that they have a complete ignorance of the power of moral standards and of human emotion. . . . They have no recognition of personal feelings.

During the course of his stay in Hong Kong, George gradually reintegrated himself into the pattern of his family, somewhat in the fashion of a traditional Chinese son. He and his father became more moderate in their behavior toward each other, and George began to feel "a little apologetic" over past disrespectful behavior. He adopted a policy of "outwardly agreeing with everything father says," avoiding conflict wherever possible, and—despite his continued reservations—making every effort to accept his father as the "moral authority" in the family. George extended his concern for personal morality to the behavior of others: he criticized a female cousin for what he considered to be indiscriminate behavior with men, and even called his older brother to task for spending a great deal of time with a girl friend at the expense of scholarly pursuits. He remained equally strict with himself in his disciplined life of writing and study, although he too began to demonstrate an increasing, if shy and hesitant, interest in girls.

When I saw him during my follow-up visit three years later, he had become a confident youth in his mid-twenties, and had improved his English enough for us to dispense with an interpreter. He no longer wished to discuss in any detail his mainland experiences, and preferred to look ahead to his study in America, having almost completed visa and scholarship arrangements. His family had already moved to the United States. But once more there had been a change in his plans: no longer a student of science, he was perhaps following his more natural bent in pursuing a program in literature and dramatics.

Compared with Chao's and Hu's, George Chen's thought reform had initially been more successful; but his family identifications, more consistently binding than theirs, played a large part in undoing these reform influences. Neither a perpetual rebel nor a frustrated careerist, George Chen was an impressionable youngster torn between youth group and family loyalties, the first of which offered a path to Chinese Communism, and the second the possibility of a liberal alternative.

In his sequence of identity patterns, George covered less emotional distance than either Chao or Hu. Coming from an urban, somewhat Westernized background, and having spent part of his childhood in the British colony of Hong Kong, he had experienced a good deal less of traditional Chinese life. Like the others he was brought up to be a filial son, obedient to his elders, loyal to his family. But as a member of a younger, more "modern" generation, he had fewer Confucian influences to contend with, and had from the beginning been exposed to a compromise Chinese-Western family atmosphere. This, along with his family's opportunity to keep together, gave him a greater sense of cultural continuity than either Chao or Hu: less "Chinese" to begin with, he had less need to break with his Chinese past. Offered love and support from his family, his filialism, compared to Hu's, was neither a pseudo identity nor an archaic one.

Yet George too felt the chaos of his society and the effects of strained family relationships. As a weak, dislocated, and dependent child, he was aware early of his refugee status; he needed more nurturing than was available, and developed a psychological escape into illness. His infantile depression at the time of the departure of his first *amah* was the prototype of a later tendency toward depression and despair.[2] As a melancholy isolate, he developed an undercurrent of introspective brooding and a keen sense for the sadness of life. Far from incapacitating him, however, these qualities contributed to a rich inner life to which he later clung tenaciously. And they also became associated with a personal pattern of death and rebirth—a tendency to hit rock bottom in despairing indecision and doubt, and then to emerge strengthened by his own inwardness.

Like Hu, George longed for the return of an absent father; and he too built up personal myths in which he was hero and redeemer. But in contrast to Hu, these myths did not involve vengeance and retaliation toward hated family members; rather, they contained the filial wish to deliver both the family and himself from positions of shame and weakness. And he found his means of personal deliverance, not through heroic action, but by continuing to turn inward, by developing—as a creative seeker—the artist's urge for self-expression as well as the scientist's urge to know. Such creative urges, whatever their origins and whatever suffering may accompany them, contribute to a sense of identity which transcends one's immediate environment, even one's culture. Both the artist and the scientist in George were involved in his search for the meaning of life. However immature and unstable this quest may have been, it was at least his own, and it required him to weigh every experience against standards that were both personal and universal.

In his early teens, George became both a romantic and a moralist. These two sides of him were symbolized in his description of his two grandmothers—one a spontaneous and affectionate lover of nature, the other a stern (and personally wronged) representative of God's most severe judgments. We cannot, of course, claim that these ladies were entirely responsible for shaping the two identities. But grandparents have a strong influence within a Chinese family, even when they preach a Western Christian message; and there is no doubt that they played an important part in bringing out these two potential aspects of George's character. The romantic in him thrived upon sensation, craving an idealized world of beautiful words, sights and feelings. The moralist in him condemned these very yearnings, both in himself and in others; it was guilt-ridden, judging, ever on guard against temptation. For it was compounded of a sensitive child's susceptibilities to shame and guilt (including the probable childhood fantasy that he was in some way responsible for such catastrophes as his *amah's* departure and the family's dislocation); of Christian notions of sin and evil, and of Confucian-derived standards of personal propriety. The moralist in him condemned his father, on the basis of both the latter's real shortcomings and George's intolerance for a rival for his cherished mother. And the moralist in him also kept a steady and critical eye on the activities of all other family members as well.

On the subjects of sex and religion, the romantic and the moralist joined forces. Feeling guilty and ashamed about his sensual urges, George found sanction (incomplete, but meaningful all the same) in D. H. Lawrence's hymn of praise to the sensual, in a novel which has been described as expressing "Lawrence's romantic religious, antinomian, ecstatic faith that sex is holy." [3] George's early attraction to Christianity reflects both the moralist's need for responsible doctrine and relief of guilt, and the romantic's quest for eternal beauty and eternal meaning.

It is as the romantic moralist, then, that George judged both the declining Nationalist regime and the oncoming Communists. He condemned the immorality of the former although retaining his family-based emotional loyalty for it. But very quickly after the onset of Communist thought reform, he experienced a romantic conversion against a dimly-lit background, with lonely and mystical overtones. Also involved was the romantic's need to submit to the natural elements, since George felt strongly Communism's claim to be the wave of the future.

In comparing George's approach to Communism with Hu's, George was more the visionary and less the political activist, more the inner man (or boy) and less the power seeker. But George shared with Hu the extremely important urge, so characteristic of youth everywhere during our era, to find group acceptance and an emotional home among his peers. Both used this acceptance to free themselves from family controls and enter into manhood. George too had his political mentor, the rational and giving instructor, who contrasted sharply with the irrational and self-centered (or absent) father of George's childhood. Like Hu (and like Dr. Vincent) George was an isolate who craved intimacy with other people; unlike either of them, he had known enough love in his life to have become quite capable of achieving this intimacy.

As the modern student, George felt a strong urge to remain in step with his fellow students and his country. George did not, like Hu, seek in Communism an outlet for personal hostilities; he felt, in fact, the need to repress these hostilities, both toward his family and the Communists themselves. This nonhostile compliance may be regarded as an inability to tolerate conscious resentment, but it is also related to a pattern of receptivity frequently present in creative people: a tendency to open oneself completely to new influences as a way of knowing them. It is also the romantic's eternal quest for an atmosphere of love.

These tendencies are part of the reason George was such a perennial backslider, why he underwent so many conversions and counterconversions. There were no less than six of these in relation to Communism, both for and against, and still another in his earlier response to Christianity. Any explanation must be, as usual, overdetermined, and must be based on both George's personal character and on the historical and cultural circumstances. The most obvious factor, but a very important one, was that his family had re-established itself in Hong Kong, the scene of so much of his childhood, and had once more assumed a collective refugee identity. These circumstances not only created a reason for George to travel back and forth, but gave him an emotional sense of living in two separate homes, of having two distinct centers—or, to put it another way, of commuting between the two identities of the filial son and the modern student. Moreover, at the time of these journeys, George was an adolescent, going through the stage of life during which conversions are most natural, identity experiments most necessary, and utopian visions most appealing. More than this, he was a Chinese adolescent, who although modern and Western in his direction, was still emotionally tied to traditional Chinese notions of propriety and harmony. Both in denouncing his parents to fulfill Communist requirements, and in giving up a career in Communist China in response to family loyalties, he felt he was doing the proper thing under the circumstances, adapting himself to the demands of a group which had just claims upon his allegiance.

Then, too, the nature of the Communist demands was such that they always carried with them the potential for rebound. Even among the most rebellious of Chinese youth, filial identifications were likely to reappear. One public denunciation cannot wipe out four thousand years of filial ethos. The potential for backsliding would always be there, especially if the environment supports it, and most especially in the company of parents.

In view of all this, one could hardly expect any Chinese youngster to steer a perfectly straight identity course. But two features of George's personal character—his unusually strong dependency needs and his pattern of ambivalence—made him especially susceptible to vacillation. His ties to his mother (she too was indecisive), and his guilt and shame-filled sentiments toward his father and brother (for unfilial acts or thoughts) made it impossible for him to cast off family attachments. Yet his equally compelling quest for group belonging made it almost impossible for him to live up to them. Never having felt himself to be fully nurtured in an emotional sense (and perhaps constitutionally in need of an unusual amount of nurturing, of a very special kind), George tended to hold on to those things which had nourished him, and to waver between choices when something had to be given up.

Here again is the death-and-rebirth pattern previously mentioned. In each of George's conversions and counterconversions there was a somewhat depressive tendency: a pattern of mourning, preoccupation with and guilt toward the lost object, and a need for a working through of these emotions before he could enjoy the fruits of the actual conversion. But perhaps of greater significance was George's capacity to enter into a variety of personal ideological experiences and still retain a strong core of self. Never prone to a totalism like Hu's, his stress upon his own inner life—his creative urge to experience and to know—buffered him against complete self-surrender, and helped to preserve his personal identity. George resembled Professor Castorp in his seemingly submissive tendency to give up so much of himself while really holding on to what was most vital. His unusually strong urge toward self-realization enabled him to use his conversions to enhance his own intellectual and emotional development.

Although George's family ties were undoubtedly the crucial factor in his decision to remain in Hong Kong, he was able to take advantage of these to reawaken parts of himself (especially his urge to know) which had been temporarily stifled under Communism. Nonetheless his over-all responses make it clear that, had there been a bit more pressure from the other direction, he might well have made the opposite decision. Not only did he resent his parents for their part in separating him from the appealing group life within China, but he also partially condemned himself for succumbing to their influence and deserting the vast team effort in which he had been involved. The full effects of the hold which the Communists had upon him were apparent in his sudden decision to abandon plans to study in Taiwan: this hold was the combination of residual fear and guilt also observed in Hu and in most Western subjects as well (it must also be remembered that at the time the Communists were threatening to "liberate" Taiwan through military action). Even here, however, George's identity-preserving, creative urges probably had some importance, joining with his fear and guilt in steering him to better opportunities for his own self-expression.

It is interesting to note the interplay of identity and ideology which finally took shape within George. He called forth his most basic components, with the emphasis on compromise alignments. He partially returned to filial obligations (going as far as he felt capable in this direction) in adapting himself to his father's authority, even if with inner reservations. At the same time, he maintained group ties and kept his identity of the modern student and patriot active: through further study in Hong Kong, through work with anti-Communist press organizations, and in his plans to study in America. Thus he maintained both traditional and modern Chinese influences in taking on the ideology of democratic liberalism. At different times, he continued to express attitudes of the moralist, the romantic, and the rational scientist. But the effective combination of this array of different identities marks the emergence of the creative artist in George. While this identity is far from the most "practical" for his American future, it seems to be the one most precious to him.

CHAPTER 18

GRACE WU: MUSIC AND REFORM

What of the experiences of young Chinese women?

The last case I shall discuss is that of a female musician whose thought reform took place during four years of attendance at two universities.

Grace Wu was one of the few Chinese subjects I was able to interview within a few weeks after arrival in Hong Kong. Although she had fled from her reform, and had lived quietly at home for more than a year before she left China, she had by no means recovered from its emotional effects at the time that a mutual acquaintance made arrangements for our first interview. A tense and intelligent girl of twenty-four, with sharp features, wearing steel-rimmed glasses, she looked both determined and fragile. She dressed neatly, but not in a particularly feminine manner. With a more Westernized background than any of the Chinese subjects previously described, her English was fluent. The combination of her Westernized upbringing and her agitated emotional state swept away cultural barriers. She plunged into her story without hesitation because she had a great need to tell it, and to understand what had happened to her. The freshness of her material and her desire for therapy increased her resemblance to my Western subjects. We had thirteen sessions, totalling about twenty-eight hours, and the last part of our work together was more like psychotherapy than anything else.

The daughter of a customs official (in a customs service separate from the Chinese government, for many years run by foreigners) Grace grew up in the cosmopolitan treaty port cities of Tientsin and Shanghai. Her father, whom she described as "not too strong," had in later years entered private business without great success, and was frequently unemployed. She spoke of her mother as a more dominant influence and at the same time a more sympathetic person. Mrs. Wu's father had been a Protestant minister, and she was not only deeply concerned with imbuing in her daughter her own values, but also wished to develop in Grace a capacity beyond her own to realize these values—in religion, in education, and especially in music. When Grace began to show outstanding musical talent, after beginning to study piano at the age of five, her mother did everything to encourage its development. Mrs. Wu was easily upset, however, and always nervous; and Grace as a child showed similar characteristics: "I was more quiet than other girls. I was more nervous, and scared easily. I was mentally not strong."

During much of Grace's childhood, the family lived under the Japanese occupation, and these were hard times. Her father lost his job, and was even arrested and briefly detained by the Japanese. Mr. Wu felt that because of the family's difficult straits Grace should give up her musical studies. She has always remained grateful to her mother for insisting that she be permitted to continue. Grace was absorbed in her music, playing, listening, and reading biographies of great musicians. She also did some painting, and when she began to attend missionary schools, she became interested in dramatics and in journalism. But she avoided social activities, and continued to spend a good deal of time alone.

During her teens, Grace faced a series of personal dilemmas relating to family, friends, sex, religion, and music—and also to her struggles to make sense out of a distressing torrent of emotions. She regarded her friends' interest in boys as frivolous, and felt "disgust" when she herself was approached by a boy. Rather than displaying conventional Chinese female shyness, she was frequently outspoken and aggressive, and this led to considerable friction with her female classmates. She wanted to transfer from her secondary school to a special music school, but this time even her mother opposed her, insisting that she acquire a strong general education. Her father was of little help and expressed only mild disapproval of both musical training and of the missionary school (he was not a Christian) which she was already attending. Since "mother was strong-willed," it was mother's decision which prevailed.

Inwardly, she was torn between her quests for both musical passion and religious calm, regarding the two emotions as incompatible:

> I felt strongly for religion . . . but I felt it was in conflict with music. . . . You are born with emotions that should be changed by religion. But in music, people must use real emotions and express them. . . . An artist must have strong feeling. . . . Music requires emotions which religion condemns—such as passion and hate. . . . In religion this would be sinful, you have to hold them back. . . . I talked to the minister about it and to others, but I got no good answer. . . . The minister and the musician said opposite things. . . . I had to postpone this problem.

Overwhelmed on all sides, Grace experienced at the age of eighteen what she described as a "breakdown," with both physical and psychological symptoms:

> My health failed. I collapsed. I was in bed for one year. . . . It was in my lung and I was told it would develop into TB if I wasn't careful. The symptoms were weakness and I tired easily. I stayed in bed for one year. I got up a little in the afternoons. I was weak and I had fever. I spent the time reading and listening to the radio.

She recognized that emotional elements were important in her illness, and she thought these were the product of her own evil:

> The feeling I had then was that I was selfish. . . . I couldn't get what I wanted so I felt different from others, angry and frustrated. . . . Now I realize that I created these feelings . . . inside of myself.

But her illness was not without its rewards:

> After one or two months I got used to it. Friends came to visit once in a while. People are nice to you when you are sick.

Returning to senior high school after a year of absence, Grace continued her journalistic interests and was caught up in postwar political currents. At first she had been excited by the restoration of Chinese sovereignty and the end of the Japanese occupation; but like most of her fellow students, she soon became disillusioned with the Nationalist regime, and condemned its use of personal privilege and "squeeze." She contributed her share of critical statements about the government to the student newspaper, and influenced by a few enthusiastic Communist students, she began, with many classmates, to take an interest in Russian writers and in other Communist programs. She was just finishing high school at the time of the Communist takeover. Although she had heard stories of Communist atrocities ("their killing church congregations, taking anything they wanted, acting like monsters"), she shared the general feeling of sympathy and expectation:

We students had lost hope in the Nationalists. We welcomed the Communists. . . . We waited to see and felt that they might be better. I was of the young generation and looked forward to change and improvement.

The Communists' exemplary behavior seemed at first to support these expectations. Grace and her friends were impressed by the discipline of their armies ("the Chinese saying, 'Good men do not become soldiers' did not seem to be true of these men"), and with the initial atmosphere of freedom.

A few months later, Grace entered a local missionary college as a journalism major, bowing to her parents' insistence that she remain at home (this time her father had his say) because of the uncertain political situation, rather than attend a university in Peking where a music course was available. Her journalistic work first brought her into contact with Communist pressures, and her earliest response was one of confusion:

We were told not to see things from the university's viewpoint, but from the people's viewpoint—to always think of the common people. . . . The Communists tried to organize everything, and since we never came across anything that we knew the answer to beforehand, we were quite confused. They failed a student whom they didn't want in power. . . . They were not satisfied with the facts, and would only want us to print certain items, telling us, "The paper is to educate people . . . not simply to bring news." At first we spoke in a straightforward manner, but later we learned not to.

Soon intensive political studies were inaugurated, as well as the beginning of a program of student thought reform. Despite her discomfort, Grace began to come under Communist influence, an influence which, in retrospect, she considered pernicious:

They are careful at first to do things step by step, gradually . . . you don't feel guilty [about following the Communist line] because they explain it all to you. You feel you are doing a big thing. They make a standard for you to follow and you say that I am doing things right according to their standard . . . . If you once believe in them, it's natural to go on believing. . . . It's just like poisoning . . . it goes deeper and deeper.

As the pressures mounted, Grace began to feel increasingly anxious. As an editor of the school paper, she attended a large number of meetings and was generally in the center of these new activities. She began to become painfully aware of restrictions upon personal freedom and of tightening controls—especially when a prominent newspaper had its publication suspended for three days for stating that North Korea had invaded South Korea. She became increasingly critical of the Communists: "I gradually began to feel that what they said was not what I thought. I was disappointed in the Communists and had a strong feeling of dissatisfaction." She felt it necessary to extricate herself from a threatening situation, and to choose a field of study other than journalism.

She decided to take advantage of a promise made earlier to her by her parents, that, should she become dissatisfied with journalism, she would be permitted to return to her musical studies. During her sophomore year, she arranged to transfer to Yenching University in Peking, one of China's major institutions of higher learning, and one with long-established American missionary and educational associations.[1] There, in a class of twenty-five music majors, she studied in a department run by three professors, two American and one Chinese. She worked hard and made progress in her musical development. She was especially close to one of the American professors, Mr. Moore, and came to value both his musical guidance and his friendship. During her lessons with him, they discussed not only music, but also philosophy and to some extent the immediate problems of life in Communist China. She felt greatly inspired by him and developed for him "an affection . . . a kind of love." As the atmosphere began to tighten, however, she noted that he and all of the other American professors were being repeatedly denounced at student meetings, and she advised him to leave the country for the sake of his personal safety.

During the winter of 1951–52, a little more than a year after her transfer, Grace was suddenly put in a situation much more painful than any she had yet experienced at either of the universities. Until this time, she had managed to avoid trouble by burying herself in her work and doing nothing antagonistic to the Communist program; she was considered a promising musician, if politically "a bit lagging behind." But now she was approached by a newly appointed and highly "progressive" Chinese music instructor who began to exert strong pressures on her, first to inform upon Mr. Moore, and later to denounce him publicly as a "reactionary." She became embroiled in a series of demands and threats, which she somehow managed to resist:

He told me that this was to be a big movement, and that it was my chance to have a bright future. He said I should try to search out Mr. Moore's faults and then come back and tell him about them. He said that since I was friendly with Mr. Moore, I could give important information about him. . . . He said that this was a challenge, and if I accepted it I would be safe. . . . I told him I did not want to do anything which I didn't believe in, and that I didn't think that things should be done this way. I said that Mr. Moore was an American and was not "progressive," but there was nothing more I could tell him. He said, "You are not smart. You won't have a bright future in spite of being a good musician. . . ."

Weeks later, I heard that the police had taken Mr. Moore's cook into custody, and again the new teacher came to me. He said, "The cook has confessed, and now it is your turn. I give you three days. Otherwise you might go to prison or to labor reform. If you do confess, you will get a new life." I was startled, I didn't know if the cook had confessed or what he confessed. Moore had told me I could say anything about him since he was safe as a foreigner, while I could get into trouble. I had no one to consult during this time. I knew that if I did say anything, I could start anew, but I knew it would be bad for Moore. I believed that what they said was not true, so I did not want to say anything. The students were against me, as they felt I knew something I wasn't telling. . . . For two nights, I could not sleep. I made the decision not to say anything. At the end of two days, I went to them. I said I could not confess an untruth. . . . Finally they admitted that they had not gotten the cook and he had not confessed and I was allowed to leave.

This incident—which extended over several months—took its emotional toll.

At this time my nerves were shot. I got neurotic diarrhea. I could never relax. It got worse. They were suspicious of me and the doctor said I was neurotic. They asked me why I was so nervous. I asked for sick leave at the hospital for one week and got it. The diarrhea stopped and I went back to school . . . but I knew I had won.

I realized that I must go. They hadn't got me this time, but the next time they would. I was also worried about Moore. I asked a boy student to take a walk on campus with me. If I went with a girl it would look more suspicious than being with a boy. We went past Moore's house, and I heard him playing so that I knew he was not in prison. I saw a policeman there who was watching his house. From the way he played a Chopin waltz I knew he was upset. He never played like that ordinarily. I left without his knowing I had been there.

Grace was also disturbed by much else that went on during the general thought reform movement, which was compounded of the "Three Anti" and "Honesty and Frankness" campaigns.

She felt "disgusted" by what she considered to be the Party's view toward love and sex:

If a boy was interested in someone, he would check with the Party to see if it was all right to be in love. Then if the Party gave the go-ahead, he would go to the girl and say, "So-and-so, I am interested in you. Can we develop?" The girl would then give an answer, "We can try." Three weeks later they would announce that they were lovers. If the girl would say, "I cannot develop," he would continue arguing and returning. The girl is supposed to be honored if a progressive person asks for her love. . . . If she spurns a progressive man, the Party will come and talk to her. If she has a good reason, the Party will give in or they will ask if there is some way the man might change to be acceptable. . . . Many girls have babies. At first a pregnancy was news, but later it was not. They would say, "Sooner or later, they will be married, so what does it matter?" They made love a kind of business.

She was both shocked and impressed when the president of the university was publicly denounced by his own daughter.

The president of our university had three children, two sons and one daughter. The Communists went to them and asked them to help against their father. The sons refused. The daughter was a graduate of the physics department doing research work. They went to her and told her that her father, Dr. Lu, was a traitor. . . . They persuaded the daughter to accuse him during a small meeting. It was very dramatic. She cried and shouted, called him by his first name. He sat there with his head lowered and was very ashamed of her. Her mother was there and cried. Her father had been a doctor of psychology and was sixty years old. The daughter was so successful that they put her in a large meeting of the whole student body and she repeated her accusations. Everyone began to listen to her and her father's reputation now began to fall.[2]

Grace described the special exhibits at which letters from the university president's files were displayed, demonstrating his American connections and his alleged part in making Yenching a "stubborn castle of reaction." Student guides took other students around the exhibit and explained "why we are poisoned here at Yenching," always ending their tour with the impassioned conclusion: "There is no way out but reforming. Hate your past, and you will find your way for the future."

In music, Communist attitudes violated her aesthetic standards, and greatly confused her.

The Communists called modern Western music unhealthy. . . . We had many meetings on this. . . . They wanted a new form of music. . . . Modern music is too abstract and uncontrolled for them. French composers like Debussy they feel are unhealthy for the people. They say that this music gives the people queer thoughts and funny ideas. That if we listen to Debussy we will feel as though we are under water or watching the sea. They say that since there is really nothing like this, we will begin to think abnormally. . . . To them anything fantastic or abstract is abnormal and unhealthy. . . . They wanted us to learn folk songs and folk dances, to go among the common people who need healthy recreation. . . . They liked songs that named all of the historical figures—like Mao. They said that these songs enable people to get educated with a healthy spirit. . . . I couldn't find a solution. . . . I thought, maybe their music was healthy, but it was not inspired.

She noticed that many of the other music students also had difficulty absorbing these policies. Some became so involved with meetings and reform activity that they did not have enough time to practice; others were in such psychological distress that they could not play; and many vocal students thought their voices unsuitable for folk songs. The authorities recognized that "thought problems" were likely to be particularly common among music students because of their artistic sensitivities, and usually approached them with a certain amount of delicacy, allowing for individual variations. The net result was that Grace saw almost everybody around her succumbing to the thought reform program:

My friends changed their minds after a while. . . . They really did. They tried to give me advice. They told me that when they had believed in Western music, they were merely looking at life from the narrow standpoint of their own personal enjoyment. They found that the country people enjoy folk music, and that there modern music was not welcome. What is most important, they said, was that somebody appreciated their music. Sooner or later we must change our minds, they said, and it is easier to do it now. There were others who hadn't believed strongly in their own music, and they changed right away. Almost everyone changed. I began to wonder what was right.

At first, there were at least ten people who were strongly against the Communists. But gradually, as the pressure mounted, they turned over. . . . They would say, "Why should I lean on decayed theory?" They read only Communist books, saw things only from that point of view, and when they had a conflict they went to a Party member for advice. Some went over without a struggle, but even those with strong convictions finally gave up and went over to the Communist side.

She felt increasingly isolated, out of step with all that was going on around her. Her difficulty was that she could neither completely deny to herself the validity of what the Communists were putting forward, nor wholeheartedly go along with it.

I was very confused. . . . I felt lonely. . . . I wanted to keep putting off the problem, to not think of it until the next day. At times they seemed reasonable by their logic and theory. You got so you had to think back on your own logic and theory to understand how you really felt. . . . I found it hard to be alone with all the world on the other side. You feel like a stranger in that environment if you don't go over.

Singled out for much special attention, she was constantly accused of having a "technical point of view":

I was a hard worker, and was criticized for being seven hours at the piano and only two hours at the meetings. They said, "To you there is nothing but a piano. Think of the millions of your country's people."

She observed the other's confessions and conformed to the extent she thought necessary, but she did not always have complete control of her feelings.

The secret in writing a confession is to make up your mind what your deficiency is in their thinking. You won't get past this otherwise, unless you understand what they want to hear. . . . I made several points. You always need several points. . . . I said that before I was too much in music, and now I will do the work that people want me to do, be more practical and less technical in my approach. . . . That I despised Chinese music before, but now I have a new appreciation of it and hate Western music, that I must learn to love Chinese music and do my best with it. . . . That in the past I was unable to tell the difference between my friends and my enemies, that I trusted certain persons like Mr. Moore but now I know I should not have, and that I should be more careful in the future. . . . That before I was isolated from the group and interested only in my own work, not interested in concentrating on the people whom I should be representing, but only on myself, and that now I would spend more time with the other students. . . . But after you have made all of these points, sometimes you wonder if you have been acting all of this or not.

Yet despite her concessions, she resisted active participation. When she was asked to play the accordion before labor or peasant groups, she insisted it was too heavy for her; and her one attempt to play before a group of workers was a fiasco.

After the first piece they didn't know enough to applaud. On the second piece they applauded at a pause. I stopped and they stopped. I started and they began to applaud again. I got mad. I refused to play to the ignorant workers. The Communists tried to apologize, saying, "We had no idea they were so uneducated."

She also retained a strong inner resistance to the conversion that was demanded of her.

I had no idea of what would happen to me, but I thought I would rather give up my future than change. . . . What prevented me from turning over was a kind of belief. I believed that the world could not be like this.

Grace could not stand up under these pressures, however, and once more began to react with frequent bouts of diarrhea and other psychogenic symptoms.

I began to be sick quite often and this made them suspicious. . . . An activist came to my room and asked about my health. I said I get tired if I work too much. He asked me if I was really too busy, or if there was something on my mind, something in the subconscious which I didn't know. He said: "You must have been poisoned from so many years in missionary schools . . . maybe you are not open enough. We will try to solve things with you. We know you will change."

Her symptoms continued, and became especially severe after some inoculations in connection with the alleged American bacteriological warfare threat.[3]

Everyone was compelled to take injections against the germ warfare. . . . In Peking we were the first to get them. . . . There were four things combined in an injection but I am not sure what they were. . . . They were very strong and many people died. Because I was so nervous and upset the nurse told me she was only giving me half. But I had two days of fever from it and then some heart trouble. My pulse was one hundred and twenty and one hundred thirty. I didn't know what was happening. The doctor said it was a reaction to the injection. I decided that I must get away.

She continued to feel ill for weeks afterward. At the end of that semester, although she needed only one more term to graduate, she decided to apply for sick leave from the university, pressing her case with an insistence that would not be denied:

At first the school doctors would not write my excuse. I went to the infirmary almost every day so that they would know I was sick. . . . I was determined to go. Finally they granted me sick leave for six months.

Almost immediately after she got home, she went to see a doctor who was also an old friend of the family. He told her that her illness was psychological, due to the "shock" from the injection and the general tension of the situation she was in. He advised her to "go away someplace where you don't have to think so much." Grace was not certain whether this was indirect advice to leave the country, but she was in any case hoping to do so.

Her family situation in Tientsin was far from calm: her father had lost his job; her mother was in the midst of a "nervous breakdown," easily excitable and unable to sleep; and her younger brother and sister were also both home on sick leave, with illnesses apparently related to physical and emotional pressures of their work environments. Grace was particularly upset to find that her parents were not completely sympathetic with her antagonism to the new regime. At first they advised Grace to make a greater effort to get along with the Communists; and only later, after they themselves had had difficulty, did they come around to her point of view.

Despite her problems, she managed to "rest, relax, and rebuild myself," during the year she spent at home, at the same time continuing with music lessons. She wanted to leave for Hong Kong as soon as possible, but her parents objected because she had no relatives there. Finally, at her insistence, they permitted her to work out an arrangement by which a friend of hers from Peking, already in Hong Kong, posed as her fiancé, and sent her letters and telegrams urging her to join him there. These Grace took to the local officials when she applied for her exit permit. The ruse was so thoroughly carried out that even her brother and the family servants believed she was to be married, and her mother went so far as to go through the motions of preparing a trousseau. At first Grace encountered some resistance from the officials in her attempts to get the permit, but she wore them down with her usual histrionic persistence.

I went to the police station often—sometimes twice a day. . . . I showed the letters. . . . At first I was afraid, as the application was turned down. I know that when they investigated at my school, they were told to detain me because musicians might be needed later on. . . . They asked me why my fiancé didn't return to be married. Finally I went to them with a letter saying he was very sick. I told them I would kill myself if he died. I cried and cried. . . . After I had gone to the police station forty times, they gave in. . . . They gave me a one-way visa. They told me that once people go out, they never come back.

In Hong Kong Grace was not only still reverberating from these experiences—she also encountered new difficulties. Although she received a great deal of help from a minister to whom she had been referred by family friends, her legal status was uncertain and she had no regular means of financial support. She reacted to her problems with British immigration officials (they even advised her to wait in Macao until things were cleared up) with nervousness, headaches, palpitations, and diarrhea ("the old feeling returns"). And she stated (referring partly to our interview situation) that she felt as isolated in Hong Kong as she had on the mainland.

I used to feel lonely in Peking and that feeling still lingers on. Certain people are sympathetic about this or that, but not about everything. No one can really understand all. I can't tell them every trouble. I am still a stranger. . . . When people are nice to me it is because they know I am out of luck—not because they take me as a friend.

She also found much to criticize in Hong Kong. The atmosphere reminded her of a treaty port in China—just the sort of thing she had always disapproved of. She was especially uneasy about the immorality—commercial and sexual—of musicians.

Things are different in a colony. I have found people who were respected on the mainland, but here they have changed. There's one vocal professor . . . who has a reputation for going out with women students. He told me he kept the tuition high so that those who could not pay would not come to see him. He said he cares only to make more money. People who come here seem to change entirely. All standards of morals are different here.

These feelings about Hong Kong, along with her other conflicts, led her to wonder whether the Communists might not have been, after all, on the right path.

When you are young and trying to find an answer, you wonder, "Am I wrong and are they right?" You are still on the point of trying to build something for yourself. . . . Should an individualist work with others or stay apart? The Communist theory is to work for the mob, the ordinary people. . . . They can give them what they need. If conditions get better they'll make things better for the ordinary people. . . . I am trying to see both sides. Maybe people have more trouble in a free system. Maybe it is easier in the Communist system. . . . I am sure I am doing the right thing. I couldn't fit in so I got out. . . . I gave up. But I am wondering about all of the others who are still there. . . . When you think of things like that you just can't get an answer. Too much is involved.

Her troubles in Hong Kong continued. She felt that as a northerner, she was discriminated against by the Cantonese who made up the bulk of the Chinese population. She sometimes wondered if a stranger standing near the house where she lived was a Communist agent sent to spy on her. And in addition, an old fear of the spirit world entered into her immediate living arrangements. She and others who lived in her boarding house began to hear strange sounds at night, including the sound of snoring, which seemed to come from the garden outside. One girl reported that she had seen the offending ghost, and Grace, along with most of the others, decided to move from that house. She explained her point of view with unintentional humor:

In China, if you are born of a nature called "the killing nature," you cannot hear a ghost. My roommate was of this nature. She had been to a fortune teller who told her this. . . . A person of this nature is harmful to his family. . . . And she had not married for fear something would happen to her husband or her family. . . . She seemed to have something go wrong with every man she met. . . . I do not possess the killing nature. . . . I was told this by a fortune teller whom I went to with my mother in Tientsin. . . . So it is possible for me to hear a ghost, although I have never seen one. . . . It is a sign of bad luck to hear or see a ghost. . . . If one appears, harm will come to the family. . . . The landlady and the minister say that we are Christians and should not believe in ghosts. . . . I do not believe in ghosts because I am a Christian, but I cannot help it if I hear them.

For a while she could not even find relief in her music, in the past her means of "forgetting everything." She had great difficulty in locating a piano for regular practice; and even after she did, her anxiety interfered with her musical expression: "I couldn't control my hands. . . . I couldn't get hold of them."

During the latter stages of our work together, Grace expressed some of her broad emotional conflicts in her descriptions of her dreams, and in her associations to these dreams. The first dream was related to her general fears, to family conflicts and to her residual doubts about having left the mainland and come to Hong Kong.

I dreamed that I was back on the mainland with my family. I talked again to my father. I was scared. I couldn't tell him what happened. Then I got afraid. I couldn't get an exit visa out again this time. I don't know whether I went to help the family or not. I woke up upset. I didn't know what the dream meant.

In her associations to this dream, Grace expressed her apprehension about her situation in Hong Kong: "Sometimes I think the Communists will come here. . . . I cannot feel secure." She went on to speak at length of her feelings of helplessness and guilt at being unable to arrange for her parents and for a close girl friend to join her in Hong Kong.

Concerning her parents, there was no clear need for her to do anything, but she was troubled all the same.

My parents would like to come here, but it would be hard for my father to start all over in Hong Kong. . . . I feel very uneasy. I received a letter from them saying I shouldn't write much until I'm settled and have more time. . . . I feel duty towards them . . . not because I owe them anything . . . but I thought I could help.

Her feelings about her girl friend were equally strong, and enmeshed in more complicated external arrangements. Grace had been trying to set up a scheme to get her out of China similar to the one through which she herself had come to Hong Kong, involving a young man's writing romantic letters from Hong Kong to her friend in China. The contrived correspondence seemed to be working well until Grace and the correspondent in Hong Kong came into conflict.

At first I wrote the letters and he copied them. She sent the answers to him. . . . At first he promised to do what I said. He thought it was romantic and exciting. I thought it was business. Then he felt he was being pushed by me. He wanted to be on his own or else quit. I said he could not write love letters himself, as he wouldn't know how to word it for the Communists. He wrote a letter to her saying that I was unreasonable and he had had enough of me and would do things by himself. . . . She wrote me that something was wrong. I told her to drop the correspondence. . . . I had an argument with the boy and he said to me, "You came out cold-hearted and half-dead. I am still human." Maybe people think that Communism does this to people. . . . I have become more calculating, but this does me good. Sooner or later one must be practical. But people here say it comes to me too early.

These two themes—her guilty involvement with her girl friend, and her anxiety over her own conflict with the boy—were brought out in her further associations. She and the girl had been roommates at college, and Grace had advised her about many problems and had influenced her regarding her approach to the Communists. She felt responsible for the girl, and was distressed that her argument with this boy had brought about an end to the attempted arrangements. It also came out that part of the difficulty was Grace's "disgust" toward the boy when he began to make romantic overtures toward her as well as to her friend in China.

Her second dream was primarily a plea for help, partly directed at me; but at the same time it was also an attempt at reconstructing her life and her sense of self:

Last night I dreamed I met a pianist from my home town. She had always been a great success, and had studied in the States with Schnabel. . . . So last night I dreamed of her. . . . I met her on the train and was so glad to see her. . . I asked her many things but I don't remember what she said. I was asking from a musical point of view. Shall I take other work than music if I am offered it? Should I try to get a piano? Should I go to a teacher? . . . I even asked her what books I should read. . . . But I don't remember what she told me. . . . It's funny I didn't get any answers from her.

As she talked more about this dream, it became evident that both the girl and the girl's father had played a very important inspirational role in Grace's past.

She is twelve or thirteen years older than I am. When I was very young I was influenced by her. I knew everything she played by heart. . . . I called her Elder Sister. . . . After I left college and returned home, I went to see her father and he gave me books and advice in literature and history. He said to me, "You must read as well as play." He talked to my parents to help them understand.

She went on to talk of her immediate life situation, and contrasted its tenuousness with the more secure sense of personal growth during her earlier days: "Now if the weather is cold, I am cold. . . . I feel almost transparent, so tiny, so little, that I don't exist." Yet she still expressed affirmation in her expectation of a solution from within: "I must get answers from myself, though it takes a long time."

Although she valued her new freedom to engage in such a search, she felt that her past had not prepared her for this self-concern. She expressed this in relationship to our interviews.

I have found it difficult to talk to you. It is nothing personal, just that I have never before had the chance to express myself. All of these years I was told not to think of myself or my own ideas—and it faded out. Now I don't feel embarrassed. I feel better to talk and to reach scientific conclusions.

She compared her suppressed personal past to the demands of the Communist regime.

Under the Communists, because of the outside pressure, you think less about yourself. . . . I tried to think less of myself because it becomes too complicated if you don't. . . . It becomes a habit not to think too much about your own feelings.

She vividly described the pleasure and pain of her new self-expression.

It was like being shut in a tight room and suffocated. Then you are thrown open into a desert. You can have free air but it has its disadvantages. . . . Thinking brings more confusion. In China it is simple just being against things. But when you come to the real world, you find everything is not like that. . . . Freedom makes things more complicated.

During the six months in which I knew Grace in Hong Kong, she periodically lapsed into psychosomatic illness, usually diarrhea. After such bouts, she appeared to be more calm and composed. Once, following a week of bed rest, she expressed to me both the type of guilty conflict which contributed so much to her illnesses, and the secondary gain—that is, the satisfying respite—which the illness provided.

I keep thinking, am I asking or wanting too much for myself, and is this what makes me feel so bad? . . . When I was young I always expected too much—so now I expect the worst. . . . I am glad I got sick. I had time, and didn't have to rush.

She wondered how much any residual effects of thought reform might be contributing to her problems; at the same time she thought she had survived and gone beyond thought reform.

The more I tried to explain all of these things, the more complicated it gets. . . . I feel a person is hurt by a Communist education. But we have a saying in China that a lotus is grown from the mud, yet is still pure.

She recognized, however, that elements of reform were still with her, and that at times she could not avoid judging herself by Communist standards.

Sometimes I feel subconscious influences from the Communists. If I make a decision I think that I shouldn't go through with it because *they* would disagree. . . . Or I think back and feel that one or two of their theories are right.

But despite this stormy course, her adjustment in Hong Kong gradually improved. She was greatly helped by an older woman she met through friends ("a mother more or less") who began to take a great personal interest in her, accepted her as one of her own family, encouraged her to play the piano at her home, and also served as an understanding confidante. First she helped Grace find young pupils as a means of support, and then helped her make arrangements to continue her musical studies in Europe.

Three themes dominate Grace Wu's life story, from early childhood through thought reform and her Hong Kong experiences: her Westernization, her musicianship, and her illnesses.

She encountered Westernizing influences far stronger than those met by George Chen. Her treaty port background, her father's occupation, and her mother's staunch Christianity all placed the family in a special Chinese subculture, removed from a good deal of Chinese life. This subculture had its particular heritage of identity strengths and weaknesses. Its strengths lay in its sense of being modern and progressive, and in its relationship to Christian ideological supports; its weaknesses in its partial severance from Chinese roots, in the often shallow, imported middle-class ethos (the Communists did not entirely make this up) which Grace herself condemned, and in the intensified susceptibilities to guilt created by the superimposed Christian conscience. It is true that when under great duress, Grace reverted to pre-Christian ghosts (and it was her Christian mother who took her to the fortune teller); but her sense of being the Westernized Christian girl was nonetheless very basic to her character.

Grace became the dedicated musician early in life. This also was an identity closely tied to her relationship with her mother, but it was a good deal more. Rather than developing generalized artistic sensibilities, as George Chen did, she possessed a focused talent which became one of the main centers of her existence. To be a dedicated musician meant, for her, to have a form of self-expression which could not be denied, a refuge from emotional blows, and a sense of being a unique human being. This kind of identity can survive almost anything, even if it must be temporarily modified or subdued.

Closely associated with Grace's musicianship, however, were

feelings of evil, of selfishness, of hating and being hateful—all of which went into her negative identity. To be sure, these feelings must have originated in Grace's early sense of being emotionally deprived and frustrated. But they were also related to her quest for artistic expression—to the artist's need to ignore ordinary amenities of life and to selfishly insist on the opportunity to develop talent, even at the expense of others' sacrifices. Her negative identity was enhanced by her father's deprecation of her musical interest (an attitude which was undoubtedly shared by many others around her), and by her awareness that in the difficult family circumstances such an interest could be considered something of a luxury.

An outgrowth of her negative identity was her pattern of escape from emotional problems through illness. She carried with her— always ready for use—the identity of the invalid. The psychological sequence involved, first, a sense of being denied her wishes, along with an unusually strong need to obtain what she was after; then a feeling of anger and frustration; a sense of guilt over both her demands and her anger; the illness itself; and the combination of attention, sympathy, and relief which it afforded her.

Of central importance was the dilemma of a girl endowed with unusually strong passions who felt the need to repress and deny these passions almost entirely. Hence her "disgust" (a word which she used constantly) over sexuality and her use of Christian ideology as an aid in the struggle against her passions. As a musician, she became aware that she could hardly dispense with strong feelings of love and hate, feelings which she could justify in herself *only* as a musician. Her music-versus-Christianity conflict was essentially an expression of this same inner struggle. It is true, of course, that Christianity, and perhaps especially her polite form of Chinese Christianity, has long recommended the taming of sexual and of hateful impulses; but she could have—had she felt the need— just as well found Christian support for her artistic passions in the music of Bach or the paintings of El Greco.

Her adolescent identity crisis therefore took the form of illness. With the intensification of passions characteristic for that stage of life, her problem became not only what to *be*—how much the musician, the journalist, the Christian, the Chinese, and the woman —but what she could safely permit herself to *feel*.

Taking a journalism course was submission to her parents; at the same time, her emergence as the "progressive" journalist allowed an alternative form of self-expression, one by which she could avoid the emotional conflicts which surrounded her music. This identity compromise, however, could not work: not only was music too basic a part of her to be long denied, but, as it turned out, being a journalist in Communist China involved her in a new set of passions (or rather, an arduous reshaping of the old ones). Returning to the identity of the dedicated artist could not protect her from these passions, but it could at least permit her to meet them with her strongest weapons.

Grace's constellation of identities gave her encounter with thought reform an unusual emotional coloring. As a Westernized Christian girl, she was immediately identified (and not entirely inaccurately) as one of the opposition. Studying in a missionary-established "castle of reaction," she was in this respect by no means alone. But she was particularly vulnerable because of her close relationship with an American teacher—an artist-disciple bond, in which, protected by barriers of culture and status, she could experience a form of love. This does not however account for the extreme emotional pain she suffered during thought reform; her inner stress was greater than any of my other Chinese subjects, with the possible exception of Hu. The explanation lies partly in her long-standing attitude toward any form of strong emotion: suddenly confronted with mass frenzy, with the exaggerated passions unleashed by the Communists, it is not surprising that she became terrified. And when she was urged to join in with these passions, to denounce her revered teacher, she was overwhelmed by fear and by guilt—guilt both over refusing and thereby resisting the authorities, and over tendencies within her to comply and make the denunciation. Similarly, the denunciation of her university president by his daughter revived her own complicated feelings of guilt and resentment toward her parents. The hateful emotions so central to thought reform were precisely the kind she had been warding off all her life.

These emotional patterns led her to distort sexual matters. It is true that in the Communist environment politics came first and love often was mechanical; but other students reported an atmosphere more puritanical than the uninhibited one Grace described. As can occur in any moment of crisis, Grace's fears about sex and hostility became confused. Thus, all of her anxieties came to a head in her response to the germ warfare inoculation, and she experienced the injection as an assault upon her entire person. In making her exit from thought reform through illness, she brought a tremendous histrionic force to the old identity of the invalid, which was also in keeping with her previous use of hysterical mechanisms. Grace's negative identity was therefore an important factor in both her pain and her escape.

It would be wrong, however, to stress only this side of her character. In her resistance to thought reform, she also gave evidence of the surprising strength inherent in her sense of being the Western Christian girl and the dedicated musician. Her previous exposure to Western liberalism and her absorption with Western classical music supported her in her belief that "the world could not be like this" (or at least that it *need* not be like this). These two identities, and perhaps especially the one of the dedicated artist, gave Grace extraordinary staying power. Not only did they help her survive thought reform pressures, they also served as important sources of stability during her tribulations in Hong Kong.

There she had to face—at first in lonely isolation—both the confusing aftereffects of thought reform, and an external environment which was unusually provocative for someone like her. So great was her identity diffusion that she reverted to every pattern of self-destructive emotional behavior, and every level of sexual and family conflict she had known since early childhood, to the point where she felt her sense of existence almost entirely fading away. Yet on her own emotional terms her movement toward renewal of identity was active from the first. In her dreams, in her relationships in Hong Kong, and in her attitudes toward me, she was searching for help, but she insisted on being the arbiter of her own life. Among my Chinese subjects, she was unusual in her ability to face and to talk about both the difficulties of freedom and the extent of residual Communist influences. Her return to a mildly Christian, firmly Westernized, and profoundly artistic way of life (as well as extreme good fortune) led her to her new "mother," and to the promise of a creative personal future. Her old emotional patterns were of course still very much with her, as was also some of the message of thought reform; but equipped with a newly-integrated adult self and a clear sense of direction, she would probably manage to live with them.

CHAPTER 19

CULTURAL PERSPECTIVES:
THE FATE OF FILIAL PIETY

Each of the four Chinese subjects I have described experienced first an immersion into thought reform—the beginnings of a personal change—and then a recoil from its demands. What brought about this recoil, which contrasted with the continued enthusiasms of more successfully reformed Chinese intellectuals? Without a comparative study of the latter group, no certain answer can be given to this question. But from the evidence at hand, we can say that some features of personal character and identity were consistently important in resistance to thought reform, not only for these four people, but for the remainder of my subjects as well. These are: tendencies toward rebelliousness and fear of domination (especially marked in Hu); strong need for individual self-expression (George Chen and Grace Wu); binding family ties (George Chen); previous patterns of anomie and of emotional escape (Robert Chao, Grace Wu, and Hu); and a significant degree of Westernization, whether Christian or otherwise (Robert Chao, Grace Wu, and George Chen). These tendencies are not simply rallying points of resistance; the conflicts existing around them can also create specific susceptibilities to thought reform.

Even more important, these are themes which have long been at

the very center of the personal struggles of most Chinese intellectuals. Tension about rebelliousness, self-expression, family loyalties, alienation, and Westernization have particular significance
for Chinese at this point in their history—as they must for the
intellectual vanguard of any society whose traditional patterns are
being replaced. In other words, these four case histories have introduced a set of conflicts relating to identity and ideology which no
Chinese intellectual, in facing thought reform, could really avoid.

The roots of such tensions lie in the interplay of individual emotions with cultural and historical influences. I have chosen, as the
title of this chapter suggests, to group all of these psychological
factors around the concept of filial piety, a basic theme of Chinese
culture, and one which has specific bearing upon the tensions just
enumerated. And the historical vicissitudes of filialism, or rather of
Chinese intellectuals (or literati) in relation to filialism, have special psychological importance for thought reform itself.

The individual lives we have been studying in many ways mir-
ror the history of China itself: early years of filial identities derived
from traditional Chinese culture; attraction during adolescence and
young adulthood to more modern and Western influences; and
finally, a third phase of Communism or thought reform. It seems
that each Chinese intellectual has had to recapitulate personally
the larger experiences of his culture in a psychocultural counterpart
of the biological tenet that ontogeny recapitulates phylogeny.

Filial influences are part of the entire history of China's traditional culture, going back to the Han dynasty (206 B.C.–220 A.D.)
and before, and extending through the Ch'ing Dynasty (1644 A.D.–
1911 A.D.) to the revolution of 1911. "Modern" (I am using the
term in a more restrictive sense than the way it is employed by
historians) Chinese identities emerged during a transitional period
which can be roughly located in the first half of the twentieth century, although it had its beginnings about fifty years before that.
The third phase, of course, began with the Communist takeover
of 1948–49.

For each of these historical stages a distinct pattern of Chinese
cultural identity, based on shared individual experiences, can be
delineated. To be sure, we must discuss ideal types, in some ways
over-simplified, and by no means completely inclusive. But these
can enable us to place both thought reform and the people under-

going it in a perspective which, for being historical, is all the more psychological.[1]

Traditional Filialism and the Filial Son

In traditional Chinese culture (I refer here most specifically to the period of the Ch'ing Dynasty), one was expected to be filial if nothing else. For the son or daughter of a gentry-literati family, the principle of *hsiao* or filial piety was at the very center of personal, family, and social existence. Its mystique was so powerful and so pervasive that Fung Yu-lan, a leading contemporary Chinese philosopher, has called it "the ideological basis of traditional [Chinese] society." [2]

Whether he was seven or seventy, a son's attitude toward his parents was expected to be one of reverence, obedience, and loyalty. Nor was this to be a token response, since if it did not stem naturally from his inner being, he was not being truly filial. He learned how to be a filial son from his parents and his older brothers and sisters, through the unconscious transmission of cultural forms as well as through their conscious elaboration. And the indoctrination began early: when only three or four, a child might be told stories (in a culture very fond of storytelling) of the famous "Twenty-four Examples of Filial Piety." These included such tales as that of the eight-year-old boy who allowed mosquitoes to "feed without restraint upon his blood until they were satisfied" in order to prevent them from biting his parents; of the seventy-year-old man who dressed himself in gaily-colored garments and played like a child "in order to amuse his parents"; and the most impressive story of all, entitled "On Account Of His Mother He Buried His Child," which is worth quoting in full:

During the Han dynasty, Ko Keu, whose family was very poor, had a child three years old. Keu's mother usually took some of her food and gave to the child. One day he spoke to his wife about it, saying, "We are so poor that we cannot even support mother. Moreover, the little one shares mother's food. Why not bury this child? We may have another; but if mother should die, we cannot obtain her again."

His wife did not dare to oppose. Keu, when he had dug a hole more than two feet deep, suddenly saw a vase of gold. On the top of the vase was an inscription, saying, "Heaven bestows this gold on Ko Keu, the dutiful son. The officers shall not seize it, nor shall the people take it." [3]

The father-son relationship was most important, the ultimate model for almost all other relationships in Chinese society. It combined love and respect and a certain distance, the last created both by family ritual and by the limited role which the father played in the child's early upbringing. A child was to feel similar emotions toward his mother, although here the barriers were down a bit and there was room for more indulgence; but, as Ko Keu's story suggests, there was no less responsibility.

The filial principle extended into all important family and social ties. Of the "Five Most Important Human Relationships" described by Confucius (between Sovereign and Subject, Father and Son, Husband and Wife, Elder and Younger Brothers, and Friend and Friend) three were within the family, and the other two were based upon specific family models.

One of these, the relationship between Sovereign and Subject, has special importance for us. It was conceived as an extension of the relationship between father and son: "From the way in which one serves one's father, one learns how to serve one's sovereign. The respect shown to them is the same." [4] At the same time, it differed by being a "social or moral" relationship rather than a "natural" (or blood) tie. Therefore, one felt respect but not love for one's sovereign. This attitude was compared to that between man and wife, in which respect and duty were also emphasized more than love. The analogy was especially important for the government official (the standard career of the literati class), since he was considered "married" to the sovereign. He was expected to emulate the bride who transfers her loyalties from her family to her husband and his family: "Before marriage she was the daughter of her parents; after it, she became the wife of her husband"; in becoming "married" to the royal family, a man was expected to experience a similar "transformation of filial piety into loyalty to the sovereign." But here too there was a distinction, for in this transformation "the filial son does not cease to be a filial son"; in fact, in his new situation, this transformation "is the only way in which he can continue to be a filial son." The point is that loyalty to one's sovereign should be part of, rather than conflict with, one's sense of being a filial son. [5]

There was thus in the filial identity a strong sense of personal continuity, continuity between family and society, and in fact in the entire life cycle. The male infant was made much of because, as one of his most important filial duties, he would continue the family line. From the first stories casually (or not so casually) told to him, through a period of childhood and youth devoted largely to a study of the classics (The Book of Filial Piety, The Book of Rites, the Confucian Analects, The Great Learning, The Doctrine of the Mean, The Spring and Autumn Annals, The Work of Mencius), his education was to a great degree an uninterrupted in-doctrination for this identity. As his first exercises in reading and writing, he began to memorize filial principles long before he could understand what they meant. Most of his education was under his family's control; sometimes his tutor was directly employed by his family, sometimes he was taught in a clan or village school. Advanced institutions for the study of Confucianism did exist in large cities; but a gentry youth need not attend one of these to pursue his studies of the classics in preparation for state examinations, nor did these schools appear to provide the opportunity for youthful self-expression that we associate with European and American universities.

In traditional China, there was no institutionalized youth culture or youth rebellion.[6] There was a group of *ch'ing-nien jen* (young people, or literally, "green-years men")—male youths between sixteen and thirty not yet married—who did to some extent associate with each other, but not to the extent of developing a collective voice or an organized group life. And since marriages took place early—bridegrooms were often in their late teens and brides even younger—a youth was not likely to remain in this category for long. Even more important in preventing youthful rebellion was the ethos that youth was to serve age: whether indulged during early childhood, strictly disciplined during later childhood, or allowed a modicum of personal freedom during his teens, one's importance lay, not in the youth he was, but in the man he would become, and mainly in relationship to his family and his society. A Chinese youth became a man not by casting off his father's influence and control, but rather by adapting himself to them, by becoming like him, by identifying with him in attitude and belief, as generations before had done with their fathers.[7] A recent sociological observer has claimed that "for hundreds and thousands of years there was no conflict of generations in China."[8] This statement is surely extravagant, especially since it ignores inner conflict; but it does indicate the *ideal* of father-son continuity which held sway in China for so long.

To marry and have children of one's own were in themselves filial tasks; as Mencius pointed out, "there are three unfilial acts, and of these lack of posterity is the greatest." And as a mature man and a father himself, the filial son reinforced his filialism by teaching its principles to others. At the same time his responsibility for the care of his own parents increased, and still included the most personal form of attention—a responsibility he could never shirk no matter where in the empire he served, or how high in the bureaucracy he rose. When his parents died, the filial son was expected not only to arrange a proper burial, but subsequently to "love what they loved" and "revere what they reverenced." Only when he himself became an old man was he able to relax into a more carefree existence. Then he finally reaped the full benefits of filial piety and enjoyed the solicitude of his family, for it was the old whose happiness mattered most.

A woman's life cycle, despite her shift from her own to her husband's family, had similar continuity, since her marital relationship was but another dimension of filial responsibility. Men, however, were the main repositories of the filial mystique: their studies and writings perpetuated its classical ideology; their patriarchal position made them its more symbolically important practitioners; and in a patrilineal society, it was through the male that the filial chain was extended.

Ancestor worship was the filial son's spiritual expression. As practiced in literati families, it emphasized the personal, rather than the supernatural or absolute. The worshiper was to try to recall the faces and mannerisms of his departed parents so that "the eyes of the son should not forget the looks (of his parents) nor his ears their voices; and that he should retain the memory of their aims, likings, and wishes." [9] Ancestor worship was a reinforcement of one's sense of biological immortality, and the quest for this immortality was itself at the root of the filial ideology.

Needless to say, nobody could completely satisfy these filial requirements. Indeed, the filial son was attracted from time to time to trends in Chinese culture specifically antagonistic to filialism. In the ideology of Legalism, which prevailed for a brief period during the third century B.C., he found an authoritarian doctrine which advocated loyalty to a centralized warlike state rather than to the family, and the use of coercion rather than the moral exhortations of filial piety. In Taoism, as old and as basic a Chinese doctrine as Confucianism, he found an opposite extreme, a mysticism which viewed earthly obligation as transient and unimportant, and which offered a call to withdraw from these in body and spirit to find The Way. And later, for several centuries after the first century B.C., Buddhism had a similar appeal. Each of these three doctrines made contact with (and itself reflected) a special facet of Chinese character. Taoism and Buddhism, in particular—although they were most widely accepted by the common people—had lasting appeal to the gentry as well, satisfying their more passive, imaginative, and nonrational impulses.

Even while he clung to his rationalistic Confucianism, the filial son was likely to feel deeply attracted to the escape into nothingness of Taoist hermits and Buddhist mystics. This attraction is described in the great eighteenth-century novel, *The Dream of the Red Chamber*, whose youthful hero, Pao Yu, abandons both an official's career and his pregnant bride for a supernatural Buddhist-Taoist destiny. Generations of gentry youth have since vicariously experienced Pao Yu's escape from filial obligation, neglecting Confucian volumes for the surreptitious pleasures of *The Dream of the Red Chamber*. But even Pao Yu squares his filial account before his departure: he applies himself to his Confucian studies and passes his state examinations with distinction, thereby bringing great honor upon his family; he impregnates his bride, thereby insuring his posterity; and as his last act before disappearing, he seeks out his stern father and bows four times before him "in a solemn *k'o-t'ou*," thereby expressing his symbolic filial submission.[10]

Thus the filial son could be both Confucian in his worldly obligations and Buddhist and Taoist during inner moments of flight from them. Or he might express other forms of antagonism toward the filial web—an admiration of outlaw heroes, heavy gambling, or opium smoking—all strongly-developed cultural patterns. One Western authority, C. P. Fitzgerald, was so impressed with these escapist tendencies in Chinese character that he regarded filial piety as an essentially compensatory phenomenon: "The Confucian insistence on filial duty and the strict training of the young would seem harsh until it is realized that the Chinese, a people naturally over-kind and indulgent to children, are also averse to discipline." [11] Yet during the traditional period Confucianism prevailed over all rival ideologies, for its stress upon filial piety gave it a biologically-based social ethic of great force, an ethic known in all societies, but brought to its highest development in China.

Did this ethic allow for maximum personal growth? Could the identity of the filial son provide a rewarding sense of existence? Fung Yu-lan answers in the affirmative:

It is by becoming a father or a son, a husband or a wife, that an individual enlists himself as a member of society and it is by this enlistment that a man differentiates himself from the beasts. In serving his father and sovereign, a man has not given up his personality. On the contrary, it is only in these services that his personality has its fullest development.[12]

Hu Shih, another contemporary Chinese scholar, expresses the opposite opinion:

All the much-idealized virtues of filial piety simply could not exist; and in those rare cases where they were consciously cultivated, the price paid for them was nothing short of intense suppression, resulting in mental and physical agony.[13]

There is no doubt truth in both views. Filialism offered one a firm and respectable self-image; but many outwardly filial sons must have experienced profound inner hostilities toward their ostensibly revered fathers. And there is no doubt that society feared this hostility: in rare cases where parents accused their sons of being "un-filial," the latter were publicly disgraced, sometimes whipped by a magistrate to the point of death. Crimes of parricide were treated as desecrations of the most dangerous sort: the culprit was not only beheaded and his body mutilated, but his house was razed to the ground, his immediate neighbors and teacher were punished, the district magistrate deprived of his office and disgraced, and higher provincial officials degraded in rank.[14]

Clearly then, rebelliousness had to be repressed, which must have resulted in a significant amount of unconscious guilt. The prohibition and repression of rebelliousness also undoubtedly contributed (at least during the Ch'ing Dynasty) to the stagnation within Chinese society, to individual passivity, to rationalization of the existing order, and to impotence rather than action in the face of a declining civilization.

How did Confucian proponents of filialism deal with such grave emotional problems? They returned, in true fundamentalist fashion, to the classical texts, seeking to sanctify their message on the basis of such passages as the following:

The body is that which has been transmitted to us by our parents. Dare any one allow himself to be irreverent in the employment of their legacy? If a man in his own house and privacy be not grave, he is not filial. If in discharging the duties of his office, he be not serious, he is not filial. If with friends he be not sincere, he is not filial. If on the field of battle he be not brave, he is not filial. If he fail in these five things the evil (of disgrace) will reflect on his parents. Dare he be but serious?

The fundamental lesson for all is filial piety. . . . True love is the love of this; true propriety is the doing of this; true righteousness is the rightness of this; true sincerity is the being sincere in this; true strength is being strong in this. Music springs from conformity to this; punishments come from violations of this. . . . Set up filial piety, and it will fill the space from heaven to earth. Spread it out and it will extend over all the ground to the four seas. Hand it down to future ages and it will be forever observed. Push it on the eastern sea, the western sea, the southern sea, and the northern sea, and it will be everywhere the law of men, and their obedience to it will be uniform.[15]

Whatever its strains, filialism was the source of the predominant identity of traditional China, a basic ideal against which any other form of self-image had to be judged. To be regarded as "unfilial" was to be placed beyond the pale. The heritage of the filial son was one of the strongest and most enduring national identities ever created.

Transitional Rebellion: The Modern Student

By the second decade of the twentieth century, the world of the young Chinese intellectual had drastically changed, especially in his relationship to the ideology of filial piety. In fact, he had apparently made a complete about face: "The new China must eradicate the Confucian rules of obedience which make slaves of men." [16] These words, written in 1916, typify the spirit of the "New Tide" or "Renaissance Movement" which was then beginning to flourish among rebellious avant-garde intellectuals, and especially among the young. Rather than being considered "the root of all virtue," filial piety was being denounced as "the source of all evils." To be sure, not every young intellectual felt this way; but such was the power of this cultural countertrend [17] that all were significantly affected by it. As one Chinese commentator observed,

The inner life of the youth of China was thus completely changed, for the ancient motto of China was: "Walk slowly behind the elders; revere the past," while the motto of China's youth today is "self-expression." [18]

During the most active years of this movement (1915–1920), matters came to a head for China both in its national history and in the life patterns of its young students. China had long been lagging in its cultural creativity, deficient in social progress, woefully behind the West in technology. Although the Ch'ing Dynasty had been overthrown in 1911, the revolutionary movement had foundered; political chaos went hand in hand with social deterioration. And young intellectuals were aware of a similar sense of discontinuity in their own lives. Although traditional forms had already lost much of their hold, the emotions lingered on. Parents continued to convey to their children in one way or another the filial principles upon which moral behavior *should* be based, even if (as was true of Hu) the social structure made it impossible to practice these principles. No longer capable of offering a sense of existential harmony, the identity of the filial son now seemed archaic and intolerably passive. Confucianism had become a rigid and narrow orthodoxy: its voice was still heard, but to young ears it had a hollow ring. To Chinese youth, Western ideas and techniques seemed much more attractive than did the decaying institutions immediately around them. The cohesion and continuity of the traditional period disappeared, to be replaced by intellectual shopping and acute ideological hunger.

There had been important attempts at reform before this, beginning in the latter part of the nineteenth century. But they had usually followed the characteristic Chinese pattern of "finding in antiquity the sanction for present-day changes." Faced with overwhelming threats from the West, both ideological and technological, reformers had maintained the ethnocentric hope of using Western knowledge for practical purposes only, while maintaining the more precious Chinese "essence." [19] They had wished to revitalize, rather than replace, the ideology of filial piety. This was even to some extent true for those early reformers to whom the modern student looked for inspiration, among them men still intellectually active at the time of the New Tide.

K'ang Yu-wei (1858–1937) was one of these early leaders. First at the turn of the century and then again during the New Tide itself, he bitterly criticized both the practices of traditional Chinese families ("They present a harmonious picture from the outside, but inside there is an unescapable and overwhelming atmosphere of hatred"), and the demand for filial piety within them ("Birds and animals care for their young but ask no reward. Real love does not ask for recompense"). Yet in his prescription for utopia [20] (*Ta-tung Shu, The Book of Great Unity*) he took Confucius himself as his authority, painting the Sage as a misunderstood Messiah. K'ang's famous pupil, Liang Chi-chao, went even further in his condemnation of the old order, and in his acceptance of Western ideas; but he returned from a post-World War I trip to Europe disillusioned with the West, and looked again to China's past for spiritual values.

In the New Tide, the modern student found something different from all that had gone before: a movement which advocated a break with tradition that would be both deliberate and decisive, and which made a special plea for young people to assume leadership within it. "It is the youth who must save this great revolution from the powers of the past," wrote Ch'en Tu-hsiu, one of the leading figures of the New Tide, in the magazine which he edited appropriately entitled *The New Youth*. The modern student was even given a blueprint for the identity change asked of him: the "old youth"—weak, effeminate, devoid of militancy, seeking only wealth and high position—was to be supplanted by the "new youth"—courageous, strong, free of parental domination, idealistic, and patriotic.[21] In this national and personal transformation, the "two gentlemen" to follow, according to Ch'en, were "Mr. Democracy" and "Mr. Science." Democracy and science were defined specifically in relationship to the problem at hand: democracy meant release from the bondage of Confucian filial piety, the attainment of equality between men and women, the opportunity for individual expression; science meant opposition to traditional Chinese thought, and its replacement by modern Western learning.[22] Here was the dichotomy (relived by Hu and George Chen) between the "irrational past" and the "rational future." And in the accompanying literary renaissance, the "new youth" were urged to express themselves in clear, forceful, conversational language—"in the living language of the people"—rather than in the effete and frequently obscure classical style.[23]

This was precisely the direction in which the modern student wished to go. His group identity had come into being with modern schools and universities during the late nineteenth and early twentieth centuries. The emergence of a Youth Movement gave him sudden prominence. The universities and upper middle schools offered him a forum for his rebellion, and an identity to challenge that of the filial son (as was true for Hu and George Chen). Frequently feeling persecuted by his family (and sometimes, like Hu, suffering at the hands of members of older generations made desperate by the crumbling of the world they had known) the modern student plunged eagerly into the new group life. Thus, a celebrated and widely-read novel of the thirties, *The Family*, whose story is laid during the time of the New Tide, describes the young hero's isolation and misery when among family members: "He was suddenly overwhelmed by a strange feeling of solitude. It was as if all the other members of his family were far away, as if they lived in a different world. He felt cold, as though he were oppressed by unspeakable sorrow and anguish," and contrasts this with his joy and trust when working among his friends for the new ideals they shared.

Here he feels that he is not an outsider, not a lonely man. He loves the other young men around him; they love him. He understands them; they understand him. He can trust them; they can trust him.[24]

Although these feelings are in many ways very similar to those experienced by generations of Westerners as they emancipate themselves from family control, this youth identity was in China a vitally important part of the cultural countertrend. The term *ch'ing-nien*, "youth," which had little significance in the past, took on a new and revealing meaning: it came to suggest articulate young advocates (including women, and to some extent peasants and laborers, rather than only male gentry-literati) of political radicalism and social reform: new generations of youth who married later, often resisting their parents' marital arrangements for them, and who demanded independent lives physically and emotionally separate from parental control.[25]

Almost overnight the modern student seemed to step into an identity which allowed him to be active rather than passive, which offered him a sense of logic and purpose rather than meaningless compliance with tradition, and an opportunity for self-realization rather than self-denial. So strong was the reaction against Confucianism, and so timely the New Tide's appeal, that the Chinese student movement during the transitional period achieved a power and influence unmatched by any similar movement in the modern world. This power was demonstrated in the celebrated "May 4th Movement" of 1919, in which student demonstrations sparked an effective national protest against the humiliating Versailles Peace Treaty; in the "May 30th Movement" of 1925, another mass demonstration against imperialism; and in the continuous student agitation against the Nationalist Government (in which Hu and Grace Wu participated) prior to the Communist takeover. The first of these, the 1919 May 4th Movement, was particularly significant as a turning point: as one authority put it, "Henceforward, agitation by students gave an ever more powerful impetus to the release, slow or violent, of the forces of change in China." [26]

In simultaneously rebelling against his family and usurping social authority, the modern student was being far from filial, and this was bound to cause him suffering. Even if he went on to become (like Hu) an extreme rebel, an avenger, or a would-be martyr, the filial son within him was likely to remain very much alive. After thousands of years, it was not to be easily destroyed. In this respect, the modern student's inner life resembled the state of his country: immobile tradition, petrified into traditionalism, existed side-by-side with iconoclastic and totalistic revolutionary urges. Indeed, the psychological strength of the filial tradition was attested to by the immense energies necessary to attack it: that part of the past which resides within oneself is most difficult to sweep away.

No one expressed this inner dilemma more powerfully than Lu Hsun, the greatest of modern Chinese writers and the leading literary spirit of the New Tide Movement. His short story, "The Diary of a Madman," which appeared in *The New Youth* in 1918, is one of the most effective condemnations of traditional Chinese society ever written. The author speaks through his hero, a madman-sage, who, in his persecutory fears, evokes a twilight world between delusion and reality. The story's theme is the "man-eating"

nature of traditional Chinese society, a theme which is expressed on
several simultaneous levels of symbolism. The hero notices the
threatening faces of the people around him, and from various bits
of evidence concludes that they are going to kill and eat him.
Wondering what he has done to cause their enmity, he decides that
it must result from his earlier rebellion:

Twenty years ago I trampled the daily account book [a derogatory allusion to the Classics] of Mr. Hoary Tradition under my feet. . . . I
did not think that I could be considered a wicked man, but . . . I am
no longer so sure. They seem to think so . . . they have a way of brand-
ing anyone they don't like as a wicked man.

In a further quest for understanding, he studies ancient history.
He finds that despite the high moral claims ("over every page was
scrawled the words 'Benevolence and Righteousness'"), in reality
"the book was nothing but a record of man-eating"; and that "this
world in which I had moved about for half a lifetime has been for
over four thousand years a man-eating world." He thinks of can-
nibalistic practices which actually occurred in Chinese society and
decides, "Everyone wants to eat others but is afraid of being eaten
himself, and so everyone looks at everyone else with such profound
distrust and suspicion." The leader of the man-eaters around him,
he discovers, is none other than his older brother (the father's
representative in the family, and here a symbol of family authority);
he decides to begin with his brother, first in "cursing man-eating
men," and then in converting them from their evil ways. But his
pleas ("you must repent . . . change at once . . . you must know
that the future has no place for man-eating men") are ignored—
out of wickedness and because of the habit of rationalization.
"Some felt that it had always been so and that it was as it should
be, while others knew that it was wrong, but wanted to eat just the
same."

Only then does he come to a terrible realization that he too is
among the guilty. He recalls his older brother's having taught him
an old principle of filial piety: the belief (which really has existed)
that if a parent is sick, the child should cut off a piece of his own
flesh, boil it, and feed it to the parent as medicine. Since this
brother was in charge of the family at the time of his sister's death,
he decides (with the logic of a madman-sage) that "they ate my

younger sister"; and since he also partook of the family meals, "it is not at all impossible that I had myself eaten a few slices of my sister's flesh!" He comes to know "how difficult it is to find a true and innocent man." The only hope lies with the young, and the story ends: "Maybe there are still some infants that have not yet eaten men. Save, save the infants." [27]

Commentators have rightly emphasized this story's assault upon traditional Chinese society, but they have overlooked something else in it which is equally important: the desperate psychological plight—the intolerable anger and overwhelming sense of guilt—of the man who has chosen the path of rebellion. The story's hero is burdened by three great sins: first, having participated in and "tasted" the rewards of the "man-eating" society which he now condemns; second, defying four thousand years of authority in making this condemnation; and third, harboring within himself such explosive hatred.

Through his imaginative use of his hero's psychosis, Lu Hsun made contact with the emotions of the Chinese modern student as no other creative writer had before or has since. "The Diary of a Madman," described as "the overture and finale" of his writings, evoked a sensational response. Young intellectuals found "man-eating" an apt description of their own attitudes toward their filial heritage, and the psychotic's suffering an expression of their own pain.

The antitraditional passions of the New Tide Movement—in both its political and literary expressions—set the tone for the entire transitional period. Emotions and ideas which had been smoldering for several previous generations were now forcefully articulated on a mass scale, and they continued to be shared and reinforced by succeeding generations of modern students until the Communist takeover in 1948–49. But the undermining of the general principle of filial piety (which the New Tide accelerated rather than initiated), far from satisfying the widespread ideological hunger, created an even greater ideological vacuum. Chinese intellectuals sought a more comprehensive set of beliefs and a more specific program of action.

What psychological characteristics did they require of a unifying ideology they might embrace? Any such ideology would have to be rebellious in tone to encourage full expression of great hostility, to offer some relief for feelings of guilt, and to provide a solution to the broad crisis in identity which I have described. It would have to be a "modern" (and therefore Western) movement, and offer a program for economic development as well as some form of popular participation in government. It would inevitably call for a national resurgence achieved by casting off both Confucianism and Western imperialism. Consequently it had to supply some way to attack the past and yet feel pride in it, to condemn the West and yet use Western ideas to find a solution to Chinese problems. This was a big order, and contending ideologies were tortuously examined, experienced, and refashioned in a series of desperate attempts to find answers to problems which seemed always deepened rather than resolved by time.

The modern student (both during and after his student days) was confronted by three ideological alternatives, two of them organized movements: the Chinese versions of Nationalism, liberal democracy, and Communism. Without attempting to trace a full history of any of these, we may ask to what extent each was able to satisfy the psychological requirements just mentioned.

By Nationalism, I mean the revolutionary movement initiated by Sun Yat-sen, and subsequently embodied in Chiang Kai-chek's leadership of the Kuomintang, or Nationalist Party. Both Sun and Chiang won great personal acclaim; their call for a strong, modern Chinese government was supported fervently by modern students as well as by much of the rest of the Chinese population. Just after Sun's death, which occurred during the period following the May 30th incident of 1925, Chiang brought the Nationalist movement to its greatest momentum and highest point of popularity. The "Second Revolution" of 1926–27 was successfully carried out in the midst of a wave of popular sentiment, mass demonstrations, and boycotts of Japan and the West. The atmosphere was violently anti-imperialist, and therefore anti-Western.

Shared angers and shared hopes did at first unite intellectuals and peasants. But Nationalism's effectiveness as an ideology virtually stopped here: it was able to gain the allegiance of modern students, but as these students matured into harassed intellectuals they could not find within it a sustained program or a set of ideas to satisfy their emotional urges and their rational standards. Sun's "three people's principles" (Nationalism, People's Rights or Democracy, and People's Livelihood) were acceptable enough but amorphous, and only the first was convincingly put into action. These principles came to be more a catechism recited by school children than a set of living beliefs. Nationalism took its forms from both Western liberalism and Russian Communism, but in a way which was frequently devoid of the inner meaning. It placed great stress upon modernization, but at the same time it joined forces with the traditionalists in hollow and ritualistic revivals of ancient Confucian values. The modern student usually found this combination of filial piety and Westernization an incompatible ideological admixture, which intensified rather than solved his guilt and identity problems. Increasingly, the intellectual drew a sharp line between himself and the bureaucrats, financiers, and military men of the Nationalist regime, and looked elsewhere for his ideological nourishment. Nationalism was indispensable to him, but he found in it no more than half an ideology.

The failure of liberal democracy is a much more complex story. By liberal democracy I mean that loose tradition developed in Europe and America which advocated social reform, parliamentary government, and full expression of individual rights. It would be too facile to state categorically, with retrospective wisdom, the reasons why it could *not* have succeeded, although it did face extraordinary problems in meeting existing emotional demands. Its achievements in China were in fact considerable. It supplied the original inspiration for China's trend toward Westernization during and before the transitional period, and was the model for individual expression which lay behind the attack on filial piety.

Ch'en Tu-hsiu's ringing declarations inaugurating the New Tide movement, for instance, were inspired by the Manchester liberalist-like philosophy which he then espoused,[28] although he later shifted his position and became one of the founders of the Chinese Communist Party (and still later was deposed as one of its first villains). Hu Shih, also a leading spirit in the New Tide, remained one of the most articulate spokesmen for liberal democracy throughout the transitional period. A disciple of John Dewey, he sought in the Chinese past a basis for the pragmatic, scientific approach of his teacher; and he accompanied the American philosopher on his celebrated and highly influential lecture tour of China in 1919–20. And Lu Hsun, although deified by the Communists and certainly a militant leftist, held fast to the liberal principles of "the right to life, the right to food and shelter, and the right to the unlimited development of the individual." [29]

Spread by missionaries, by Western and Chinese educators, and by Chinese students returning from the West, liberalism had tremendous appeal for the Chinese intellectual. But it could never satisfy his need for totalism, and its "drop-by-drop" moderation (in Dewey's phrase) seemed weak in contrast with the messianic tone of its ideological competitors. Liberalism was least able to make sustained use of feelings of hostility and rebellion, and although its stress upon individualism inspired Chinese to challenge family authority, it offered little help for the resulting guilt and identity stress. It offered no lasting group identity to a people who had become dependent upon one, and no substitute for the filial loyalties being cast off. In addition, because of its Western origins, it bore the stigma of Western imperialism, no matter how strongly Chinese and Western liberals opposed to imperialism sought to dissociate themselves from this stigma. Liberalism also created a problem about "Chineseness" (as, for example, for Robert Chao and Grace Wu), since the individual Westernization which was likely to accompany any profound acceptance of liberal democratic ideas often led to a sense of being severed from Chinese roots.

Without entering further into the question of potential compatibility between traditional Confucian humanism and modern liberal democratic ideals (and a case can be made for such compatibility), we can say that no effective political-ideological form was evolved to unite them. Liberal democratic ideology during the transitional period therefore proved more effective in stimulating opposition to the past than in resolving pressing emotional conflicts of the present.

Every Chinese intellectual to whom I spoke emphasized just how pressing these conflicts were. Even taking into account the general tendency during any such transitional period to stress only chaos (some intellectuals must have lived relatively stable lives), there is no doubt that emotional chaos was widespread. Generations of young students had their patriotic emotions aroused but unsatisfied, their rebellious feelings frustrated, their guilt unresolved, their self-definition obscured. Sons and daughters clashed openly with their parents in a society ill-equipped to deal with such strife. While great strides were made in youthful self-assertion and in the position of women, much remained confused. In father-son conflicts, compromises were often achieved at the price of great anguish for both parties. And the breakdown of clear-cut male and female roles often resulted in uncomfortably overt female domination, a recurrent theme in our case histories.[30]

Once initiated into the antitraditional, modern Western world, the Chinese intellectual could never reverse the psychological forces generated within him. The intense conflicts and visions experienced during youthful struggles to attain adult identity often remained throughout life, and the struggles of the modern student in many ways came to characterize the entire transitional period. Sometimes the former student activist, as he got older, seemed to slip back into a traditional pattern, honor his filial duties, then see his own rebellions mirrored in those of his son. But no matter how filial or how "modern" the Chinese intellectual appeared on the surface, some conflict between these two emotional tendencies was bound to be taking place underneath. His undigested combination of filialism, Nationalism, and Western liberalism was likely to leave him— at different times and in different degrees—rebellious, withdrawn, disillusioned, despairing. Continuous war and plunder further sapped energies and hopes—early revolutionary battles, encounters between warlords, Japanese invasions, World War II, and the Communist-Nationalist Civil War. Governed during the latter phase of the transitional period by a group which had become "conservative and antirevolutionary" and out of touch with his own aspirations, the modern student shared in the "general bankruptcy of morale" [31] and turned his gaze toward Communism—if it was not already there.

Thought Reform: The Filial Communist

In Communism, his third ideological alternative, the Chinese intellectual found a no-nonsense solution for his spiritual predicament. What role did thought reform play in this solution? Was the cure worse than the disease?

The interplay between Chinese intellectuals and Communism began, not in 1948, but in 1919, immediately following the Russian Revolution. From then on, Communism became linked with

China's own continuous revolution—emotionally, organizationally, and ideologically. Of all Chinese mass movements, Communism was most capable of harnessing the powerful emotions released in the youth-age cultural reversal; [32] moreover, its revolutionary inspiration and practical techniques were attractive to Nationalist leaders like Sun and Chiang, and its emphasis upon social reform was much admired by Westernized Chinese liberals.

Communism's greatest ideological weapon was perhaps the "grandiose, starkly melodramatic image of the world" [33] provided by the Leninist theory of imperialism, the doctrine which placed on the Western nations and their international finance capital virtually the entire onus for China's (or any other "backward" country's) wretched condition. Intellectuals of all shades of political opinion found in this theory a focal point for hostilities, a reassuring interpretation of a humiliating situation, a way to avoid the pain of their own struggles with shame and guilt by centering their accusatory emotions upon an outside enemy, and a rationale for rejecting that Western enemy even while borrowing his knowledge and methods. This kind of emotional relevance leads to great oversimplifications, and Chinese intellectuals magnified the part-truths of the Leninist theory into a "scientific" gospel.

Liberals, Nationalists, and even traditionalists espoused this theory, but it was really Communist property, an integral part of the broader Communist scheme. As the modern student moved from the Leninist theory to its surrounding Marxist-Leninist principles, which had great currency even outside the Communist movement, he found that this hostile critique reinforced his own Chineseness, so that even when he severely criticized China's past, he was able to avoid a sense of being completely alienated from it. And the unwavering boldness of Marxist-Leninist and Communist attacks on both Chinese tradition and the modern West saved him from both the confusing complexities of liberalism, and the fluctuating ethics of Kuomintang Nationalism. The three-fold Communist program was clear enough: break filial bonds, expel the harmful Westerner, and follow the Communist Party on the path to total redemption. Thus the modern intellectual could begin to see a possible solution for his long-standing emotional torment; not only could hostility be expressed and guilt atoned for, but there seemed to be the promise of an identity which was both new and Chinese.

Yet at first, for most intellectuals, all of this was no more than a possibility, and here is where thought reform enters the picture. In the mid-1930's intellectuals recruited to the Communist-held border area—just a handful from among the great numbers who were embracing Communism—were already undergoing a kind of re-education which closely resembled later thought reform programs. From that time on, thought reform took shape as the Communists' conveyer of a new Chinese identity. It won adherents, trained cadres, ensured compliance to Communist doctrines, and instilled inner warning signals of anxiety to guard against potential deviation. Yet transcending all of these very important functions was (and is) thought reform's role in directing the human aspect of China's vast culture change—or to put it more accurately, in redirecting on its own terms a culture change which was already well under way.

To influence this change, thought reform had to deal with the problem of filial piety, less with its traditional ideology than with its modern emotional remnants. This involved thought reform in four basic identity tasks.

First and most obvious was the problem of coming to grips with filial emotions which have a way of outlasting even the most extreme kind of transitional rebellion. Emotions of loyalty, self-discipline, and respect for authority remained alive side-by-side with their negation, and these were emotional commodities too valuable for the Communists to waste, even if it were possible to dispel them. "Hate your past to win your future," the reformers urged, and they meant it. But they might well have added, "Do not hate it so much that you cannot bring us its sense of filial dedication." The reformed intellectual was expected to be, as before, loyal, self-disciplined, and obedient—now a filial son of the Communist regime.

Thought reform placed equal stress on its second task, the undermining of lingering effects of Western liberalism. Liberalism was a dangerous rival; it still appealed to many intellectuals as an inner alternative to Communist discipline. In personal terms, this task meant that an intellectual had to be taught to stigmatize as evil and selfish those aspects of himself which desired moderation, wished to live and let live, considered both sides of any question, or favored any form of gradualism. Hu Shih was an obvious choice for the symbolic liberal villain. He has been denounced in almost all

thought reform curricula, and during 1954 and 1955 a special national campaign was conducted during which his personal life and
his political, historical, and literary opinions were subjected to a
Communist-style dissection. Hu was condemned as an "extreme
liberal," a "pro-American," and "worshiper of America," a purveyor
of "anti-Marxist pragmatism"; and it was made clear that these
pernicious influences still exterted considerable influence upon intellectuals.[34] The liberal identity may not have been as deep-rooted
as that of the filial son, but its relationship to rival political forces
make it, in Communist eyes, a more dangerous one.

The third task was a mopping-up operation directed against transitional chaos and against the psychological patterns which accompanied it. Confusion was to be replaced by certainty, wavering
speculation by absolute knowing. Under attack were many relatively indefensible identities—those related to cynical detachment,
asocial self-seeking, or hollow despair, and those associated with nonideological personal loyalties to questionable political, military, or
financial leaders. In this area the Communists were able to mobilize
considerable moral force.

Finally, thought reform has had a synthesizing function, the
building of a new identity. Resurrected filial emotions, much of the
identity of the modern student, and a sizable chunk of the international Communist were all to be a part of it.

An awareness of these four identity tasks enables us to read between the clichés of thought reform, and construct an analysis based
on the principle of imposed identity change. We then discover
that its language and its demands, stereotyped as they are, have a
special set of emotional meanings for Chinese intellectuals. In both
sequence and content, the thought reform process bears down on the
historical and cultural conflicts I have enumerated.

The first stage of thought reform (the great togetherness) offers
a prelude of promise—the sense of effortlessly merging with a
dedicated group which is basic to any utopian quest. This stage
revives the group identity of the modern student, and gives an
immediate sense of release from the emotional chaos of the transitional period (the third of the four identity tasks). "Thought
mobilization" then reminds everyone that inner chaos is not to be
so easily cleared up, that the infection is deep-seated. As Mao himself explains: "The first method is to give the patients a powerful

stimulus, yell at them, 'You're sick!', so that the patients will have a fright and break out in an over-all sweat; then, they can be carefully treated." [35] The intellectual is reminded that he has inner conflicts (indeed they are made to seem worse than he thought they were); but the accompanying rationale gives him a feeling that Communist "doctors" possess both the knowledge of cause and the means of cure. The treatment will be difficult, but if he will submit himself to it totally and trust in his physicians, he will acquire a new self, and be better than ever. The stress upon promise and need, and the accusations leveled at the distant and recent past indicate the general direction of the treatment. This first stage thus focuses the intellectual's full attention on the identity tasks at hand.

Stage two (the closing in of the milieu) brings on the struggle phase: the pain which the intellectual must experience in order to realize the utopian promise, the psychological surgery necessary to rid him of the disease. The "logical dishonoring" of this stage of the re-education process can be understood in terms of the specific conflicts of Chinese intellectuals.

For instance, the Chinese intellectual is vulnerable to the accusation of "individualism"—the most basic criticism, since in the eyes of the Communists it "sums up in one term the ideological characteristics of the petty bourgeois class" [36]—on all identity fronts. When individualism is defined as "ultra-democratic ideology, tendency for independent action, excess emphasis upon individual liberty," [37] it is obviously being directed at the Western liberal in him. When it is defined as "individual firstism" to include those who "both adulate and pull strings," who believe that "what is mine is mine and what is yours is also mine," [38] he can feel its valid application to highly-personalized acquisitive patterns which became so prominent during the transitional phase. When individualism is described as "placing personal honor, status, and interests above other things," [39] the intellectual feels it directed against traditional patterns still part of himself—especially against the traditional stress on preserving individual dignity and social standing which is inherent in the Chinese concept of "face." [40] And the criticism of "individual heroism" applies both to the traditional Chinese ideal of the *chien-hsia* or "knight errant" and to more modern ideals of "the hero" brought in from the West. Each of these forms of "individualism" is equated with selfishness, hypocrisy, and insincerity;

each is rendered immoral because it allegedly conflicts with the greater group interest.

The Chinese intellectual has similar vulnerabilities to the accusation of "subjectivism." When this fault is ascribed to those "who simply quote the words of books they have studied as the sole basis for the solution of problems," it is being directed at a long-standing Confucian pattern which persisted in the approach of Chinese intellectuals to Western knowledge as well as to Confucianism itself.[41] When Communist reformers denounce the "subjective idealism and mysticism" of such liberal approaches as those of John Dewey and Hu Shih,[42] they are dealing with a more recent set of hopes and visions so consistently shattered that many Chinese intellectuals are now willing to view them as illusory. "Worshipping blindly Western culture" [43] is another accusation which makes effective contact with the modern student identity in all Chinese intellectuals (but since the Communists could themselves be accused of doing the same thing, much depended on which aspects of Western culture were chosen as objects of worship).

Just as the "sincere man" (one who submits totally to the Communist movement) is offered as the identity alternative to individualism, so the "scientific" practitioner of Marxist-Leninism is the alternative to subjectivism: "Marxism-Leninism, derived from objective reality and tested by objective reality, is the most correct, scientific, and revolutionary truth." [44] This form of *scientism* (I use the term to mean both a false claim of precision based upon an alleged natural science model, and a deification of science itself) has a very special appeal for those rebelling against a non-Western, nonscientific cultural tradition. Scientism was thus a comfortable ideological resting place for many Chinese intellectuals after the confusing array of ideas to which they had been so recently exposed.

The Communists equated most additional criticisms either with individualism or with subjectivism, but two of their other epithets —"liberalism" and "sentimentalism"—have special importance for the problems under discussion.

I have already mentioned the accusation of "extreme liberalism" applied to Hu Shih; closely related is the charge of "extreme democratic tendencies." Both these accusations have direct application to those Western liberal influences which the Communists seek to undermine; but there is also a specifically Chinese connotation for "liberalism." In an essay devoted to this question, "In Opposition to Liberalism," Mao's first illustrative bad example is "failing to start an argument in principle with a person, even when you know he is in the wrong, letting things slide for the sake of peace and cordiality, all because he is an old friend, a fellow villager, a fellow student, a close friend, someone beloved, an old colleague, or an old subordinate . . . or speaking about [the error] in allusions in order to preserve harmony and unity." Mao is referring here mainly to the principles of personal loyalty, propriety, and harmony carried over from the filial identity of traditional Chinese culture. All these principles are then viewed in terms of individual character, and "liberalism" is extended to include "refusing to consider correction of your errors even when you recognize them, adopting a liberal attitude toward yourself." [45] Liberalism becomes equated with laxity, softness, and self-indulgence. Here, the traditional Chinese considerations for "human feelings"—that special tolerance for individual frailty which gave balance to an otherwise rigid Confucian system—is under fire; and so is the modern liberal ethic which also urges respect for individual differences.

"Sentimentalism" has essentially the same significance as the personal side of "liberalism," and refers mainly to a reluctance to sacrifice personal loyalties, and especially those of family, to political (Communist) considerations. This is primarily an attack upon traditional practices, although a modern liberal can also be guilty of sentimentalism in connection with his concern for other people as individuals. A deep reluctance to sever his personal ties was often more than offset by the Chinese intellectual's rebellion from these ties, as well as by his conviction that sentimentalism and nepotism had long been barriers to Chinese progress. He was, moreover, offered an identity alternative which was just the opposite of liberal and sentimental softness: that of a "straightforward, loyal, and positive" person who would, "no matter where or when, uphold correct principles and struggle untiringly against all incorrect thoughts and actions" [46]—in other words, he was to become definite rather than wishy-washy, active and "masculine" rather than passive and "feminine."

The methodical criticisms and self-criticisms of thought reform's second stage are thus aimed at breaking down every emotional identification which could interfere with the full acceptance of the new Communist identity. Authorities from outside the Communist camp are devalued (as, for instance, the university professors who were publicly humiliated) until they too fall into step with the Communist program. Nothing in one's heritage is to remain worthy of respect unless it contributes to the "new man" being shaped.

The final stage (submission and rebirth) completes the four identity tasks. In this stage the intellectual symbolically acts out his "turning over," and at the same time commits himself to it by his written analytic statement.

The denunciation of one's father is the symbolic act par excellence. Through it the intellectual is to cast off his tie to filialism entirely; after this let no man regard him as a traditional filial son. The act also severs him from his more recent past, and allows him to disown the identities derived from the transitional period. It has this last effect because in China the father has always been especially representative of a man's past, and because the fathers of contemporary intellectuals were very apt to have been associated with Nationalist, liberal, or other transitional Western influences (as they were for three of my four Chinese subjects). Indeed, the most celebrated denunciations of fathers were cases in which the fathers had distinguished themselves mostly in connection with Western learning: Lu Chih-wei, the former president of Yenching University, whose humiliation by his daughter was described by Grace Wu, was an American-trained psychologist; Liang Chi-ch'iao, who was posthumously condemned by his son, himself a university professor, was one of the great early reformers; and a widely-publicized attack was made upon Hu Shih (in absentia) by his son. The latter called his father a "public enemy of the people, and an enemy of myself" and went on to state the identity issue in very clear terms: "I feel it is important to draw a line of demarcation between my father and myself." [47] The "line of demarcation" is between father and son, old regime and new, family and Party, past and future.

The final thought reform summary, with its detailed class analysis, codifies and conceptualizes the identity shift, and puts it on permanent record. The class analysis is based on Communist psychological theory, the crux of which is that "in a class society, man's class character forms the very nature and substance of man . . .

the class character of man is determined by his class status." [48] The thought reform participant can draw upon this concept for a correlation of class and character: those from "exploiting classes" are extravagant, competitive, cruel, abusive; those of proletarian origin seek solidarity, mutual co-operation, have a "sense of organization and discipline," and are also characterized by "progressive outlook and demand of public ownership of property," revolt against all exploiters, militancy, tenacity, and so on—in other words, the ideals of the Communist Party as an organic representative of the working classes. Intellectuals, since they have bourgeois and petty bourgeois backgrounds, must inevitably reflect the characteristics of these classes: idealism, greed, objectivism, individualism, and stress on personal honor and status. In this sense, all of thought reform is an attempt to emulate Mao Tse-tung's own example and "outgrow" one's class characteristics by changing from one class to another. If an intellectual cannot achieve this ideal of becoming "one with the masses of workers and peasants" [49] he can at least do the next best thing and "accept the direction of the ideology of the working class"—in other words, of Marxism-Leninism and "the thought of Mao Tse-tung." [50] These views on class character, derived from earlier Communist writings, have limitations as psychological theory, but they do serve as a framework for the content of the final thought summary or personal confession. They supply the necessary theoretical basis for commitment.

The third stage ends on a note of togetherness very similar to the one with which the program begins. The pattern of thought reform thus follows the classic Marxist sequence of harmony, struggle, harmony; in psychological terms—group identification, isolation and conflict, and reintegration. At every moment of thought reform, the intellectual has revised, rejected, and modified elements of his past in order to dislodge himself from what he was, and become someone else.

As painful as it is, thought reform would never have a lasting effect if it did not offer a new and appealing sense of identity as its reward. I have so far mentioned only a few of the character traits which thought reform attempts to instill. In general, the reformed identity is based upon principles originally applied to Communist party members, the élite of the Communist movement. This identity is therefore not an exact blueprint, but rather an ideal which neither the dedicated Communist nor the ordinary intellectual can hope to realize fully. But like the identity ideal of the filial son, it is one against which everything else must be weighed.

Partly for this reason I have called the thought reform identity the "filial Communist"—but not for this reason alone. For in becoming a filial Communist, the Chinese intellectual becomes part of a new mystique, also vast in its scope and stringent in its demands, one which, like the old Chinese family system, envelops almost his entire life space. The filial Communist draws upon traditional sources for its all-important ethic of loyalty, and taps the values of the transitional period for its stress upon progress, science, and change. It is thus a culmination of the historical Chinese identity shifts we have been discussing.

What is the "new man" of thought reform to be like? Many of his characteristics were described by Liu Shao-chi in the famous pamphlet, "How to be a Good Communist." Liu's criteria, those from other Communist writings, and the attitudes expressed by my subjects allow us to summarize the personal qualities of the ideal filial Communist as follows: he is active, energetic, decisive, unambivalent, forceful, masculine, unwavering in his thoughts and actions; he is logical, scientific, materialistic, and disdainful of mysticism, of notions of spiritual values, and of philosophical idealism; he is realistic, down to earth, simple in his tastes, deeply respectful toward labor and toward the masses, critical of artistic and intellectual efforts that are not of practical value; he is selfless and totally dedicated, subordinating his own interests to those of the Party and the People in every conceivable manner, ready to make any sacrifices, including that of his life, and to be, in so doing, the happiest of men; he is humble, self-critical, receptive to criticism from others, eager to improve himself in order to be able to do still more for his cause; he is always enthusiastic, confident, high-spirited, totally sincere in his manner and in his beliefs, well-integrated within himself and in harmony with his society; he is modern, progressive, forward-looking, disdainful of traditional cultures and of requirements dictated by past custom; he is conscious of his relationship to a great international movement, of his role in liberating human beings from their bondage, and of having participated in "the remoulding of the substance of mankind"; yet he is proudly Chinese, intensely patriotic, nationalistic, aware of being part of an old and great civilization, of a nation far exceeding any other in population and in potential power.

While no such man could possibly exist, the identity ideal is impressive in its excess of both crassness and nobility. It contains in its totalism the psychological potential for wide-ranging accomplishment as well as for bitter disillusionment. No more radical change in Chinese character has ever been called for.

Do these identity shifts mean that filial piety, in the original family sense, no longer has any emotional appeal for Chinese intellectuals? We can draw no such conclusion. The history of other mass movements teaches us that attacks upon family ties are most characteristic of early phases. We can expect in China, as happened in Russia, a revival of support for the family—that is, for a form of "new Communist family," regarded as an extension of rather than a threat to the regime. It is doubtful whether anything approaching the old ideology of filialism can ever reappear in China, but its central principle of obedience and loyalty of children to their parents is too basic an emotional phenomenon, and one too deeply rooted in Chinese life, to be long negated. Not only does the new Communist man bear the stamp of his filial past; his creators—perhaps more than they realize—are influenced by that same cultural heritage.

CHAPTER 20

CULTURAL PERSPECTIVES: ORIGINS

Where did the Chinese Communists learn their reform skills? How did they get to be such master psychologists?

These are questions I have frequently been asked, and as often as not the questioner has in mind a theory of his own: the Chinese have studied Freud on individual psychology, or Kurt Lewin on group dynamics, or Pavlov on conditioned reflexes. The first two of these theories (Freud and Lewin) are products of a cultural and professional ethnocentrism among Western psychiatrists and social scientists; actually, neither Freud nor Lewin has had much influence in China or Russia. The Pavlovian theory is more generally held. It is based on a chain of associations that goes something like this: Pavlov—Russian scientist—supported by Soviet regime—Soviets use his theory of conditioned reflex for propaganda purposes—they taught his techniques to the Chinese—result, thought reform. But there is no convincing evidence that thought reform developed this way. It is true that academic psychology in Communist China does follow the Soviet lead in emphasizing Pavlovian theory, but academic psychologists apparently have had nothing to do with thought reform. And even in the Soviet Union, according to an American authority, there has been nothing to indicate that psychiatrists or psychologists have shaped confession or indoctrination techniques, or even that Pavlovian theory has been an important model for propaganda approaches.[1] In all three of these theories there is the twentieth-century tendency to single out the scientific specialist both as the fountain of all knowledge and the perpetrator of all evil. Moreover, all of them neglect the two great historical forces which shaped thought reform: Chinese culture and Russian Communism.

The Russian Communist contribution to thought reform is immediately apparent in much of the content and many of the forms of the process: the allegedly scientific Marxist-Leninist doctrine; the stress upon criticism, self-criticism, and confession as features of "ideological struggle"; the organizational techniques of "democratic centralism"; the combination of utopian imagery and iron discipline; the demands for purity of belief and absolute obedience; and the practice of informing upon others in the service of the Party. Certainly, many of the pressures used to extract confessions in penal thought reform closely resemble techniques used by the Russians during the great Soviet purge trials of the late 1930's: the irresistible demand for an admission of criminal guilt, however distorted or false, and the prolonged interrogations, physical pressures, and incriminating suggestions used to obtain it.[2] Eastern European Communist nations have employed similar confession methods, for instance, in the widely publicized cases of Cardinal Mindszenty, William Oatis, and Robert Vogeler.

Russian Communist influences are also responsible for thought reform's immense stress upon sin and evil, and for its continual manipulation of feelings of guilt within all who take part in the program. Such a focus upon sin and guilt has never been prominent in traditional Chinese culture. These Soviet Russian contributions are in turn derived from the many cultural influences which fed modern Communism: the Judeo-Christian religious tradition, the utopian secular ideologies of the eighteenth century, mystical elements of German romanticism, and the authoritarian excesses of traditional Russian and Byzantine culture, including the heritage of the Russian Orthodox church.

But after acknowledging these Russian and Western debts, we must still ask why it was the Chinese who developed thought reform. Other Communist countries have, to be sure, used elaborate propaganda techniques and various psychological pressures, but never with thought reform's meticulous organization, its depth of psychological probing, or its national scale. Nowhere else has there been such a mass output of energy directed toward changing people. In Russia confessions have generally been associated with the purge —the "ritual of liquidation"; in China, confession has been the vehicle for individual re-education. What is the source of this special *reform* emphasis?

Communist leaders reveal the source in some of their thought reform writings. Liu Shao-chi, for instance, in "How to be a Good Communist" enjoins Party neophytes to pursue diligently their "self-cultivation." And he quotes as an example the experience and the words of none other than Confucius himself:

At fifteen, I had my mind bent on learning. At thirty, I stood firm. At forty, I had no doubts. At fifty, I knew the decree of Heaven. At sixty, my ear was an obedient organ for the reception of truth. At seventy, I could follow my heart's desire, without transgressing what was right.

Liu also makes reference to the Confucian disciple who said: "I reflect on myself three times a day," and to the Book of Odes which suggests that one cultivate oneself "as a lapidary cuts and files, carves and polishes." He refers to the Confucian principles expressed in the following quotation from *The Great Learning*:

The ancients who wished to illustrate illustrious virtue throughout the kingdom first ordered well their own states. Wishing to order well their own states, they first regulated their families. Wishing to regulate their families, they first cultivated their persons. Wishing to cultivate their persons, they first rectified their hearts. Wishing to rectify their hearts, they first sought to be sincere in their thoughts. Wishing to be sincere in their thoughts, they first extended to the utmost, their knowledge. . . . from the Son of Heaven down to the mass of the people, all must consider the cultivation of the person the root of everything besides.[3]

These principles echo in the thought reform program, although Liu does of course emphasize the Communists' needs to stress materialism rather than classical "idealism," and to achieve their self-cultivation not through passive meditation but rather by means of active participation in the Communist movement.

Yet the concept of self-cultivation is distinctly Confucian, as is Liu's injunction to Communist cadres that each "watch himself when alone." Liu and other Communist theorists may refer to these traditional principles in order to introduce the alien words of Marx, Lenin, and Stalin in a familiar idiom; but this Confucian idiom does have deep emotional meaning even for anti-Confucian reformers, and it is this lingering Confucian spirit which has caused the Chinese Communists to make an ideological fetish of moralistic personal re-education.

Similarly, the Confucian principle of "rectification of names" (which according to the Sage was the first and most important task for a new ruler) has important bearing upon thought reform's approach to the reshaping of identity. In both cases, "rectification" means changing not the "name" or category of man, but rather changing the man himself until he fits that category—the Confucian or Communist ideology, of course, being the arbiter of proper standards. This principle is expressed in Confucius' demand, "let the ruler be ruler, the minister be minister; let the father be father and the son, son," and in the Communist demand that the intellectual be the "progressive" or "proletarian" intellectual or the "good Communist." For Confucianism shares with Communism the assumption that men can and should remake themselves, first as part of a process of changing their environment, and then as a means of adapting themselves to their environment. Both systems always involve a subtle interplay between role and identity: one first learns the more or less formal requirements for thought and behavior, and only much later becomes in his essence the thing aspired to. This is called achieving complete "sincerity."

And in Confucianism, just as in thought reform, the ideal of sincerity is made almost sacred:

Sincerity is the way of heaven. The attainment of sincerity is the way of men. He who possesses sincerity is he who, without an effort, hits what is right, and apprehends without the exercise of thought;—he is the sage who naturally embodies the *right* way. He who attains to sincerity is he who chooses what is good and firmly holds it fast.[4]

This Confucian (and later neo-Confucian) notion of sincerity depends very much upon the principle of harmony: harmony within, permitting one to act correctly in an automatic fashion, and harmony without, enabling one to find his proper behavior in relationship to other men. To be sincere, in traditional China, meant to possess an inner urge toward fulfilling one's obligations, including both the desire and the means for conforming to the filial ideology. Only the sincere man could give full expression to his nature, possess genuine self-knowledge, exert a beneficial influence upon others, and achieve a complete union (both organic and mystical) with Heaven and Earth. Thought reform is a way to achieve such sincerity in relationship to Communist doctrine. As in Confucianism, it is finding the correct path; as in neo-Confucianism it is combining knowledge and action. And the man who is truly sincere, like his Confucian and neo-Confucian counterparts, is said to possess superhuman powers.[5]

These traditional Chinese themes could be expressed in thought reform only because they were also consistent with Marxist-Leninist principles. And this double fit has enabled the Chinese Communists to pursue them so energetically. Marxist-Leninist writings, for instance, are replete with references to personal reform; a similar Chinese cultural tradition has enabled Chinese Communists to be good Marxists. Communist practice in any country requires role-playing and identity change; but the Chinese bring to this a more concrete and explicit—not to say diligent—emphasis. In the matter of sincerity, Leninists too stress uniting theory and practice; but it is thought reform's combination of Marxist-Leninist (including Christian and Russian) with Confucian influences that has produced the bizarre extremes described in this book: for when the Eastern notion of The Way was combined with the Western ideal of credal purity, sincerity came to mean nothing short of absolute submission.

It is impossible to document all the ways in which traditional Chinese and Russian Communist styles come together in thought reform, but a few of the more important convergences are worth listing. We have already noted the great sweep of both Confucianism and Communism; both cover all aspects of human existence in their stress upon loyalty and orthodoxy. In addition, both have a tradition of benevolent leadership by a small élite, within a strongly authoritarian framework. They also share an emphasis upon the responsibility of the individual person to the larger human group, upon his impotence when he stands alone, and upon the dangers of deviant individual initiative. In both there is the conviction that human nature is essentially good, although the extent to which both seek to control human behavior makes one wonder whether their advocates really believe this. The Russian Communist reliance upon emotionally charged slogans has an analogue in the traditional Chinese style of thinking in wholes rather than in parts, of using proverbs and metaphor to envelop a subject emotionally as well as intellectually.[6] There is some similarity (along with a good deal of difference) between the Soviet Communist dualism of the dialectic and the traditional Chinese dualism of *Yin* and *Yang*.[7] The traditional blood brotherhood of Chinese rebel bands and secret societies resembles Communism's sense of cloak-and-dagger intimacy and moral mission. The Soviet Communist stress upon personal confession (the main source of this ethic for thought reform) had some relationship to the traditional Chinese practice of requiring local officials to accept blame for such things as natural catastrophes and to "confess" that their own unworthiness may have been responsible. And in the prison setting, Russian Communist pressures to confess (themselves apparently derived from practices of the Tsarist *Okhrána*) come together with a traditional Chinese custom of requiring a prisoner to confess his crime before being judged, while granting the judge considerable latitude in the methods he could employ to extract this confession.[8]

How did this blending of cultural styles occur? The extensive thought reform program which the Communists had ready at the moment of the takeover was obviously the product of years of preparation. I was fortunate in being able to discuss this question in some detail with Mr. Chang Kuo-t'ao, one of the leading figures of the early Chinese Communist movement until his defection in 1938. According to Mr. Chang, the Communists began to employ systematic, if crude, reform techniques as early as the late 1920's. Communist leaders commanding small and relatively isolated military units began to devote much attention to the problem of winning over captured enemy soldiers and groups among the general population. Their task was complicated by the differences among their prospective converts: peasants, opium-smoking bandits, disgruntled conscripts in the Kuomintang armies, old-time Kuomintang supporters, uninvolved bystanders, and idealistic intellectuals. They first utilized international Communist principles, learned from Soviet contacts, dealing with "agitation and propaganda." But very soon they began to modify these and develop their own programs derived from their special Chinese environment.

They approached uneducated peasants on a simple colloquial level. Ordinary enemy soldiers were first treated with unexpected "leniency"; then they were encouraged to vent all of their grievances against such past authorities as landlords and officers (to "vomit bitter water"); next they were taught to recognize the social evils of the Kuomintang regime as the source of their suffering ("dig the bitter roots"). The soldier was then offered an opportunity to remain with the Communists—to join the "one heart movement" to combat Chiang Kai-shek and create a new China; or he was given the option of returning to his home village as a person ostensibly sympathetic to the Communist cause. As in later programs, participants quickly became themselves active reformers: peasant soldier captives showing signs of "progress" were encouraged to circulate among new arrivals with similar class backgrounds, and help in the latter's "vomiting" and "root digging" by recounting their own happy reform experiences.

With captured officers the Communists employed more sophisticated and individualized approaches. After separating the officer from his men, they would assign to him some of their most articulate and persuasive spokesmen, and then subject him to prolonged analytic discussions of his personal relationship to the Chinese Civil War. Struggle procedures were used upon the most recalcitrant, and those known to be responsible for the death of large numbers of Communists were often executed; but there was an attempt to win converts whenever possible.

Chang emphasized that, with both officers and men, the Communists were consciously aware of the importance of setting an impressive personal example in their own dedication, discipline, and personal morality. After their first more or less experimental military efforts, the Communists proceeded in twenty years of trial-and-error improvement to make their program increasingly efficient. They extended the reform efforts to Japanese prisoners captured during the thirties and later to American prisoners captured during the Korean war. But their main efforts were concentrated upon their own countrymen during the phases of the long Chinese Civil War, so that by the time of the takeover, they had learned how to apply them quickly and effectively to entire armies of prisoners.

The reform program specifically for intellectuals, as opposed to that for military captives, was developed by Communist groups operating in the outlying border areas during the Yenan period (1935–45). In order to absorb the large numbers of intellectuals, sympathetic but inexperienced (at least in the ways of revolution), who made their way to these Communist areas, a number of special training centers were set up. Those in the Yenan area of northwest China—the Anti-Japanese University, North Shensi Academy, and Marx Lenin Institute (later renamed Lu Hsun Academy)—gave rise to the thought reform programs for intellectuals we have been studying.

Here, as elsewhere, the Communists started with a prescribed Russian Communist model: the Yenan institutions were set up as replicas of Sun Yat-sen University in Moscow, an early training center for Chinese Communist intellectuals. This model was then adapted to their own revolutionary style. The Communists improvised as they went along, hardly following a precise scientific "methodology." Indeed, Mr. Chang felt that an important factor in the introspective *hsüeh hsi*, or group study process, was the isolation of many of these early institutions, and the lack of qualified teachers and textbooks, so that much of the subject matter studied had to come from the participants. This comment, while far from a full explanation, does make clear how important the external circumstances were under which the Chinese Communist revolutionary movement synthesized Chinese and Russian Communist themes. Nor were Chinese improvisations always approved by Russian advisors: Chang mentioned that on several occasions Chinese Communist leaders were criticized for being "too much influenced by Confucian ethics." Yet this moral and psychological emphasis seemed to come naturally to them; according to Chang, they were "good psychiatrists." And although the Nationalists made similar efforts to "reform" Communists and Communist sympathizers in special "repentance camps," their efforts were (according to Chang and many other observers) much more clumsy and much less effective.

Perhaps the crucial step in the development of the Communist reform program for intellectuals was the *Cheng Feng* (literally, reform of work style or "spirit") conducted within the Communist Party, mostly in Yenan, from 1942 to 1944. (Mr. Chang was no longer with the Communists then; my information here is based on written studies and on the impressions of my subjects.) During this campaign, the basic techniques, as well as the widely-circulated *Reform Documents* from which I have been quoting, were evolved.

At the time of the *Cheng Feng*, the Party faced the problem of the threat of unorthodoxy among its heterogeneous recruits, and especially among its intellectuals; it was also confronted with the task of Sinifying a Marxist movement whose ideology had heretofore been entirely foreign, and it had to invigorate intraparty morale.[9] It is of the greatest significance that the Chinese Communists solved these problems through personal confession and re-education, that these forms of introspection were used to produce within each Party member the desired blend of Leninism and Chineseness, along with a sense of personal revitalization. From this movement the Chinese Communists' own ideology (mostly in the form of "the thought of Mao Tse-tung") emerged; the importance of this ideology lay not in any brilliant originality, but more in its organizational and psychological usefulness, and in the renewed sense of group identity to which both the campaign and its ideology contributed. After the *Cheng Feng*, the die was cast; just a year later, "the documents of the movement had become Party dogma, and the reform process had become a continuing organizational mechanism." [10] Even such a brief outline of the history of thought reform confirms what I have already suggested— that the reformers evolved their psychological skills by combining elements from their cultural heritage and their own revolutionary needs with principles of Russian Communist theory and practice.

One other important factor in the Chinese heritage also played a part in the evolution of reform techniques: human-centered psychological skills. No other civilization has paid so much attention to the conduct of human relationships. An American anthropologist has claimed that "Chinese culture has developed inter-personal relationships to the level of an exquisite and superb art." [11] It is not that Chinese are incapable of obtuseness and insensitivity; but a particular kind of psychological mindedness has long been cultivated in Chinese life. The Chinese family, with its characteristically complicated inner maneuvering, has been an excellent psychological training ground: in order to be "proper," Chinese children have had to learn to be aware of the emotional currents in their milieu. And this personal emphasis has extended from the family into the rest of Chinese life: whether performing official duties or seeking personal objectives, Chinese have always put great stress on exerting influence upon the people involved—and there is only a fine line between influence and manipulation. These human-centered skills have been carefully nurtured over centuries, and emphasized at the expense of technical achievements (even the gods play psychological games).[12] In this sense, thought reform is the modern totalitarian expression of a national genius.

But the spirit in which these human-centered skills are used in thought reform is certainly alien to the traditional Chinese cultural style. In the past, the stress was upon individual and social harmony; the ideal was that of quiet wisdom and unbroken calm. The *chuntze*, or superior Confucian man, was expected to be contemplative and reserved in his bearing: "the master was mild yet dignified; majestic and yet not fierce; respectful and yet easy." [13] Above all, he was to be in full control of his emotions: "if a man be under the influence of passion, he will be incorrect in his conduct." [14] For the withdrawn Taoist sage, restraint was equally essential: "So long as I love calm, the people will be right themselves." [15] Such a cultural stress upon moderation, balance, and harmony—which we may call a *cult of restraint*—insures a certain degree of preservation of self.

Thought reform has the opposite ethos, a *cult of enthusiasm* (*enthusiasm* in the religious meaning of rapturous and excessive emotional experience),[16] with a demand for total self-surrender. It is true that thought reform implies a promise of a return to restraint, and of an attainment of relaxed perfection some time in the mystical Communist future, just as Confucius claimed that these ideals had existed during an equally mystical past or "golden age"— but enthusiasm and restraint, once established, are not always so easily controlled.

The spirit of enthusiasm seems to have entered China from the outside, carried in on the ideological wings of Western nationalism, international Communism, and displaced Judeo-Christian demands for ecstatic repentance and histrionic remorse. Yet the intellectual descendants of the staid literati have shown themselves to be quite capable of orgiastic display—in fact, more capable of it than their counterparts in Western Communist countries who have a much greater tradition for this type of emotional excess. Apparently any culture, or any person within a culture, is potentially capable of either restraint or enthusiasm, depending upon individual and collective historical experience. Those cultures in which restraint has been long maintained (again we may use the analogy of the individual) are likely to experience an explosive emotional breakthrough once the restraint begins to loosen; and the new enthusiasm becomes the means of putting to rout what remains of the older pattern.

Just as thought reform draws upon psychological skills of both traditional China and Western Communism, it also brings out the inquisitional tendencies of both worlds. From each of the two great cultural streams, it stresses what is most illiberal. Inquisitorial dogmatism, skillful human-centered manipulation, and ecstatic enthusiasm combine within it to produce an awesome quality. Consequently, relatively moderate Russian and Eastern European Communists look warily at China's totalism (and Stalinism); and people like Bishop Barker (something of an enthusiast himself) envy the energies and the psychological cleverness of a respected rival. For in breaking out of its traditional cult of restraint, while retaining its old penchant for the reordering of human emotions, China has created a cult of enthusiasm of such proportions that it must startle even the most immoderate Christian or Communist visionary.

CHAPTER 21

CULTURAL PERSPECTIVES: IMPACT

How have the majority of Chinese intellectuals responded to the cult of enthusiasm? Has thought reform really been successful with them? What has been its immediate and long-range impact upon them? These questions demanded a follow-up evaluation of the continuing thought reform program.

The evaluation had to be made cautiously, since most Chinese intellectuals remain within China, quite inaccessible to me. Yet I believe I have enough evidence to make a few generalizations —evidence derived from my original research, from Chinese Communist press reports of the next few years, and from my follow-up visit to Hong Kong during the summer of 1958.

Most of my Chinese subjects had participated in the first great national wave of thought reform which took place from 1948 to 1952. These were the years of maximum activity in the revolutionary universities (afterward, many of them were converted into more conventional Marxist-Leninist training centers), of sweeping reforms in regular universities, and of the histrionic early campaigns —"The Suppression of Counterrevolutionaries," the *hsüeh hsi* program, the "Three-Anti" and "Five-Anti" movements, the ideological struggles of "culture workers" (everyone concerned with the arts) centering around the motion picture *The Life of Wu Hsun*, and the Thought Reform Campaign itself. My subjects' accounts of these campaigns always included a description of others' responses along with their own. I also made a point of asking each of them to estimate the general effects of thought reform within his immediate environment.

The estimates I got were remarkably consistent, and were also confirmed by other Chinese and Westerners who had been in China at the time. I was led to the conclusion that thought reform, at least during its early phase, had been much more successful with Chinese than with Westerners—largely because of the immense appeal of nationalism, the reinforcement of thought reform by the Chinese Communist environment, the sense of belonging to a group within one's own society, as well as many of the other historical and cultural influences already mentioned. Yet it was possible to identify in the Chinese intellectuals three kinds of response roughly analogous to (although by no means the same as) those I have described in Westerners.

Chinese *zealous converts* underwent a profound religious experience. They regarded thought reform as fine and ennobling and felt genuinely reborn, along with their society. The zealous convert was usually youthful, either an adolescent or a young adult. Although he may not have been completely free of inner doubt even after his thought reform, his conversion was generally much more profound than that of the apparent converts among the Westerners. (This was, after all, *his* world, and in it his future seemed unlimited.) None of my subjects fit exactly into this category; of them, George Chen's early responses came closest. Perhaps better examples of zealous converts were the middle-school and university students around him whom he described as being completely immersed in the general enthusiasm. It was probably true that a sizable number, perhaps even a majority, of Chinese between the ages of fifteen and twenty-two were at that time zealous converts. The incidence of conversion apparently decreased in direct proportion to age, and most of my informants expressed the opinion that thirty was an important dividing line. Zealous converts were probably rare in the upper age groups, and they seemed to be a distinct minority among Chinese intellectuals as a whole.

At the other extreme were the *resisters*, those who felt suffocated by the program and considered it bad and coercive. As with some of my subjects (Mr. Hu and Grace Wu for instance), they were apt to have been a good deal more sympathetic to Communism before their reform than after. But the resister who stayed in China could not, at least during this early period, reveal himself; clear-cut acts of resistance were virtually confined to the few who fled. And the responses of those who did leave China led me to conclude that the program had been massive enough to make even the resister question his own attitude and feel guilty for being against the majority —perhaps even more guilty than the Western apparent resister felt. It is probable that the resisters were most frequently older intellectuals, especially those who in the past had been significantly exposed to the West. But resisters too seemed to constitute a minority among Chinese intellectuals.

The most usual response lay between these two extremes, and most Chinese intellectuals may be called *adapters*. An adapter was partially but not entirely convinced by the program; essentially he was concerned with the problems of coping with a stressful experience and finding a place in the new society. His feelings about thought reform may have been similarly complicated; he may have experienced it as painful, perhaps even coercive, but at the same time possibly beneficial—like medicine which may do some good just because it tastes so bad. The adapter, while by no means unaffected by ideology, was likely to be (as was Robert Chao) less affected by it than either a convert or a resister. Of course, both convert and resister also did some adapting. The adapter underwent his share of confusion and identity crisis, but not to the extreme degree of the obviously confused among Westerners; for he was not (except in rare cases) forced to make a sudden transition from one world to another. He often tried to dispel his doubts by behaving like a zealous convert, and in doing so, may have resembled a Western apparent convert immediately after his reform experience. In a historical sense, the adapter was following a long-established pattern of Chinese intellectuals: accepting the change in dynasty as part of the order of things, placing his talents at the disposal of the new rulers, and seeing in the reign both good and evil, but not enough good to win his absolute enthusiasm nor enough evil to provoke his unqualified opposition.

Apart from these response categories, I gained the impression that this first wave of thought reform had served the over-all function of setting the standards for intellectual and emotional existence under Communism. Not only was The Way pointed out, but it was, to a large extent, internally imposed.[1] Early enthusiasm for Communism and residual bitterness toward the old regime made this the period of thought reform's greatest opportunity—an opportunity furthered by the patriotic sentiments aroused by the Korean war, and by the special campaign appeals ("Resist America, Aid Korea," "Enlist For The Army," and even the hygiene enthusiasms) which went along with it. But we cannot judge the effects of this initial phase of thought reform without examining the events which followed.

After two years of relative ideological calm, Chinese intellectuals were swept up into the second great wave of thought reform campaigns. During 1954 and 1955, organized emotional frenzy was renewed—first over the lingering "poisons" related to the liberalism of Hu Shih; then over the proper critical approach to the novel, *The Dream of the Red Chamber;* and then over the "criminal acts" of the independently-minded left-wing writer and former disciple of Lu Hsun, Hu Feng. Each of these campaigns served to stimulate new displays of confession and repentance, and each outdid its predecessor in thought reform efforts; the vituperative intensity and the scope of this second wave of thought reform were, if anything, even greater than those of the first.

Yet when the frenzy of this push-button enthusiasm had abated, the Party leaders indicated that there was still much more to be accomplished, and in late 1955 and early 1956 convened a series of conferences on "the question of intellectuals." At one of these, Chou En-lai expressed the belief that great progress had been made, and quoted from surveys: "According to statistical data on 141 teachers in four higher institutes of Peking, Tientsin and Tsingtao, for example, in the past six years the progressive elements have increased from 18 per cent to 41 per cent, while the backward elements were reduced from 28 per cent to 15 per cent." [2] He summed up his statistics as follows: 40 per cent were "progressive elements" actively supporting the regime; 40 per cent were "middle-of-the-road elements" who supported the regime but were "not sufficiently progressive"; a little over 10 per cent were "backward elements" who "lack political consciousness or ideologically oppose socialism"; and "only a few per cent"—presumably the rest—were "counter-revolutionaries and other bad elements." Chou of course concluded that intellectuals require "continued ideological reform," but his tone was conciliatory, and he proposed a series of improvements (soon put into effect) in general working and living conditions relating to such things as housing, salary, equipment, and availability of needed reference materials. He proposed that five-sixths of intellectuals' working time, or forty hours a week, be made available for their professional activities; the remaining time was to be used for "political study, attending necessary meetings, and taking part in social activity." This soft approach contrasted sharply with the vindictive excesses of the recently-completed Hu Fung campaign, and it inaugurated the third and perhaps most remarkable of all thought reform phases—the period of the "Hundred Flowers."

That the Communists should adopt as a slogan the phrase, "Let the hundred flowers bloom, let the hundred schools of thought contend" (a classical allusion to the hundred schools of philosophy which flourished during the Chou Dynasty before Confucianism became the official ideology) was ironic enough, but no less ironic than the events which followed. Mao Tse-tung is said to have first suggested the expression in an unpublished address before a Party conference in May, 1956; and it was first publicly stated a few weeks later by the director of propaganda of the Party's Central Committee. Thought reform was to continue, but thought reform of a new kind: there was to be "freedom of independent thinking, freedom of debate, freedom of creative work, freedom to criticize, to express one's own views." [3]

Intellectuals were understandably slow to respond to the invitation until it was again extended by Mao himself almost a year later in his widely publicized speech, "On the Correct Handling of Contradictions among the People," and still again in another speech a few weeks later. The invitation was then formalized into a national campaign for the "Rectification of Party Members," and the strange spectacle was seen of all the usual organizational paraphernalia—newspaper editorials, radio and loud-speaker broadcasts, and word of mouth evangelizing—being directed at provoking criticism (constructive, of course) of Communist Party members. The idea behind the campaign was apparently a tentative policy of liberalization, a controlled opportunity for non-Party intellectuals to vent their grievances and thereby improve their working relationship with the Party. In converting the invitation to a command performance, Communist leaders may have been influenced by an uneasiness they sensed in the intellectuals, about events elsewhere in the Communist world (the Hungarian uprising and the publication of Khrushchev's speech on Stalin), and about economic difficulties within China.

In any case, it was all meant to be a friendly version of thought reform. Everyone was to speak out freely and air the "contradictions" between the leaders and the led. There were to be no mass meetings or "struggles," only small discussion groups and "comradely heart to heart talks"; the campaign was to be carried out, according to its directive, "as gently as a breeze or a mild rain."

But when the intellectuals finally spoke out, the "mild rain" quickly assumed hurricane proportions. Far from limiting themselves to polite suggestions, they bitterly criticised every phase of Communist rule, including Party infallibility, the benevolence of the Peking regime, and the integrity of Mao Tse-tung himself. One group of intellectuals (sometimes sounding like the Yugoslav Communist, Milovan Djilas) centered their fire upon the Party's abuse of power and privileges: a newspaper editor complained that the Party was highhanded ("I think a Party leading the nation is not the same as a Party owning the nation"); other critics equated Communist leadership with traditional despotism ("Local emperors," "Party dynasty," "empire of the Party"), and urged high Communist officials to "alight from their sedan-chairs"; still others condemned the priority given to Party members in such matters as promotion, living subsidies, medical care, school facilities for children, and opportunities to travel abroad.

Many intellectuals said that their initial enthusiasm for Communism had given way to disillusionment. A lecturer in science warned the regime that things had gotten so bad that unless it gave up its "arrogant and conceited" attitudes, "the masses will bring you down, kill the Communists, and overthrow you."

One university professor, after an articulate statement on the limitations of Marxism-Leninism ("no doctrine can embody the whole truth"), had the audacity to suggest that it be dispensed with as an ideological guide. Others advocated the formation of genuine opposition parties, free elections, and other elements of parliamentary democracy. The absence of civil rights and legal safeguards was noted, and the regime's constitution was denounced as a "scrap of paper not observed by the Party." Critics condemned Communist manipulation of information; and one journalist chided the country's newspapers for "playing the role of a notice board, a gramophone, and a pirated edition of a book"; another objected to the practice of reproducing editorials from the *People's Daily*—the spokesman of the Peking regime—in newspapers throughout China, pointing out that "the editorials of the *New York Times* are not reproduced by other American papers."

And perhaps most important, many of the critics struck out at thought reform itself. A Peking University professor minced no words: "I find the term *thought reform* rather repulsive. . . . I am not aware that there is anything wrong with my thought. . . . No style of thought is made up entirely of cream or scum." Many condemned the abuses of the national campaigns ("People who have gone through these movements will remember the terror and feel their flesh creep whenever they think of them") and demanded that the Party admit its mistakes in humiliating, imprisoning, and even putting to death many innocent people. One highranking government official referred to the repeated re-education programs as "disgusting," and felt that rather than winning over the intellectuals, they had done much to embitter them. Others found the programs "a total mistake" and "rotten to the core," claiming that thought reform "has made everybody live in insecurity," and using such terms as "assault on the person" and "blindfold of the mind."

Some of the most heated criticisms were made by Communist Party members. One compared the relationship between the leaders and the led (placing intellectuals in the latter category) to that between mistress and slave girl:

A slave girl is the dowry or appendage of her mistress. She has to win the favor and avoid the hate of her mistress. In her spiritual world there are only submission and flattery. She looks upon the swallowing of the saliva of her mistress as an honor. This is the true philosophy of the slave girl.

Another, in condemning Party orthodoxy, defended his own "rebellious character," and quoted Maxim Gorki's phrase, "Man comes into the world to rebel." Still another expressed the dilemma of a Party member asked to participate actively in the rectification campaign and at the same time observe Party discipline: "This amounts to sealing our mouth while expecting us to speak."

This critical outburst was permitted to last for about one month, during which time the Party leadership apparently experienced hesitancy and confusion. Although they had themselves set off the campaign, they seemed to be totally unprepared for its vehemence. At the beginning, Party organs praised its own critics for their participation in the "blooming and contending," and for having become "inflamed with enthusiasm." After that, there were a few expressions of concern about the tone of the criticisms, but still no clear policy was taken about them.

Finally, six weeks after the beginning of the rectification movement, a full-scale counterattack was launched. An editorial in the Peking *People's Daily*, appropriately entitled, "What is This For?", gave the signal for a reversal of the critical tide. It labeled the most outspoken critics "rightist elements," and accused them (accurately enough) of "challenging the political leadership of the Communist Party . . . and even openly clamoring for the Party's 'quitting the stage' . . . in the name of 'helping the Communist Party rectify its working style.' " In subsequent editorials (and presumably in instructions passed down through the Party's ranks), the order was given to oppose "incorrect criticisms" and "firmly develop correct countercriticisms." Soon it was the critics themselves (no longer simply "rightist elements" but "bourgeois rightists"), rather than Party members, who were being "rectified." These critics then became targets of the most extreme "ideological struggle" and the most abusive hostility, as the "blooming and contending" abruptly gave way to a new "Anti-Rightist Campaign." Many of them were accused of participating in the subversive "Chang-Lo alliance" (Chang and Lo, both leading members of "democratic" parties who had held rather high positions in the regime, had been among the most outspoken, and were cited as prominent bad examples).

The regime was particularly sensitive about the criticisms of thought reform. It countered these with the claim that the Hundred Flowers incident left no doubt that more, rather than less, thought reform was needed, and promised the intellectuals that they would in the future be given refresher courses of thought reform every year or even every six months. The results of the first of these refresher courses soon become apparent. True to form, each of the former critics in turn renounced his criticisms of the regime; each condemned the remaining bourgeois influences within himself, and many emphasized their having been influenced by the notorious "Chang-Lo alliance." Many Party members were expelled (not for being themselves "bourgeois rightists," but for having allegedly been influenced by them), critics were removed from office, some were arrested, and there were reports of suicides, and even of executions. The soft policy toward intellectuals was suddenly replaced by hard disdain: intellectuals were ridiculed, unfavorably compared (even in regard to intelligence) with "the masses," told that it was necessary to be first "Red" and then "expert," and in many cases were sent to rural areas to learn their lessons. The experiment with liberalization was over and the old variety of thought reform was back.

One particularly significant aspect of the Hundred Flowers outburst was the behavior of China's students. In 1958, I obtained firsthand descriptions of this behavior from two young men who had participated in the campaign the year before while attending universities in Peking. Their reports on the attitudes of university students—the age group which has been most responsive to thought reform—were extremely revealing.

Both were in their early twenties; in 1957 Wang had been a junior at Tsing Hua, and Li a senior at Peking University. Each had gone through thought reform at middle school; both had then shared in the general sense of exhilaration and had accepted the Communist point of view fully, though Li felt that because he was a Christian, he might have been a bit less enthusiastic than some of the others. Both described the strong impact upon the Chinese students of events in European Communist countries—Khrushchev's denunciation of Stalin, the Hungarian revolution, and unrest of Polish intellectuals—despite the limited and highly-slanted coverage of these events in the Chinese Communist press. Since many students had, according to Li, a "religious" belief in Communism's perfection, their disillusion was "like that of a person with a sincere belief in God who suddenly discovers there is no God." He said the Hungarian revolution was particularly important to them, and estimated that only about one-third of the students accepted without question the Party's official version that it was a reactionary uprising brought about by American imperialist activity. Reports of Russian intervention bothered the students, although most eventually rationalized this as "probably necessary to preserve socialism."

Li himself shared the general feeling of uneasiness and had an urge to "talk to the others about these things."

Wang stressed the effects of Khrushchev's revelations about Stalin. I asked him how he and the other students had learned about this, since the Chinese Communist regime, deeply identified as it was with Stalinism, had suppressed most of the details. Wang gave a surprising answer: someone had discovered the text of the speech in a copy of the New York *Daily Worker* in a library. The *Worker* was, of course, the only American newspaper available to students. This information was spread by word-of-mouth, and many students went to the library to read the speech. It was a shock to them to learn that the Russian system was "not democratic" and that the man held up to them as such a humane leader, whose writings they used in their courses, had put so many people to death.

Both Li and Wang emphasized, however, that almost 90 per cent of the students were members of the Communist Youth Corps, and that the students continued to identify themselves with the regime. Some consoled themselves with their faith that Chinese Communism was superior to European Communism. Although occasionally aware that individual freedom was curtailed, they did not experience a continuous sense of suppression, and were usually "too busy studying to think too much about it." But Li thought that in 1957 most students would have favored China's following Poland's example in granting additional self-expression, although few said so outright.

In any case, in the months just before the release of Hundred Flowers emotions both Li and Wang were aware of widespread "restlessness" and "frustration." The students, like their teachers, were slow to respond to the invitation to speak out. But when they did, they were second to none in the vigor of their criticisms, and much more prone than other groups to convert their sentiments into action. As usual, it was Peking University which led all the rest.

There the students set up a "Democratic Wall," a large bulletin board devoted to criticism and protest. The wall space near the bulletin board was devoted to the same purpose, and, true to the horticultural metaphor, was called "The Garden of Democracy." Students, individually or in groups, prepared sharp commentaries, satirical poems, cartoons, and slogans. And soon, as the Party press reported, "enthusiastic discussions and debates were developed near the walls, in the dormitories, in the passageways of the classrooms, or on the meadows by the side of the lake." The spontaneous debate was "like in Hyde Park," and "the atmosphere of free contention engulfed the whole university." Students brought up the same complaints as other critics. They also raised issues particularly important to them as a group. They complained of the Party's arbitrary control over their programs of study and of their later job assignments; they asked for free expression of student opinion; they praised the "courageous" actions of their fellow-students in Hungary and Poland. One of the most persistent themes, expressed both on the bulletin board and during debates, was, "We should find out what freedom and democracy mean."

At one point, a Party official tried to restrain the Peking University students, and told them that bulletin boards were "not a good medium" for the rectification campaign. But this attitude was bitterly denounced on the Democratic Wall, and soon afterward a higher official apologized to the students for the erroneous views of his subordinate. And according to Li, many Party members and Youth Corps leaders from among the students were in the vanguard of the protest activities.

Very quickly, Democratic Walls appeared at universities all over China (press reports and letters exchanged among students had publicized the original). Wang told me that Khrushchev's anti-Stalin speech was posted on Tsing Hua's Democratic Wall. In some other cities, the students acted with even greater vehemence, staging riots, beating up Party members, and destroying Party property. Prominent among the demonstrators were middle-school students. Once more there was student agitation in China, but this time the Communists were its targets rather than its beneficiaries.

Immediately after the "What is This For?" editorial, however, Party members and supporters were able to gain full control of university environments. The students abruptly ceased their protests, and the attack upon "rightists" in their ranks began. According to Li, students were not surprised when the government stepped in; but they did resent its rough treatment of those who had spoken out. Li said that many of the students who had previously been most vehement in their criticisms were now the loudest voices in the anti-rightist chorus, and compared their actions to the betrayal of Jesus by his own disciple.

The government made sure that the counterattack was launched from Peking University. A reorganized Peking University student association sent an open letter to student leaders in all of the other major universities, denouncing "rightist activities," and supporting the government's countermeasures. The Democratic Wall was retained; but the essays, poems, and cartoons on it now attacked the "rightists," and its new slogan—posted in large whitewashed characters—read: "Any word or act alienated from Socialism is completely erroneous."

Li estimated that about one-third of the students agreed fully with the government's intervention, feeling it necessary and just; the sentiments among the rest varied greatly—some were bitterly resentful, others of two minds, and still others blandly compliant. Many students, in explaining these difficult matters to themselves and to each other, resorted to traditional Chinese ideas about the rise and fall of great dynasties; they concluded that since Communism had been active in China for only about twenty-five years, it had "not yet used up its history," and one might as well continue to support it.

Li told me that he had decided to leave China because he feared that if he ever expressed his resentments about the regime, he might cause difficulty for himself and others. Chang gave similar reasons; during the Hundred Flowers campaign he had compared Stalin to Hitler, and spoken out strongly against Party control of the university, so that he felt that his position was already precarious. Nor were his apprehensions unfounded: the *People's Daily* had already announced that graduates of Peking University were to be subjected to a special "political examination" consisting of a detailed scrutiny of their attitudes and behavior during the "anti-rightist struggle." The results of this examination were to be kept as official records and used as a basis for job assignments: "We will never let anyone politically questionable assume duties that he should not assume." And during the wave of thought reform which followed, many students and recent graduates were sent to work in the countryside, many others placed under various forms of special surveillance, and a few were sent to prison for reform through labor.

I believe the Hundred Flowers episode has great significance for an evaluation of thought reform's effectiveness. One cannot draw statistical conclusions from an event so massively emotional; and there is no way of knowing what percentage of Chinese intellectuals shared the feelings of the regime's critics. Yet the sudden intensity of both the antiregime outburst and the "anti-rightist" counterattack illuminate the limitations as well as the accomplishments of the thought reform program.

Looking first at the program's limitations, the Hundred Flowers incident reveals the potential of a reform-saturated environment for a sudden reversal of sentiment, for the release of bitter emotions directed both at thought reform and at the regime which perpetuates it. Behind such a reversal lies the latent resentment which thought reform builds up in varying degrees within virtually all who are exposed to it. This resentment originates in a basic human aversion to excessive personal control, a phenomenon which I call the hostility of suffocation (discussed further in Part IV). Thought reform constantly provokes this hostility, first by stimulating it within individual participants, and then by creating conditions of group intensity which can magnify it to frenzy. In other words, thought reform is able to promote an emotional contagion—of resentment as well as enthusiasm. These emotions are closely related, and easily changed from one to the other. Individual feelings of hostility and resentment toward reform may exist consciously, or may be deeply repressed, but when encouraged by external conditions, they can emerge suddenly and unexpectedly.

One external condition which encourages their expression is the release of environmental controls. This in turn leads to the breakdown of the individual's defense mechanisms, particularly repression, which ordinarily keep resentment in check. Thus, liberalization of the milieu can create a quick surge of resentment, which mounts until it is again forced underground by the restoration of a suppressive atmosphere. This leads to more hostility of suffocation, and thought reform is then on a treadmill of extremism.

Another limitation in the effectiveness of thought reform is its dependency on the maintenance of a closed system of communication, on an idea-tight milieu control. If information from the outside which contradicts thought reform's message breaks through this milieu control, it can also be a stimulus for resentment. This was true of the news from Hungary, Russia, and Poland at the time of the Hundred Flowers. As the students' use of the New York

Daily Worker reveals, the increase in international communication makes strict milieu control difficult to maintain; and if information from outside includes evidence of brutality within the Communist system, the hostility of suffocation becomes combined with a sense of having been betrayed.

The break in milieu control need not come from so great a distance: life experiences within Communist China, outside of the immediate thought reform process, can also serve the same function. Thus, thought reform extolled the brilliance of the Communist Party's economic planning, but Chinese intellectuals, like everyone else, were suffering from shortages; thought reform preached austerity, but intellectuals saw a privileged class of Party members emerge. This kind of information is of course even more accessible to a thought reform participant than news from the outside world. All of which suggests that thought reform cannot be conducted in a vacuum; milieu control can never be complete. The one-sided visions of thought reform are always threatened by the world without, a world which will neither live up to these visions nor cease to undermine them.

The Hundred Flowers experience also seems to indicate that thought reform is subject to a law of diminishing conversions. Repeated attempts to reform the same man are more likely to increase his hostility of suffocation than to purge him of his "incorrect" thoughts. With each histrionic show of repentance, his conversion becomes more suspect. This hypothesis is confirmed by the revised official estimates of the intellectuals' ideological status after the Hundred Flowers episode. In 1958, commentators placed "only a few" of China's intellectuals in the category of fully acceptable "working class intellectuals" (fewer than Chou En-lai's 1956 estimate of 40 per cent), characterizing the majority of intellectuals as "middle-of-the-roaders" (more than Chou's 1956 estimate of 40 per cent). Although these estimates are hardly precise (they may have been exaggerated to spur the intellectuals on to greater efforts), the Hundred Flowers incident itself suggests that they may correctly indicate a trend. By "middle-of-the-roaders," the Communists did not mean "bourgeois rightists" (who presumably had already been dealt with), but rather those intellectuals who had reacted with emotional passivity and partial withdrawal to an overdose of thought reform. Such passive tendencies can be observed in Chinese intellectuals (Robert Chao, for instance) who are faced with unpleasant environmental realities. At the beginning, perhaps, thought reform can frequently break through these patterns and even utilize the emotional conflicts which accompany them; but over a period of time it runs the risk of itself stimulating a protective inner passivity and withdrawal even among those who outwardly seem active and involved.

The Chinese Communists seem to interpret these passive tendencies not as evidences of too much reform but rather of too little, and their treatment is always the same—more reform. We can only conclude that Chinese leaders are by no means as logical and calmly methodical about their reform programs as many outsiders assume them to be. Indeed, they themselves appear to be caught up in an irrational urge to reform, an urge which frequently works against their own interests. I estimate that thought reform's maximum (post-takeover) effectiveness was reached sometime during its first wave (about 1951 or 1952), and that after this the balance between enthusiasm and coercion has shifted to a decrease of the former and an increase of the latter. This too is part of the Communist leaders' own treadmill, since it means that they can neither achieve their perfectionistic thought reform goals, nor cease trying to; and every wave of thought reform makes the next wave even more necessary. The stagers of thought reform are in this sense the victims of their own cult of enthusiasm.

Yet all of this is just one side of the story. The repetitive waves of thought reform diminish spontaneity and stimulate resentment, but they also help to achieve what is perhaps thought reform's major goal, the rapid establishment of a Chinese Communist ideological culture—a prescribed system of feeling and belief against which everything is critically judged. A variation of thought reform got the Party into difficulty during the Hundred Flowers outburst; a hyperorthodox thought reform came to the rescue. Although the counterattack was neither as significant nor as unexpected as the critical outburst which preceded it, the almost immediate recantation made by all who had spoken out was nearly as impressive a spectacle, and was certainly a highly convincing display of the recuperative powers of thought reform. Those who recanted must have been very fearful, and their performances were perhaps even more than usually ritualistic. Yet they may also have felt some genuine repentance, for thought reform had applied to them its special techniques for reclaiming backsliders. By its mobilization of mass emotions, it could have convinced them that their critical views were out of step with the march of history, and that they had helped their country's enemies and harmed a noble cause. Thought reform can so envelop the backslider in his guilt that, however sincere his original protest, he is made to doubt himself enough to return to the fold—if not as a true believer, then as a humiliated, fearful, confused, and impotent follower. We saw vestiges of this reclaiming power in many of my subjects: the guilty sense of having been a betrayer, along with a paralyzing fear of the Communists (especially in Hu and in George Chen), persisting long after the escape from Communist control. For thought reform achieves a degree of psychological control over the individual as strong as any yet devised.

Accompanying this control is thought reform's extraordinary capacity for personal manipulation. We need not accept, of course, the regime's later claim to infallibility in relationship to the Hundred Flowers episode—its innuendoes that it had inaugurated the campaign in order to expose the "poisonous weeds" (a view also held by many cynical outsiders). The evidence suggests that the Communists were as surprised as anyone else at the response. Yet this *ex post facto* claim does have a kernel of truth: for in any system as total as thought reform, liberalization is at best a device, a purposeful technique rather than an expression of genuine conviction. Thought reform manipulates the sequence of suffocation-liberalization-suffocation, and in so doing ensures that Communist realities remain at the center of the stage, whatever the degree of enthusiasm or resentment of the players.

I am aware that I have presented versions of thought reform's limitations and accomplishments which seem almost contradictory. I have done this intentionally, because these opposing effects can and do co-exist, sometimes even within the same person. A true picture of the program's impact can only be obtained by visualizing within the emotional life of individual Chinese intellectuals a fluctuating complex of genuine enthusiasm, neutral compliance, passive withdrawal, and hostility of suffocation—along with a tendency to accept much that is unpleasant because it seems to be a necessary part of a greater program, or the only way to get things done.

Will thought reform continue indefinitely? No one can be sure. Its intensity may diminish as the Chinese Communists move beyond the acute ideological stage of revolution. This would be in keeping with their contention that the need for thought reform arises solely from the contaminations of the old order: new generations of intellectuals, brought up entirely under Communism, should—according to this logic—have no reason to reform. Yet matters may not turn out to be quite so simple. The psychological forces which originally set thought reform in motion will continue to be felt; and perhaps for as long as this strange marriage between Communism and Chinese culture remains solvent (despite the early clash of temperaments, the union looks like an enduring one), Chinese intellectuals will find themselves subjected to some kind of periodic "rectification."

PART FOUR

TOTALISM AND ITS ALTERNATIVES

For my part, I detest these absolute systems which represent all the events of history as depending upon great first causes linked by the chain of fatality, and which, as it were, suppress men from the history of the human race. They seem narrowed to my mind, under their pretense of broadness, and false beneath their air of mathematical exactness.

Alexis de Tocqueville

If to see more is really to become more, if deeper vision is really fuller being, then we should look closely at man in order to increase our capacity to live.

Pierre Teilhard de Chardin

CHAPTER 22

IDEOLOGICAL TOTALISM

Thought reform has a psychological momentum of its own, a self-perpetuating energy not always bound by the interests of the program's directors. When we inquire into the sources of this momentum, we come upon a complex set of psychological themes, which may be grouped under the general heading of *ideological totalism*. By this ungainly phrase I mean to suggest the coming together of immoderate ideology with equally immoderate individual character traits—an extremist meeting ground between people and ideas.

In discussing tendencies toward individual totalism within my subjects, I made it clear that these were a matter of degree, and that some potential for this form of all-or-nothing emotional alignment exists within everyone. Similarly, any ideology—that is, any set of emotionally-charged convictions about man and his relationship to the natural or supernatural world—may be carried by its adherents in a totalistic direction. But this is most likely to occur with those ideologies which are most sweeping in their content and most ambitious—or messianic—in their claims, whether religious, political, or scientific. And where totalism exists, a religion, a political movement, or even a scientific organization becomes little more than an exclusive cult.

A discussion of what is most central in the thought reform environment can thus lead us to a more general consideration of the psychology of human zealotry. For in identifying, on the basis of this study of thought reform, features common to all expressions of ideological totalism, I wish to suggest a set of criteria against which any environment may be judged—a basis for answering the ever-recurring question: "Isn't this just like 'brainwashing'?"

These criteria consist of eight psychological themes which are predominant within the social field of the thought reform milieu. Each has a totalistic quality; each depends upon an equally absolute philosophical assumption; and each mobilizes certain individual emotional tendencies, mostly of a polarizing nature. Psychological theme, philosophical rationale, and polarized individual tendencies are interdependent; they require, rather than directly cause, each other. In combination they create an atmosphere which may temporarily energize or exhilarate, but which at the same time poses the gravest of human threats.

Milieu Control

The most basic feature of the thought reform environment, the psychological current upon which all else depends, is the control of human communication. Through this milieu control the totalist environment seeks to establish domain over not only the individual's communication with the outside (all that he sees and hears, reads and writes, experiences, and expresses), but also—in its penetration of his inner life—over what we may speak of as his communication with himself. It creates an atmosphere uncomfortably reminiscent of George Orwell's 1984; but with one important difference. Orwell, as a Westerner, envisioned milieu control accomplished by a mechanical device, the two-way "tele-screen." The Chinese, although they utilize whatever mechanical means they have at their disposal, achieve control of greater psychological depth through a human recording and transmitting apparatus. It is probably fair to say that the Chinese Communist prison and revolutionary university produce about as thoroughly controlled a group environment as has ever existed. The milieu control exerted over the broader social environment of Communist China, while considerably less intense, is in its own way unrivalled in its combination of extensiveness and depth; it is, in fact, one of the distinguishing features of Chinese Communist practice.

Such milieu control never succeeds in becoming absolute; and its own human apparatus can—when permeated by outside information—become subject to discordant "noise" beyond that of any mechanical apparatus. To totalist administrators, however, such occurrences are no more than evidences of "incorrect" use of the apparatus. For they look upon milieu control as a just and necessary policy, one which need not be kept secret: thought reform participants may be in doubt as to who is telling what to whom, but the fact that extensive information about everyone is being conveyed to the authorities is always known. At the center of this self-justification is their assumption of omniscience, their conviction that reality is their exclusive possession. Having experienced the impact of what they consider to be an ultimate truth (and having the need to dispel any possible inner doubts of their own), they consider it their duty to create an environment containing no more and no less than this "truth." In order to be the engineers of the human soul, they must first bring it under full observational control.

Many things happen psychologically to one exposed to milieu control; the most basic is the disruption of balance between self and outside world. Pressured toward a merger of internal and external milieux, the individual encounters a profound threat to his personal autonomy. He is deprived of the combination of external information and inner reflection which anyone requires to test the realities of his environment and to maintain a measure of identity separate from it. Instead, he is called upon to make an absolute polarization of the real (the prevailing ideology) and the unreal (everything else). To the extent that he does this, he undergoes a *personal closure*[1] which frees him from man's incessant struggle with the elusive subtleties of truth. He may even share his environment's sense of omniscience and assume a "God's-eye view"[2] of the universe; but he is likely instead to feel himself victimized by the God's-eye view of his environment's controllers. At this point he is subject to the hostility of suffocation of which we have already spoken—the resentful awareness that his strivings toward new information, independent judgment, and self-expression are being thwarted. If his intelligence and sensibilities carry him toward realities outside the closed ideological system, he may resist these as not fully legitimate—until the milieu control is sufficiently diminished for him to share these realities with others. He is in either case profoundly hampered in the perpetual human quest for what is true, good, and relevant in the world around him and within himself.

Mystical Manipulation

The inevitable next step after milieu control is extensive personal manipulation. This manipulation assumes a no-holds-barred character, and uses every possible device at the milieu's command, no matter how bizarre or painful. Initiated from above, it seeks to provoke specific patterns of behavior and emotion in such a way that these will appear to have arisen spontaneously from within the environment. This element of planned spontaneity, directed as it is by an ostensibly omniscient group, must assume, for the manipulated, a near-mystical quality.

Ideological totalists do not pursue this approach *solely* for the purpose of maintaining a sense of power over others. Rather they are impelled by a special kind of mystique which not only justifies such manipulations, but makes them mandatory. Included in this mystique is a sense of "higher purpose," of having "directly perceived some imminent law of social development," and of being themselves the vanguard of this development.[3] By thus becoming the instruments of their own mystique, they create a mystical aura around the manipulating institutions—the Party, the Government, the Organization. They are the agents "chosen" (by history, by God, or by some other supernatural force) to carry out the "mystical imperative,"[4] the pursuit of which must supersede all considerations of decency or of immediate human welfare. Similarly, any thought or action which questions the higher purpose is considered to be stimulated by a lower purpose, to be backward, selfish, and petty in the face of the great, overriding mission. This same mystical imperative produces the apparent extremes of idealism and cynicism which occur in connection with the manipulations of any totalist environment: even those actions which seem cynical in the extreme can be seen as having ultimate relationship to the "higher purpose."

At the level of the individual person, the psychological responses to this manipulative approach revolve about the basic polarity of trust and mistrust. One is asked to accept these manipulations on a basis of ultimate trust (or faith): "like a child in the arms of its mother," as Father Luca accurately perceived. He who trusts in this degree can experience the manipulations within the idiom of the mystique behind them: that is, he may welcome their mysteriousness, find pleasure in their pain, and feel them to be necessary for the fulfillment of the "higher purpose" which he endorses as his own. But such elemental trust is difficult to maintain; and even the strongest can be dissipated by constant manipulation.

When trust gives way to mistrust (or when trust has never existed) the higher purpose cannot serve as adequate emotional sustenance. The individual then responds to the manipulations through developing what I shall call the *psychology of the pawn*. Feeling himself unable to escape from forces more powerful than himself, he subordinates everything to adapting himself to them. He becomes sensitive to all kinds of cues, expert at anticipating environmental pressures, and skillful in riding them in such a way that his psychological energies merge with the tide rather than turn painfully against himself. This requires that he participate actively in the manipulation of others, as well as in the endless round of betrayals and self-betrayals which are required.

But whatever his response—whether he is cheerful in the face of being manipulated, deeply resentful, or feels a combination of both —he has been deprived of the opportunity to exercise his capacities for self-expression and independent action.

The Demand for Purity

In the thought reform milieu, as in all situations of ideological totalism, the experiential world is sharply divided into the pure and the impure, into the absolutely good and the absolutely evil. The good and the pure are of course those ideas, feelings, and actions which are consistent with the totalist ideology and policy; anything else is apt to be relegated to the bad and the impure. Nothing human is immune from the flood of stern moral judgments. All "taints" and "poisons" which contribute to the existing state of impurity must be searched out and eliminated.

The philosophical assumption underlying this demand is that absolute purity (the "good Communist" or the ideal Communist state) is attainable, and that anything done to anyone in the name of this purity is ultimately moral. In actual practice, however, no one (and no State) is really expected to achieve such perfection. Nor can this paradox be dismissed as merely a means of establishing a high standard to which all can aspire. Thought reform bears witness to its more malignant consequences: for by defining and manipulating the criteria of purity, and then by conducting an all-out war upon impurity, the ideological totalists create a narrow world of guilt and shame. This is perpetuated by an ethos of continuous reform, a demand that one strive permanently and painfully for something which not only does not exist but is in fact alien to the human condition.

At the level of the relationship between individual and environment, the demand for purity creates what we may term a *guilty milieu* and a *shaming milieu*. Since each man's impurities are deemed sinful and potentially harmful to himself and to others, he is, so to speak, expected to expect punishment—which results in a relationship of guilt with his environment. Similarly, when he fails to meet the prevailing standards in casting out such impurities, he is expected to expect humiliation and ostracism—thus establishing a relationship of shame with his milieu. Moreover, the sense of guilt and the sense of shame become highly-valued: they are preferred forms of communication, objects of public competition, and the bases for eventual bonds between the individual and his totalist accusers. One may attempt to simulate them for a while, but the subterfuge is likely to be detected, and it is safer (as Miss Darrow found) to experience them genuinely.

People vary greatly in their susceptibilities to guilt and shame (as my subjects illustrated), depending upon patterns developed early in life. But since guilt and shame are basic to human existence, this variation can be no more than a matter of degree. Each person is made vulnerable through his profound inner sensitivities to his own limitations and to his unfulfilled potential; in other words, each is made vulnerable through his existential guilt. Since ideological totalists become the ultimate judges of good and evil within their world, they are able to use these universal tendencies toward guilt and shame as emotional levers for their controlling and manipulative influences. They become the arbiters of existential guilt, authorities without limit in dealing with others' limitations. And their power is nowhere more evident than in their capacity to "forgive." [5]

The individual thus comes to apply the same totalist polarization of good and evil to his judgments of his own character: he tends to imbue certain aspects of himself with excessive virtue, and condemn even more excessively other personal qualities—all according to their ideological standing. He must also look upon his impurities as originating from outside influences—that is, from the ever-threatening world beyond the closed, totalist ken. Therefore, one of his best ways to relieve himself of some of his burden of guilt is to denounce, continuously and hostilely, these same outside influences. The more guilty he feels, the greater his hatred, and the more threatening they seem. In this manner, the universal psychological tendency toward "projection" is nourished and institutionalized, leading to mass hatreds, purges of heretics, and to political and religious holy wars. Moreover, once an individual person has experienced the totalist polarization of good and evil, he has great difficulty in regaining a more balanced inner sensitivity to the complexities of human morality. For there is no emotional bondage greater than that of the man whose entire guilt potential—neurotic and existential—has become the property of ideological totalists.

The Cult of Confession

Closely related to the demand for absolute purity is an obsession with personal confession. Confession is carried beyond its ordinary religious, legal, and therapeutic expressions to the point of becoming a cult in itself. There is the demand that one confess to crimes one has not committed, to sinfulness that is artificially induced, in the name of a cure that is arbitrarily imposed. Such demands are made possible not only by the ubiquitous human tendencies toward guilt and shame but also by the need to give expression to these tendencies. In totalist hands, confession becomes a means of exploiting, rather than offering solace for, these vulnerabilities.

The totalist confession takes on a number of special meanings. It is first a vehicle for the kind of personal purification which we have just discussed, a means of maintaining a perpetual inner emptying or psychological purge of impurity; this *purging milieu* enhances the totalists' hold upon existential guilt. Second, it is an act of symbolic self-surrender, the expression of the merging of individual and environment. Third, it is a means of maintaining an ethos of total exposure—a policy of making public (or at least known to the Organization) everything possible about the life experiences, thoughts, and passions of each individual, and especially those elements which might be regarded as derogatory.

The assumption underlying total exposure (besides those which relate to the demand for purity) is the environment's claim to total ownership of each individual self within it. Private ownership of the mind and its products—of imagination or of memory—becomes highly immoral. The accompanying rationale (or rationalization) is familiar to us (from George Chen's experience); the milieu has attained such a perfect state of enlightenment that any individual retention of ideas or emotions has become anachronistic.

The cult of confession can offer the individual person meaningful psychological satisfactions in the continuing opportunity for emotional catharsis and for relief of suppressed guilt feelings, especially insofar as these are associated with self-punitive tendencies to get pleasure from personal degradation. More than this, the sharing of confession enthusiasms can create an orgiastic sense of "oneness," of the most intense intimacy with fellow confessors and of the dissolution of self into the great flow of the Movement. And there is also, at least initially, the possibility of genuine self-revelation and of self-betterment through the recognition that "the thing that has been exposed is what I am." [6]

But as totalist pressures turn confession into recurrent command performances, the element of histrionic public display takes precedence over genuine inner experience. Each man becomes concerned with the effectiveness of his personal performance, and this performance sometimes comes to serve the function of evading the very emotions and ideas about which one feels most guilty—confirming the statement by one of Camus' characters that "authors of confessions write especially to avoid confessing, to tell nothing of what they know." [7] The difficulty, of course, lies in the inevitable confusion which takes place between the actor's method and his separate personal reality, between the performer and the "real me."

In this sense, the cult of confession has effects quite the reverse of its ideal of total exposure: rather than eliminating personal secrets, it increases and intensifies them. In any situation the personal secret has two important elements: first, guilty and shameful ideas which one wishes to suppress in order to prevent their becoming known by others or their becoming too prominent in one's own awareness; and second, representations of parts of oneself too precious to be expressed except when alone or when involved in special loving relationships formed around this shared secret world. Personal secrets are always maintained in opposition to inner pressures toward self-exposure. The totalist milieu makes contact with these inner pressures through its own obsession with the exposé and the unmasking process. As a result old secrets are revived and new ones proliferate; the latter frequently consist of resentments toward or doubts about the Movement, or else are related to aspects of identity still existing outside of the prescribed ideological sphere. Each person becomes caught up in a continuous conflict over which secrets to preserve and which to surrender, over ways to reveal lesser secrets in order to protect more important ones; his own boundaries between the secret and the known, between the public and the private, become blurred. And around one secret, or a complex of secrets, there may revolve (as we saw with Hu) an ultimate inner struggle between resistance and self-surrender.

Finally, the cult of confession makes it virtually impossible to attain a reasonable balance between worth and humility. The enthusiastic and aggressive confessor becomes like Camus' character whose perpetual confession is his means of judging others: "[I] . . . practice the profession of penitent to be able to end up as a judge . . . the more I accuse myself, the more I have a right to judge you." The identity of the "judge-penitent" [8] thus becomes a vehicle for taking on some of the environment's arrogance and sense of omnipotence. Yet even this shared omnipotence cannot protect him from the opposite (but not unrelated) feelings of humiliation and weakness, feelings especially prevalent among those who remain more the enforced penitent than the all-powerful judge.

The "Sacred Science"

The totalist milieu maintains an aura of sacredness around its basic dogma, holding it out as an ultimate moral vision for the ordering of human existence. This sacredness is evident in the prohibition (whether or not explicit) against the questioning of basic assumptions, and in the reverence which is demanded for the originators of the Word, the present bearers of the Word, and the

Word itself. While thus transcending ordinary concerns of logic, however, the milieu at the same time makes an exaggerated claim of airtight logic, of absolute "scientific" precision. Thus the ultimate moral vision becomes an ultimate science; and the man who dares to criticize it, or to harbor even unspoken alternative ideas, becomes not only immoral and irreverent, but also "unscientific." In this way, the philosopher kings of modern ideological totalism reinforce their authority by claiming to share in the rich and respected heritage of natural science.

The assumption here is not so much that man can be God, but rather that man's *ideas* can be God: that an absolute science of ideas (and implicitly, an absolute science of man) exists, or is at least very close to being attained; that this science can be combined with an equally absolute body of moral principles; and that the resulting doctrine is true for all men at all times. Although no ideology goes quite this far in overt statement, such assumptions are implicit in totalist practice.[9]

At the level of the individual, the totalist sacred science can offer much comfort and security. Its appeal lies in its seeming unification of the mystical and the logical modes of experience (in psychoanalytic terms, of the primary and secondary thought processes). For within the framework of the sacred science, there is room for both careful step-by-step syllogism, and sweeping, nonrational "insights." Since the distinction between the logical and the mystical is, to begin with, artificial and man-made, an opportunity for transcending it can create an extremely intense feeling of truth. But the posture of unquestioning faith—both rationally and nonrationally derived—is not easy to sustain, especially if one discovers that the world of experience is not nearly as absolute as the sacred science claims it to be.

Yet so strong a hold can the sacred science achieve over his mental processes that if one begins to feel himself attracted to ideas which either contradict or ignore it, he may become guilty and afraid. His quest for knowledge is consequently hampered, since in the name of science he is prevented from engaging in the receptive search for truth which characterizes the genuinely scientific approach. And his position is made more difficult by the absence, in a totalist environment, of any distinction between the sacred and the profane: there is no thought or action which cannot be related to the sacred science. To be sure, one can usually find areas of experience outside its immediate authority; but during periods of maximum totalist activity (like thought reform) any such areas are cut off, and there is virtually no escape from the milieu's ever-pressing edicts and demands. Whatever combination of continued adherence, inner resistance, or compromise co-existence the individual person adopts toward this blend of counterfeit science and back-door religion, it represents another continuous pressure toward personal closure, toward avoiding, rather than grappling with, the kinds of knowledge and experience necessary for genuine self-expression and for creative development.

Loading the Language

The language of the totalist environment is characterized by the thought-terminating cliché. The most far-reaching and complex of human problems are compressed into brief, highly reductive, definitive-sounding phrases, easily memorized and easily expressed. These become the start and finish of any ideological analysis. In thought reform, for instance, the phrase "bourgeois mentality" is used to encompass and critically dismiss ordinarily troublesome concerns like the quest for individual expression, the exploration of alternative ideas, and the search for perspective and balance in political judgments. And in addition to their function as interpretive shortcuts, these clichés become what Richard Weaver has called "ultimate terms": either "god terms," representative of ultimate good; or "devil terms," representative of ultimate evil. In thought reform, "progress," "progressive," "liberation," "proletarian standpoints" and "the dialectic of history" fall into the former category; "capitalist," "imperialist," "exploiting classes," and "bourgeois" (mentality, liberalism, morality, superstition, greed) of course fall into the latter.[10] Totalist language, then, is repetitiously centered on all-encompassing jargon, prematurely abstract, highly categorical, relentlessly judging, and to anyone but its most devoted advocate, deadly dull: in Lionel Trilling's phrase, "the language of nonthought."

To be sure, this kind of language exists to some degree within any cultural or organizational group, and all systems of belief depend upon it. It is in part an expression of unity and exclusiveness:

as Edward Sapir put it, " 'He talks like us' is equivalent to saying 'He is one of us'." [11] The loading is much more extreme in ideological totalism, however, since the jargon expresses the claimed certitudes of the sacred science. Also involved is an underlying assumption that language—like all other human products—can be owned and operated by the Movement. No compunctions are felt about manipulating or loading it in any fashion; the only consideration is its usefulness to the cause.

For an individual person, the effect of the language of ideological totalism can be summed up in one word: constriction. He is, so to speak, linguistically deprived; and since language is so central to all human experience, his capacities for thinking and feeling are immensely narrowed. This is what Hu meant when he said, "using the same pattern of words for so long . . . you feel chained." Actually, not everyone exposed *feels* chained, but in effect everyone *is* profoundly confined by these verbal fetters. As in other aspects of totalism, this loading may provide an initial sense of insight and security, eventually followed by uneasiness. This uneasiness may result in a retreat into a rigid orthodoxy in which an individual shouts the ideological jargon all the louder in order to demonstrate his conformity, hide his own dilemma and his despair, and protect himself from the fear and guilt he would feel should he attempt to use words and phrases other than the correct ones. Or else he may adopt a complex pattern of inner division, and dutifully produce the expected clichés in public performances while in his private moments he searches for more meaningful avenues of expression. Either way, his imagination becomes increasingly dissociated from his actual life experiences and may even tend to atrophy from disuse.

Doctrine Over Person

This sterile language reflects another characteristic feature of ideological totalism: the subordination of human experience to the claims of doctrine. This primacy of doctrine over person is evident in the continual shift between experience itself and the highly abstract interpretation of such experience—between genuine feelings and spurious cataloguing of feelings. It has much to do with the peculiar aura of half-reality which a totalist environment seems, at least to the outsider, to possess.

This tendency in the totalist approach to broad historical events was described in relationship to Chinese Communism by John K. Fairbank and Mary C. Wright:

. . . stock characters like capitalist imperialists from abroad, feudal and semi-feudal reaction at home, and the resistance and liberation movements of "the people" enact a morality play. This melodrama sees aggression, injustice, exploitation, and humiliation engulf the Chinese people until salvation comes at last with Communism. Mass revolutions require an historical myth as part of their black and white morality, and this is the ideological myth of one of the great revolutions of world history.[12]

The inspiriting force of such myths cannot be denied; nor can one ignore their capacity for mischief. For when the myth becomes fused with the totalist sacred science, the resulting "logic" can be so compelling and coercive that it simply replaces the realities of individual experience. Consequently, past historical events are retrospectively altered, wholly rewritten, or ignored, to make them consistent with the doctrinal logic. This alteration becomes especially malignant when its distortions are imposed upon individual memory as occurred in the false confessions extracted during thought reform (most graphically Father Luca's).

The same doctrinal primacy prevails in the totalist approach to changing people: the demand that character and identity be reshaped, not in accordance with one's special nature or potentialities, but rather to fit the rigid contours of the doctrinal mold. The human is thus subjugated to the ahuman. And in this manner, the totalists, as Camus phrases it, "put an abstract idea above human life, even if they call it history, to which they themselves have submitted in advance and to which they will decide quite arbitrarily, to submit everyone else as well." [13]

The underlying assumption is that the doctrine—including its mythological elements—is ultimately more valid, true, and real than is any aspect of actual human character or human experience. Thus, even when circumstances require that a totalist movement follow a course of action in conflict with or outside of the doctrine, there exists what Benjamin Schwartz has described as a "will to orthodoxy" [14] which requires an elaborate façade of new rationalizations designed to demonstrate the unerring consistency of the doctrine and the unfailing foresight which it provides. The public operation of this will to orthodoxy is seen in the Party's explanation of the Hundred Flowers Campaign. But its greater importance lies in more hidden manifestations, particularly the totalists' pattern of imposing their doctrine-dominated remolding upon people in order to seek confirmation of (and again, dispel their own doubts about) this same doctrine. Rather than modify the myth in accordance with experience, the will to orthodoxy requires instead that men be modified in order to reaffirm the myth. Thus, much of prison thought reform was devoted to making the Westerner conform to the pure image of "evil imperialist," so that he could take his proper role in the Communist morality play of Chinese history.

The individual person who finds himself under such doctrine-dominated pressure to change is thrust into an intense struggle with his own sense of integrity, a struggle which takes place in relation to polarized feelings of sincerity and insincerity. In a totalist environment, absolute "sincerity" is demanded; and the major criterion for sincerity is likely to be one's degree of doctrinal compliance—both in regard to belief and to direction of personal change. Yet there is always the possibility of retaining an alternative version of sincerity (and of reality), the capacity to imagine a different kind of existence and another form of sincere commitment (as did Grace Wu when she thought, "the world could not be like this"). These alternative visions depend upon such things as the strength of previous identity, the penetration of the milieu by outside ideas, and the retained capacity for eventual individual renewal. The totalist environment, however, counters such "deviant" tendencies with the accusation that they stem entirely from personal "problems" ("thought problems" or "ideological problems") derived from untoward earlier ("bourgeois") influences. The outcome will depend largely upon how much genuine relevance the doctrine has for the individual emotional predicament. And even for those to whom it seems totally appealing, the exuberant sense of well-being it temporarily affords may be more a "delusion of wholeness" [15] than an expression of true and lasting inner harmony.

The Dispensing of Existence

The totalist environment draws a sharp line between those whose right to existence can be recognized, and those who possess no such right. In thought reform, as in Chinese Communist practice generally, the world is divided into the "people" (defined as "the working class, the peasant class, the petite bourgeoisie, and the national bourgeoisie"), and the "reactionaries" or "lackeys of imperialism" (defined as "the landlord class, the bureaucratic capitalist class, and the KMT reactionaries and their henchmen"). Mao Tse-tung makes the existential distinction between the two groups quite explicit:

Under the leadership of the working class and the Communist Party, these classes [the people] unite together to form their own state and elect their own government [so as to] carry out a dictatorship over the lackeys of imperialism. . . . These two aspects, namely, democracy among the people and dictatorship over the reactionaries, combine to form the people's democratic dictatorship . . . . to the hostile classes the state apparatus is the instrument of oppression. It is violent, and not "benevolent." . . . Our benevolence applies only to the people, and not to the reactionary acts of the reactionaries and reactionary classes outside the people.[16]

Being "outside the people," the reactionaries are presumably nonpeople. Under conditions of ideological totalism, in China and elsewhere, nonpeople have often been put to death, their executioners then becoming guilty (in Camus' phrase) of "crimes of logic." But the thought reform process is one means by which nonpeople are permitted, through a change in attitude and personal character, to make themselves over into people. The most literal example of such dispensing of existence and nonexistence is to be found in the sentence given to certain political criminals: execution in two years' time, unless during that two-year period they have demonstrated genuine progress in their reform.

In the light of this existential policy, the two different pronunciations of the word *people* ("people" and "peepúl") adopted by the European group described in Chapter 9 was more than just a practical maneuver. It was a symbolic way to cut through the loaded totalist language and restore the word to its general meaning,

thereby breaking down the imposed distinction between people
and nonpeople. Since the Westerners involved were themselves
clearly nonpeople theirs was an invention born of the negative status
dispensed to them.

Are not men presumptuous to appoint themselves the dispensers
of human existence? Surely this is a flagrant expression of what the
Greeks called *hubris*, of arrogant man making himself God. Yet one
underlying assumption makes this arrogance mandatory: the conviction that there is just one path to true existence, just one valid
mode of being, and that all others are perforce invalid and false.
Totalists thus feel themselves compelled to destroy all possibilities
of false existence as a means of furthering the great plan of true
existence to which they are committed. Indeed, Mao's words suggest that all of thought reform can be viewed as a way to eradicate
such allegedly false modes of existence—not only among the nonpeople, within whom they supposedly originate, but also among
legitimate people allegedly contaminated by them.

The [function of the] people's state is to protect the people. Only
where there is the people's state, is it possible for the people to use democratic methods or a nationwide and all-round scale to educate and reform themselves, to free themselves from the influence of reactionaries
at home and abroad . . . . to unlearn the bad habits and ideas acquired
from the old society and not to let themselves travel on the erroneous
path pointed out by the reactionaries, but to continue to advance and
develop towards a Socialist and Communist society accomplishing the
historic mission of completely eliminating classes and advancing toward
a universal fraternity.[17]

For the individual, the polar emotional conflict is the ultimate
existential one of "being versus nothingness." He is likely to be
drawn to a conversion experience, which he sees as the only means
of attaining a path of existence for the future (as did George
Chen). The totalist environment—even when it does not resort
to physical abuse—thus stimulates in everyone a fear of extinction
or annihilation much like the basic fear experienced by Western
prisoners. A person can overcome this fear and find (in Martin
Buber's term) "confirmation," not in his individual relationships,
but only from the fount of all existence, the totalist Organization.
Existence comes to depend upon creed (I believe, therefore I am),
upon submission (I obey, therefore I am) and beyond these, upon

a sense of total merger with the ideological movement. Ultimately of course one compromises and combines the totalist "confirmation" with independent elements of personal identity; but one is ever made aware that, should he stray too far along this "erroneous path," his right to existence may be withdrawn.

The more clearly an environment expresses these eight psychological themes, the greater its resemblance to ideological totalism; and the more it utilizes such totalist devices to change people, the greater its resemblance to thought reform (or "brainwashing"). But facile comparisons can be misleading. No milieu ever achieves complete totalism, and many relatively moderate environments show some signs of it. Moreover, totalism tends to be recurrent rather than continuous: in China, for instance, its fullest expression occurs during thought reform; it is less apparent during lulls in thought reform, although it is by no means absent. And like the "enthusiasm" with which it is often associated, totalism is more apt to be present during the early phases of mass movements than later—Communist China in the 1950's was generally more totalist than Soviet Russia. But if totalism has at any time been prominent in a movement, there is always the possibility of its reappearance, even after long periods of relative moderation.

Then too, some environments come perilously close to totalism but at the same time keep alternative paths open; this combination can offer unusual opportunities for achieving intellectual and emotional depth. And even the most full-blown totalist milieu can provide (more or less despite itself) a valuable and enlarging life experience—*if* the man exposed has both the opportunity to leave the extreme environment and the inner capacity to absorb and make inner use of the totalist pressures (as did Father Vechten and Father Luca).

Also, ideological totalism itself may offer a man an intense peak experience: a sense of transcending all that is ordinary and prosaic, of freeing himself from the encumbrances of human ambivalence, of entering a sphere of truth, reality, trust, and sincerity beyond any he had ever known or even imagined. But these peak experiences, the result as they are of external pressure, distortion, and threat, carry a great potential for rebound, and for equally intense opposition to the very things which initially seem so liberating. Such imposed peak experiences [18]—as contrasted with those more freely and privately arrived at by great religious leaders and mystics— are essentially experiences of personal closure. Rather than stimulating greater receptivity and "openness to the world," they encourage a backward step into some form of "embeddedness"—a retreat into doctrinal and organizational exclusiveness, and into all-or-nothing emotional patterns more characteristic (at least at this stage of human history) of the child than of the individuated adult.[19]

And if no peak experience occurs, ideological totalism does even greater violence to the human potential: it evokes destructive emotions, produces intellectual and psychological constrictions, and deprives men of all that is most subtle and imaginative—under the false promise of eliminating those very imperfections and ambivalences which help to define the human condition. This combination of personal closure, self-destructiveness, and hostility toward outsiders leads to the dangerous group excesses so characteristic of ideological totalism in any form. It also mobilizes extremist tendencies in those outsiders under attack, thus creating a vicious circle of totalism.

What is the source of ideological totalism? How do these extremist emotional patterns originate? These questions raise the most crucial and the most difficult of human problems. Behind ideological totalism lies the ever-present human quest for the omnipotent guide—for the supernatural force, political party, philosophical ideas, great leader, or precise science—that will bring ultimate solidarity to all men and eliminate the terror of death and nothingness. This quest is evident in the mythologies, religions, and histories of all nations, as well as in every individual life. The degree of individual totalism involved depends greatly upon factors in one's personal history: early lack of trust, extreme environmental chaos, total domination by a parent or parent-representative, intolerable burdens of guilt, and severe crises of identity. Thus an early sense of confusion and dislocation, or an early experience of unusually intense family milieu control, can produce later a complete intolerance for confusion and dislocation, and a longing for the reinstatement of milieu control. But these things are in some measure part of every childhood experience; and therefore the potential for totalism is a continuum from which no one entirely escapes, and in relationship to which no two people are exactly the same.

It may be that the capacity for totalism is most fundamentally a product of human childhood itself, of the prolonged period of helplessness and dependency through which each of us must pass. Limited as he is, the infant has no choice but to imbue his first nurturing authorities—his parents—with an exaggerated omnipotence, until the time he is himself capable of some degree of independent action and judgment. And even as he develops into the child and the adolescent, he continues to require many of the all-or-none polarities of totalism as terms with which to define his intellectual, emotional, and moral worlds. Under favorable circumstances (that is, when family and culture encourage individuation) these requirements can be replaced by more flexible and moderate tendencies; but they never entirely disappear.

During adult life, individual totalism takes on new contours as it becomes associated with new ideological interests. It may become part of the configuration of personal emotions, messianic ideas, and organized mass movement which I have described as ideological totalism. When it does, we cannot speak of it as simply a form of regression. It is partly this, but it is also something more: a new form of adult embeddedness, originating in patterns of security-seeking carried over from childhood, but with qualities of ideas and aspirations that are specifically adult. During periods of cultural crisis and of rapid historical change, the totalist quest for the omnipotent guide leads men to seek to become that guide.

Totalism, then, is a widespread phenomenon, but it is not the only approach to re-education. We can best use our knowledge of it by applying its criteria to familiar processes in our own cultural tradition and in our own country.

CHAPTER 23

APPROACHES TO RE-EDUCATION

Throughout this book I have been discussing what Milton called "the bitter change of fierce extremes." This kind of discussion, especially when it is critical in tone, implies that there are alternative possibilities for human change less bitter and less extreme. By *human change* I mean those shifts and alterations in the sense of inner identity which occur within individuals during late adolescence and adult life. My concern in this chapter is with the great agencies of such change—educational, psychological, religious, and political—and with their resemblances to, and their possibilities for avoiding, ideological totalism.

All these agencies make use of four general approaches to changing people: coercion, exhortation, therapy, and realization. Ideological totalism utilizes all four, as this study of thought reform makes clear; but it leans most heavily upon the first two. The approaches, therefore, are by no means mutually exclusive; however, each conveys a distinct message, a specific goal, and an appeal to a particular aspect of human nature.

The message of coercion is: you *must* change and become what we tell you to become—or else. The threat embodied in the "or else" may be anything from death to social ostracism, any form of physical or emotional pain. The goal of naked coercion is to produce a cowed and demoralized follower. It is directed at the most primitive of human emotions, and stimulates the desire to flee, or to fight back, to freeze in fear, or submit completely. A good example of the coercive approach to changing people was the Nazi concentration camp. There, as Bruno Bettelheim has described,[1] the intent was "to break the prisoners as individuals and to change them into docile masses. . . . useful subjects of the Nazi state." Gestapo authorities made no effort to indoctrinate the inmates, and in fact treated them in an unprecedentedly cruel, sadistic, and degrading fashion. Yet it is significant that even under such conditions some ideological conversions occurred: some long-term prisoners eventually adopted Nazi views on Aryan racial supremacy and on the legitimacy of German expansionism—a literal expression of the psychological mechanism of "identification with the aggressor." [2] In thought reform, coercion is greatest during the early stages of the prison process; but it is an essential ingredient of all varieties of thought reform and of all phases, however much it may temporarily be shunted to the background.

The message of the exhortative approach is: you *should* change —if you are a moral man—and become what we (in the name of a higher moral authority) tell you to become. Exhortation seeks to create converts and disciples, people who have been changed in accordance with the specific ideological convictions of the mentor. It appeals to the individual's wish to be a good man, or to become a better one; to pre-existing tendencies toward experiencing guilt and shame, including existential guilt. It is the method par excellence of religions and of pseudo-religious secular ideologies, both of which reinforce their moral appeal by their promise of reward, earthly or supernatural. Exhortation is, as I have already emphasized, always extremely prominent in thought reform, and is perhaps the most prominent of thought reform's approaches.

The message of the therapeutic approach is: you *can* change —from your sickly state, and find relief for your suffering—if you have a genuine urge to become healthy; and if you are willing to follow my (or our) method and guidance. Its goal is physical and emotional health (in the sense conveyed by the words *hale* and *whole*), freedom from incapacitating disease and defect. It makes its appeal to that part of a man that is most reasonable, healthful, health-seeking, and balanced. This has been the traditional approach of the medical profession, and in the emotional sphere it is best exemplified by psychotherapy and psychoanalysis.

But religious and secular ideologies also use this approach, or at least make claims on it. Thought reform is extravagant in its referral to "illness," "health," and "cure," following Mao Tse-tung's original lead; this usage implies biological restoration, and places reformers in the role of social physicians.

The message of realization is: you *can* change—in such a fashion that you will be able to express more fully your own potential—if you are willing to confront yourself with ideas and approaches which challenge your present ways of knowing and acting. Its goal is to produce a person who expresses his creative potential to the full, one who extends his faculties to their utmost in the effort to appreciate and produce at the highest level at which he is capable. Although this goal is closely related to that of the therapeutic approach, it is by no means the same; it may cause rather than relieve pain, and may promote within a person periods of incapacity alternating with creative peaks rather than a balanced continuity of health and strength. Each of the major agencies for change at times emphasizes the approach of realization; at other times, each strays from it. It has been an avowed ideal of such diverse groups as political forces associated with traditional liberalism; various psychoanalytic groups,[3] most recently those influenced by existentialism; mystics of all major Eastern and Western religions and practicing Zen Buddhists; and educators influenced by the philosophy of John Dewey. Other historical variations are the Confucian concept of self-cultivation, and the Greek notion of *aretê*—the view that life exists for the purpose of reaching the full expression of one's inborn capacity.[4] But the approach of realization is the most difficult of all to maintain: many have violated it even as they theoretically proclaimed it, and it is notorious for its quick mortality rate. Indeed, the very formation of an institution around it has too often signified the beginnings of its disappearance. Here thought reform's claim is frequently the bitterest of ironies, since totalism does more to stifle than to realize the human potential. Yet the claim is not entirely false, since sometimes, especially among the young, thought reform has been experienced as a pathway to self-realization.

In practice, no one of these approaches ever appears in pure form (even the Nazi concentration camp must have been influenced by the exhortative spirit of the mass movement behind it), and significant attempts at changing people usually embody elements of all four. There is, moreover, considerable overlapping among them, and distinguishing them can become difficult. Thought reform in particular shows the complexities of interplay between exhortation and coercion: the use of coercion to stimulate excessive guilt and shame so that these in turn create an inner exhortation; and the use of exhortation to stimulate negative conscience so powerful that it becomes in effect a form of self-coercion. At its other end, exhortation merges with therapy, as therapy merges with re-alization. Yet these four approaches can and should be distinguished from one another in any attempt at re-education, if not as absolute alternatives, at least as predominant emotional tones.

In discussing the broader agencies of change—education, psychiatry, religion, and politics—I shall make no attempt to list every possible similarity and dissimilarity with thought reform. Rather, I shall point up those aspects in each of these agencies which can be illuminated by our general study of totalism.

Education and Re-education

I can best introduce the subject of the relationship of education to thought reform and to ideological totalism by presenting the several points of view which emerged at a small faculty seminar held at an American girls' college. After I had described the thought reform process at a revolutionary university, a lively debate began among the participating teachers about the relevance of thought reform to practices at their own institution (which I shall call Arly College).

Professor A made a blunt accusation:

I think we are doing the same thing. We are brainwashing the girls here at Arly. When the girls arrive as freshmen, they are herded together, greeted by seniors and other students who help them and show them around so that when they get to a class they can be relaxed and they can listen. They can agree with what is said and then we can be sure they will not leave Arly and go home. Then they can settle down to learning how to become good Arly girls. . . . In most of our classes, the teacher has a definite idea of what we expect, and will view the student's past as evil until the student comes to this idea. There is no difference at all.

As I listened to Professor A's accusation (and self-accusation), I felt that she was taking her extreme stand partly for its shock value, partly because she wished to air her worst fears (and have them relieved), and partly to express a certain amount of hostility toward her profession. Her attitude was manifestly open-minded, but it was also intellectually inadequate. Impressed by the similarities, and unable to immediately fathom the differences, she had in effect concluded: education is "brainwashing."

Her words did not go unchallenged. Professor B became visibly upset, and firmly disagreed:

What we do is entirely different. The point is that at a revolutionary university they demand a specific product, and insist that everyone emerge as this. Here at Arly we do not care about such things. We do not care what the girls believe when they graduate. Our main concern is that they learn something from their college experience.

Professor B compassionately defended an institution to which she was deeply committed, and in her emphasis on the "expected product," she made an important point. But the threat to her self-esteem, implicit in Professor A's comparison, led her to overstate her defense; for when the others questioned her more closely she admitted that as a serious educator she could not avoid caring about what her students believed and about what kind of young women they were encouraged to become during their college years. She was taking an equally simplistic intellectual position: namely, that good education has absolutely no connection with "brainwashing" (or with ideological totalism).

A young professor of English, also troubled, but more wary of facile conclusions, restated the issue as a dilemma:

Much of what we teach depends upon some kind of group agreement on standards of quality and truth of concepts. At the same time, one of our main troubles is getting people to speak up and offer criticisms of others' ideas based upon their own genuine opinions. . . . But just by simply saying that Shakespeare was the greatest poet in the English language—an assumption on which any English teacher would find widespread common agreement—and by then expecting the student to hold this opinion, aren't we really indulging in the same kind of process as thought reform?

After considerable additional discussion, during which I mentioned some of the features of ideological totalism, Professor C made a thoughtful attempt at resolution:

Perhaps we can avoid this by holding our beliefs with a certain amount of tension . . . with an attitude that "I believe in this, but recognize that there can be other beliefs in opposition to it." In this way we can subject any belief which we hold to the tension or pressure of its own limitations and of other alternative beliefs.

By neither denying the continuities with thought reform nor overstating them in nihilistic despair, but instead by facing them as an unavoidable paradox, Professor C opened the way to a more fundamental approach. He grasped the necessity for both commitment and flexibility in education, and especially the necessity for its inclusion of what Michael Polanyi has called "personal knowledge"—knowledge neither strictly objective nor strictly subjective which demands active participation and responsibility on the part of the knower.[5]

Later, as I thought about these three positions, I realized that Professors A and B had gone astray largely because they were unable to understand the relationship between education and re-education. In the broadest sense, these amount to the same thing. For in the student's act of attaining knowledge, his previous patterns of identity as well as belief must be altered, however slightly. Every new idea or technique requires a complex rearrangement of what existed before. And this rearrangement is necessary from the moment of birth, since the infant begins not as a *tabula rasa* but as an organism with innate behavioral tendencies (whether we call these tendencies drives, instincts, or needs). Re-education is inevitably influenced by the attitudes and beliefs (personal and institutional) conveyed by the mentors who guide it, and thus has something in common with thought reform. Professor A perceived some of this and was overwhelmed by her perception. Professor B had to deny both the relationship between education and re-education and the extent of the mentor's involvement in the educational process. Professor C was searching for a formulation which would account for the relationship between education and re-education, for the mentor's influence upon it, and also for his being himself bound by certain group standards; but he transcended these similarities by distinguishing between good educational practice and ideological totalism. His concept of tension in the educational process was thus an affirmative addition to the negative criteria of ideological totalism described in the previous chapter.

Any educational experience is a three-way interplay among student, mentor, and the ideas being taught—ideally it is an interplay of stimulating tension. Such tension includes the mentor's forceful presentation of ideas within the context of the cultural traditions in which they arose; his demand that each student permit himself to be challenged by these ideas; and his allowance for each student's individual relationship to the ideas. When this tension does not exist, education is apt either to move in the direction of totalism or else simply fail. If, for instance, the idea or the subject matter becomes so predominant that mentor and student come to see themselves as mere vehicles for it, education encounters the totalistic dangers of doctrine over person and of the implied claim of a sacred science. Either the student will be completely uninvolved, or else he will be coerced by seemingly mysterious ahuman forces. The same totalist trends are present when mentor and idea come together in an incontestable, omnipotent combination which makes no provision for the student; also present in these circumstances are milieu control, mystical manipulation, and—depending upon the forms of discipleship which the mentor's individual and institutional character dictate—the possibility of the demand for absolute purity, the cult of confession, and the dispensing of existence.

This situation might exist, for instance, in a graduate school department of, let us say, economics, sociology, or literature, dominated by a forceful, authoritarian department head who is a single-minded devotée of one particular doctrinal approach to his subject and who considers alternative views "erroneous," and "unscientific." His students' assigned reading matter would be limited to this "correct" approach, except possibly for a few readings among "incorrect" writers included for the sake of gathering ammunition with which to ridicule them; students would be unable to question the ultimate truth of the prescribed doctrine and approach; they would feel guilty, frightened, and ashamed if they began to suspect that a rival approach might be a better one; and each would be under great pressure to reshape his identity in such a way that it could encompass the correct doctrine—especially those who might be seeking the good will of the department head in relation to their future careers. This is, of course, the educational situation which most closely approximates totalism, although the ultimate availability of alternative life choices outside the correct doctrine does distinguish it from thought reform.

Finally, at the opposite extreme is the teaching situation in which ideas are considered to have little importance and are presented (and are expected to be received) with minimal involvement on everyone's part. In these circumstances, a disinterested withdrawal on the part of both mentor and student occurs, or else a compensatory overfocus on the student-mentor relationship, so that both become bogged down in a psychological morass which neither understands.

In each of these imbalances within the three-way relationship, the student's intellectual growth and his quest for realization are both hampered.

Three-way tension does not in any way imply absolute equality of mentor and student; on the contrary, it demands that the former accept the responsibility of his intellectually superior position, and that the latter surrender himself to the extent that he becomes receptive rather than refractory to what is being taught. Moreover, temporary discipleships and educational environments of near-totalism (such as sometimes exist in Jesuit-run schools) offer distinct intellectual advantages if the student goes on from these to the world outside. Even relatively coercive institutional demands for a particular identity product—transmitted by faculty and advanced students through a number of well-defined hazing rituals—can provide emotional benefits: strong identifications, the opportunity to test one's capacity for rebellion against respected authorities, and an experience of personal trial and initiation which, although painful at the time, is nostalgically recalled forever after. Relatively coercive environments can come close enough to totalism to do their damage, especially at lower age levels (for instance, the British public schools described by George Orwell).[6] But in pluralistic societies, even the most extreme of these institutions see themselves as part of the individual's continuing educational process. They may try to influence him as much as possible during his stay; but it is assumed that he will go on to new ideas and different identities in the future. They become most harmful when they approach the totalist extreme of claiming to offer the student a single path of absolute perfection whose limits he is never to exceed.

The alternative to totalism in education then is a liberalism based upon the three-way tension described above, a liberalism that in Lionel Trilling's words can recapture its "essential imagination of variousness and possibility," without losing the "awareness of complexity and difficulty." It is, as Trilling goes on to say, "a large tendency rather than a concise body of doctrine." [7] In this "tendency" there is a rejection of omnipotence on the part of the mentor even when the student seeks to thrust it upon him; and a balance between a vigorous presentation of available knowledge and the encouragement of those elements of the student's imagination which may someday transcend that knowledge in new discovery.

Psychological Re-education

Psychotherapy and psychoanalysis are forms of psychological re-education; but they focus less upon man's knowledge of the world about him than upon his understanding of his own self. Their concern with the most fundamental and the most hidden of human emotions adds a special depth to their re-educating efforts, and a special intensity to their influence. Their avoidance of totalism is therefore a matter of particular importance. [8]

The ethos of psychoanalysis and of its derived psychotherapies is in direct opposition to that of totalism. Indeed, its painstaking and sympathetic investigations of single human minds place it within the direct tradition of those Western intellectual currents which historically have done most to counter totalism: humanism, individualism, and free scientific inquiry. Because of its continuing concern for individual differences and for flexible personal development, it is not surprising that psychoanalytic work has never been permitted under totalitarianism (or political totalism). And psychoanalytically-derived insights, as I have attempted to suggest throughout this book, provide one of the best ways to counter totalism through shedding light on its manner of functioning.

But in its organizational aspects, psychoanalysis—like every other revolutionary movement, whether scientific, political, or religious

—has had difficulty maintaining its initial liberating spirit; it has had its full share of bitter ideological controversy and schism. Moreover, certain social and historical features of the psychoanalytic movement—its early struggle with the unusually strong hostilities stimulated by its "shocking" doctrines, the novelty and isolated intensity of its therapeutic relationship, the brilliant virtuosity and "grandiose one-sidedness" [9] of its originator, and the subsequent intellectual and emotional appeal of its doctrine among practitioners and patients to the point of sometimes substituting for religious or political beliefs—have given rise to special problems in relationship to its scientific pursuits. These problems, and especially the effect they have on the psychoanalytic training situation, have been commented on by many psychoanalysts.[10] I can add little to what has already been written except to place some of these issues in the perspective of this study of totalism.

Psychoanalytic training is a form of personal re-education, in preparation for re-educating others. During his years of apprenticeship the trainee develops three important identities. He becomes first a *patient*. Through his own free associations in the "faceless" encounter with his analyst, he comes to grips with previously buried emotions in a way that "can play havoc with . . . his adjustments to the individuals close to him, who cannot for the life of them see why a person has to get sick in order to learn how to cure others." [11] This training analysis is his means of gaining insight into and mastery over those psychological tendencies which might otherwise interfere with his own therapeutic work. He is also a *student*. He attends seminars on psychoanalytic theory and technique, sees these principles demonstrated in his own analysis, and learns how to utilize them in the analyses he later conducts under the supervision of senior analysts. And he is a *candidate*. He seeks to qualify for membership in the local institute, and in the national and international psychoanalytic organizations—for eventual "confirmation" as a psychoanalyst. Erikson has referred to this training as "a new kind of asceticism," one that "demands a total and central personal involvement . . . which takes greater chances with the individual's relationship to himself . . . than any other professional training except monkhood." [12]

From the standpoint of the criteria for ideological totalism, we may raise the following additional questions: Does this combination of personal therapy, professional instruction, and organizational influence—all mediated by a single training institute—create a tendency toward milieu control? Does it cause the institute itself to become surrounded with a near-mystical aura? Do these circumstances—especially the candidate's learning a scientific doctrine in connection with its therapeutic application to his own psychological distress—create an implicit demand for ideological purity? And do they raise the possibility that his analyst and his institute, by bringing about his "cure," will become (even if inadvertently) the arbiters of his neurotic and existential guilt? Could the confession process of therapy in this way take on an extratherapeutic function of binding the candidate to the psychoanalytic movement, thereby making him hesitant to criticize its teaching? Is there sometimes a tendency, in the descriptive and reductive overemployment of a particular school's or institute's favorite technical terms, to load the language or to suggest a sacred science? Is there thus a danger of establishing (perhaps unconsciously on everyone's part) a pattern of intellectual conformity as a prerequisite for a successful training experience—or in other words, establishing a primacy of doctrine over person? And when questions of ideological difference influence decisions about who is to be recognized as a legitimate psychoanalyst, is there a tendency toward the dispensing of existence?

It is perhaps unnecessary to stress that the psychoanalytic training procedure never approaches the totalist actualities of thought reform, and for this reason I raise questions about "tendencies" and "dangers." [13] Nor can the problems involved in preparing men and women for psychoanalytic work in a manner that offers maximum protection for future patients be ignored. Indeed, it may be that the psychoanalyst often requires something stronger than a working hypothesis—something closer to a dogma—as a combined protective shield and sorting mechanism for the extraordinary rush of emotions released by the psychoanalytic process. But psycho-analysis is able to look critically at itself, to experiment, correct, and change. As early as 1937, Franz Alexander, then President of the American Psychoanalytic Association, warned against these dangers and urged that psychoanalysis divest itself of its own "movement"; [14] others subsequently have suggested diminishing the institutes' power, [15] and dividing the therapeutic and didactic aspects of the student's training so that they are no longer controlled by the same institute.[16] Studies of the training procedure are being conducted; and the general trend is toward a more "open" environment, toward a better balance in the educational tension among doctrine, mentor, and student. Thus the sweeping accusation that "psychoanalysis is brainwashing" is as false as the statement that "education is brainwashing." Insofar as tendencies toward totalism exist, however, they are bound to interfere with intellectual progress, and with the emergence of those creative spirits which any discipline requires if it is to continue to contribute to the stream of human thought.

I shall mention briefly just a few more of the many implications of this study of thought reform for the theory and practice of psychiatric re-education. The first pertains to the concept of "resistance," which is basic to most psychotherapy. Since thought reform has its own notion of "resistance," the caricatured exaggerations of ideological totalism can be helpful in examining some of the presuppositions of more moderate and more genuinely therapeutic work. Chinese reformers are apt to consider any inner opposition or outer hesitation—in fact anything at all that stands in the way of thought reform—as "resistance." The psychotherapist similarly regards almost any attitude or behavior standing in the way of cure—but especially the reluctance to bring unconscious ideas into consciousness—to be expressions of resistance to therapy. These resistances are the real experience of any therapist; but after a study of thought reform one cannot help but be a bit chastened in the use of the concept. That is, as a psychotherapist I would consider it important to ask myself whether what appears to be resistance is truly a reflection of inner opposition to cure, or whether it might be inner opposition to my concept of the necessary direction of cure. And I would also wonder whether such resistance might not be a reflection of poor communication between the patient and myself, or of the absence between us of shared values [17] and assumptions about the therapy, both of which might be profitably investigated along with any psychological barriers within the patient.

The psychoanalytic concept of "transference"—a concept which is constantly being studied and reformulated—may also be re-examined in the light of questions of totalism. The therapist's recognition of the existence of transference—that is, of the patient's tendency to re-experience, in relationship to the therapist, earlier attitudes and fantasies developed originally toward parental authorities—is on the whole an extremely important check *against* totalism. For it provides a theoretical framework within which any tendencies in the patient to grant omnipotence to the therapist can be questioned by both, as well as a means of inquiring therapeutically into the sources of such tendencies, and a rationale for resolving these emotions—however difficult a task this resolution may be. In thought reform an opposite policy prevails. Transference occurs there too, not so much in relationship to one "therapist" as to the entire ideological movement; but instead of attempting to understand and ultimately resolve this transference, the reformers seek to enlarge and perpetuate it in the participant's permanent surrender of self to the authoritarian organization.

Like many other useful concepts, however, the notion of transference, if it is overemphasized, can produce the very results against which it ordinarily guards. Thus, if the therapeutic relationship is viewed as exclusively one of transference—with the actual person of the therapist and the adult self of the patient ignored—the danger arises that the patient will come to see himself almost entirely within his infant-child identity, and that his bestowal of omnipotence upon the therapist will be inadvertently encouraged. Psychoanalysts have recognized this problem and have emphasized the necessary dialectic in every therapeutic relationship between actual encounter and transference, as well as the inevitability of the therapist's own emotional involvement (or countertransference reactions).[18] Especially relevant is Janet Mackenzie Rioch's concern [19] that the psychotherapist do all possible to offset rather than perpetuate the patient's frequent "willingness to surrender," and that he take cognizance of the "symbolically submissive position" inherent in the psychoanalytic treatment situation. Her warning to the analyst to avoid the role of the "chronic hypnotist" amounts to a warning against totalism—since hypnosis is in effect a situation of interpersonal totalism in which the subject's perceptual world is reduced to the highly-focused influence of the omnipotent hypnotist.[20]

Another important issue which thought reform raises for psychiatric therapy is the use of the concept of "reality." The totalist environment (in a Chinese prison, for instance) can literally stand reality on its head: demand that all within its sway commit themselves to altered versions of external events, and then insist that these falsehoods constitute "objective reality." Psychiatrists are familiar with distortions like these, but arising in the minds of individuals rather than resulting from group manipulations; and as psychiatrists we consider them signs of mental illness, thereby implying that we expect psychologically healthy people to be able to adhere to a reality of external events. We also recognize the great variation in interpretations of reality, especially in relationship to the "psychological realities" of individual patients. And we extend the concept of reality to suggest something on the order of the way things are, as opposed to the way that the patient imagines them to be. In fact, we regard the therapeutic relationship as a means of enhancing the patient's reality-testing, of helping him to recognize his own distortions.

All of these usages have validity; but the therapist's notion of reality is nonetheless highly colored by his own ideological convictions about such matters as psychological health and illness, social conformity and rebelliousness, commitment and detachment, and especially about what constitutes wise or mature attitudes and behavior. Moreover, it is precisely these issues—and their relationship to problems of personal identity—which trouble patients in psychotherapy in America today, rather than the more clear-cut symptom neuroses described during the earlier days of psychoanalysis. This means consequently that unless the therapist can sort out his own reality prejudices, he may inadvertently transmit his personal ideologies within the treatment situation and require a successful implant upon the patient as a criterion for cure. Since ideological convictions about all of these matters are never absent, and indeed are necessary for any constructive change in therapy, they are better openly discussed as a part of the therapeutic process, and discussed in a manner that allows for their subjectivity and tentativeness. To do this requires the view that reality is both definite (in relationship to external events), and highly relative (in relationship to any observer's interpretation of such events).

Concerning milieu therapy, I have already mentioned thought reform's demonstration of the tremendous influence which a particular milieu—and the psychological themes contained therein—can bring to bear upon the individual person. This has great importance for psychiatric practice in a variety of ways, but I shall limit myself here to mentioning the harmful effects of environments that are "extremist" in regard to the magnitude of stimuli which they offer. At one pole is the deprived milieu—the milieu of "sensory deprivation" [21]—in which stimuli are so sparse as to be insufficient for the maintenance within the individual person of a reasonable degree of interest in and responsiveness toward his surroundings. Such an environment has been created under experimental conditions, and it produces patterns of boredom, restlessness, stimulus-hunger, extensive day-dreaming, loss of organized thinking, hynogogic states, and a variety of hallucinatory experiences. The rough equivalent of a deprived milieu within a psychiatric environment is the old-fashioned back ward in which patients sat about (and unfortunately still sit about) aimlessly, with little or no challenge or activity-evoking stimuli from their external surroundings. The opposite pole is the milieu of ideological totalism, in which the individual is bombarded with stimuli to the point of suffocation. The counterpart of this kind of environment within a psychiatric hospital would be (again speaking very roughly) the "total push" approaches adopted during the recent past by many institutions as a reaction against the stagnancy of the back wards atmosphere. While this was a definite improvement, it sometimes led to activity for activity's sake; a revealing comment on this was made to me by a schizophrenic patient after a few weeks' exposure to total push: "Gee, Doc, I wish I had a minute to sit down and think."

There is a certain similarity in these two types of extreme environments: both are overcontrolled milieux, and both interfere with the variety and balance of environmental stimuli required for optimal psychological function. Both are thus ultimately "deprived," although we cannot say (as has sometimes been suggested) that the milieu of sensory deprivation is an experimental model for thought reform.

Psychiatric hospitals have learned to avoid both extremes, and to develop programs and activities which offer a better balance between individual and milieu, so that the patient is neither overwhelmed by external stimuli nor so cut off from them that he is thrown back entirely upon his already malfunctioning internal life. Recent workers have stressed both socialization and individual creativity, the increase of "open" (unlocked) wards, and the therapeutic community. They have advocated patient participation in the planning of hospital programs, a balance between ordered and spontaneous activities, and finally, an avoidance of the identity of permanent patienthood through emphasizing the patient's connections with and educational preparation for—rather than his medical isolation from—the outside world.[22]

Finally, thought reform also has sobering implications for psychiatric theory. Despite contrivances and crudities, Chinese Communist theory about the "class character of man" was made operative and—at least to a certain extent—could be shown to "work." Theories have an irrepressible tendency to confirm themselves, especially when one deals with human beings; in Alfred North Whitehead's phrase, "the idea is a prophecy which procures its own fulfillment." This does not mean that we need despair and give up theorizing entirely (I certainly have shown no such tendency in this book); but it does suggest that psychiatrists can learn from physical scientists to look on theory not as a permanent and unalterable structure but rather as a useful and relatively valid means of ordering the data of experience within the framework of existing knowledge. Everyone of course recognizes this about theory—except when it comes to *his* theoretical beliefs.

Similarly, thought reform should make us somewhat cautious about those claims to "unification" of the behavioral sciences which imply an ultimate monopoly of one approach or an ultimate ideal of incontrovertible truth. A plunge into this kind of theoretical closure would be but another example of an intolerance for confusion driving us into the seductive embrace of totalism. I do not suggest that we can afford to rest content or cease being critical of faulty and ill-conceived theory and research; nor is there any doubt about our need for greater unity in our knowledge of man. But thought reform illustrates (and scientific experience strongly affirms) the importance of remaining open to knowledge from all sources, even (or especially) the most unlikely. I am convinced that we need new approaches to psychiatric theorizing based upon humanized notions of style, pattern, and configuration in the interplay of internal and external psychological forces, rather than upon the more simplistic cause-and-effect mechanical images of nineteenth-century physics now so widely employed. Such new approaches seem to be necessary if we are to learn more about the nature of man's emotional involvement in his changing physical environment, the ways in which he is himself undergoing change, and the relationship of this change to psychological health and disease, and to the realization of human potentialities. They will require outlooks which are the very antithesis of totalism: a subtle and flexible historical perspective beyond that of the individual life-history, a certain degree of boldness in the application of disciplined imagination, and a willingness to risk being wrong—or to expose (in Riesman's term) the "nerve of failure."

Religion, Political Religion, and Science

I have already suggested that thought reform bears many resemblances to practices of organized religion, and to various kinds of religious re-education. Indeed, most of the psychological themes of ideological totalism can be found somewhere in the Judeo-Christian tradition, however indirect any such theological influences may have been in the development of thought reform itself. These totalist tendencies have usually been related either to the theocratic search for heresy or to patterns of revitalizing enthusiasm—or (as in thought reform) to both.

In the first of these, the theocratic search for heresy, the inevitable assumption is that the administrators—whether themselves secular or clerical—rule their community and carry out their ideological purifications only as agents of a perfect and omniscient deity. The classical examples are the Inquisition of the middle ages and the treason and anti-Papist trials of sixteenth-century England. Both of these movements were characterized by orgies of false confessions, apparently produced by psychological manipulations of reality, identity, and guilt similar to those of thought reform. Thus the Inquisition created its own witches, much as thought reform created its spies and reactionaries—this despite the fact that Inquisitors were specifically cautioned in one of their "technical manuals" (*Malleus Maleficarum* or *Witches' Hammer*) [23] against the undesirable possibility of producing false confessions. And prominent persons in Tudor England, impressed by "the brilliant aura of divinity, the inscrutable light of infallibility which emanated from the royal person" denounced themselves for crimes they had never committed.[24] Chinese Confucianism (whether or not one considers it a religion) on the whole avoided such tendencies, although it too at times became sensitive to heresy and moved in the direction of totalism; for the most part it created something closer to what Whitehead has termed a "genial orthodoxy," and allowed a considerable amount of personal leeway within the limits of its unchallengeable assumptions (in this respect not unlike some phases of medieval Catholicism).

The second variety of religious totalism, that associated with revitalizing enthusiasm, has been widespread enough: it can be found in the more extreme practices of early Lutheranism and Calvinism,[25] in the Chiliastic sects of the middle ages [26] and in many post-Reformation fundamentalist and revivalist cults. All of these movements, according to Ronald Knox, reflect the "overmastering influence" of St. Augustine—even if "exaggerated now from this angle, now from that." [27] Usually laying great stress upon the dramatic personal conversion experience, while varying in their relative emphasis upon confession and re-education, they have sought to purify man in accordance with a particular vision of Biblical truth or prophecy; as in thought reform, this vision has sometimes been so urgent that men have been physically and psychologically brutalized in its name.

Beyond these theological excesses, thought reform has a more fundamental relationship to religion in general, a relationship noted by almost every priest and minister who has come into contact with it. One Jesuit priest who was studying Chinese indoctrination methods in Hong Kong emphasized to me the following parallels with Christianity: the concept of love (of country, "the people," labor, science, and public property); the concept of hope in the future (through the accomplishments of socialism); faith (in Communist ideology); a deity (the Communist movement); a spirit of martyrdom, of sacrifice and suffering, an aspiration to sainthood; stress upon humility and selflessness; and the stress upon converting theoretical principles into a way of life. (Many secular writers—Bertrand Russell, for instance—have made similar comparisons.) Others among my subjects compared thought reform to their own Jesuit training, although they were usually quick to distinguish the two on the basis of ultimate moral purpose. A Protestant missionary was struck by its similarity with the Moral Re-

armament movement in which he had at one time been active—
especially in regard to such things as group manipulation of guilt
and planned spontaneity.[28] One or two priests spoke of Communism as "nothing but a Christian heresy"—a statement which
perhaps says both too much and too little; and few among my
subjects, whatever their clerical or secular status, failed to comment
upon the "religious" nature of thought reform's emotional in-
tensities, moral energies, and exhortative demands.

Keeping in mind thought reform's close relationship to religion,
how can we distinguish totalist practice within religious institutions
from more balanced forms of spirituality? Rhadakrishnan, the distinguished Indian philosopher and statesman, points to organizing
tendencies within religion as the specific danger:

> When religion becomes organized, man ceases to be free. It is not God
> that is worshipped but the group or the authority that claims to speak
> in His name. Sin becomes disobedience to authority and not violation
> of integrity.[29]

I believe we must consider also the prevailing themes within a
particular religious milieu. Thus religious totalism can be recognized
by the criteria outlined in Chapter 22, and especially by the following trends: exaggerated control and manipulation of the individual, the blanketing of the milieu with guilt and shame, the
emphasis upon man's hopeless depravity and worthlessness, and
upon his need to submit abjectly to a vengeful deity—all within the
framework of an exclusive and closed system of ultimate truth.

Contrasting with religious totalism are those religious situations
which stress man's worth and his possibilities as well as his limitation; his capacity to change as well as the difficulties inherent in
bringing about such change; and faith and commitment without
the need for either self-negation or condemnation of nonbelievers.
These attitudes leave room for emotional and intellectual growth
as opposed to static doctrinal repetitions, and a broadened sensitivity to the world rather than a retreat into religious embeddedness.
Since each of the world's major religions has at one time or another demonstrated both of these contrasting tendencies, any
particular religious environment must be judged according to its
own characteristics.[30]

Man is unlikely to give up his need for the sense of awe and devotion inherent in the religious experience; but there are indications from many parts of the world that organized religion is playing a diminishing role in mediating human change. Religious institutions, while highly influential, tend to assume a relatively conservative stance, and political movements, as well as scientific and technological innovations, have become the great regulators of change. During the past century, emotions formerly directed toward organized religion have been expressed in relationship to politics and science. This rechanneling of emotion is not without its dangers; as Camus said, "Politics is not religion, or, if it is, then it is nothing but the Inquisition." [31] Such political inquisitions occur —as in thought reform—when ideological totalists set up their own theocratic search for heresy.

One example of this variety of totalism in recent American history would be McCarthyism, a bizarre blend of political religion and extreme opportunism. True, this movement never developed the scope or the organization of a full-scale thought reform program, either during the lifetime of its leader or after his death; yet it had many uncomfortable resemblances, including most of the characteristics of ideological totalism. In particular: the "big accusation" accompanied by "small facts" (like that described by Father Vechten); the quick development of a relationship of guilt between the accused and his environment, along with ruthless exploitation of ostracism and shame; a cult of confession and repentance; a stress upon self-betrayal and a bond of betrayal between accusers and accused; the creation of a mythological doctrine (the State Department was being overrun by Communist "subversives" who were in turn responsible for "losing China"); and the demand that victims take on a new identity in accordance with this myth. The ostensible purpose of McCarthyism was of course that of fighting Communism; in the end, it not only did great service to Communism throughout the world, but also became a poor imitation of its declared enemy. Indeed, the focus of so much of McCarthyism's ideological mythology upon China seems more than coincidental. It suggests that the American emotional involvement in that country, based on years of missionary activity and wartime alliance, was so great, and the events of the Communist revolution so far-reaching and unpalatable, that the American public was receptive to a rewriting of history no less distorted than that of thought reform's own myth. And among those most actively engaged in the McCarthyist movement were many former Communists turned anti-Communist—all of which again seems to confirm (at varying levels of politics and individual emotion) the principle that totalism breeds totalism.

But McCarthyism was not simply a reaction to Communism; it had close connections with specific religious and secular currents in American life. Edward Shils has convincingly demonstrated its relationship to religious fundamentalism and to the demagogic strain of political populism.[32] This relationship suggests that the political inquisition and its related totalist phenomena find fertile soil in a wide variety of social and historical conditions and in virtually any culture. It also reveals the source of one of McCarthyism's fatal weaknesses—its antiscientific bias.

As Shils points out, the McCarthyist harassment of scientists within and without the government was not only a reflection of its general mania concerning "security," but also of the fundamentalist's long-standing distrust of the scientist, and of the demagogue's resentment of the intellectual. The thought reform movement also shows great distrust of the intellectual, but in contrast worships science and scientists. In these extreme attitudes we see a modern shift of the god-devil axis from religion to science.

The god side of the axis (by no means confined to the Communist world) is expressed vividly by Michael Polanyi:

. . . just as the three centuries following on the calling of the Apostles sufficed to establish Christianity as the state religion of the Roman Empire, so the three centuries after the founding of the Royal Society sufficed for science to establish itself as the supreme intellectual authority of the post-Christian age. "It is contrary to religion!"—the objection ruled supreme in the 17th century. "It is unscientific!" is its equivalent in the 20th.[33]

Accompanying this deification is the expectation that science will supply a complete and absolutely accurate mechanistic theory of a closed and totally predictable universe. Modern physics has long disowned this ideal, but it persists in the human sciences—biological, psychological, and social—and is particularly damaging there. Thought reform is its ultimate expression—a mechanized image of man within a closed society, and a claim to scientific method in the remaking of man in this image. There is the assumption that science—that is, the "social science" of Marxism—can liberate men from the encumbrances of all past institutions, family ties, social loyalties, professional affiliations, and religious and philosophical commitments: first by exposing these as "unscientific," then by demonstrating that they are no longer necessary in a truly "scientific" environment. It is true that this faith in science can produce much that is humane and beneficial: a distinguished British physician, for instance, after his return from a visit to China termed the Chinese Communist Party "probably the best instrument ever devised for cleaning up a slum, for instructing its inhabitants in hygiene and for getting everybody immunized." [34] But men also require institutions and conventions of varying degrees of rationality; and thought reform, rather than eliminating such institutions, has established new ones even more encompassing than the old, and a good deal more blinding in relationship to knowledge and truth.

While this god-pole of science seems now to predominate almost everywhere, it is possible that there lurks beneath it more of the devil-pole than might be suspected. For there are also suggestions (evident in many kinds of literature, including science fiction) of great hostility toward science, hostility beyond the fundamentalist prejudices of McCarthyism. Men resent the power of science to change familiar landscapes and to reshape the world in ways that make them feel less at home in it. Above all, they fear the destructive power of science, its capacity to create weapons which could destroy mankind. Science becomes, if not a disguised devil, at least a vengeful god to be feared beyond all others, and people begin to believe that if only we could be rid of science and scientists the world would be left in peace. God-pole and devil-pole, equally misleading and dangerous in their extremism, may even exist concurrently within the same mind.[35]

There are more constructive approaches to science, and there are alternatives to the kinds of totalist imbalance we have described among science, politics, and religion. An extensive discussion of these would be beyond both the scope of this book and my personal capabilities; but I would like to indicate a few of the possibilities which have been suggested by scientists themselves.

Albert Einstein, for instance, stressed the need for an equilibrium between science and nonscientific tradition:

> . . . the scientific method can teach us nothing else beyond how facts are related to, and conditioned by, each other . . . the aspiration toward such objective knowledge belongs to the highest of which man is capable. . . . Yet it is equally clear that knowledge of what *is* does not open the door directly to what *should be*. . . . To make clear these fundamental ends and valuations, and to set them fast in the emotional life of the individual, seems to me precisely the most important function which religion has to perform in the social life of man. And if one asks whence derives the authority of such fundamental ends, since they cannot be stated and justified merely by reason, one can only answer, they exist in a healthy society as powerful traditions, which act upon the conduct and the aspirations and judgments of individuals.[36]

Einstein does not claim for science the omnipotence which totalists bestow upon it, nor the authority to dictate or replace the full complex of ideals that men live by.

Indeed, the greatest of scientists have frequently spoken of their own need for faith—or trust—in the order of the universe, of their awe and humility before it, of the inevitable incompleteness of their understanding of it. Thus, Robert Oppenheimer writes about his profession:

> In it we learn, so frequently that we could almost become accustomed to it, how vast is the novelty of the world, and how much even the physical world transcends in delicacy and in balance the limits of man's prior imaginings. We learn that views may be useful and inspiriting although they are not complete. We come to have a great caution in all assertions of totality, of finality or absoluteness.[37]

It seems clear that scientific practice should lead one to reject, rather than embrace, totalism of any variety. J. Bronowski carries this view further in his discussion of "the scientific spirit" as a mode of thinking, with its emphasis upon "the creative mind," the "leap of imagination," and the "habit of truth"; and its requirement that "the society of scientists . . . be a democracy [which] can keep alive and grow only by a constant tension between dissent and respect, between independence from the views of others and tolerance for them." [38]

Science can advance greatly even in a totalitarian society, but it always requires a special enclave in which there exist speculative freedom and the "habit of truth." (Genuine science can serve as an escape from philistine sacred science and becomes in such a society one of the few professions in which unhindered creative work is possible. Indeed the attractions of this relatively free and highly-respected enclave within an over-controlled society are inevitably felt by that society's most talented young men and women, and may have much to do with the impressive scientific progress which has taken place in Russia.)

The ideas of Einstein, Oppenheimer, and Bronowski suggest the possibility of a society in which politics and science coexist neither in total isolation nor in suffocating embrace; in which political bodies help to guide scientifically-based change with sensitive concern for the simultaneous altering, elimination, and preservation of various traditional institutions; in which science itself is free to explore all aspects of the human and nonhuman realms, while actively resisting anyone's claim to a mechanized absolute: and above all, of a society supporting a variety of clerical and secular approaches to knowledge and to faith, no one of which is permitted to impose upon the others the threats and restrictions of self-acclaimed final truth.

We need not dwell upon the difficulties of achieving such a vision, and during the last half-century the world has, if anything, moved further from it. Nor is the task made simpler by the dramatic transformations which science is helping to promote everywhere, the significance of which is baffling to nonscientists and by no means fully clear to scientists themselves. Yet this vision can provide not only an alternative to totalism but also an approach toward restoring a more favorable balance in the creative-destructive potential always inherent within this three-way interplay. If religion, politics, and science can reach such an equilibrium, they will become less the objects of extremist emotions and more the rightful agents of three vital tendencies of individual mental life: spirituality, judiciousness, and the mastery of the unknown.

CHAPTER 24

"OPEN" PERSONAL CHANGE

Nontotalist approaches to re-education can encourage an experience of individual change very different from that promoted by thought reform—one characterized by "openness to the world" rather than by personal closure. Not much has been written about the psychology of this open form of personal change, and I will attempt only to suggest some of its features in relationship to the general problem of human change at this historical moment. I do so well aware of the difficulties involved both in formulating such change and in actually achieving it; yet it would seem to me less than responsible to conclude this study in any other way.

Any statement about human change depends upon one's assumptions concerning the extent to which adult and near-adult people can change. Chinese reformers seem to assume an extreme malleability of human character. They go far beyond conventional Marxist-Leninist approaches in their conviction that even those who have been exposed to the most pernicious influences of the "exploiting classes" can "change their class" and personally "turn over." They look upon human beings, at least implicitly, as wrongly-molded clay, needing only new molds and proper remolding from ideological potters—a remolding process which they themselves are willing to pursue with the hottest of fires and the most suffocating of kilns. Theirs is the totalist vision of change, what J. L.

Talmon has called "the sustained and violent effort to make all things new." [1]

Psychiatric experience can support no such view. As psychiatrists, we are in fact constantly impressed with the enduring quality of emotional patterns developed during infancy and childhood, and with the difficulties involved in changing these. We are also struck by the importance of certain universals of emotional life—ambivalent admixtures of love, hate, shame, guilt, striving, and dependency. These exist partly outside of conscious awareness, and none can be completely eliminated even by the dramatic type of change which thought reform proposes. It may be, however, that in psychiatry we err in the opposite direction, that we underestimate the possibilities for adult change. Thus some psychiatric writing seems to express the ultra-conservative notion that there is nothing new under the sun, that man is so "determined" by his instincts and by the events of his childhood that all suggestion of later change is illusory.

Recent work in the human sciences, however, suggests a middle ground,[2] and it is this approach I wish to pursue here. For I believe that change during adult life is real and perpetual; significant change may be extremely difficult to consolidate, but the capacity to change significantly during adult life has become in this historical epoch increasingly necessary for emotional survival. Thus, in the individual subjects of this study, important changes occurred during late adolescence and adulthood, although impressively consistent behavioral patterns remained throughout their lives. And more universally, we find imaginative expression of this capacity to change in the great mythological theme of "death and rebirth," a theme given coercive expression in thought reform.

I wish to describe in rough outline a pattern of personal change, another symbolic form of death and rebirth, parallel to but significantly different from that imposed by totalist practice. Such a change can occur through more or less formal association with education, religion, therapy, or politics; it can also take place through less structured encounter with new people, new ideas, or new landscapes. We may conveniently envision it within a three-step sequence: confrontation, reordering, and renewal.

By *confrontation* I mean the combination of inner impulse and external challenge which creates within a person the simultaneous recognition of the need and the possibility for change. I stress the element of inner impulse because I believe that there is in man a fundamental urge toward change—a force which propels him in the direction of what is new and unknown—ever battling with his opposing tendency to cling exclusively to what is emotionally familiar. In this sense man is never simply "changed" by external forces, but rather finds his individual impulses toward change activated and manipulated by these forces. Without such inner assistance from each individual person, the agencies of change could have little success, and little justification for their existence. External challenge is thus always related to internal urges to know and to master.

This open confrontation causes a questioning of identity rather than thought reform's assault upon identity. It calls forth the most specifically human of faculties—introspection and symbolization—rather than stunting these faculties by use of totalist coercion and dogma. The person so challenged is thrown back upon the resources derived from his own past without being thrust into thought reform's regressive stance. He experiences anxiety at the prospect of emerging from the security of existing identities and beliefs, possibly even the severe anxiety of potential nothingness, but not the sense of being annihilated by all-powerful manipulators of anxiety. He feels the guilt and shame of unfulfillment—the "shock of recognition" of neglected personal capacities—but without the virulent self-hatred demanded by the accusatory totalist milieu. He may experience a deep sense of inner and outer disharmony, of uncomfortable personal alienation, but not the antagonistic estrangement of thought reform. The rebel who undergoes "a feeling of revulsion at the infringement of his rights," [3] the prospective religious convert who becomes aware of his "divided self," [4] the seeker of psychotherapy who comes to recognize the debilitating nature of his neurosis, the artist who feels himself drawn into a new creative realm, and the ordinary man who at some point questions the pattern of his existence—all of these are examples of confrontation.

To act upon this confrontation is to advance to the next phase, that of *reordering*; and this means embarking upon the work of re-education and change. As in thought reform, reordering is likely to include a personal "emptying" process—some form of confession and exploration of existential guilt—in the service of exposing and altering past emotional patterns. But the personal exposure is dignified by privacy and balance; insights and interpretations are neither coercively publicized nor artificially guided along the negative thought reform channels of self-betrayal and logical dishonoring. The involved individual cannot avoid the impact of his negative identity, but he is not forced to view himself as *nothing but* this most debasing of self-images. In dealing with the harsh realities of his own limitations and of the world outside himself, he is by no means guaranteed a happy ending: he may indeed experience the terror and dread of a true sense of tragedy, but not the humiliating command performance of thought reform's manipulated pseudo-tragedy.

Symbolic emptying is accompanied by a corresponding absorption of new or refashioned ideas and emotions; this absorption can be accomplished by relatively free learning rather than by the narrow impositions of a sacred science. This learning requires a measure of personal isolation, and even a temporary refractoriness to alternative influences, but not the hermetic self-sealing of totalism. There is the opportunity to test the personal validity of new ideas, to experiment with new forms of human relationships and creative expression, rather than the demand that all of these be subjugated to prefabricated totalist ideology and language. Through emptying and absorption, the individual (as in thought reform) constantly reinterprets his own past. He cannot reinterpret without ideological bias, without a certain amount of emotional polarization and an overcritical attitude toward his past conditioned by his urge to change; but he can find ways to moderate his judgments (through both introspection and outside influences), rather than having them further distorted by the always immoderate, guilt saturated totalist milieu.

The third and final stage consists of a sense of open *renewal*, contrasting with thought reform's closed form of rebirth. Renewal depends upon the new alignment—the new sense of fit—between personal emotions and personally-held ideas about the world; in other words, on a new interplay between identity and ideology in which both have been changed. Through renewal, the individual can free himself from exaggerated dependencies and experience an "emergence from embeddedness" [5] rather than a plunge into a new form of totalist embeddedness. He can accomplish this only by viewing his relationships to old authorities as steps along his personal path toward greater independence, not by making the illusory totalist effort to annihilate their inner remnants or deny their existence.

He is free to experience a new or reinforced commitment to an ideal or a cause, but a commitment made autonomously and in the face of alternatives, rather than as a compulsory loyalty associated with a bond of betrayal. Instead of totalism's highly-simplified and distorted pure image approach to knowledge, he may acquire an enlarged receptivity to intellectual and emotional complexities around him. Nor can this renewal be consolidated by the symbolic submission of a "final confession" or a "final thought summary"; rather, there must be an awareness (whether gradual or sudden) of genuine self-knowledge and a readiness to accept its consequences. These include: a personal responsibility for expressions of love and hate, rather than a submission to their legislation by push-button enthusiasm or by ideological command; and a recognition of social identifications beyond the self—free of ideological exclusiveness, and including yet transcending family, profession, culture, and nation.

A person so renewed, instead of being coercively reshaped according to an imposed ideological myth, will be able to call forth the "submerged metaphor" [6] of his own mythologically nourished imagination to further his efforts at self-expression. He will feel himself to be connected with his past, however critical he may be of it, and will not try, in the totalist manner, to cut himself off from it completely. This new harmony, however, cannot afford him total relief from personal conflict and confusion. A certain amount of conflict and confusion are in fact inherent in the enlarged life space which he attains, in contrast to their attempted elimination by totalist constriction. Such renewal, whether achieved through personal search or by guided secular or clerical change, places one in more viable relationship to the universal human experience, or to "the principle of continuous life." [7]

In contrasting this open style of change with the closed thought reform mode, I am admittedly speaking in ideal terms. No such change can proceed entirely unhindered, as closed-system emotional patterns always exist within any person—patterns of regression, mistrust, and of incapacitating dependency—which undermine open change at every turn. The three steps I have described are, of course, schematic, since each is likely to be incomplete and all three can occur simultaneously.

Yet open change does occur and has been described. We can see it in the lives of great men: in, for instance, Camus' emergence from the "burning and disordered" years of his experiments with totalism (both Communism and nihilism) to become perhaps the most articulate moralist and exponent of autonomous commitment in our century.[8] We see it also in what William James described as the "willingness to be" of religious converts and the "states of knowledge" and "states of insight" of Eastern and Western mystics;[9] and in what Michael Balint calls the "new beginning of love" of successfully treated psychoanalytic patients.[10] We have also observed change of this kind among the subjects of this study, in their casting off the closed influences of thought reform and undergoing a personal experience of renewal (for example, Father Vechten, Father Luca, George Chen, and Mr. Hu). I would make the further claim that in the completion of every genuinely creative act, and in fact at some time during virtually every adult life, changes of this open variety take place.

Whether a change is open, closed, or something of each, it involves the entire person. For this reason I have stressed throughout this study the relationship of personal identity to specific attitudes and values as well as to larger ideologies; and I have used the concept of identity as a large configuration rather than a localized subdivision in the mental topography. Similarly, I have spoken little of "persuasion" and much of pressures toward identity change. For I feel that belief and identity are so intimately related that any change in one must affect the other. This means that anyone's approach to ideologies, within his own culture or without, will invariably be strongly influenced by existing group identifications (or more broadly, by the need to belong), as well as by the ever-present inner struggle for a self-respecting personal definition. Also of great importance is the question of guilt, and especially existential guilt. That which will permit a man to come to terms with his own feeling of limitation and at the same time afford him a sense of group affiliation and personal continuity is that which he will come to believe.

This psychological interplay is always related to broader historical influences. Problems of identity and belief are likely to become more widespread and intense when individual change is associated with rapid culture change—and during our epoch rapid culture change has become the rule rather than the exception. Thus the changing identity sequence we described for China in Chapter 19 has important meaning for other countries still emerging from traditional individual and social patterns—countries in Asia, the Middle East, parts of Europe, Africa, and South America. Nations in all of these areas have, in widely diverse ways, shared an ethos of filialism and an identity of the filial son. Now mostly in some kind of transitional stage, they show strong evidence of rebellion against filialism and of adopting the identity of the modern student. Highly vocal "youth cultures" are appearing where they had never existed before—young people in great conflict with their parents and with family-oriented customs, demanding self-expression in place of youthful deference, seeking active patterns (or even activism) rather than passive ones, experiencing bitter anger and painful guilt in connection with their rebellion, undergoing considerable confusion in identity, and feeling desperate ideological hunger. This seems to be the individual pattern of culture change within any recently traditional society. And contesting ideologies—nationalism, liberal democracy (or democratic socialism), and Communism—are also still battling as they did in China.

Certainly a major task of the human sciences is to relate knowledge of specific cultures to existing universal alternatives in the direction of change—and to gain more understanding of the actual process of change in both cultures and individual people.[11] As John Dewey wrote in 1949, "Social 'science' waits upon a grasp of the fact that the only possible stable coordinations are *equilibria of movements* in respect to one another. . . . Now that practically all things are 'in process,' failure to study the direction in which they are moving constitutes the present . . . disorganization." [12]

In pursuing this problem, we will do well to pay special attention to youth groups, to men and women from sixteen to thirty years old. It is they who most enthusiastically espouse the change-stimulating ideas and ideologies. And there is good reason to believe that in these youth groups we can regularly see, as we saw in China, a culture's experimentations with its own possible future courses. I do not wish to imply that these youth group phenomena alone initiate culture change, for there is no denying the importance of technological and industrial development, of altered patterns in child-rearing and education, and of new ideologies and social institutions. But I do suggest that youth groups represent a human vanguard in the sense that they are the first and most intense indicators of the kinds of psychological experience and identity shift which will occur subsequently in adult populations throughout a particular society.

Thus, I believe that the developmental phase of late adolescence and early adulthood has special significance for all subsequent personal change. This is the period in which adult identity takes shape, and it is the time of strong enthusiasms, of a marked tendency toward emotional polarization, of great ideological receptivity, and of maximum experiential intensity. I suspect that during any adult change it is necessary to revive in some fashion—or else perpetuate—the predominant patterns of this phase of life, perhaps even more than those of the earlier phases of childhood to which psychiatry presently directs so much attention. This is not to minimize the importance of character formation during early life, but rather to suggest that the altering of adult identity depends upon a specific recapturing of much of the emotional tone which prevailed at the time that this adult identity took shape. This view is consistent with William James' association of religious conversion with "the ordinary storm and stress and moulting-time of adolescence," and his conviction that "conversion is in its essence a normal adolescent phenomenon, incidental to the passage from the child's small universe to the wider intellectual and spiritual life of maturity." [13] The "moulting-time" of youth, then, establishes within each man a model for later adult change; and the sudden emergence of youth cultures can similarly provide a social model (or several alternative models) for later historical change.

All of this has much bearing on the problem of ideological totalism. For the more intense the identity strains and patterns of alienation among the modern students of any country emerging from filialism, the greater the possibility of this group's adopting extremist approaches to the resolution of such strains. In China these took the form of Communist ideology, and the "therapy" of thought reform. Other countries may respond similarly to the attractions of totalism, as a means of achieving rapid economic and technological growth and of simultaneously dealing with identity tasks similar to those described for China: the destruction of traditional filialism, the undermining of Western liberalism, the mopping up of transitional chaos, and the resurrection of filial emotions in the service of a closed mass movement. These countries, insofar as their specific cultural traditions allow, could conceivably also adopt some thought reform-like process for the purpose of carrying out a similar program. In studying patterns of historical change, we should divest ourselves of the psychological illusion that a strong filial tradition is a bulwark against modern ideological totalism (or most specifically, Communism). The opposite seems to be true. It is precisely the desperate urge to sweep away decaying yet still powerful filial emotions and institutions that can call forth political totalism.

Nor are post-industrial cultures—including our own "affluent society"—immune from identity strains of equal severity, or from possible attractions to various forms of totalism. In our country, these attractions could stem from a sense of purposelessness, confusion, and lack of commitment; of dissatisfaction with the ritualism and roteness created by overorganization of our professional and social spheres (big society and mass society); of mounting evidences of corrupt and irresponsible practice in public life and within communication media; and of our relative ineffectuality in the face of the gains of ideological rivals (including some envy of their apparent totalist efficiency). Again some of the patterns of youth culture may be revealing; and in American youth we encounter—amidst much quiet conformity—rebellion which concerns itself less with political preoccupations and more with patterns of social nihilism, iconoclastic criticism of existing cultural forms, and an urge for direct and absolute "experience." Indeed, the Zen Buddhist plunge of the American beatnik has in it some of the same element of total rejection of one's past, in exchange for another's past, as the Chinese intellectual's initial plunge into Western sociopolitical forms.

This is not to say that totalism is by any means the sole (or even most probable) eventuality, either for ourselves or for the transitional cultures of which we have spoken. It rather suggests the faltering state of liberal alternatives to totalism, the paucity of nontotalist social visions for the future, and the urgent necessity for such visions. It may be that the most fervent of liberal antitotalists —those most confident of their moral stand—are among those intellectuals who have known the most extreme forms of totalism— among Chinese, Poles, and Hungarians who have spoken out against their regimes. The actions of these groups have an additional significance, for they demonstrate that the open nontotalist mode of existence has been sufficiently experienced to have become part of the broad human consciousness, and is therefore likely to continue to endure everywhere as a viable alternative to totalism. The youth rebellions opposing totalism in Eastern Europe, Russia, and China seem to combine urges toward privacy, personal freedom, and self-expression (frequently manifested by interest in non-Communist literature, art, and jazz music, or by "bourgeois romance") with patterns of nihilism not too different from those found in the United States and among youths throughout the world.

Surely the craving and the search are universal: man seeks new modes of existence—blending the scientific, the political, the artistic, and the spiritual—which will provide liberal alternatives to totalism along with the sense of feeling meaningfully related to a world whose most constant feature is change. No one can predict from what quarter such a vision, or elements of it, may emerge.

We can be sure that these alternative visions will in part depend upon a more accurate perception of current human transformations —individually, by generations, and in terms of the broader evolutionary process. It may be that this knowledge will teach us that we require—as has been suggested in relationship to primitive societies—wholistic configurations of change which take into account all aspects of human life while at the same time permitting a sense of continuity with one's personal past.[14] But perhaps we shall also have to make a more conscious effort to preserve specific elements within our heritage even as so much of it is in the process of being altered. Certainly we must learn to live with a good deal of conflict, confusion, and ferment, and at the same time cultivate the emotional balance of "thought which recognizes limits."[15] By "we" I mean mankind: "the community today is the planet,"[16] and it is indeed already beyond that.

In studying thought reform and related expressions of totalism,

I have been profoundly impressed with the dangers which face this expanding human community, dangers which arise from man's tendency to symbolize his universe within a suffocating circle of hatred. I have been equally impressed with his ingenuity in breaking out of that circle, with his physical and emotional resiliency, and with the extraordinary scope of his imaginative faculties at moments when he feels his existence most threatened.

APPENDIX, NOTES, AND INDEX

APPENDIX

A CONFESSION DOCUMENT

The following is the confession of Professor Chin
Yüeh-lin, made during the thought reform campaign
of 1951–52, as translated in *Current Background*, No. 213, American Consulate General, Hong Kong, October 1, 1952. Professor Chin, who spent a number of years studying in this country, mostly at Harvard University, has been regarded as China's leading authority on formal logic.

CRITICIZING MY IDEALISTIC BOURGEOIS PEDAGOGICAL IDEOLOGY

By Chin Yüeh-lin

(Peking *Kuang Ming Jih Pao*, April 17, 1952)

Born of a bureaucratic landlord family, I have always led a life of ease and comfort. I went abroad at nineteen and stayed there for eleven years to absorb the way of life and the predilection for pleasure of the European and American bourgeoisie. The principal source of my various pleasures lay in the decadent philosophy of the bourgeoisie, and for thirty years I played a game of concepts. I was engrossed in this game of concepts because it was the only way for me to feel happy and free, and to escape from the restrictive realities of society. I thus cultivated the habit of running away from realities, despising realities, and leading a life isolated from realities. However, since I still had to live in a society of realities, the only way for me to maintain this life isolated from the realities was to gain certain privileges. I needed those privileges, and I thus fell a victim to the ideology of special privileges.

MY CRUST OF SELFISHNESS

My life in school served to form this outer crust of mine which can conveniently be divided into three phases:

I. *My decadent bourgeois philosophy.* While in school, I incessantly disseminated the trivialities of metaphysical idealism, in particular the inanities of metaphysical philosophical methods. As I gradually assumed a position of leadership within the Philosophy Department of Tsinghua, all sorts of injuries to the people's enterprises inevitably resulted as manifested in: (1) I obstructed the development of the philosophy of materialistic dialectics in Tsinghua's Philosophy Department. Though I never actually tried to stop the discussion of materialistic dialectics among teachers and students, I nevertheless throttled the development of materialistic dialectics in Tsinghua's Philosophy Department by subjecting it to attacks by a circuitous system of philosophical debate. (2) I trained those who concerned themselves only with the game of concepts, were not interested in politics, and were even reactionary. As for instance, Yin Fu-sheng, one of the reactionary elements for whose training I was responsible, is now serving the Chiang bandits in Taiwan. I was further possessed of the bourgeois viewpoint of the education of the talented. I was thus very much struck by Professor Shen Yüeh-ting's powers in playing the game of concepts. As a result of my evil influence, Professor Shen is even now seriously isolated from the realities. (3) I disseminated the purely technical viewpoint in logic. For twenty years I taught logic to numerous students. All the time, however, I only tried to teach logic from the formalistic viewpoint, as for instance I was only concerned with the correctness of the reasoning without caring about the truthfulness of the premises. My mistaken viewpoint of education for the talented led me to think highly of Wang Hao, who even now is serving the interests of American imperialism by being connected with an American university. (4) I encouraged the development of sectarianism within Tsinghua's Philosophy Department by stressing the highly involved analysis of concepts and the formulation of circuitous systems of philosophy as the most important aspects of philosophy. I then thought that the Philosophy Department of Tsinghua was very good in these respects. This sort of sectarianism was inevitably one of the facts which obstructed the regulation of the departments and colleges.

II. *My decadent "above-politics," "above-class," "out-of-the-world", and "above-humanity" philosophy of life.* Before the liberation, having absolutely no idea of the truth that the human world is created through labor, I mistakenly took the human race to be insignificant and the history of the human race to be but a minor episode in the main stream. I therefore tended to despise the world, and to become above-politics and above-class. My preoccupation with this decadent philosophy of life led me to despise administrative work. I consequently tried by all means to minimize my personal affairs and adopted an attitude of absolute indifference toward all things. When I was charged with administrative work after the liberation, my mistaken attitude inevitably resulted in idiotic bureaucratism. Though a member of the University Administration Committee, I spoke up only once in all its meetings, and I honestly had nothing to talk about; and though the Dean of the College of Arts really had very little to do, what little there was I neglected altogether. For instance, I never seemed to remember that I was actually the Dean of the College of Arts when handling such matters as the resumption of publication of the Tsinghua Journal, the maintenance of proper relationship between the different colleges and departments, etc. As Chairman of the Philosophy Department, I left the affairs of the department to take care of themselves, and I never bothered to do anything about personnel appointments within the department.

III. *My ideology of special privileges.* In order to maintain my way of life, I had to have special privileges. I felt the need for these privileges, I enjoyed these privileges, became obsessed by the ideology of special privileges, and I became one of the privileged few of Tsinghua. Though I was privileged, I yet refused to shoulder the accompanying responsibilities. Thus, while I enjoyed special privileges in Tsinghua, yet I never burdened myself with administrative work.

The three above-mentioned phases constituted the main ingredients of my crust. The scope of the crust was moreover variable: one crust represented my individual self, one crust the Philosophy Department, while another represented Tsinghua. My personal crust being the "core" of this miniature universe, I accordingly remained completely indifferent to things which had little to do with my personal interests. Whenever the matter in question was in conflict with my personal crust, I always sallied forth to give battle. As for instance, when the son of Professor Liang Ssu-ch'eng wanted to change his registration from the History Department to the Architecture Department, I, as an old friend of the family who knew him when he was born, tried to help him, in the thought that he was more suited to the study of architecture. Though there are certain strict restrictions in connection with the change of registration from one department to another, yet I made use of my special privileges to work on his behalf which resulted in a series of serious mistakes. This is but one example of a situation which conflicted with my personal crust. I opposed the reform of curriculum because I wanted to maintain the crust of the Philosophy Department in Tsinghua. When the regulation of departments and colleges started in 1950, I was dead against it, for my most outstanding crust was Tsinghua University. Motivated by departmentalism, sectarianism, and the educational ideology of the bourgeoisie, I was of infinite harm to the program for the regulation of departments and colleges. Had the regulation of departments and colleges been carried out in 1950, then Tsinghua alone would have turned out another 5,000–6,000 cadres, and a far larger number would have been turned out throughout the country. Incalculable harm has thus been caused the democratic construction program of the entire country. For this I now hate myself beyond measure.

MY POLITICAL ATTITUDE

My crust is based on the past prevailing economic social foundation, that is, the capitalistic social system. In order to protect this crust, I had to give my political support to the old system of democracy. As a confirmed individualistic liberal, I have always based my political attitude upon this point of view. Only now have I realized that fact that the old democracy is but the dictatorship of the bourgeois class, and the so-called individual freedom is but the "freedom" for the bourgeoisie to exploit and oppress the laboring people. My numerous criminal deeds of the past should thus be attributed to my acceptance of individual liberalism.

With regard to my attitude toward American imperialism, as a result of long years of studying in America, the evil influences of bourgeois education, my large number of American friends, and my constant contact with Americans, I became instilled with pro-American thoughts which prevented me from realizing American imperialism's plots of aggression against China during the past hundred years, and turned me into an unconscious instrument of American imperialistic cultural aggression. I cried bitterly over the Twenty-one Demands, but took no notice of the Sino-American Treaty of Friendship, Commerce and Navigation. While I was highly indignant at the time of the Tsinan Incident during the Northern Expedition, and was all for resisting Japan when the Mukden incident and the Luguochiao Incident took place, I nevertheless remained blind to the misdeeds of American soldiers in China. In 1943 I was one of the Chinese professors who went to America on the invitation of the American State Department. There, totally deprived of my national standpoint as a result of my pro-American thoughts, I even tried to persuade the American State Department to force bandit Chiang to practice democracy.

With regard to my attitude toward the Soviet Union, in always looking at the USSR from the viewpoint of old democracy, I consistently distorted and slandered the Soviet Union, and right up to the liberation I thought that individual "freedom" does not exist in the Soviet Union. I considered both the October Revolution and the purges within the Party to be "going too far," and that the Soviet Union made use of the Communist Party in other countries to interfere in their internal affairs. All these ideas were of course mistaken and reactionary. My principal mistake lay in thinking of the Soviet Union as devoid of individual freedom. At that time, in failing to take the October Revolution as an epoch-making great event of history, I only tried to antagonize the Soviet Union on the basis of my individual liberal pro-America ideology. It was only after the liberation that I succeeded gradually in gaining an understanding of true freedom, and thus to change my attitude toward the Soviet Union.

With regard to student movements, I nearly always maintained a negative and double-faced attitude toward all the student movements I came across in my teaching career. On the one hand I "loathed" the Kuomintang of the Chiang bandits, while on the other hand I opposed the Communist Party of China. I say "loathed" advisedly, because I never tried to oppose them by any positive effort. Before I left for America in 1943, I had to go through five days of Kuomintang training in Chungking before I could get my passport, and had to write a short essay of two hundred words on the advisability for local officials to visit the central government. This was really a shame. Though I honestly loathed the Kuomintang, this was not what mattered. The important thing was that I opposed the Chinese Communists. This dualism in my make-up was best shown at the time of the December First Incident [a student movement which took place in 1945 in Kunming]. Though I was highly enthusiastic at the start of the movement, when I followed the footsteps of the progressive elements, I later lost my interest and finally I stood for the resumption of class. This was because I opposed the Communists. Soon after the end of the movement I quarreled with Professor Chang Hsi-jo and I told him in the sternest manner and in tears that, "It is you people who made such a mess of China. After depriving China of 'freedom,' it will take I don't know how many years to have it restored."

As viewed from the three above-mentioned aspects, my political attitude was truly intolerable. How was it possible that though early in life I loved my country and wanted to save her from the fate of partition, yet I turned out to be such a fool later? On this point I have to charge the American imperialists who made use of a mission school, that is, Tsinghua College, and of the education I received while in America, to turn me into an instrument of American imperialistic cultural aggression, deprived me of my national standpoint, prevented me from making a distinction between our friends and our enemies, and led me to do things detrimental to the people.

MY IDEOLOGICAL CHANGE

My preliminary understanding of the People's Liberation Army and the Communist Party. The miracles of the People's Liberation Army demanded my whole-hearted respect. I never thought such discipline possible, and they love the people so much. In the early days after the liberation, I was highly moved by an episode involving the son of my maid Liu. When her son, who was working in a certain factory, misbehaved himself, certain soldiers of the PLA stationed in that factory tried to reform him by education. When this failed, two comrades of the PLA approached Liu to request her to go and reform her son. In the end, the two soldiers treated the mother to a meal and finally saw her home. I consider such a fighting force as unique in history. In the spring of 1949, I was fortunate enough to have the chance to listen to a series of reports rendered by various senior Party cadres. There attitude was so very honest and sincere and they were always prepared to practice what they preach. Though all occupying senior positions within the Party, they yet were always ready to admit their mistakes publicly before the masses. Such a party I consider unprecedented in China. However, this kind of recognition was only the preliminary stage of cognition through emotion, something within the capability of all Chinese.

My change in philosophical ideology. Generally speaking this change can be divided into three periods. During the first period, I was still unable to link up the actualities of the revolution with Marxism-Leninism. Though I had already acquired a preliminary understanding of the Communist Party and the PLA, yet this did not mean that I was ready to accept materialistic dialectics and historical dialectics. When Comrade Ai Ssu-ch'i lectured in Tsinghua, I even tried to argue with him. Starting from the months of March and April 1949, I began to attend various meetings for the exchange of philosophical opinions. Even at that time I still held two mistaken points of view: in the first place I still looked upon materialistic dialectics and the old philosophy as equals, and, under the illusion that our Communist comrades were ignorant of the old philosophy, had the wish to initiate them in the mysteries of old philosophy; in the second place, in the mistaken idea that materialistic dialectics and historical dialectics were not well systematized, I thought of putting them to order by means of my trivial system of analysis. My unbelievable arrogance and ignorance was the result of the fact that I was still looking at materialistic dialectics on the basis of the old philosophy. As I took part in the first attempt at curriculum reform in the above mentioned spirit, naturally nothing was accomplished. The Philosophy Department was thus prevented from making any progress.

The second period lasted roughly from the start of the second attempt at curriculum reform in 1950 to the spring of 1951. From the very start of this period I had already accepted the leading position of materialistic dialectics, and rectified my two above-mentioned mistakes. I then considered materialistic dialectics as a piece of red string linking up all different branches of knowledge. Yet, though I admitted its importance in an abstract fashion, my real interests were still focused on philosophy, as one of the branches of knowledge linked up by materialistic dialectics. In this manner I was still trying to oppose the new philosophy by the old. Both on the basis of my mistaken views and in compliance to the then prevailing conditions in Tsinghua's Philosophy Department, I proposed to divide the departments into three groups: history of philosophy, logic, and history of art. Since this amounted to change in name only but not change in substance, I again succeeded in preventing Tsinghua's Philosophy Department from making any progress.

In the spring of 1951, I went regularly into the city to make a study of *On Practice* [an essay by Mao Tse-tung]. It was during this period that a radical change began to take place in my ideology. For almost two years before this, I had been going to the city regularly every Sunday to take part in the study activities of the Chinese Philosophy Society. Whatever I gained in the course of these two years, coupled with my study of *On Practice*, enabled me to realize the fundamental difference in nature between materialistic dialectics and the old philosophy. The old philosophy, being metaphysical, is fundamentally unscientific, while the new philosophy, being scientific, is the supreme truth. It was during the Curriculum Reform Campaign of 1951 that I succeeded in realizing that the mission of the Philosophy Department lies in the training of propaganda personnel for the dissemination of Marxism-Leninism. This time the curriculum reform was carried out in a comparatively thorough manner. However, insofar as my understanding of materialistic dialectics was still based on abstract concepts, it inevitably brought serious consequences to Tsinghua's Philosophy Department.

THE DANGERS OF IDEALISM AND BOURGEOIS PEDAGOGICAL IDEOLOGY TO THE PHILOSOPHY DEPARTMENT

Idealism and bourgeois pedagogical ideology have always occupied a leading position in Tsinghua's Philosophy Department, and I have all the time been an outstanding representative of this decadent ideology. This situation has remained more or less unchanged right from the liberation up to the moment. This naturally resulted in huge losses. In the main, our principal defects lay in our low level of political consciousness and the dislocation of theory from practice. The concrete manifestations are as follows:

To deal with materialistic dialectics by means of the analysis of concepts really amounts to the exposition of Marxism-Leninism by means of idealistic metaphysical methods. As for instance, should we try to carry out in class a conceptual analysis of "necessity and contingency" and "relative truth and absolute truth," we would inevitably fall into the trap of running around in abstract circles of concepts, with the students getting more and more confused. To teach Marxism-Leninism in such a manner can only result in the distortion of Marxism-Leninism. Marxism-Leninism which in itself is concrete, militant, and should serve as the guide for our action, has, in our hands, been turned into a lifeless and abstract heap of concepts.

Under the influence of this kind of idealistic bourgeois pedagogical ideology, certain students naturally fell a victim to idealism. A student by the name of Li Hsüeh-chin is, in this respect, an outstanding example. Li entered Tsinghua in 1951, and within half a year he managed to read up on Wang Yang-ming [the idealist philosopher of the Ming Dynasty], the Buddhist philosophy of Hsiung Shih-li, Moslem philosophy, and various other obscure books. When certain students felt they were unable to study the subjects they needed, they naturally changed their registration to other departments. Of the thirteen students of the class of 1949, nine decided to enter other departments; of the seven students of the class of 1950, five changed to other departments; and of the eight students of the class of 1951, two are going to change their registration to other departments.

Another undesirable manifestation in pedagogy lay in the dogmatic attempt to stuff the students with various theories, without taking pains to solve the ideological problems of the students. Inasmuch as materialistic dialectics is one of the subjects taught in the general political course attended by the entire school, I only tried to deal with materialistic dialectics in a supplementary manner, in the mistaken idea that the responsibility for the solution of ideological problems lay with the general political course, while in teaching materialistic dialectics in the Philosophy Department we only had to deal with the theoretical aspects. I thus erred in idealistically divorcing the problems of ideology and theory to cause the students great confusion.

Though Marxism-Leninism is designed to solve practical problems, yet in our hands, it is fundamentally unable to solve the ideological problem of the students. To cite three graduates of the 1950 class of the Philosophy Department as examples: one by the name of Tang entered the graduate school of the Philosophy Department, but he was all the time more interested in mathematics; another graduate by the name of Chou gave up all his former training to enter the Physics Department of Peita; while still another graduate by the name of Shui, though he had already qualified for the graduate school of the Philosophy Department, yet chose to enter Peita to study chemistry. Though all three students had ideological trouble, yet neither I nor the other teachers of the Philosophy Department succeeded in giving them timely assistance. Of this year's freshman students in the Philosophy Department, eight have already signified their wish to change their registration. With the situation in our department even as serious as it was, we still failed to notice it, not to say remedy the situation. It is entirely due to the fact that we were so badly poisoned ourselves that we failed to notice the seriousness of the situation and to rectify it.

In the bourgeois pedagogical method there is fundamentally no relationship between the teacher and the student. I myself only went to class to lecture, without caring whether the students understood me or whether they had any problems. I often missed classroom discussions, and I had no concern for the life, ideology, and state of health of the students. In adopting a liberalist attitude towards the students' studies, the teachers of the Philosophy Department always left everything to the individual efforts of the students. As for instance, we remained ignorant of the fact that a certain student studied for as many as seventy hours a week, and we certainly would not have done anything had we known it.

Though the mission of the Philosophy Department lies in the training of cadres for the dissemination of Marxism-Leninism, yet as a result of the predominance of idealistic philosophy and pedagogical practice within the department, we inevitably failed to carry out this task, thus bringing about the above-mentioned harmful effects. Whereas this responsibility should be borne by all the professors of the Philosophy Department, the greater part of the guilt should be attributed to me for I led them to become estranged from politics and isolated from realities.

THE TEACHERS' STUDY MOVEMENT AND THE THREE-ANTI CAMPAIGN

As stated above, it was in the spring of 1951 that I began to realize the scientific and truthful nature of Marxism-Leninism, though this realization was even then abstract and conceptual. Before the start of the study movement for the teachers of Peking and Tientsin and the Three-Anti Campaign, I failed to link up Marxism-Leninism both with the realities in general and with my personal case. Though I took part in numerous activities in and out of Tsinghua, these activities never influenced me to any appreciable degree. It was only at the start of the teachers' study movement that I succeeded in linking myself up, criticizing my old democratic individual liberalistic ideology, and taking the first step in gaining a correct understanding of the Soviet Union and of American imperialism. I was still unable to gain a correct understanding of my former ideological self. It was only at the start of the Three-Anti Campaign that I began to understand my former self, my crust of selfishness, and my ideological shortcomings. Late in the spring of 1951, I began to try to become a good teacher of the people. However, I never was able to succeed in this. Not only did I fail, but I even committed the gravest mistakes. With the assistance of others and following my own preliminary analysis, I now consider the fundamental ideological source for my personal crust of selfishness to be the extremely depraved, epicurean, liberalist, and bourgeois ideology of striving after individual freedom. The philosophical manifestation of this ideology was found in my preoccupation with the completely impractical and extremely abstract game of concepts. In personal philosophy of life, this ideology was manifested in my decadent "above-politics," "above-class," "above-the-world," and "above-humanity" viewpoint. In actual life at school, this ideology was manifested in my attempt to maintain my life of ease and comfort and to build up a crust of special privileges. This kind of ideology was the ideology of the exploitative class, or rather the exploitative ideology of the "share-holders" and "behind-the-scene-boss" of the exploitative class. It was owing to this ideology that I was led to become estranged from the social realities and prevented from gaining a correct understanding of the people even after the liberation. I shall smash my personal crust and eradicate the bourgeois ideologies which have for years dominated my life.

MY DETERMINATION

He who loves New China well must know that in New China the people are on their feet and have come into their own. There are 470,000,000 Chinese in New China and I am one of them. This New China is working for the interests and welfare of the people of China as well as of the world. I have no wish to be an onlooker both in connection with the revolution and with the people's construction enterprises. I want to take part in the glorious and mighty enterprises which should be participated in not only by the young, but by the people of all ages, including the old. I am now close to sixty, and I am a criminal for having sinned against the people. From now on, however, I shall strive to become a new man and a teacher of the people in substance as well as in name. I shall exert myself to study, as well as to work, for one year, two years, three years, or even five or ten years. Provided I am able to keep up my efforts, I shall ultimately succeed.

NOTES

CHAPTER 1 (3–7)

[1] Edward Hunter, *Brain-washing in Red China*, New York, Vanguard Press, 1951.

[2] Robert J. Lifton, "Home by Ship: Reaction Patterns of American Prisoners of War Repatriated from North Korea," *American Journal of Psychiatry* (1954) 110:732–739. This book does not concern itself with the military application of thought reform to Westerners. Much valuable work on the subject can be found in the contents and the references of the following three symposia: "Methods of Forceful Indoctrination: Observations and Interviews," Group for the Advancement of Psychiatry, Symposium No. 4, July 1957; "Brainwashing," *The Journal of Social Issues* (1957) XIII, No. 3; and "Communist Methods of Interrogation and Indoctrination," *Bulletin of the New York Academy of Medicine* (1957) 33:599–653. Edgar H. Schein has done especially comprehensive work with American prisoners of war ("The Chinese Indoctrination Program for Prisoners of War: A Study of Attempted 'Brainwashing'," *Psychiatry* (1956) 19:149–172), as have Hinkle and Wolff ("Communist Interrogation and Indoctrination of 'Enemies of the State'," *Archives of Neurology and Psychiatry* (1956) 76:115–174).

CHAPTER 2 (8–16)

[1] Mao Tse-tung, "Correcting Unorthodox Tendencies in Learning, the Party, and Literature and Arts," in C. Brandt, B. Schwartz, and J. Fairbank, *A Documentary History of Chinese Communism*, Cambridge, Harvard University Press, 1951, 392.

[2] This "argument" is extracted and quoted from two authoritative statements on the rationale of thought reform made by a leading Party theorist: Ai Ssu-ch'i, "On Problems of Ideological Reform," *Hsüeh Hsi*, III, January 1, 1951; and "Recognize Clearly the Reactionary Nature of the Ideology of the Bourgeois Class," *Current Background*, No. 179, American Consulate General, Hong Kong, May 6, 1952, translated from *Hsüeh Hsi*, March 16, 1952, a later "self-criticism" by Ai of his earlier article.

[3] "Reform Through Labor of Criminals in Communist China," *Current Background*, No. 293, American Consulate General, Hong Kong, September 15,

1954. This passage was translated from an editorial in *Jen Min Jih Pao* (*The People's Daily*).

⁴ "Regulations Governing Labor Service for Reform of the People's Republic of China," adopted by the Government Administration Council of the Peking Central People's Government, Aug. 26, 1954, tr. in *Current Background*, No. 293. The practices described in these regulations had apparently been in force long before this code was enacted.

CHAPTER 3 (19–37)

¹ Vincent, like many of my Western subjects, knew enough spoken Chinese so that most of his reform could be conducted in that language; and his fluency greatly improved during his ordeal. A bilingual fellow prisoner (or, during interrogations, an official translator) was always available for Chinese-English interpretation, however.

² The judge is actually a high-ranking prison official, and the interrogations which he presides over are official court proceedings; other prison officials of less exalted rank may conduct ordinary interrogations. These distinctions do not always hold.

³ The italics used in quotations from subjects during this and subsequent chapters are, of course, my own.

⁴ Here, and in the next case as well, I could not be sure that the recollection of sleep-deprivation was completely accurate; I believe that in both cases it was reasonably so, although the subjects may have neglected to report brief periods of dozing. The officials always allowed prisoners to get sleep enough to be able to participate in the interrogations, but sometimes during this early period of imprisonment they were permitted little more.

CHAPTER 4 (38–64)

¹ This was part of a widespread change in prison policy in 1952 and 1953. Some, but not all, of the extreme practices, especially those within the cells, were curbed. After this change, in many prisons individual prisoners were prohibited from discussing the criminal details of their cases with cellmates; these were to be reserved for sessions with prison officials. A prisoner was still expected to confess details of personal evil within the cell, but primarily in connection with the re-education process.

CHAPTER 5 (65–85)

¹ These have been altered and expanded from an earlier analysis presented in: Lifton, "Thought Reform of Western Civilians in Chinese Communist Prisons," *Psychiatry* (1956) 19:173–195.

² Erik H. Erikson, "On the Sense of Inner Identity," *Health and Human Relations*, New York, 1953. See also Erikson's, "The Problem of Ego Identity," *Journal of the American Psychoanalytic Association* (1956) 4:56–121.

³ Some prisoners are held in isolation for a few weeks at police headquarters before being assigned to a prison cell group. They experience particularly disturbing feelings of loneliness, hopelessness, and abandonment; their interrogations become their only form of direct communication with others. Through

a slightly different route they too experience a similar regressive stance, assault upon identity, and loss of personal autonomy.

⁴ Much of the intense anxiety stimulated during this early phase thus becomes associated with guilt. But in addition, a certain amount of anxiety arising in connection with the developing sense of guilt may be perceived simply as anxiety, while the guilt remains unconscious. Piers has proposed the term "guilt anxiety" as a more accurate description of this phenomenon. I have not used it here because I have found that it also can be a source of confusion. See Gerhart Piers and Milton B. Singer, *Shame and Guilt*, Thomas, Springfield, Ill., 1953. See also H. Basowitz, H. Persky, S. J. Korchin, and R. R. Grinker, *Anxiety and Stress*, New York, McGraw-Hill, 1955.

⁵ This analogy, or one very similar to it, was originally suggested by Margaret Mead. See her discussion in: Lifton, "Chinese Communist Thought Reform," *Group Processes*, Transactions of the Third Conference, Josiah Macy, Jr. Foundation, New York, 1956, 249.

⁶ See Gert Heilbrunn, "The Basic Fear," *Journal of the American Psychoanalytic Association* (1955) 3:447. This basic fear is similar to what Erikson has called "an ego-chill . . . the sudden awareness that our nonexistence . . . is entirely possible," *Young Man Luther*, W. W. Norton & Co., New York, 1958, 111. William James has also described "the fear of the universe" of "sick souls" prior to the experience of religious conversion: *The Varieties of Religious Experience*, Longmans, Green and Co., London, 1952.

⁷ Erving Goffman reports that, in the parlance of the society of the mental hospital, a psychotic episode is "hitting the bottom"; this phrase contains an element of affirmation—the understanding that the patient to whom this has happened "can come up in some sense a changed person." See Goffman's discussion in "Chinese Communist Thought Reform," *Group Processes*, *supra*, 265. See also, in the same volume, Goffman's paper, "Characteristics of Total Institutions."

⁸ The alternation between kind and vindictive interrogators, like the more general alternation between leniency and assault, is a technique of thought reform which is also widely used in penal and interrogative settings everywhere. But the possibility always exists that the solicitous concern of a particular officials—such as the doctor mentioned in this passage, or one of the interrogators—is genuine, and independent of reform policy. Even if it is, however, it may have the same effects upon the prisoner; he is indeed hard put to distinguish between the technical maneuver and the humane sentiment.

⁹ This concept was originally elaborated by Theodor Reik, *The Compulsion to Confess*, Farrar, Straus and Cudahy, New York, 1959. It has also been used extensively by Joost A. M. Meerloo (*The Rape of the Mind*, World Publishing Co., New York, 1956, and in earlier articles listed therein) in connection with various forms of totalitarian mental coercion. I use the concept somewhat differently from either of these writers, although I have profited from both of their work. See also James Clark Moloney, "Psychic Self-Abandon and Extortion of Confessions," *International Journal of Psychoanalysis* (1955) 36:53–60.

¹⁰ Erikson, *Young Man Luther*, 102.

¹¹ See Rollo May, "Contributions of Existential Psychotherapy," in Rollo May, E. Angeo and H. F. Ellenberger, *Existence*, Basic Books, New York, 1958, 52–55. May uses the term "ontological guilt" which he considers to be "rooted in the fact of self-awareness" and which he distinguishes from neurotic guilt.

He also stresses, as I wish to stress here, that such guilt is universal, occurring in all cultures, and that under ordinary circumstances its recognition can lead to highly constructive effects. See also, Paul Tillich, *The Courage to Be*, New Haven, Yale University Press, 1952, 52.

[12] Some of the communication concepts which I employ here and in later sections have been suggested by the writings of Jurgen Ruesch and Gregory Bateson. See J. Ruesch and G. Bateson, *Communication: The Social Matrix of Psychiatry*, New York, Norton, 1951; and Ruesch, "Synopsis of the Theory of Human Communication," *Psychiatry* (1953) 16:215–243.

CHAPTER 6 (86–116)

[1] Erikson locates the identity crisis "in that period of the life cycle when each youth must forge for himself some central perspective and direction, some working unity, out of the effective remnants of his childhood and the hopes of his anticipated adulthood; he must detect some meaningful resemblance between what he has come to see in himself and what his sharpened awareness tells him others judge and expect him to be" (*Young Man Luther*, 14).

[2] The immense personal value of such a research attitude in "extreme situations" was movingly demonstrated by Bruno Bettelheim in a report of his observations made while he was in a Nazi concentration camp. He describes this as follows: "The study of these behaviors was a mechanism developed by him [Bettelheim—he refers to himself in the third person] *ad hoc* in order that he might . . . in this way be better equipped to endure life in the camp. His observing and collecting of data should . . . be considered as a particular type of defense developed in such an extreme situation . . . based on this particular prisoner's background, training, and interests. It was developed to protect this individual against a disintegration of his personality." The two situations differed in many respects, but the investigative attitude was helpful in both. See Bettelheim, "Individual and Mass Behavior in Extreme Situations," *Journal of Abnormal and Social Psychology* (1953) 38:417–452.

[3] Men and women in this category were in fact frequently capable, just after their release, of making the kind of probing (and sometimes exaggerated) criticisms of the West characteristic of those who have become acutely alienated from—and hypersensitive to the shortcomings of—their own cultural institutions. Thus, when Dr. Vincent spoke of the wasted time spent by the Westerners living in Hong Kong ("spending four hours for nothing—between one drink and another smoke and wait for tomorrow"), he was of course expressing his own sense of dislocation; but he was also observing, through magnifying emotional lenses, real problems of purposelessness within the non-Communist world.

CHAPTER 7 (117–132)

[1] A conscience is "negative" when it is based upon an exaggerated sense of sin. See *Young Man Luther*, 193.

[2] Erikson, "Wholeness and Totality—A Psychiatric Contribution," *Totalitarianism*, edited by Carl J. Friedrich, Harvard University Press, Cambridge, Mass., 1954, 156–171.

CHAPTER 8 (133-151)

[1] Karl Stern, *The Pillar of Fire*, Harcourt Brace & Co., New York, 1951.

[2] The importance of anticipation and anticipatory behavior in human interchange is generally neglected in psychological theory. See David McK. Rioch, "Psychiatry as a Biological Science," *Psychiatry* (1955) 18:313-321. Rioch stresses the importance of anticipatory influences in thought, reverie processes, and other subjective experience. He goes on to state that "behavior in anticipation of probable environmental responses . . . is the behavior primarily studied in psychiatry."

[3] Avoidance of emotional participation was extremely difficult in Chinese prisons because of the environment's constant demand for active involvement. Within the less intensive thought reform programs of Chinese-run prisoner-of-war camps in Korea, however, psychological withdrawal was widespread. It was associated with "playing it cool," which meant being unresponsive and minimally communicative, co-operating to some extent with captors, but only to the degree considered necessary to avoid reprisals. (One repatriate expressed this to me in a vivid, characteristically American, automotive metaphor: "I just put my mind in neutral.") This useful form of withdrawal must be distinguished from more profound—and frequently self-destructive—forms of apathy. See H. D. Strassmann, Margaret Thaler, and E. H. Schein, "A Prisoner of War Syndrome: Apathy as a Reaction to Severe Stress," *American Journal of Psychiatry* (1956) 112:998-1003; Schein, "The Chinese Indoctrination Program," *supra*; and Lifton, *Home by Ship*, Note 2, Chapter 1.

[4] Prison officials do take great pains to prevent martyrdom, suicide, death, and irreversible psychosis; but the prisoner is nonetheless inevitably made to feel that his physical and emotional survival is at stake. And in such an extreme atmosphere, the danger always exists that the officials themselves will lose control over their self-restraints to the extent of genuinely threatening the prisoner's survival—as did happen to Father Luca.

[5] T. W. Adorno, Elsa Frenkel-Brunswik, D. J. Levinson, and R. N. Sanford, *The Authoritarian Personality*, Harper and Bros., New York, 1950; see also Erich Fromm, *Escape from Freedom*, New York, Farrar & Rinehart, Inc., 1941; *Man for Himself*, New York, Rinehart & Co., 1947.

[6] This similarity may have some relationship to an observation made on the basis of psychological tests about repatriated prisoners of war: namely, that the two extreme groups—resisters and collaborators, both of which were opposed to the in-between group of neutrals—shared a common tendency toward action, active involvement, and acting out in the face of stress, a tendency which testers felt was related to their greater self-confidence. See Schein, in "Methods of Forceful Indoctrination," *supra*; and Margaret Thaler Singer and E. H. Schein, "Projective Test Responses of Prisoners of War Following Repatriation," *Psychiatry* (1958) 21:375-385. It is impossible to say to what degree these traits among prisoners of war may be aspects of totalism, and the different nature of the activity-inactivity and activity-passivity problems existing within prisoners of war camps must be kept in mind. But it does seem significant that these investigators found, as I did, important psychological similarities within subjects at the two extreme poles of response.

[7] The various patterns described for the three categories of response also appear in written accounts by those who have undergone prison thought reform. For an example of the obviously confused, see Arthur W. Ford, *Wind Between the Worlds*, New York, David McKay Co., 1957. For an example of apparent converts, see Allyn and Adele Rickett, *Prisoners of Liberation*, New York, Cameron Associates, 1957. And for an example of an apparent resister, see Harold Rigney, *Four Years in a Red Hell*, Chicago, Henry Regnery, 1956.

CHAPTER 9 (152–184)

[1] See Lifton, "Leadership under Stress," *Symposium on Preventive and Social Psychiatry*, Walter Reed Army Institute of Research, Washington, D.C. (U.S. Government Printing Office) 15–17 April, 1957, 365–377. This is a much briefer version of the material presented in this chapter.

[2] Such re-examination is constantly taking place in social and psychological research. I will not attempt to cite the vast literature on this subject; the following two reports do seem to me to evince the same spirit as my own approach: Fritz Redl, "Group Emotion and Leadership," *Psychiatry* (1942) 5:573–596; and James S. Tyhurst, "Problems of Leadership: in the Disaster Situation and in the Clinical Team," *Symposium on Preventive and Social Psychiatry, supra.*

CHAPTER 10 (185–206)

[1] His urge to "be free" was also involved in this exaggerated activity. I am not certain of its full significance, but there is evidence (for instance, his statement about not having left the cell for a year and a half) that he was experiencing a delayed sense of confinement carried over from his imprisonment, as if he were perceiving for the first time the full impact of those years of physical and emotional restraint. This, plus the confining elements of his new environment—its real intellectual, geographical, and interpersonal limitations as compared with the exhilarating and adventurous life he had led in China before his imprisonment and to some extent during his imprisonment as well—seemed to create within him an oppressive sense of spiritual claustrophobia. He could find no outlet for his special creative talents, particularly his talent for personal mediation; and his impulses toward flight and escape must have added to his burden of guilt.

CHAPTER 12 (222–239)

[1] Sigmund Freud, *Beyond the Pleasure Principle*, Hogarth Press, London (Strachey translation), 1950, 21.

[2] E. H. Erikson, *Childhood and Society*, W. W. Norton & Co., New York, 1950, 189.

[3] The process described in these last two paragraphs follows the general principles of what Freud termed the "work of mourning," the more or less normal response to the loss of a loved one. I am taking the position here that the same process can occur when one is separated from an environment which holds special emotional significance for him. See Sigmund Freud, "Mourning and Melancholia," *Collected Papers*, Vol. IV, Hogarth Press, London, 1924.

⁴ Malcolm Cowley, in his description of the post-World War I "lost generation" of American writers, *Exile's Return* (Viking Press, New York, 1956), speaks of their combined adventure and nostalgia ("in Paris or Pamplona, writing, drinking, watching bull fights or making love, they continued to desire a Kentucky hill cabin, a farm house in Iowa or Wisconsin, the Michigan woods, the blue Juniata . . . a home to which they couldn't go back," [9]), then concludes that "when all the paths are seen from a distance they seem to be interwoven into a larger pattern of exile (if only in spirit) and return from exile, of alienation and reintegration" (292). My phrase, "expatriate's return," was partly inspired by Cowley's title, and this section owes much to his stimulating views of his literary generation.

⁵ Kenneth S. Latourette, *A History of Christian Missions in China*, New York, The Macmillan Co., 1929, 279–280.

⁶ Paul A. Varg, *Missionaries, Chinese, and Diplomats*, Princeton, N.J., Princeton University Press, 1958, 194.

⁷ Joseph R. Levenson, " 'History' and 'Value': The Tensions of Intellectual Choice in Modern China," *Studies in Chinese Thought*, edited by Arthur F. Wright, Chicago, University of Chicago Press, 1953, 151–152. Their policy of entering into Chinese life, however, sometimes led them to engage in questionable practices for which they were severely criticized later on: for instance, supervising the manufacture of cannon for use against enemies of the reigning dynasty, and entrepreneurial activities for support of their missions, including money lending.

⁸ Columbia Cary-Elwes, *China and the Cross*, New York, Longmans, Green & Co., 1957, 83.

⁹ *Loc. cit.*

¹⁰ *Ibid.*, 85.

¹¹ *Ibid.*, 109.

¹² *Ibid.*, 110–111.

¹³ Latourette, *op. cit.*, 131–155, presents a comprehensive discussion of the entire Rites Controversy. He expresses the view that Papal policy "tended . . . to keep the Roman Catholic church [in China] a foreign institution"; but he does not believe that had the opposite decision been made, the Jesuits would have succeeded—as many have thought possible—in creating a Chinese Church which would have won the entire country to Christianity. Although this early Jesuit mission effort failed to accomplish its evangelizing task in China, however, it did succeed in making the virtues of Chinese Confucianism known to educated Europeans, and especially to the leading philosophers of the Enlightenment. Men like Leibniz and Voltaire delighted in the democratic and rationalist elements of Confucianism, although they were not fully aware that the Confucianism about which the Jesuits reported in their letters to Europe was the classical ideal rather than the orthodoxy which already had come into being, or that the Jesuits themselves tended to exaggerate these virtues because of their urge to mediate between the two cultures. It is undoubtedly going too far to call Confucius, as some have, "the patron saint of the Enlightenment," or to claim that "Chinese philosophy was without doubt the basic cause of the French Revolution"; but there is a good deal of evidence that the early Jesuit missionaries did as much to spread Confucian ideals in Europe as Christian ideals in China. See H. G. Creel, *Confucius, The Man and The Myth*, Routledge & Kegan Paul, Ltd., London, 1951, 276–301,

for an interesting if somewhat overstated discussion of this Confucian influence upon the West.

[14] Harold R. Isaacs, *Scratches on Our Minds*, New York, John Day Co., 1958, 151.

[15] Cary-Elwes, *op. cit.*, 236–240.

[16] Martha Wolfenstein, in her psychological study of disaster, speaks of the "post-disaster Utopia" (*Disaster*, Glencoe, Ill., The Free Press, 1957, 189–221); and G. P. Azima and F. J. Carpenter note the beneficial effects, as yet difficult to evaluate, of the reorganization of psychic structure following its disorganization through sensory deprivation (*Diseases of the Nervous System*, 17:117, April 1956). The formulations made in these two studies do not exactly coincide with the ideas I have expressed here, but I believe that these phenomena are all related.

CHAPTER 13 (243–252)

[1] See Brandt, Schwartz, and Fairbank, *op. cit.*, 19–20 and 475–481; and Maria Yen, *The Umbrella Garden*, New York, Macmillan, 1954.

[2] Chung Shih, *Higher Education in Communist China*, Communist China Problem Research Series, the Union Research Institute, Hong Kong, 1953, 36.

[3] For the description of the events of this campaign I have used, in addition to the reference cited above and information given me by research subjects, the following sources: *Current Background* (translations from the Chinese Communist Press, American Consulate General, Hong Kong) Nos. 169, 182, and 213, "The Communists and the Intellectuals," Stages One, Two, and Three respectively; and Richard L. Walker, *China Under Communism: The First Five Years*, New Haven, Yale University Press, 1955.

[4] Chung Shih, *op. cit.*, 36.

[5] L. S. Yang, "The Concept of *Pao* as a Basis for Social Relations in China," *Chinese Thought and Institutions*, edited by John K. Fairbank, Chicago, University of Chicago Press, 1957, 291.

CHAPTER 14 (253–273)

[1] I include under this general heading three kinds of institutions: those set up primarily for intellectuals, those for both intellectuals and nonintellectuals, and those for people of relatively limited educational background. The center described in this chapter is of the first type. These centers were sometimes referred to as simply "universities" or "research institutes," with no "revolutionary." These distinctions were not always followed, however, and since the over-all emotional pattern was the same in all three, I have referred to "revolutionary university" and "revolutionary college" interchangeably.

[2] For an enlightening essay on the Chinese Communist cadre—his importance for the regime, his group mind, and his training—see Walter E. Gourley, "The Chinese Communist Cadre: Key to Political Control," Russian Research Center, Harvard University, February 1952.

[3] Such symptoms of general stress were always common, but it is difficult to evaluate the relative occurrence of the more malignant psychological experiences of suicide and psychosis. One must keep in mind that a certain number of

these occur among young people at educational institutions of any kind; but it is likely that the reform pressures were of great importance in precipitating the ones described here.

CHAPTER 15 (274–300)

[1] In addition to his erudite theoretical statements on thought reform rationale (quoted in the notes to Chapter 2, *supra*), Ai Ssu-ch'i produced, in his earlier writing, a number of popular statements on Marxism. The most famous of these was a book actually called *Popular Philosophy*, to which Hu was probably referring. Although originally aimed at the relatively uneducated common man, this book achieved immense popularity among secondary school and university students as well, and went through thirty-two editions during the twelve years after its publication in 1936. Part of its appeal lay in its utter simplicity and in its promise of total salvation through Marxism; see Gourley, *op. cit.*, Note 2, Chapter 14, 45–50.

[2] Erikson, *Young Man Luther*, especially Chapters III, IV, and VI.

[3] It is striking to note how many ways Hu's life history corresponds to the universal myth of the hero, as extracted from mythologies of cultures throughout the world: the hero is a child of distinguished parents (or, in Hu's case, of one distinguished parent); his origin is preceded by difficulties; as a child he is surrendered to the care of others, frequently "suckled by a common woman"; he has a "call to adventure" (Hu's first summons to leadership by fellow students); then faces a series of "difficult tasks" or "road of trials" (for Hu, before and during thought reform); and finally achieves "atonement with the father," a reconciliation which combines revenge, submission, and diminution of early fear. In the myths, the hero's final accomplishment is to right the wrongs done his people, and achieve for them a higher level of accomplishment and wisdom. Hu has already done some of this, but his present fate seems to be that of additional personal trials. See Joseph Campbell, *The Hero with a Thousand Faces*, New York, Meridian Books, 1956; Otto Rank, *The Myth of the Birth of the Hero*, New York, Vintage Books, 1959; and Clyde Kluckhohn, "Recurrent Themes in Myths and Mythmaking," *Daedalus*, Spring, 1959, 268.

[4] Thus Gourley, *op. cit.*, ii–iii, states, "A cadre is an 'activist', a dynamic element, who serves as the transmission belt between the Party, the State, and the masses. He . . . is at all times connected with the activity of the Party, and expresses the point-of-view of the Party."

CHAPTER 16 (301–312)

[1] I gave Thematic Apperception Tests to all my Chinese subjects, and found the results useful in helping me to understand interview data. I did not attempt any separate, systematic interpretation of TAT responses, and I mention them only when they illuminate something important which was not brought out by the interviews themselves.

[2] For discussions of extreme adaptability to change as a modern character trait, see David Riesman, Nathan Glazer, and Reuel Benny, *The Lonely Crowd*, New Haven, Yale University Press, 1950; and Allen Wheelis, *The Quest for Identity*, New York, W. W. Norton & Company, 1958.

CHAPTER 17 (313–337)

[1] For analyses of the techniques through which these "bacteriological warfare" confessions were extracted, see papers by Biderman, West, and by Hinkle and Wolff contained in the symposia cited for Chapter 1.

[2] See the work of René Spitz on infantile depression, especially "Anaclitic Depression," *The Psychoanalytic Study of the Child*, Vol. II, International Universities Press, 1946, 313–342.

[3] Alfred Kazin, "Lady Chatterley in America," *The Atlantic Monthly*, July, 1959, 34.

CHAPTER 18 (338–358)

[1] Yenching University was established in 1919, and subsequently supported, by American Protestant missionary groups. For some years before the Communist takeover it maintained an affiliation with Harvard University.

[2] For additional accounts of this widely-publicized event, see Maria Yen, *op. cit.*, Note 1, Chapter 13, 260–261, and *Current Background*, No. 182, 14–15, and No. 213, 3–4; for earlier Communist attitudes toward Yenching University, see *Current Background*, No. 107, " 'Cultural Aggression' in American Missionary Colleges in China."

[3] Chinese health authorities apparently took advantage of the germ warfare scare to carry out a general program of inoculations.

CHAPTER 19 (359–387)

[1] The historical themes discussed in this chapter will necessarily be selective, chosen because of their important bearing upon the psychological issues with which this book is concerned. Thus I wish to stress that filialism is just one strain of traditional Chinese Confucianism—a vital strain, and crucial to all patterns of authority, but by no means encompassing the entire social and philosophical world of traditional China. Similarly, in discussing certain basic psychological trends, I do not wish to lose sight of the diversity and conflict always present in traditional China; these are revealed in Wright's and Fairbank's volumes on Chinese thought already referred to, and by a third volume in the series, *Confucianism in Action*, edited by David S. Nivison, Stanford, Calif., Stanford University Press, 1959.

[2] Fung Yu-lan, "The Philosophy at the Basis of Traditional Chinese Society," *Ideological Differences and World Order*, edited by F. S. C. Northrop, New Haven, Yale University Press, 1949, 18.

[3] Rev. Justus Doolittle, *Social Life of the Chinese*, New York, Harper & Bros., 1865, Vol. I, 456–457. As told routinely within the culture these stories might not have had the emotional impact which they convey to us as outsiders, but there can be little doubt of their symbolic significance.

[4] *Hsiao Ching* (*Book of Filial Piety*), translated by Ivan Chen, London, J. P. Murray, 1908, quoted in Fung, *op. cit.*, 27. Subsequent quotations in this paragraph are also from Fung's article, and represent his interpretation of filial patterns in traditional China as prescribed by classical ethics.

[5] Conflicts could arise, however, between the two commitments—between the filial son and the loyal official. This happened to Chao Pao, the governor of a frontier province during the second century A.D. Enemy forces captured Chao's mother and threatened to put her to death unless he surrendered his armies. Faced by this moral dilemma, he fought and defeated the enemy, thus sacrificing his mother's life. After the war, he was said to have died of grief at his mother's grave. But in subsequent commentaries (this incident was a frequent subject for ethical discussion for more than a thousand years) Chao was criticized—for being an "extremist" who took only one aspect of the situation into account, and for failing to make some attempt, even if unsuccessful, to save his mother's life. The prevailing principle (strongly reinforced in the writings of Mencius) was that if such a conflict should arise, the duty of the son as a son should receive first consideration. (Fung, in Northrop, ed., *op. cit.*, 29–30).

[6] There are reports of protests against government corruption and inefficiency by students of the Imperial College during the Han Period (25–220 A.D.) and Southern Sung Period (1127–1279 A.D.); and of scholars leading political criticism for some time during the Ming Dynasty (1368–1644 A.D.). But these were essentially demands for adherence to the ideals of traditional ethics— examples of scholars serving as guardians of principles—rather than youth rebellions in the modern sense. See Wen-han Kiang, *The Chinese Student Movement*, New York, King's Crown Press, 1948, 8.

[7] See Marion J. Levy, Jr., *The Family Revolution in Modern China*, Cambridge, Harvard University Press, 1949, 63–208.

[8] Olga Lang, *Chinese Family and Society*, New Haven, Yale University Press, 1946, 10.

[9] *Book of Rites*, in *Sacred Books of the East*, edited by F. M. Muller, Oxford, Vol. XXVIII, 428, quoted in Fung *op. cit.*, 33.

[10] *The Dream of the Red Chamber*, New York, Pantheon Books (Kuhn translation), 1958, 579.

[11] C. P. Fitzgerald, *China, A Short Cultural History*, London, The Crescent Press, 1935, 88.

[12] Fung, in Northrop, ed., *op. cit.*, 20.

[13] Hu Shih, *The Chinese Renaissance*, Chicago, University of Chicago Press, 1934, 110.

[14] Doolittle, *op. cit.*, Vol. I, 140.

[15] *Book of Rites*, quoted by Fung, *op. cit.*, 22. W. M. Theodore De Bary similarly stresses the "fundamentalism" and "restorationism" characteristic of Confucianism; see his "Common Tendencies in Neo-Confucianism," in Nivison, ed., *op. cit.*, 34–37.

[16] Ch'en Tu-shiu, *The New Youth*, Vol. I, No. 5, quoted in Lang, *op. cit.*, 110.

[17] See R. Bunzel and J. H. Weakland, *An Anthropological Approach to Chinese Communism*, Columbia University, Research in Contemporary Cultures, mimeographed.

[18] Tsi C. Wang, *The Youth Movement in China*, New York, New Republic, Inc., 1928, 6–7.

[19] Levenson, " 'History' and 'Value' . . . ," in Wright, ed., *op. cit.*, 156.

[20] K'ang Yu-wei, *Ta-tung Shu* (*The Book of Great Unity*), quoted in Lang, *op. cit.*, 111.

[21] Lang, *op. cit.*, 110.

[22] Benjamin I. Schwartz, *Chinese Communism and the Rise of Mao*, Cambridge, Harvard University Press, 1951, 9.

[23] Hu Shih, *op. cit.*, 44.

[24] Pa Chin, *The Family*, quoted in Lang, *op. cit.*, 297–298.

[25] Levy, *op. cit.*, 294–302.

[26] Conrad Brandt, *Stalin's Failure in China*, Cambridge, Mass., Harvard University Press, 1958, 48.

[27] "The Diary of A Madman," *Ah Q and Others, Selected Stories of Lu Shun*, translated by Wang Chi-shen, Columbia University Press, 1941, 205–219. The character of Ah Q, who appears in the title story of this volume became a symbolic rallying point for protest. He was a caricature of all that Lu Shun condemned in Chinese culture: the tendencies, in the face of personal oppression, to remain passive, to rationalize philosophically, or to take out resentment on those lower in the social hierarchy. "Ah Q-ism" became a term of rebuke, usually referring to these influences from the past, in contrast to the ideals of the "modern student"—*active* self-assertion, a feeling of personal dignity, and commitment to social change.

[28] Schwartz, *op. cit.*, 9.

[29] Lu Shun, in Wang, ed., *op. cit.*, 16.

[30] Apart from the case histories in this study, much evidence of intensified intra- and extra-family conflict can be found in the sociological studies of Levy and Lang, cited above.

[31] The last two quotations are from Brandt, Schwartz, and Fairbank, *op. cit.*, 19–20.

[32] These youthful emotions were frequently in advance of, and more extreme than, the Party's own program. The formation of the Socialist Youth Corps, which later became the Chinese Communist Youth Corps, antedated the formation of the Communist Party; and it maintained considerable autonomy even after the Party had been organized (Brandt, *op. cit.*, 46–49).

[33] Schwartz, *op. cit.*, 21.

[34] See *Current Background*, Nos. 315 and 325; and Theodore Hsi-en Chen and Sin Ming Chiu, "Thought Reform in Communist China," *Far Eastern Survey*, 24:177–184.

[35] Mao Tse-tung, "Opposing Party Formalism," Brandt, Schwartz, and Fairbank, *op. cit.*, 396.

[36] Ai Ssu-ch'i, "On Problems of Ideological Reform," Note 2, Chapter 2.

[37] *Ibid.*

[38] Mao Tse-tung, "Correcting Unorthodox Tendencies in Learning, The Party, and Literature and Arts," Brandt, Schwartz, and Fairbank, *op. cit.*, 386.

[39] Ai, *op. cit.*

[40] Hu Hsien-chin, "The Chinese Concept of 'Face,'" *American Anthropologist* (1944) 46:45–65.

[41] This injunction from Ai could also apply to those who found Party policy

inconsistent with Marxist-Leninist writings, or who had difficulty accepting official attempts to reconcile the two.

[42] Ai Ssu-ch'i, "Recognize Clearly."

[43] *Ibid.*

[44] Mao Tse-tung, "Correcting Unorthodox Tendencies," Brandt, Schwartz, and Fairbank, *op. cit.*, 382.

[45] Mao Tse-tung, "In Opposition to Liberalism," in Boyd Compton, *Mao's China: Party Reform Documents, 1942–44*, Seattle, University of Washington Press, 1952, 184–185.

[46] *Ibid.*, 187.

[47] From Hu Shih-tu, "Confession," reprinted by the *Hong Kong Standard*, September 24, 1950, and also in Edward Hunter, *Brainwashing in Red China*, 303–307.

[48] Liu Shao-chi, "The Class Character of Man," written in June, 1941, included in an undated edition of *How to be a Good Communist*, Foreign Languages Press, 109–110.

[49] "The May 4 Movement," *Selected Works of Mao Tse-tung*, London, Lawrence & Wishart, 1954, Vol. III, 11. Mao's description of his personal transformation is recorded in one of his speeches reprinted in Brandt, Schwartz, and Fairbank, *op. cit.*, 410–411.

[50] Ai Ssu-ch'i, "Recognize Clearly," *supra.*

CHAPTER 20 (388–398)

[1] Raymond A. Bauer, "Brainwashing: Psychology or Demonology?", *Journal of Social Issues* (1957) 13:41–47. See also, by the same author, *The New Man in Soviet Psychology*, Cambridge, Harvard University Press, 1952.

[2] These trials are discussed in Nathan Leites and Elsa Bernaut, *Ritual of Liquidation*, Glencoe, Ill., The Free Press, 1954. They were fictionalized, with great psychological accuracy, by Arthur Koestler in the novel, *Darkness at Noon*, New York, Macmillan, 1941. Both of these books deal with the special ethos of the "old Bolshevik." F. Beck and W. Godin, *Russian Purge and the Extraction of Confession*, New York, Viking Press, 1951, conveys vividly the experiences within a Soviet prison of outsiders caught up in the great purge.

[3] *The Great Learning*, in *The Four Books*, translated by James Legge, London, Perkins, 310–313. All subsequent references to Confucian writings are to this translation.

[4] *The Doctrine of the Mean*, Legge, 394.

[5] See David S. Nivison, "Communist Ethics and Chinese Tradition," *The Journal of Asian Studies* (1956) 16:51–74; and the same author's, "The Problem of 'Knowledge' and 'Action' in Chinese Thought since Wang Yang-ming," *Studies in Chinese Thought*, 112–145.

[6] Lily Abegg, *The Mind of East Asia*, Thames and Hudson, London, 1952, Chapters 2 and 3.

[7] In terms of logic, both follow the "law of opposition," rather than the traditional Western pattern of the "law of identity"; but their difference lies in the Chinese emphasis upon "adjustment" in relationship to this opposition, in contrast to the Marxist emphasis upon "struggle." See Chang Tung-sun, "A

Chinese Philosopher's Theory of Knowledge," *The Yenching Journal of Social Studies* (Peking, 1939) 1:155–189.

[8] Robert Van Gulik, *The Chinese Bell Murders*, New York, Harper Bros., 1958, 258.

[9] Boyd Compton, *op. cit.*, xv–lii; and Brandt, Schwartz, and Fairbank, *op. cit* 372–375.

[10] Compton, *op. cit.*, xlvi.

[11] Weston LaBarre, "Some Observations on Character Structure in the Orient: II. The Chinese," *Psychiatry* (1946) 9:215–237.

[12] Once during a discussion with one of my Chinese interpreters, I mentioned the interest of American psychiatrists in the subject of interpersonal relations. His immediate reply was, "What else *is* there?" In this interest in what goes on between people, there is something Sullivanian in every Chinese. See also John H. Weakland, "The Organization of Action in Chinese Culture," *Psychiatry* (1950) 13:361–370.

[13] *Confucian Analects*, Legge, 94.

[14] *The Great Learning*, Legge, 326.

[15] *The Texts of Taoism*, translated by James Legge, London, 1891, Part I, 70.

[16] Ronald Knox, *Enthusiasm*, London, Oxford University Press, 1950. See also William Sargent, *Battle for the Mind*, New York, Doubleday, 1957, for a different approach to relating thought reform to ecstatic religious practice.

CHAPTER 21 (399–415)

[1] In this sense, thought reform had some similarity to a primitive initiation ceremony; it initiated one into the world of Chinese Communism. See Branislaw Malinowski, *Magic, Science, and Religion*, New York, Doubleday, 1955, 37–41.

[2] *Current Background*, No. 376, February 7, 1956.

[3] See Theodore Hsi-en Chen, "The Thought Reform of Intellectuals," *Annals of the American Academy of Political and Social Science* (1959) 321:82–89, 86. For my discussion of the Hundred Flowers episode, I also drew on the following sources: "Contradiction" and "The Storm," pamphlets published by *China Viewpoints*, Hong Kong, 1958; Benjamin Schwartz, "New Trends in Maoism?", *Problems of Communism* (1957) 6:1–8, and "China and the Communist Bloc: A Speculative Reconstruction," *Current History* (1958) 35:321–326; Michael Walzer, "When the 100 Flowers Withered," *Descent*, Autumn 1958, 360–374; and Chinese Communist Press reports translated by the American Consulate General in Hong Kong and reproduced in the *New York Times* from April, 1957, through the following year.

CHAPTER 22 (419–437)

[1] Personal "closure" implies abandoning man's inherent strivings toward the outer world as well as much of his receptivity to his own inner impulses, and retreating into what Ernest Schachtel has called "the closed pattern of relatedness to the world institutionalized in . . . [a] particular culture or cultural subgroup (*Metamorphosis*, New York, Basic Books, 1959, 75).

[2] Helen Lynd, *On Shame and the Search for Identity*, New York, Harcourt, Brace & Co., 1958, 57.

[3] Alex Inkeles, "The Totalitarian Mystique: Some Impressions of the Dynamics of Totalitarian Society," *Totalitarianism*, edited by Carl Friedrich, Cambridge, Mass., Harvard University Press, 1953, 88 and 91.

[4] *Ibid.*, 91.

[5] In Camus' novel, *The Fall* (New York, Alfred A. Knopf, 1957, 127), Clamence states: "My great idea is that one must forgive the Pope. To begin with, he needs it more than anyone else. Secondly, that's the only way to set oneself above him. . . ."

[6] Helen Lynd, *op. cit.*, 57.

[7] Camus, *The Fall*, 120.

[8] *Ibid.*, 8 and 138.

[9] A somewhat similar point of view is expressed by Hannah Arendt in her comprehensive study, *The Origins of Totalitarianism*, New York, Meridian Books, 1958, 468–474.

[10] In this respect, thought reform is clearly a child of its era, for Weaver claims that "progress" is the "'god term' of the present age," and also lists "progressive," "science," "fact," and "modern" as other widely-used "god terms" ("Ultimate Terms in Contemporary Rhetoric," *Perspectives* (1955), 11, 1–2, 141). All these words have a similar standing in thought reform. Thought reform's "devil terms" are more specifically Communist, but also included are such general favorites as "aggressor" and "fascist."

[11] Edward Sapir, "Language," *Culture, Language and Personality*, Berkeley, Calif., University of California Press, 1956, 17.

[12] John K. Fairbank and Mary C. Wright, "Documentary Collections on Modern Chinese," *The Journal of Asian Studies* (1957) 17:55–56, intro.

[13] Camus, *The Rebel*, New York, Alfred A. Knopf, 1954, 141.

[14] Benjamin Schwartz, *op. cit.*, 4–5.

[15] Erik Erikson, "Wholeness and Totality," in Friedrich, ed., *op. cit.*, 165.

[16] Mao Tse-tung, "On the People's Democratic Dictatorship," Brandt, Schwartz, and Fairbank, *op. cit.*, 456–457.

[17] *Ibid.*, 457.

[18] I have borrowed the term "peak experiences" from A. H. Maslow (Presidential Address, Division of Personality and Social Psychology, American Psychological Association, Chicago, Ill., September 1, 1956, mimeographed), although my use of it is perhaps somewhat broader than his. In his terminology, he might see the imposed "peak experience" as lacking in genuine "cognition of being."

[19] "Openness to the world," or "world-openness," and "embeddedness" are conceptualized by Schachtel (*Metamorphosis*, 22–77), as perpetually antagonistic human emotional tendencies.

CHAPTER 23 (438–461)

[1] Bettelheim, "Individual and Mass Behavior," Note 2, Chapter 6.

[2] Anna Freud, *The Ego and the Mechanisms of Defence*, New York, International Universities Press, 1946.

[3] Erich Fromm, throughout his writings, frequently uses the term, "self-

realization" to suggest the goal of psychotherapy and of life itself. Kurt Gold-stein speaks similarly of the organism's "trend to actualize itself."

⁴ C. M. Bowra, *The Greek Experience*, New York, World Publishing Co., 1957, 198–201.

⁵ Michael Polanyi, *Personal Knowledge*, Chicago, The University of Chicago Press, 1958, 300–303.

⁶ George Orwell, "Such, Such Were the Joys," *A Collection of Essays*, Double-day Anchor Books, New York, 1954, 9–55.

⁷ Lionel Trilling, *The Liberal Imagination*, Garden City, New York, Double-day Anchor Books, 1954, 6 and 10.

⁸ In this section I shall not enter into the long-standing controversy over dis-tinctions between psychoanalysis and psychonanalytic therapy, or between medi-cal and nonmedical psychoanalytic and psychotherapeutic work. I believe that the principles expressed here apply, at least in spirit, to all of these agents of psychological re-education. What I say about psychoanalytic training is most specific to that situation, but may also be applied in lesser degree to other forms of psychological and psychiatric (or, medical psychological) training. Similarly, the ideas expressed about transference, resistance, and reality apply to all forms of psychoanalytically-influenced therapeutic work, while those about milieu therapy relate primarily to hospital settings. Ideas about theory apply to all systematic attempts to understand man.

⁹ Erik Erikson, "The First Psychoanalyst," *Freud and the 20th Century*, edited by Benjamin Nelson, New York, Meridian Books, 1957, 80.

¹⁰ See, for instance, Franz Alexander, *Psychoanalysis and Psychotherapy*, New York, Norton, 1956, Chapters IX–XII (including both the author's discussion and those of leading psychoanalysts whose opinions he solicited); Erikson, *Young Man Luther*, 151–154; Leslie Farber, "The Therapeutic Despair," *Psychiatry* (1958) 21:7–20; Erich Fromm, *Sigmund Freud's Mission*, New York, Harper & Bros., 1959, Chapters VIII–X; Thomas S. Szasz, "Psychoanalytic Training–A Socio-Psychological Analysis of Its History and Present Status," *The International Journal of Psychoanalysis* (1958), 39:598–613; Clara Thomp-son, "A Study of the Emotional Climate of Psychoanalytic Institutes," *Psy-chiatry* (1958) 21:45–51; and Allen Wheelis, *op. cit.*, Chapters II, V, and VII.

¹¹ Erickson, *Young Man Luther*, 152.

¹² *Ibid.*, 153.

¹³ Somewhat analogous ideas have been expressed by George Winokur, " 'Brainwashing'—A Social Phenomenon of Our Time," *Human Organization* (1955) 13:16–18; and by J. C. Moloney, "Psychic Self-Abandon," *supra*; and Meerloo, *Rape of the Mind*, *supra*.

¹⁴ In his presidential address of that year to the American Psychoanalytic Association (*Psychoanalysis and Psychotherapy*, 177–178), Alexander stated: "They [psychoanalysts] should lose the defensive attitude of a minority group, the militant soldiers of a *Weltanschauung* attacked by and therefore antagonistic to the world. Rather than disseminators of the gospel, they must become self-critical scientists. For psychoanalysis as a whole, this leads to the simple but unavoidable conclusion that the sooner psychoanalysis as a 'movement' disap-pears, the better."

¹⁵ Szasz, *op. cit.*

¹⁶ Thompson, *op. cit.*

[17] See John P. Spiegel's discussion of the relationship of cultural values to concepts of resistance and reality in "Some Cultural Aspects of Transference and Countertransference," *Individual and Familial Dynamics*, edited by Jules H. Masserman, Grune and Stratton, 1959, 160–182.

[18] See, for instance, Robert Waelder, "The Problem of the Genesis of Psychical Conflict in Earliest Infancy," *International Journal of Psychoanalysis* (1937) 18:473; Mabel Blake Cohen, "Countertransference and Anxiety," *Psychiatry* (1952) 15:231–243; and Leo Berman, "Countertransference and Attitudes of the Analyst in the Therapeutical Process," *Psychiatry* (1949) 12:159–166.

[19] Janet Mackenzie Rioch, "The Transference Phenomena in Psychoanalytic Therapy," in *An Outline of Psychoanalysis*, edited by Thompson, Mazer, and Witenberg, New York, The Modern Library, 1955, 498, 500, 501.

[20] Merton M. Gill and Margaret Brenman, *Hypnosis and Related States*, New York, International Universities Press, 1959, have compared hypnosis with "brainwashing," primarily in relationship to the reliance upon induced regression common to both. I would place greater emphasis upon the totalism contained in both, along the lines of my discussion in Chapter 21, and would further raise the question of whether such totalism might not be one of the truly fundamental aspects of the hypnotic process.

[21] See papers by D. O. Hebb, E. S. Heath, and E. A. Stuart, *Canadian Journal of Psychology* (1954) 8:152, and by John C. Lilly, *Psychiatric Research Reports* (1956) No. 5, 1; for a general review, see P. Solomon, H. Liederman, J. Mendelson, and D. Wexler, *American Journal of Psychiatry* (October, 1957) 114:357.

[22] See, for instance, Paul Sivadon, "Technics of Sociotherapy," in *Symposium on Preventive and Social Psychiatry, supra,* 457–464; Kai T. Erikson, "Patient Role and Social Uncertainty—A Dilemma of the Mentally Ill," *Psychiatry* (1957) 20:263–274; D. McK. Rioch and A. H. Stanton, "Milieu Therapy," *Psychiatry* (1953) 16:65–72; A. H. Stanton and M. S. Schwartz, *The Mental Hospital*, New York, Basic Books, 1954; and William Caudill, *The Psychiatric Hospital as a Small Society*, Cambridge, Mass., Harvard University Press, 1958.

[23] *Malleus Maleficarum*, translated by Montague Summers, London, The Pushkin Press, 1951. See also Henry Charles Lea, *A History of the Inquisition of the Middle Ages* (3 vols.), New York, S. A. Russell, 1956; and Giorgio Di Santillana, *The Crime of Galileo*, University of Chicago Press, 1955.

[24] L. B. Smith, "English Treason Trials and Confessions in the Sixteenth Century," *Journal of the History of Ideas* (1954) 15:471.

[25] See Fromm, *Escape from Freedom*.

[26] Norman Cohn, *The Pursuit of the Millenium*, London, Secker and Warburg, 1957.

[27] Ronald Knox, *op. cit.*, 580.

[28] See also Hadley Cantril, *The Psychology of Social Movements*, New York, John Wiley and Sons, 1951, Chapter 6.

[29] S. Radhakrishnan, *East and West*, New York, Harper and Bros., 1956, 41.

[30] Erich Fromm, *Psychoanalysis and Religion*, New Haven, Yale University Press, 1950, presents a rather similar point of view.

[31] Camus, *The Rebel*, 269.

[32] See Edward A. Shils, *The Torment of Secrecy*, Glencoe, Ill., The Free Press,

1956. I wish to emphasize that I am referring to just one theme within American populism; I would tend to be more cautious than Shils in relating the general populist movement to McCarthyism.

[33] Michael Polanyi, " 'The Two Cultures'," *Encounter* (1959) 13:61.

[34] Dr. T. F. Fox, editor of *Lancet*, quoted in *The New York Times*, October 22, 1959.

[35] This close relationship between godhood and devildom has a long tradition: Margaret Murray demonstrated, in *The God of The Witches*, New York, Oxford University Press, 1952, that the devil himself is no one but the Horned God widely worshipped during the Bronze Age and Iron Age of pre-Christian Europe, and that "the God of the old religion becomes the Devil of the new." This statement has a good deal of significance for thought reform and totalism in general.

[36] Albert Einstein, *Out of My Later Years*, New York, Philosophical Library, 1950, 21–23.

[37] J. Robert Oppenheimer, *The Open Mind*, New York, Simon & Schuster, 1955, 93–94.

[38] J. Bronowski, *Science and Human Values*, New York, Julian Messner Inc., 1956.

CHAPTER 24 (462–472)

[1] J. L. Talmon, "Utopianism and Politics," *Commentary* (1959) 28:149–154, 153.

[2] I have in mind the writings of Schachtel, Erikson, Fromm, Riesman, and Wheelis, which I have already cited; and also, recent work by Margaret Mead: *New Lives for Old*, New York, William Morrow Co., 1956; "Cultural Discontinuities and Personality Transformation," *The Journal of Social Issues* (1954) 8:3–16; and "The Implications of Culture Change for Personality Development," *American Journal of Orthopsychiatry*, 17:633–646.

[3] Camus, *The Rebel*, 19.

[4] William James, *Varieties of Religious Experience*, 163–185.

[5] Schachtel, *Metamorphosis*, p. 6.

[6] Mark Schorer, *William Blake: The Politics of Vision*, New York, Vintage Books, 1959, 27.

[7] Joseph Campbell, *Hero with a Thousand Faces*, 26.

[8] Germaine Brée, *Camus*, New Brunswick, N.J., Rutgers University Press, 1959, 21; 20–46.

[9] William James, *op. cit.*, 242 and 371.

[10] Michael Balint, "The Final Goal of Psychoanalytic Treatment," in *An Outline of Psychoanalysis*, 434.

[11] A large literature on "social influence" and "persuasibility" has recently developed. See particularly the descriptions of the already classical Asch experiments: S. E. Asch, "Effects of Group Pressures upon the Modification and Distortion of Judgment," *Readings in Social Psychology*, New York, Henry Holt, 1952. See also E. T. Borgetta and R. F. Bales, *Small Groups*, New York, Knopf, 1955; and C. Hovland and I. Janis, editors, *Personality and Persuasibility*

New Haven, Yale University Press, 1959; and Herbert C. Kelman, *Compliance, Identification, and Internalization: A Theoretical and Experimental Approach to the Study of Social Influence* (monograph in preparation).

[12] John Dewey, Letter to Corinne Chisholm (Mrs. Frank G. Frost), December 7, 1949, published in *Daedalus*, Summer, 1959, 558.

[13] William James, *op. cit.*, 196.

[14] See Margaret Mead, *op. cit.*

[15] Camus, *The Rebel*, 261.

[16] Campbell, *op. cit.*, 388.

INDEX